Digital Sovereignty in the BRICS Countries

In a world where digital development and policymaking are dominated by Silicon Valley tech giants, the BRICS countries – Brazil, Russia, India, China, and South Africa – play an increasingly important role. With 40 percent of the world's population and 25 percent of global GDP, these nations possess a vast trove of personal data. Yet, their conceptions, narratives, and initiatives of digital sovereignty remain understudied. This volume is the first to explore digital sovereignty from a Global South perspective and offers a forward-looking take on what a world less dependent on Silicon Valley might look like. It brings together excellent analyses of BRICS digital sovereignty issues, from historical imaginaries to up-to-date conceptualizations, e-payment to smart cities, and legal analysis to geopolitical assessment. By offering neglected perspectives from the Global South, this book makes important contributions to the digital sovereignty debate. This title is also available as Open Access on Cambridge Core.

Min Jiang is Professor of Communication Studies and an affiliate faculty member of International Studies at the University of North Carolina at Charlotte. She is a secretariat member of the annual international Chinese Internet Research Conference (CIRC) and CyberBRICS Visiting Professor at FGV Law School (Rio de Janeiro, Brazil).

Luca Belli is Professor of Digital Governance and Regulation at FGV Law School, Rio de Janeiro, where he heads the Center for Technology and Society and the CyberBRICS project. He is Editor of the journal *International Data Privacy Law* and Director of Computers, Privacy and Data Protection Conference Latin America.

COMMUNICATION, SOCIETY AND POLITICS

Editors

W. Lance Bennett, *University of Washington*
Regina Lawrence, *University of Oregon*

Founding Co-Editor, Emeritus

Robert M. Entman, *The George Washington University*

Communication, Society and Politics is a series that probes the political and social impacts of communication processes and systems in national, comparative, and global contexts. The series adopts a broad definition of politics as the exercise of power within and between nations, which includes the social, cultural, psychological, and institutional underpinnings of politically significant communication. The series includes a diversity of methods and views, with an emphasis on questions about democracy, equality, justice, and other normative concerns.

In recent years, politics in societies across the world have been transformed by communication technologies that blur traditional definitions of news, the nature of citizenship, and the boundaries between public and private life. Many democracies face challenges due to disruptive communication processes operating in the context of declining levels of trust in public institutions, including legacy journalism. One result of these trends is the spread of disinformation by illiberal movements and parties that aim to undermine science, the press, civil society organizations, and other traditional public information sources. A related trend involves the growth of authoritarian regimes that rely on media systems and communication strategies to manage publics.

Within these broad trends are many other important communication developments in which communication technologies and networked organization have impacted human rights, climate change, new forms of citizenship and inclusion, and personal political expression. Communication, Society and Politics provides a platform to explore how people in different societies engage with the ideas that organize their lives.

Other Books in the Series:

Min Jiang and Luca Belli, *Digital Sovereignty in the BRICS Countries: How the Global South and Emerging Power Alliances Are Reshaping Digital Governance*

Kevin Arceneaux, Johanna Dunaway, Martin Johnson, and Ryan J. Vander Wielen, *The House that Fox News Built? Representation, Political Accountability, and the Rise of Partisan News*

j. Siguru Wahutu, *In the Shadow of the Global North: Journalism in Postcolonial Africa*

Stuart N. Soroka and Christopher Wlezien, *Information and Democracy: Public Policy in the News*

Danny Hayes and Jennifer L. Lawless, *News Hole: The Demise of Local Journalism and Political Engagement*

Sabina Mihelj and Simon Huxtable, *From Media Systems to Media Cultures*

Matthew Powers and Adrienne Russell, *Rethinking Media Research for Changing Societies*

Roderick P. Hart, *Trump and Us: What He Says and Why People Listen*

Clifford G. Christians, *Media Ethics and Global Justice in the Digital Age*

Reece Peck, *Fox Populism: Branding Conservatism as Working Class*

Roderick P. Hart, *Civic Hope: How Ordinary Citizens Keep Democracy Alive*

Sue Robinson, *Networked News, Racial Divides: How Power and Privilege Shape Public Discourse in Progressive Communities*

Lynn S. Clark and Regina Marchi, *Young People and the Future of News*

Douglas M. McLeod and Dhavan V. Shah, *News Frames and National Security*

Victor Pickard, *America's Battle for Media Democracy: The Triumph of Corporate Libertarianism and the Future of Media Reform*

Erik Albæk, Arjen van Dalen, Nael Jebril, and Claes de Vreese, *Political Journalism in Comparative Perspective*

Daniela Stockmann, *Media Commercialization and Authoritarian Rule in China*

Rodney Benson, *Shaping Immigration News: A French-American Comparison*

Margaret Scammell, *Consumer Democracy: The Marketing of Politics*

Eva Anduiza, Michael James Jensen, and Laia Jorba, eds., *Digital Media and Political Engagement Worldwide: A Comparative Study*

Bruce Bimber, Andrew Flanagin, and Cynthia Stohl, *Collective Action in Organizations: Interaction and Engagement in an Era of Technological Change*

Daniel C. Hallin and Paolo Mancini, eds., *Comparing Media Systems Beyond the Western World*

Bruce A. Williams and Michael X. Delli Carpini, *After Broadcast News: Media Regimes, Democracy, and the New Information Environment*

Ruud Koopmans and Paul Statham, eds., *The Making of a European Public Sphere: Media Discourse and Political Contention*

Tim Groeling, *When Politicians Attack: Party Cohesion in the Media*

Patrick Sellers, *Cycles of Spin: Strategic Communication in the U.S. Congress*

Marwan M. Kraidy, *Reality Television and Arab Politics: Contention in Public Life*

Pippa Norris and Ronald Inglehart, *Cosmopolitan Communications: Cultural Diversity in a Globalized World*

Stephen Coleman Jay G. Blumler, *The Internet and Democratic Citizenship: Theory, Practice and Policy*

Peter Dahlgren, *Media and Political Engagement, Citizens, Communication and Democracy*

Hernan Galperin, *New Television, Old Politics: The Transition to Digital TV in the United States and Britain*

L. Sandy Maisel, Darrell M. West, and Brett M. Clifton, *Evaluating Campaign Quality: Can the Electoral Process Be Improved?*

C. Edwin Baker, *Media Concentration and Democracy: Why Ownership Matters*

Robert B. Horwitz, *Communication and Democratic Reform in South Africa*

Philip N. Howard, *New Media Campaigns and the Managed Citizen*

Frank Esser and Barbara Pfetsch, eds., *Comparing Political Communication: Theories, Cases, and Challenges*

Daniel C. Hallin and Paolo Mancini, *Comparing Media Systems: Three Models of Media and Politics*

Gadi Wolfsfeld, *Media and the Path to Peace*

Bruce Bimber, *Information and American Democracy: Technology in the Evolution of Political Power*

Myra Marx Ferree, William Anthony Gamson, Jürgen Gerhards, and Dieter Rucht, *Shaping Abortion Discourse: Democracy and the Public Sphere in Germany and the United States*

Adam F. Simon, *The Winning Message: Candidate Behavior, Campaign Discourse*

C. Edwin Baker, *Media, Markets, and Democracy*

Pippa Norris, *Digital Divide: Civic Engagement, Information Poverty, and the Internet Worldwide*

Murray Edelman, *The Politics of Misinformation*

W. Lance Bennett and Robert M. Entman, eds., *Mediated Politics: Communication in the Future of Democracy*

Pippa Norris, *A Virtuous Circle: Political Communications in Postindustrial Society*

Richard Gunther and Anthony Mughan, eds., *Democracy and the Media: A Comparative Perspective*

Digital Sovereignty in the BRICS Countries

How the Global South and Emerging Power Alliances Are Reshaping Digital Governance

Edited by

MIN JIANG

University of North Carolina at Charlotte

LUCA BELLI

Fundação Getulio Vargas Law School, Rio de Janeiro

CAMBRIDGE
UNIVERSITY PRESS

CAMBRIDGE
UNIVERSITY PRESS

Shaftesbury Road, Cambridge CB2 8EA, United Kingdom

One Liberty Plaza, 20th Floor, New York, NY 10006, USA

477 Williamstown Road, Port Melbourne, VIC 3207, Australia

314–321, 3rd Floor, Plot 3, Splendor Forum, Jasola District Centre, New Delhi – 110025, India

103 Penang Road, #05–06/07, Visioncrest Commercial, Singapore 238467

Cambridge University Press is part of Cambridge University Press & Assessment, a department of the University of Cambridge.

We share the University's mission to contribute to society through the pursuit of education, learning and research at the highest international levels of excellence.

www.cambridge.org
Information on this title: www.cambridge.org/9781009531139

DOI: 10.1017/9781009531085

When citing this work, please include a reference to the
DOI 10.1017/9781009531085

First published 2025

A catalogue record for this publication is available from the British Library

Library of Congress Cataloging-in-Publication Data
NAMES: Jiang, Min (Professor of communication studies), editor. | Belli, Luca, editor.
TITLE: Digital sovereignty in the BRICS countries : how the Global South and emerging power alliances are reshaping digital governance / edited by Min Jiang, Luca Belli.
DESCRIPTION: Cambridge, United Kingdom ; New York : Cambridge University Press, 2025. | Series: Communication, society and politics. | Includes bibliographical references and index.
IDENTIFIERS: LCCN 2024017712 | ISBN 9781009531139 (hardback) | ISBN 9781009531085 (ebook)
SUBJECTS: LCSH: Information technology – Government policy – BRIC countries. | Digital media – Government policy – BRIC countries. | Internet – Government policy – BRIC countries.
CLASSIFICATION: LCC HM851 .D5444 2025 | DDC 303.48/33–dc23/eng/20241007
LC record available at https://lccn.loc.gov/2024017712

ISBN 978-1-009-53113-9 Hardback
ISBN 978-1-009-53112-2 Paperback

Contents

Figures

Tables

Contributors

Min Jiang is Professor of Communication Studies and an affiliate faculty member of International Studies at the University of North Carolina at Charlotte. She is a secretariat member of the annual international Chinese Internet Research Conference (CIRC) and a CyberBRICS visiting professor at FGV Law School (Rio de Janeiro, Brazil). Her research focuses on the intersections of Chinese internet technologies, politics, policies, and, increasingly, their impact on the Global South and global communication. Currently, she serves as an advisory board member and China lead on a CAD $2.5 million research grant on the Global Media and Internet Concentration Project. Jiang received her BA and MA degrees from Beijing Foreign Studies University and her PhD in communication from Purdue University.

Luca Belli is Professor of Digital Governance and Regulation at FGV Law School, where he heads the Center for Technology and Society and the CyberBRICS project. Luca is also editor of the International Data Privacy Law (IDPL) Journal, published by Oxford University Press, and Director of the Computers Privacy and Data Protection conference Latin-America (CPDP LatAm). He is currently member of the Brazilian Presidency's National Cybersecurity Committee, board member of the Global Digital Inclusion Partnership and member of the Steering Committee of the Forum for Information & Democracy. He is author of more than 80 publications on law and technology, exploring data governance, cybersecurity, AI regulation, Internet access, and digital transformation.

Olga Bronnikova is Associate Professor at the University of Grenoble Alpes. She is a member of the Institute of Languages and Cultures of Europe, America, Africa, Asia and Australia (ILCEA4) and an associate member of the Center for Russian, Caucasian and East European Studies (CERCEC). For several years, she has been working on the political mobilization of

Russian-speaking migrants in the European Union (EU) countries and on the transnationalization of their political demands. She has recently started research on Russian workers in French factories in the years 1920–1930. In the scope of the L'Agence nationale de la recherche (National Research Agency) and the Net Resisters. Criticism and evasion of digital coercion in Russia (ResisTIC project), she is interested in the migration of web professionals and the circulation of knowledge on digital security between Russia and international organizations.

Enrico Calandro (PhD) is a cybersecurity capacity building consultant and researcher. In 2020, he co-founded the Cybersecurity Capacity Centre for Southern Africa at the University of Cape Town and has been a researcher at Research ICT Africa between 2010 and 2019. Furthermore, he was a board member of the Global Forum on Cyber Expertise between 2018 and 2022 and he is the Chairperson of the Research Committee of the GFCE since 2020. For more than ten years, he has explored the relationship between digitalization and development, focusing on digital inequalities. His targeted and locally-relevant research has aimed at shaping cyber policy processes and debates and at crafting evidence-based and informed capacity-building initiatives in the field of cyber and digital policy.

Stefano Calzati is currently a postdoc researcher in the Department of Urbanism at Technology University of Delft. His research interests and teaching cover technology governance, philosophy of technology, data ethics, and ICT geopolitics. Before joining TU Delft, Calzati was a postdoc fellow at Tallinn University of Technology – where he researched China–Africa relations in ICTs – and a teaching assistant at Polytechnic Institute of Milan, where he taught sociology of media and digital cultures. Calzati has authored several peer-reviewed academic articles and five books, among which *Mediating Travel Writing, Mediated China: The Middle Kingdom in Travel Books and Blogs* (Common Ground, 2018).

Wanshu Cong is a lecturer at the College of Law of the Australian National University (ANU). Her research interests include the theory and history of international law, critical legal studies, and the intersection of law and technology. Her current project draws from Marxist and Third World Approaches to International Law to examine the histories and contestations of freedom of information in international law. Cong holds a doctoral degree from McGill University and was Max Weber Fellow at the European University Institute and Global Academic Fellow before joining the ANU.

Françoise Daucé is Professor at the School for Advanced Studies in the Social Sciences (EHESS) and Director of CERCEC. Her current research work focuses on censorship in the public sphere and the framing of political criticism in Russian society. She coordinates the research project ResisTIC project (2018–2022). She published in a range of journals, including *First Monday*, *Critique Internationale*, *Revue d'études comparatives Est-Ouest*,

Europe-Asia Studies, *Problems of Post-Communism*, *Journal of Civil Society*, and *Laboratorium: Russian Review of Social Research*.

Henrique Estides Delgado is a PhD candidate in the Josef Korbel School of International Studies at the University of Denver and in the Department of Economics at G. d'Annunzio University of Chieti-Pescara. His research interests are in the politics and economics of development, with a focus on the institutions that mediate technological upgrading and the role of international flows. He has worked as a professor in Brazil (Santa Úrsula University, among others) and in the United States (University of Denver and Colorado School of Mines). Delgado currently works as a researcher in a project funded by the Italian Ministry for Education, University and Research.

Vashishtha Doshi is a PhD student in the Department of Political Science at the University of California, Santa Barbara (UCSB). His research interests include currency internationalization, politics of sovereign debt, and the geopolitics of finance and technology. His dissertation focuses on the economic statecraft of middle powers, and the policies enacted that allow them to enhance (or not) their autonomy in a hierarchically structured world of technology and finance. The research seeks to explore what differences in international relations, domestic business–state relations, and institutional setups allow developing countries to enact (or not) autonomy-enhancing policies. Vashishtha also has several years of public service and higher education administration experience. He currently serves as the Associate Director of Career Development for the M.S. in Business Analytics program at UC Davis Graduate School of Management.

Ksenia Ermoshina is a tenure researcher at the Center for Internet and Society National Centre for Scientific Research (CNRS) and an associate researcher at the Citizen Lab (University of Toronto). She holds a PhD from Mines Paris Tech and develops an interdisciplinary approach on the intersection of Science and Technology Studies, usability studies, and network measurements. As a specialist in sociology of privacy-enhancing technologies and surveillance studies, she is also involved in software development (with Delta Chat and CENO browser) as a user experience researcher.

Venkatesh Hariharan is the India Representative of the Open Invention Network, an organization that protects the open source community from patent litigation, Public Policy Director for FOSS United, and a researcher in digital public goods. Hariharan has thirty-two years of experience in journalism and public policy with organizations such as Indian Express, IIIT Bangalore, Red Hat, Google, iSPIRT, and the Data Governance Network at IDFC Institute. In these roles, he has been involved in key policy issues such as open source in government, open standards, software patents, Indian Language Computing, free speech on the internet, privacy, building and evangelizing digital public goods, and many others. His long-term interest is in democratizing access to technology and knowledge.

Valéry Kossov is an associate professor in Russian language and civilization at the University Grenoble Alpes and Director of the Centre for Contemporary Slavic Studies at ILCEA4. His recent work in the ResisTIC research project addresses the issue of the legal framework of the internet in contemporary Russia as well as the strategies of resistance and circumvention of legal constraints by Russian lawyers engaged in the defense of digital rights.

Benjamin Loveluck is Junior Professor of Political Science at Paris-Panthéon-Assas University, a researcher at Centre for the Study and Research on Administrative and Political Sciences (CERSA). His current research focuses on surveillance, censorship, and social control online (such as digital vigilantism). His wider interests include online political practices, digital governance, and the political economy of information. He has published in a range of journals including *Journal of Information Technology & Politics*, *First Monday*, *Global Crime*, and *Internet Policy Review*.

Francesca Musiani is Associate Research Professor at the CNRS. She is Deputy Director of the Center for Internet and Society of CNRS, which she cofounded in 2019. She is also an associate researcher at the Center for the Sociology of Innovation (i3/MINES ParisTech) and Global Fellow at the Internet Governance Lab, American University in Washington, DC. Francesca is the author, with Ksenia Ermoshina, of *Concealing for Freedom: The Making of Encryption, Secure Messaging and Digital Liberties* (2022, Mattering Press) and the author, coauthor, and editor of numerous other articles and books. She is the vice president for research of Internet Society France, has collaborated with the French Parliament (2014–2015) and the French Council for Audiovisual Media (2015–2018), and is the recent coauthor of a study on internet fragmentation for the European Parliament (2022).

Sarayu Natarajan is the founder of Aapti Institute, a think tank working at the intersection of technology and society. Her research and practice focus on digital public goods and infrastructures, open technology, governance, inclusion, and citizenship. Professionally, she has a background in management consulting (McKinsey & Company), venture investing (Elevar Equity), program development and management (Gray Matters Capital), and academic research. She has a PhD in political science from King's College London, an MA in public policy from the School of International and Public Affairs at Columbia University, and a BA degree in arts and law from the National Law School of India University, Bangalore.

Bella Ostromooukhova is an associate professor at Sorbonne University. She is a member of the research project ResisTIC project (2018–2022). Her research in the sociology of culture focuses on independent publishing and censorship issues, as well as on internet publishing in contemporary Russia. She has published in *First Monday*, *Terminal*, *Cahiers du*

Monde russe, Le Mouvement Social, and Laboratorium: Russian Review of Social Research.

Perrine Poupin is a sociologist, Associate Research Professor at CNRS, at the Centre for research on sound space and urban environment (CRESSON) in the Ambiances Architectures Urbanities Laboratory team in Grenoble. She works on environmental issues, protest movements, and war in Russia and Ukraine. She is a member of the research project ResisTIC project (2018–2022). In the past few years, she has focused and published on the Shies protest against government plans for a massive landfill in the Arkhangelsk Region, in Russia's north, which was launched by local habitants and lasted two years.

Johannes Thumfart is currently conducting a project on internet shutdowns within the European Union's Horizon 2020 program as a Marie Skłodowska-Curie fellow at VUB. He conducted a research project about digital sovereignty at Vrije Universiteit Brussels (VUB) from 2020 to 2022, which was supported by Gerda Henkel Stiftung. Following research and teaching positions at Humboldt University and Free University in Berlin, Paris VIII, University of Cincinnati and Universidad Iberoamericana in Mexico City, he is currently teaching ethics of international security management at the Berlin School of Economics and Law. He is a trained philosopher and historian and holds a PhD in the intellectual history of international law.

Tales Tomaz is a researcher and lecturer in media policy and media economics at the University of Salzburg (Austria) and a project manager of the EU-funded Euromedia Ownership Monitor (EurOMo: https://media-ownership.eu). Between 2019 and 2021, he managed the Media for Democracy Monitor, coedited and published a book trilogy on the topic with Josef Trappel, published by Nordicom. His current research interests are normative theories of news media, news media structure, and digital communication governance, focused especially on public regulation and alternative economic models.

Anna Zaytseva is Associate Professor at the University of Toulouse 2 Jean Jaurès, a member of the LLA Créatis laboratory, and an associate member of CERCEC/EHESS. She specializes in the sociology of arts, cultural practices, social movements, and urbanism. Her interests include transformations of cultural industries and intellectual property rights in the digital age, the evolution of cultural hierarchies and creative figures in the USSR and contemporary Russia, and the diversity and historical development of forms of engagement and protest at the intersection of art, "alternative" cultures, and activism. She is also a translator of works in the humanities and social sciences and of independent comics.

Preface

With 40% of the world's population, 25% of global GDP, and large sums of one of the world's most valuable resources – personal data – BRICS countries (Brazil, Russia, India, China, and South Africa) are playing an increasingly important role in global digital development and policymaking. Yet, their conceptions, narratives, and initiatives of digital sovereignty remain surprisingly understudied. This is the first book-length project to explore the digital sovereignty debate from a Global South perspective by analyzing BRICS countries' approaches to digital governance as well as offering a forward-looking take on what a digital world less dependent on a handful of Silicon Valley tech giants might look like and what alternatives there might be.

Just as the BRICS alliance is a developing world's response to the 2008 global financial crisis and the 2009 Euro crisis, triggered by the subprime mortgage crisis in the US, many of the BRICS digital sovereignty initiatives are also expressions of a strong desire to build a multipolar world, seeking independence from and alternatives to a US-centric model of digital development and governance. This book assembles a collection of fine academic analyses of key digital sovereignty issues in the BRICS countries from diverse and complementary perspectives: from historical imaginaries to up-to-date conceptualizations of digital sovereignty, from e-payment systems to smart cities, and from legal analyses to geopolitical assessments. Given the growing international relevance of the BRICS grouping, corroborated by its recent expansion, we expect the perspectives and issues identified in the book will be of great importance to the future debate and shape of global digital governance.

This book makes significant epistemological, theoretical, and strategic contributions to the growing research on digital sovereignty. *Epistemologically*, this is the first book-length project to explore the digital sovereignty debate from an underappreciated Global South perspective, drawing from discourses and practices in the BRICS countries. This collective effort situates the debate at a critical historical and geopolitical juncture, against the backdrop of the 2013 Snowden Affair, the Facebook–Cambridge Analytica scandal during the 2016 US presidential election, and the recent Russian invasion of Ukraine started in the middle of a global pandemic and economic recession.

The emergence of the BRICS not only represents the "rise of the rest" (Amsden, 2001) in an increasingly multipolar, *post-Western* world (Stuenkel, 2016), it also signifies a *post-global* moment when the world's subalterns recognize the US-led neoliberal globalization experiment as a failed master narrative (Lopez, 2007) in need of a substantial reboot. The ways in which such a reboot may occur, however, are far from clear and deserve great attention. In the digital realm, while once imagined as an instrument for a borderless "global village," the internet is currently undergoing complex processes of renationalization (e.g., China, Russia, and to some extent India) and regionalization (e.g., the EU). BRICS countries, like many others around the world, are grappling with conflicting sets of realities and desires – individual privacy and national security, data localization and cross-border data flows, digital self-determination and international technological trade – often driven by concurrent national priorities, international commitments, and ambitions for global expansion and influence.

Theoretically, the book also makes several important contributions to an emerging and prominent debate on digital sovereignty. Importantly, we depart from a normative, legal approach toward (digital) sovereignty centered around the nation-state. Instead, we define "digital sovereignty" as ultimately the exercise of agency, power, and control over digital infrastructure, data, services, and protocols. While Westphalian norms that undergird many of the modern nation-states such as territorial integrity, legal equality, and noninterference still dominate in academic, policy, and public debates about (digital) sovereignty, we recognize that, in reality, borders are repeatedly transgressed, international norms are frequently violated in a world of asymmetrical power, so much so that some argue sovereignty is an "organized hypocrisy" (Krasner, 1999). The gap between norms and reality is especially pronounced in the digital realm where much of the world's digital infrastructure, data, and services remain overly dependent on a handful of Silicon Valley companies that deploy a remarkable level of corporate digital sovereignty (Belli, 2022).

Further, beyond the conventional state-centric interpretation, recent literature on digital sovereignty (e.g., Belli, 2021a; Belli & Hadzic, 2023; Couture & Toupin, 2019; Pohle & Thiel, 2020) has moved to incorporate diverse discursive and policy practices. Increasing public concern over data privacy, state surveillance, corporate abuse, and digital colonialism (e.g., Couture & Toupin, 2019; Zuboff, 2019a) has given ascendance to a wide array of alternative perspectives on digital sovereignty that emphasize individual autonomy, indigenous rights, community well-being, and sustainability. Couture and Toupin's article (2019), for instance, features *five* perspectives on digital sovereignty: "cyberspace sovereignty," "digital sovereignty, governments and states," "indigenous digital sovereignty," "social movements and digital sovereignty," and "personal digital sovereignty." Our conceptual framework builds on this line of work but extends it to include *seven* theoretical perspectives that can guide contextualized analyses: state digital sovereignty, supranational digital sovereignty, network digital sovereignty, corporate digital sovereignty, personal digital sovereignty, postcolonial digital sovereignty, and commons digital sovereignty. We also demonstrated how these seven perspectives may prove to be particularly useful to inform debates in a single application area such as "data sovereignty" or "algorithmic sovereignty."

Rather than making nation-states the default actors with the legitimacy or capacity to exercise digital agency, power, and control over citizens' data and digital lives, our new theoretical framework recognizes and shows with empirical evidence that a plethora of actors including empowered individuals, companies, communities, and even supranational alliances can pursue and influence digital sovereignty. As judged by the short yet intense history of the internet, nation-states routinely fail to protect their citizens' digital rights and aspirations for self-determination. Questionable business players can also drive multistakeholder efforts in the name of human rights and democracy while stripping away human protection and dignity. Only by asking who can (legitimately) wield agency, power, and control over digital infrastructure, data, services, and protocols, who ultimately defines "digital sovereignty" and for what purposes, and to what extent a particular form of "digital sovereignty" enhances or worsens the autonomy, choices, and protection of a country's citizens can we start to have a more meaningful debate of "digital sovereignty."

Strategically, this volume acknowledges that BRICS countries' approaches offer some telling examples of not only how and why digital sovereignty may be needed and constructed but also how dysfunctional the implementation of digital sovereignty policies may become without a coherent long-term vision. BRICS countries' experiences underscore the importance of self-determination, strategic autonomy, rights-based frameworks, and governance, whether the "sovereign" is an individual, a community, a corporation, a state, or a group of states. BRICS countries have realized that without sufficient understanding, the development or control of digital infrastructures, data, and services, aspiring "digital sovereigns" are doomed to remain "digital subjects." In this perspective, they have developed technologies, implemented national policies, and made intra-BRICS arrangements to escape technological dependency and try to preserve or construct their capacity to be exert agency, power, and control online. Their digital policies, increasingly influential beyond their national borders, are often considered models in the Global South, even if they are not openly acknowledged as such by policymakers in developed countries.

Importantly, we also need to take BRICS digital sovereignty narratives, policies, and practices with a grain of salt. Indeed, digital sovereignty may be driven by a wide spectrum of motivations, including authoritarian control and protectionism, alongside self-determination and empowerment, which may produce both negative and positive outcomes. On the one hand, such policies may strongly enhance cybersecurity, fiscal justice, and innovation. China, for instance, built the only digital ecosystem that can compete with Silicon Valley over the past three decades. Brazil pioneered the national adoption of open-source software in 2003 to avoid technological dependence. Also, in partnership with the EU, Brazil constructed EllaLink, an undersea cable to connect Brazil directly to Portugal, to circumvent US surveillance and enhance its digital sovereignty. Indian activists staged the impressive #SaveTheInternet movement in 2016 to reject Facebook's dubious Internet.org initiative supposedly to offer more digital freedom to Indians in poverty. Thanks to the prohibition of zero-rating practices, India has become the only Global South country to experience meaningful connectivity, unleashing a new era of innovation and construction of easily accessible digital public infrastructure (DPI). South Africa has developed its own data protection and cybersecurity model, but pernicious practices of censorship and surveillance have also been introduced under the auspice of digital sovereignty that seriously curtail citizens' rights, privacy, and security. Under President Putin, Russia passed the Sovereign Internet Law in 2019 and pursued an intensive process of sovereignization of the Russian segment of the internet, the "RuNet" despite grassroots resistance. BRICS experiences show it is critical to examine not only the discursive claims to digital sovereignty but also the specific actions and outcomes in contexts.

Last but not the least, we are also witnessing a new generation of techno-regulatory initiatives that aim at embedding digital sovereignty into technology to purposefully shape the evolution of society and economy through digital infrastructure. This new approach to policy and regulation by technology, particularly evident in numerous BRICS experiences, deserves academic, policy, and public attention. While not necessarily a trend toward techno-authoritarianism where technology becomes an instrument of control, embedding digital sovereignty into technology can also be a positive exercise of self-determination, allowing individuals, communities, and countries to become the protagonists of their own digital development. The India Stack, for instance, fosters the digitalization of the entire country through the development of DPI based on open-source technology. While not exempt from criticism, it is a fascinating example of digital sovereignty fostered by the state but implemented in a decentralized way by technologists through technology, no less effective than state policy. Similarly, Brazil has embraced DPI by creating Pix, the national electronic payment system established by the Brazilian Central Bank, that in less than three years has become omnipresent, breaking the previous online payment (and ecommerce data) duopoly of Visa and Mastercard

(Belli, 2023). This and other initiatives from BRICS and the Global South need to be carefully studied and understood by researchers, policymakers, and civil society advocates alike, as they hold promise to create entire new avenues for governance, policy, and regulation.

Taken altogether, this edited book volume will contribute to not only epistemological and theoretical debates on digital sovereignty but also their varied applications and perspectives from the Global South and emerging power alliances, critical to the shaping of the world's digital future and policymaking. As such, this book promises to enrich the ongoing and far from settled debate on digital sovereignty and digital governance among scholars, researchers, policymakers, civil society, and businesses in both developed and developing countries.

Acknowledgments

The seeds of this book project were sown in 2018 when the CyberBRICS Project was initiated by Luca Belli as the first research initiative dedicated to exploring digital policies in the BRICS countries. It has since been hosted by the Center for Technology and Society at FGV Law School, Rio de Janeiro, Brazil.

Since the inception of the project, the FGV Rio Law School and particularly its Dean, Professor Sergio Guerra, have been constantly supportive, understanding the incredible potential of this unique project. We would like to thank FGV and CyberBRICS supporters to promote invaluable and innovative research on some of the most pressing digital issues in leading emerging economies, which were enormously underexplored previously. The CyberBRICS project is proud to have established a new network of Global South leaders and scholars, driven by their interest and passion for digital governance from the perspective of the Majority World with a platform for collaborative research.

Min Jiang joined the CyberBRICS Fellowship Program as a China fellow in 2019. She is grateful for the support from Luca and her former Dean, Dr. Nancy Gutierrez, who saw the CyberBRICS project's potential and encouraged building international connections. Having collaborated on the book *CyberBRICS: Cybersecurity Regulations in the BRICS Countries* published by Springer in 2021, Min and Luca reunited for a new endeavor focused on the digital sovereignty debate and, more broadly, digital governance in the Global South. Min wrote about Chinese internet sovereignty a decade prior. Over time, many digital sovereignty issues persisted and have become more intertwined with cybersecurity and other digital governance issues. A new project was needed to explore how BRICS countries were shaping their digital sovereignty and digital governance narratives and initiatives.

We are particularly proud that this book project is truly global and interdisciplinary in nature with contributors spanning all six continents of Africa,

Asia, Oceania, Europe, North America, and South America crossing disciplinary boundaries of communication studies, law, political science, international relations, as well as language and cultural studies. This diversity is not only a reflection of the growing international interest of the BRICS alliance and the "rise of the rest" that it represents but also the global relevance and importance of the digital sovereignty debate. We are especially grateful for the faith our authors placed in the collective endeavor as well as in us as coeditors as we continuously improved the book for almost three years. The hard work, insight, feedback, advice, and support we received from this vibrant scholarly community is inspiring. We would like to acknowledge their excellent work and warm friendship.

Our partners at Cambridge University Press deserve our heartfelt special thanks. Dr. Lance Bennett, book editor for the "Communication, Society and Politics" series, took an immediate interest in this project and helped us sharpen our arguments, thinking, and composition of the book. Ms. Rachel Blaifeder, our Cambridge editor, is another wonderful sounding board who shepherded us through the entire publishing process with care and grace., Mses. Jadyn Fauconier-Herry, Chloe Quinn, and Swati Kumari also attended to every publishing detail with expediency and professionalism. The three anonymous reviewers also provided us with sharp critique and wise feedback that helped us improve our book a great deal. We are thankful to have worked with such a stellar team at Cambridge University Press.

Also hardworking behind the scene are many of our colleagues, friends, and research assistants. Leah Woehr and Kristen Zhang, who were Min Jiang's research assistants while M.A. students at the University of North Carolina at Charlotte and who have gone on to pursue their doctoral degrees, helped with copyediting and indexing of the book manuscript. Eduardo Brasil, Nibin Babu, and João Pedro Demambro, research assistants of Luca Belli, have provided valuable editorial support.

Finally, we want to thank the institutions that provided financial support for the book to be open access to all. CTS-FGV provided the majority of the funding for this effort, thanks to the generous contributions it received from the Open Society Foundations and the Ford Foundation. Atkins Library and the College of Humanities, Earth and Social Sciences (CHESS) at the University of North Carolina at Charlotte (USA) also offered to cover the cost of open access with facilitation from Associate Dean for Collection Services at Atkins Elizabeth Siler and CHESS Interim Associate Dean for Research Beth Whitaker. Paris Lodron Universität Salzburg (Austria) covered the remaining open-access funding needs with help from Drs. Tales Tomaz, Josef Trappel, and Ursula Schachl-Raber.

A book of this scope could not have been done by us two alone. We are deeply grateful for the community and support that have nurtured it to fruition.

Special Acknowledgments: Institutional Sponsors for Open Access

FGV DIREITO RIO
CENTRO DE TECNOLOGIA
E SOCIEDADE

The Center for Technology and Society at Fundação Getulio Vargas Law School (Rio de Janeiro)

cyberBRICS

The CyberBRICS project (https://cyberbrics.info/)

UNIVERSITY OF NORTH CAROLINA
CHARLOTTE
COLLEGE OF HUMANITIES &
EARTH AND SOCIAL SCIENCES

University of North Carolina at Charlotte, College of Humanities, Earth and Social Sciences (CHESS)

UNIVERSITY OF NORTH CAROLINA
CHARLOTTE
J. MURREY ATKINS LIBRARY

University of North Carolina at Charlotte, Atkins Library

PARIS
LODRON
UNIVERSITÄT
SALZBURG

Paris Lodron University of Salzburg

Abbreviations

AI	Artificial intelligence
ASEAN	Association of Southeast Asian Nations
BRICS	Brazil, Russia, India, China, and South Africa
CAC	Cyberspace Administration of China
CPTPP	Comprehensive and Progressive Agreement for Trans-Pacific Partnership
DNS	Domain name system
DPI	Digital public infrastructure
ECJ	European Court of Justice
EU	European Union
ICANN	Internet Corporation for Assigned Names and Numbers
IMF	International Monetary Fund
ITU	International Telecommunication Union
NWICO	New World Information and Communication Order
SCO	Shanghai Cooperation Organization
SOE	State-owned enterprises
UDHR	Universal Declaration of Human Rights
UN	United Nations
UNESCO	United Nations Educational, Scientific and Cultural Organization
W3C	World Wide Web Consortium
WIC	World Internet Conference
WSIS	World Summit on the Information Society
WTO	World Trade Organization

1

Introduction

Contesting Digital Sovereignty: Untangling a Complex and Multifaceted Concept

Min Jiang and Luca Belli

1.1 DEBATING DIGITAL SOVEREIGNTY

The last decade has witnessed a series of initiatives, both top-down and bottom-up, in BRICS countries (Brazil, Russia, India, China, and South Africa) to reassert their digital sovereignty, especially in reaction to Snowden's 2013 revelations of US National Security Agency's (NSA's) massive global surveillance programs. Brazil affirmed its commitment to building EllaLink, an undersea cable to connect Brazil directly to Portugal, and connecting by proxy South America to Europe to circumvent US surveillance and enhance its digital sovereignty. Putin's Russia, in a bid to restrict foreign influence and bolster its digital borders, pursued "sovereign RuNet" after passing the *Sovereign Internet Law* in 2019 despite grassroots resistance. In India, besides state-led efforts in constructing digital public infrastructure (DPI) known as the "India Stack," activists organized the social movement #SaveTheInternet in 2016, resoundingly rejecting Facebook's Internet.org initiative (which offers free limited web access to those who cannot afford it) as a form of anticompetitive digital colonialism. China, having long filtered content at the border with the Great Firewall and avowed to defend its digital sovereignty, ramped up its pursuit of digital independence in the unfolding US–China geopolitical rivalry, following Trump administration's ban on Huawei 5G products and threat to force a sale of TikTok to a US firm in 2020 (Jiang, 2021). South Africa, like many other developing countries, tries to forge its own path of digital independence by leveraging Chinese or EU tech equipment, US digital platforms, and its newly enacted data protection policies. Across the five BRICS countries, digital sovereignty discourses, practices, and policies have unfolded differently and unevenly.

This book project, to the best of the authors' knowledge, the first of its kind to explore the digital sovereignty debate in the BRICS countries, attempts to untangle this complex and multifaceted concept from a Global South epistemic lens. As a hotly debated topic, digital sovereignty inspires interpretive diversity and disagreements rather than uniformity and consensus (Ayers, 2016; Broeders & van den Berg, 2020; Chander & Sun, 2023; Couldry & Mejias, 2019; Couture & Toupin, 2019; Duarte, 2017; Herlo, Irrgang, Joost, & Unteidig, 2022; Kukutai & Taylor, 2016; Mueller, 2017; Pohle & Thiel, 2020). The Westphalian notion of sovereignty – nation-states accorded territorial integrity, legal equality, and noninterference in international affairs monopolize the legitimate use of force and supreme authority over its territory – has not only been challenged in history repeatedly through episodes of colonial expansions and border transgressions (Krasner, 1999) but also faces an unprecedented upset in the digital era from actors ranging from individuals and civil society groups to companies and supranational entities attempting to assert their agency, power, and control.

While the nation-state has traditionally been the legal vessel of sovereignty, chasms exist between normative assumptions of sovereignty and widely uneven practices in reality. Codified into the UN Charter, the modern system of nation-states can trace its origin to the French philosopher Jean Bodin's conceptualization of sovereignty in the sixteenth century as well as the *1648 Peace of Westphalia*, which created a group of legally equal states in the Holy Roman Empire (Grimm, 2015). Yet, centuries of colonization well after the Westphalia treaties and unilateral border transgressions (e.g., invasions of Iraq and Ukraine) call into question many a time the sanctity and normativity of national sovereignty. Besides territorial infringements, asymmetric economic, political, and cultural relations have throughout history produced foreign dominations and interferences. In addition, the normative assumptions of sovereignty also suffer from logical contradictions (e.g., nonintervention versus democracy promotion) and a lack of institutional arrangements to deter dominant actors from abusing their force unilaterally in international conflicts (Krasner, 1999).

Sovereignty is frequently a function of power. Strong nation-states often engage in tactics beyond the scope of their sovereignty normatively defined; weaker states generally lack power and resources to exert effective influence, so much so that Krasner (1999), for instance, argues that sovereignty is "organized hypocrisy." Further, an absolutist notion of sovereignty is criticized to be unattainable, especially in an age of global challenges ranging from organized terrorism, regime change attempts, turbulent international financial markets to global pandemics, climate change, and digital technologies (Havercroft, 2011). In this perspective, the capability to muster digital technologies offers to a wide range of actors a new powerful tool to exercise self-determination,[1] control, and ultimately sovereignty.

[1] The right to self-determination plays an instrumental role to allow individuals to enjoy their inalienable human rights. For this reason, it is enshrined as the first article of both the *Charter of the United Nations* and the *International Covenants of Human Rights*. According

It is important to acknowledge that sovereignty is a complex concept that arose as an attempt to frame the internal structure of a state but ended up becoming the cornerstone of international public law. The German sociologist, jurist, and political economist Max Weber famously considered that states are "political enterprises" (Weber, Gerth, & Wright Mills, 1948), characterized by "the monopoly of the legitimate use of physical force within a given territory" (p. 78). Carl Schmitt (1985), an influential political theorists, argued in line with a Hobbesian reasoning that rather than a monopoly of coercion, the sovereign enjoys the monopoly to decide. In a similar way, Peter Malanczuk (1997), author of one of the most utilized international law manuals, provides a useful discussion of sovereignty, emphasizing that the sovereign enjoys the "supreme power" to decide who is "bound by the laws which he made" and that international law fundamentally interprets sovereignty as independence, stressing that "when international lawyers say that a state is sovereign, all that they really mean is that it is independent, that is, that it is not a dependency of some other state" (p. 17).

These assumptions constitute core pillars underpinning the public law's construction of national institutions and governance based on the consideration of national governments as the only entities able to craft and implement – using coercion, if necessary – their vision for the achievement of the peoples' fundamental right to self-determination. However, these key tenants of public law become considerably more uncertain when they clash with global phenomena and, particularly, digital technologies' capacity to skirt the application of national legislation. This latter dimension means that non-state actors, whether corporations, communities, or individuals, can acquire the

to these international legal instruments, states have agreed that "all peoples have a right to self-determination" and that "by virtue of that right they are free to determine their political status and to pursue their economic, social and cultural development." While self-determination is usually discussed in its external dimension, that is, territorial and political independence from external actors, it is essential to stress that here we are referring to the internal dimension of self-determination, that is, the right to freely determine and pursue one's economic, social, and cultural development, including independently choosing, developing, and adopting digital technologies. Such conception is also corroborated by the fundamental right to "informational self-determination" as an expression of the human right to have and develop a personality, first recognized by the German Supreme Court in the 1983 Census case. The fundamental right to free development of personality is also formally recognized internationally. Article 22 of the *Universal Declaration of Human Rights* affirms that "everyone is entitled to the realization of the rights needed for one's dignity and the free development of their personality." The *International Covenant on Economic, Social and Cultural Rights* consecrates this fundamental principle regarding one's right to education and to participate in public life. Particularly, the *Covenant*'s signatories have agreed that the right to education "shall be directed to the full development of the human personality and the sense of its dignity [...] and enable all persons to participate effectively in society" (Article 13.1). Moreover, the free development of personality is explicitly considered as instrumental to exercise the fundamental right "to take part in cultural life [and] to enjoy the benefits of scientific progress and its applications" (Article 15) (see further elaboration in Belli 2017, 2019).

capabilities to understand, develop, and ultimately exercise agency through technology, thus either eschewing the exercise of the classic state sovereignty or exercising a type of quasi-sovereignty (Belli, 2022).

Drawing from existing scholarship (e.g., Couture & Toupin, 2019; Floridi, 2020), we define *digital sovereignty* as the exercise of agency, power, and control in shaping digital infrastructure, data, services, and protocols. Couture and Toupin (2019) argued that digital sovereignty today is often linked to concepts such as freedom, capacity, nationalism, and increasingly control over data (p. 2310). Floridi (2020) defined digital sovereignty specifically as "the *control* of *data*, *software* (e.g., AI), *standards and protocols* (e.g., 5G, domain names), *processes* (e.g., cloud computing), *hardware* (e.g., mobile phones), *services* (e.g., social media, e-commerce), and *infrastructures* (e.g., cables, satellites, smart cities), in short, for the *control* of the *digital*" (pp. 370–371, italicized in original). Here, we join them in departing from a conventional, normative, state-centric approach that views digital sovereignty as a mere online extension of state sovereignty.

Traditional approaches tend to reify (digital) sovereignty as a self-evident thing while overlooking its often fragile, hybrid, and contested nature. In reality, borders are repeatedly transgressed, and international norms are frequently violated. The gap between the norms of state sovereignty and reality is especially pronounced in the digital realm where much of the world's digital infrastructure, data, and services are overwhelmingly dependent on a handful of Silicon Valley firms and increasingly their Chinese counterparts. By reframing "digital sovereignty" as contested rather than merely accepted, discursively and strategically practiced to articulate legitimation rather than legally binding (Couture & Toupin, 2019; Pohle & Thiel, 2020), we make room for exploring the concept at levels beyond the default plane of nation-states, thus allowing scholars, policymakers, and the public to engage with a wider range of perspectives and discourses on digital sovereignty that can provide visions for the future, especially beyond US and Chinese influence in global digital affairs and governance.

Spanning many disciplines including law, communication studies, political science, international relations, and public policy, the much-debated concept of digital sovereignty is rooted in the classic tension between the supposedly borderless nature of the internet and the bordered conceptualization of sovereign nation-states. At the onset, one must acknowledge the idea of the internet posing unprecedented challenges to state sovereignty is not new (e.g., Johnson & Post, 1996; Lessig, 1999a). Prior works in this area have explored state responses to reassert authority and power in cyberspace (Deibert, Palfrey, Rohozinski, & Zittrain, 2010; Goldsmith & Wu, 2006). However, global digital policymaking was long dominated by an "Internet freedom" agenda (Clinton, 2010a) that regards the internet as a borderless global network, able to circumvent national sovereignty to spread freedom and democracy without paying sufficient attention to the underlying security, economic, political, and cultural risks associated with such a vision (Morozov, 2011). China's assertion of "Internet sovereignty" (Jiang, 2010), that is, managing networks, information, and population within its borders based on its own laws for security and economic autonomy was scoffed at as an anachronistic, undesirable anomaly, which is understandable due to the Chinese state's instrumental use of domestic laws to implement extensive online political censorship.

In an era of globalization, rather than emphasizing "sovereignty" or "digital sovereignty," scholarly work on digital issues tends to be subsumed under a framework of internet governance or digital governance. Internet governance and digital governance can overlap a great deal, although internet governance tends to stress the governance of the internet itself through a multi-stakeholder model involving states, private sector, and civil society in developing shared principles, rules, norms, and decision-making that shape the evolution and use of the internet (Kurbalija, 2016; WSIS, 2005), while digital governance tends to underscore the use of digital technologies – including those that cannot be properly categorized as internet such as AI – in governing and government processes (Zittrain, 2019). For instance, internet governance focuses on issues such as internet domain names and addresses (Mueller, 2004; Palladino & Santaniello, 2021), internet protocols and applications (DeNardis, 2009, 2014, 2020), and internet governance process and institutions (Mueller, 2017; Palladino & Santaniello, 2021; Radu, 2019). Digital governance, on the other hand, tends to encompass a wider array of digital issues converging with and going beyond internet governance. Earlier works in digital governance tend to be primarily concerned with bridging digital divide (e.g., Norris, 2001), integrating digital technologies to improve public services and democratic participation (e.g., Milakovich, 2012), and balancing privacy and security in digital inclusion (e.g., Chen, 2017). More recent digital governance works focus more on issues of data protection (Chander & Sun, 2023; Cohen, 2019a; Weber & Staiger, 2017; Zuboff, 2019a), artificial intelligence (Crawford, 2020), and quantum computing (Hoofnagle & Garfinkel, 2021). The recent digital governance foci may be connected to the evolution and use of the internet but can also be distinct from it. In both circumstances, their development and regulation may have enormous consequences for digital sovereignty. Thus, digital sovereignty – conceived as the exercise of agency and power in shaping digital infrastructure, data, services, and protocols – crisscrosses internet governance and digital governance.

In the evolution of the digital sovereignty debate, arguably, a critical moment in the digital sovereignty debate came in 2013 with Snowden's revelation of NSA's surveillance programs. Besides a newfound distrust of the US government's "Internet freedom" agenda, US tech giants' catastrophic failures during the 2016 US presidential election also created a deep skepticism of the credibility and neutrality of such corporate entities. These pivotal moments set in motion global repercussions fueling not only critical reflections of our collective digital well-being but also the rise of all forms of "digital sovereignty." Two prominent books – Shoshana Zuboff's *Surveillance Capitalism* (2019) and Nick Couldry and Ulises Mejias's *The Costs of Connection: How Data Is Colonizing Human Life and Appropriating It for Capitalism* (2019) that do not address "digital sovereignty" directly – ushered a critical turn in scholarly and public debate of digital governance.

Following the Snowden affair, publications on digital sovereignty witnessed a sharp uptick. A burst of new voices and claims to "digital sovereignty" started to account for the diverse array of perspectives of this concept. Several well-received articles (e.g., Couture & Toupin, 2019; Floridi, 2020; Pohle & Thiel, 2020) have brought the concept to some prominence by repositioning digital sovereignty in a contested discursive field rather than accepting the normative approach to digital sovereignty. In particular, Couture and Toupin (2019) outlined *five* perspectives on digital sovereignty: "cyberspace sovereignty," "digital sovereignty, governments and states," "indigenous digital sovereignty," "social movements and digital sovereignty," and "personal digital sovereignty." Our conceptual framework builds on this line of work while modifying the terminologies and extending it to account for the claims to digital sovereignty made by tech giants as well as supranational entities such as the EU (see "Perspectives on Digital Sovereignty" in this introduction).

To date, focused book-length treatment of digital sovereignty is not abundant, much less from a Global South perspective. In the US, in the aftermath of the Snowden's revelations, there was a renewed emphasis on cybersecurity and sovereignty that produced books such as *Rethinking Sovereignty in the Context of Cyberspace* (Ayers, 2016), an effort by the US Army War College. Scholars such as Milton Mueller pondered on the prospect of a fragmented internet in *Will the Internet Fragment? Sovereignty, Globalization and Cyberspace* (2017). A notable book from China translated also into English – *Cyberspace Sovereignty: Reflections on Building a Community of Common Future in Cyberspace* – was authored by none other than Binxing Fang (2018), an architect of China's now infamous Great Firewall. This book, unsurprisingly, expounds on the Chinese state's official positions. During this period, indigenous studies also contributed to the emerging debate of digital sovereignty through books such as *Indigenous Data Sovereignty* (Kukutai & Taylor, 2016) and *Network Sovereignty: Building the Internet across Indian Country* (Duarte, 2017).

Following EU's enactment of General Data Protection Regulation (GDPR) in 2018, work on digital sovereignty gained further momentum. Scholars in diverse fields such as communication studies, political science, international relations, political economy, and law have contributed to the current debate of digital sovereignty. Relevant books include *Practicing Sovereignty: Digital Involvement in Times of Crises* (Herlo, Irrgang, Joost, & Unteidig, 2022) that showcases a large collection of articles on contemporary digital sovereignty issues, ranging from algorithmic sovereignty and geofilters to feminist approaches and collective sovereignty. Srivastava's *Hybrid Sovereignty in World Politics* (2022) also critiques the normative ideals of state sovereignty by examining public–private partnerships in structuring sovereignty and international relations in the realms of war, global firms, trade, and international human rights. Most recently, *Data Sovereignty: From the Digital Silk Road to the Return of the State* (Chander & Sun 2023) surveys and debates sovereign states' attempts to cope with the territorial control of data flows and related digital sovereignty issues. New works also pay close attention to individual nation-states' exercise of cyber sovereignty, such as that of China (Kokas, 2022; Timoteo, Verri, & Nanni, 2023).

In sum, our approach to digital sovereignty as the exercise of agency and power in shaping digital infrastructure, data, services, and protocols does not regard the nation-state as the default and only actor capable to exercise and realize sovereign powers. In the digital realm, such powers are often realized through private actors (e.g., tech giants) and desired by individuals, communities, and states that lack them. The shaping of digital infrastructure, data, services, and protocols is thus not only an expression of agency and self-determination but also a product of power and capacity in structuring and influencing digital outcomes. Multiple conceptions of digital sovereignty can overlap or clash as they are experimented with and implemented by different stakeholders in the same jurisdiction. For example, the federal government of a state may implement digital sovereignty policies based on social control through technology (e.g., backdoor mandate), while a local community based in the same state can develop technology for its own collective empowerment (e.g., constructing and managing community networks).

By problematizing "digital sovereignty" and moving beyond a state-centric conceptualization, we can start to raise fundamental questions as to who (legitimately) wields agency, power, and control over digital infrastructure, data, services, and protocols; who ultimately defines "digital sovereignty" and for what purposes; and to what extent a particular form of "digital sovereignty" enhances or worsens the autonomy of, choices by and protection for, a country's citizens. Unlike the freewheeling cyberspace dreamed up by Barlow (1996), we recognize cyberspace is not at all free from states, rules, barriers, prejudices, competing interests, or power differentials. While there is a tendency to frame Western conception of digital sovereignty in terms of public interest and democratic values and conversely brand BRICS promotion of the concept as protectionist and authoritarian, there is also a long history of state surveillance programs in both democratic and nondemocratic countries alike (Chadwick, 2006). While the legitimacy of authoritarian states to exercise "digital sovereignty," for instance to censor, is often called into question, the Snowden revelation of the far reach of NSA and its "Five Eyes" partners into global networks also casts doubt on some Western democracies' legitimacy and neutrality, especially when their actions contradict the purported principles of territorial integrity, legal equality, and noninterference.

If the nation-state is no longer the only legitimate actor with the ability to exercise agency, power, and control in cyberspace or is even capable of doing so in certain cases, it is then possible and desirable to look past the normative, idealistic, and often mythical state-centric construction of "digital sovereignty" and start to understand, describe, and assess how digital sovereignty is structured in practice. Non-state actors and the exercise of their sovereignty would enter the picture: "corporate sovereignty" embodied by the likes of Google, Facebook, and Amazon whose almighty power easily eclipses those of small nation-states (MacKinnon, 2012); "personal digital sovereignty" grounded in individual rights, autonomy, and freedom in relation to body politics and individual personhood (Koopman, 2019); "postcolonial digital sovereignty" aimed at challenging the violent dispossession of (digital) resources in the process of (digital) colonization (Couldry & Mejias, 2019; Coulthard, 2014); and "commons digital sovereignty" motivated by a desire to create alternatives to state or commercial digital technologies to achieve self-determination and sovereignty of the people through technology managed as a common good (Belli, 2017; Haché, 2017). These diverse ideas challenge the singular, normative assumptions of digital sovereignty centered on the nation-state.

Digital sovereignty thus has multiple, and often, contradictory meanings. Although it is customary to approach "digital sovereignty" from a state-centric perspective, this orthodox approach tends to ignore the alternative perspectives and claims to digital sovereignty made at the grassroots and supranational levels as well as at the intersections between them (Couture & Toupin, 2019). Rather than assuming a state-centric view of digital sovereignty as a given, our goal here is to map the wide range of interpretations of this central concept in the digital era from a BRICS perspective and showcase the plethora of actors – individuals, communities, corporations, nation-states, and supranational organizations – striving to become digital sovereigns rather than digital subjects (e.g., Cheung, 2023).

We also recognize digital sovereignty is often used interchangeably with cyber sovereignty, internet sovereignty, and closely related to data sovereignty. A meta-analysis of these concepts by Hummel, Braun, Tretter, and Dabrock (2021) reveals cyber sovereignty is often evoked by nation-states in the context of cyber defense, while internet sovereignty is more often used to reference power and control over the internet network. We consider data sovereignty a corollary, core concept that undergirds these terms with particular relevance to rights and ownership by data subjects. For us, digital sovereignty provides a much broader frame to discuss the shaping of digital infrastructure, data, services, and protocols.

As our literature review of digital sovereignty scholarship above has shown while there is growing literature on digital sovereignty, there is also a profound lack of literature to address digital sovereignty from a collective Global South perspective, especially grounded in BRICS experiences. Taking cues from such recent work as *CyberBRICS: Cybersecurity Regulations in BRICS Countries* (Belli, 2021b), this project intends to shine a spotlight on how different types of digital sovereigns besides the states are claiming sovereignty and exercising their power over digital infrastructure, data, services, and protocols in the BRICS countries. While these five developing countries – Brazil, Russia, India, China, and South Africa – are playing an increasingly important role in global digital development and policymaking, their conceptions, narratives, and initiatives of digital sovereignty remain surprisingly understudied as a collective. Contained here is an excellent collection of cutting-edge academic analyses of key digital sovereignty issues in the BRICS countries – ranging from historical imaginaries to up-to-date conceptualizations, from payment systems to smart cities as architectures of digital sovereignty, and from legal analyses to empirical accounts of the exercise of digital sovereignty by states, companies, and communities – offering much needed visibility to frequently neglected perspectives from the Global South.

Much can be gained by bringing varied BRICS digital sovereignty practices under a single umbrella to view how these Global South countries address such challenges separately and together. For instance, although Putin's Russia is known for promoting an ultranationalistic version of "Internet sovereignty" aimed at separating the RuNet from the global internet, it also routinely faces grassroots resistance with individual and collective expressions of digital sovereignty (Daucé & Musiani, 2021). While US tech giants wield immense sovereign-like power across the globe, thus exporting US state sovereignty by proxy (Belli, 2022), they have also been challenged by bottom-up social movements and connective actions (Bennett & Segerberg, 2013) such as India's #SaveTheInternet movement that rejected Facebook's Internet.org initiative seen as a form of digital colonialism (Mukerjee, 2016). China also banned many US tech giants altogether, while investing billions in the development of an indigenous digital ecosystem. The BRICS grouping, although initially an eclectic network of emerging economies interested in multilateral trade, is also increasingly cooperating on digital development and policymaking (Belli, 2021c), taking a loosely coordinated approach in contrast to EU's more uniform supranational stance toward "digital sovereignty" (Leonard & Shapiro, 2020), for instance, through GDPR.

In addition, these BRICS countries present highly relevant and intriguing case studies of digital sovereignty from the Global South with a considerable range. In the BRICS bloc, one finds not only extreme hostile countries such as Russia centralizing its internet control and manipulation in service of its ongoing war efforts in Ukraine but also a tech powerhouse such as China now locked in a new geopolitical rivalry with the US. Besides, India and Brazil – both relatively new democracies with some recent regress in democratic governance – are crucial middle-power countries with the potential to reshape the digital landscape not only in the Global South but also exert influence globally. Finally, South Africa represents a digital arrangement many other countries increasingly find themselves in, that is, relying heavily on China for cheap hardware, the US for applications/software, and its own newly enacted data protection laws to navigate the unfolding digital spaces. Taken altogether, BRICS countries offer a wide range of digital sovereignty policies and solutions from the Global South.

In Section 1.2, we provide an account of why an exploration of the digital sovereignty debate in the BRICS countries is particularly important and relevant at this moment in time. We outline seven major theoretical perspectives on digital sovereignty that serve to elucidate the different digital sovereigns operating on different planes. We close this introduction with a summary for the chapters that compose this volume to recognize their connections and valuable contributions to the digital sovereignty debate in BRICS countries.

1.2 WHY BRICS? RISE OF THE GLOBAL SOUTH AND EMERGING POWER ALLIANCES

Goldman Sachs economist Jim O'Neill first coined the term "BRIC" (O'Neill, 2001) to designate the four largest emerging economies – Brazil Russia, India and China – that experienced a similar phase of development. Geographically dispersed, economically distinct, culturally diverse, and politically different, BRICS countries may not appear to be the most coherent motley crew (Sparks, 2014), especially given the multiple economic, political, and territorial disputes among them, further complicated by the pandemic and the ongoing wars in Ukraine and Gaza. Despite their differences, BRICS nations were united since the 2000s to introduce overdue reforms at Bretton Woods institutions such as the IMF and the World Bank by demanding more transparency as well as more voting power and representation of emerging economies in the global financial system (Stuenkel, 2020). Over the years, the loosely joint bloc did not impose binding conditions on its member states and maintained an informality and a low degree of institutionalization, signaling the bloc's unwillingness to directly challenge the existing US-centered Western global order (Stuenkel, 2020). Rather than being overtly anti-West as Putin's Russia turned recently, most BRICS member states are more "non-Western," in pursuit of support and expanding influence in the existing structure.

Geopolitically, BRICS's emergence represents the "rise of the rest" (Amsden, 2001) in an increasingly multipolar world. The US as the world's sole superpower since the end of the Cold War, suffered a decline in relative power following several pivotal episodes: the highly costly and unpopular wars in Iraq and Afghanistan for two decades since 2001; the 2008 global financial crisis; the pandemic-induced recession since 2020. BRICS countries, on the other hand, include some of the world's largest growth engines (see Table 1.1), representing 25% of global GDP, 42% of the world's population or 3.2 billion (CGTN, 2022a), and 44% of the global internet population[2]. Despite suffering different degrees of economic setbacks exacerbated by the pandemic

[2] Internal issues of some BRICS countries, such as China's aging population and declining birth rate, do pose considerable challenges to their long-term sustainable development (Bai & Lei, 2020).

TABLE 1.1 *BRICS countries profiles (compared to the US)*[3]

	Brazil	Russia	India	China	South Africa	US
Population (2023)	217 million	144 million	1437 million	1425 million	60 million	341 million
Internet Population (2023)	177 million	127 million	692 million	1079 million	45 million	311 million
GDP (2020, USD)	$1.44 trillion	$1.48 trillion	$2.66 trillion	$14.72 trillion	$0.34 trillion	$21 trillion
GDP (2021, USD)	$1.61 trillion	$1.78 trillion	$3.18 trillion	$17.73 trillion	$0.42 trillion	$23.32 trillion
GDP (2022, USD)	$1.92 trillion	$2.24 trillion	$3.41 trillion	$17.96 trillion	$0.40 trillion	$25.44 trillion
GDP per capita (2022, USD)	$8,918	$15,345	$2,389	$12,720	$6,776	$76,399

Sources: WorldoMeter (2023) for population figures, Statista (2023) for internet population figures, World Bank (2022a) for 2020–2022 GDP and GDP per capita figures.

(e.g., China's strict "Zero Covid" policy), the combined GDP of the BRICS at purchasing power parity has surpassed that of the G7 since 2020 (Statista, 2024). BRICS's existence symbolizes a changing global order where the US's relative decline has paved the way for emerging powers such as China, India, Brazil, Russia, and South Africa from the Global South. It is important to pay attention to the emerging power alliances between the BRICS countries and beyond in remaking the global order.

Economically, the BRICS grouping – an unorthodox experiment – is a direct response to the 2008 global financial crisis and the subsequent 2009 Eurozone crisis that exposed the instability of the global financial system centered around the US. The initial BRIC group organized their first informal gathering in 2006. After the 2008 global economic crisis, the BRIC countries whose economies were largely spared from the crises convened their first summit in 2009 with the induction of South Africa in 2010. The grouping's cooperation, cemented by the establishment of the New Development Bank in 2015 with $100 billion initial capital and Contingent Reserve Arrangement, has come a long way. The New Development Bank, conceived not as a rival to established financial institutions such as the IMF and the World Bank, creates a parallel financial system for the developing countries and symbolizes their expectations and aspirations (Economic Times, 2015). In 2021, the New Development Bank added UAE,

[3] Note Russia's economic statistics are subject to considerable variations due to war-related sanctions since February 2022. Russia's federal statistics service announced a 2.1% GDP contraction for 2022, Business Insider reports (Tan, 2023), although World Bank data show GDP growth for the country. Russia's economy has been resilient due to gains in energy prices.

Bangladesh, Uruguay, and Egypt as new members (NDB, 2022). In 2023, the BRICS summit added four more countries – Egypt, Ethiopia, Iran, and the UAE – to the grouping (BRICS, 2023).

It needs to be acknowledged that in the decade and a half since the global financial crisis and especially since the COVID-19 pandemic, many parts of the world including the US and BRICS countries experienced sharp social divisions, economic instability, and widening wealth gaps. A World Bank report (2022b) shows the richest 1% in the world controlled 54% of new global wealth over the past decade. It accelerated to 63% in 2020 and 2021. The top 1% in America, recent research (Smith, Zidar, & Zwick, 2023) finds, owns nearly as much wealth as the bottom 90%. The pattern of widening income gap is also observed in BRICS countries such as China and India (World Bank, 2022b).

In digital matters, during a time of deep economic crisis, widespread social upheaval, and unprecedented nativist furor, the BRICS grouping provides pointers to the future shape of a new global (digital) order. The war in Ukraine marked the most significant military conflict, including cyberwarfare, in Europe since WWII. Except the Putin administration bent on restoring its sphere of influence in the former Soviet states and mounting a direct challenge to the US as a global superpower (Hinck, Cooley, & Kluver, 2019), China and other emerging powers seem more interested in rising *alongside* the US without either assimilating into the current Western-centric global order or directly challenging it (Barma, Ratner, & Weber, 2014). Instead, they have been creating a "parallel order" (Stuenkel, 2016) to accommodate and complement existent international institutions while making more room for their own autonomy and ability to bargain, compete and mitigate risks associated with dependence on external products or services in an increasingly multipolar world. China, for instance, has developed over the last 30 years the only digital ecosystem to rival Silicon Valley's in both scale and sophistication (Miao, Jiang, & Pang, 2021). India has also built a set of DPI widely known as the "India Stack" (Desai, Manoharan, Jayanth, & Zack, 2023; Raghavan, Jain, & Varma, 2019) for identity, payments, and data exchange. While not exempt from criticism, the India Stack offers an alternative framework to the private sector-led platforms created by either the US or Chinese firms (see Chapter 5 for a payment example).

Russia's invasion of Ukraine in 2022 puts its BRICS partners in a difficult bind. The BRICS bloc, notably China, endorses territorial sovereignty. Ten days after the war started, the BRICS-led New Development Bank stopped all new transactions in Russia, signaling its willingness to avert risks (USCC, 2022). Yet, as the war dragged on and motivated by self-interest, the BRICS bloc did not impose on Russia the same sanctions as the US and the EU did, citing NATO expansion as a legitimate security concern (CNN, 2022). Instead, despite some divergent opinions on the war, the group tried to maintain neutrality and continued with the annual BRICS meeting (USCC, 2022). Witnessing the severe economic sanctions the US and the EU imposed on

Russia due to its invasion of Ukraine, in particular the seizing of Russia central bank's overseas assets of $300 billion by the US government, which is not legal by US Treasury Secretary Janet Yellen's own admission (Lawder, 2022), some developing countries are reconsidering their economic, political, and technological alliances in a US dollar-denominated and US dollar-dominated global economy (CGTN, 2022b).

The 2022 BRICS summit reiterated the grouping's commitment for intra-BRICS cooperation focused on sustainable development toward building a global order more favorable to developing countries to address issues including food insecurity, energy shortage, inflation, debt crisis, and de-dollarization (CNN, 2022). After China's successful brokerage of the Iran–Saudi rapprochement, the 2023 BRICS summit further accelerated the expansion of the group under the BRICS+ model by accepting four more countries – Egypt, Ethiopian, Iran, and the UAE – with more to join in the future (BRICS, 2023). The energy-rich bloc – bolstered by Russia, Iran, and UAE – holds considerable sway in global energy and economic affairs.

Ultimately, the war in Ukraine has not changed BRICS countries' trajectory to explore alternative paths for economic and social developments that do not depend on the US-dominated international order that has failed to eradicate – and frequently condoned or produced – gross inequalities, dysfunctional democracies, environmental catastrophes, and persistent militarism. Despite mounting civilian toll, nuclear threat as well as energy, food, and economic crises worsened by the ongoing Ukraine war, the BRICS bloc has moved forward while preserving multilateral and – most importantly – trade relations critical to their own interest and the functioning of their economies and societies (Zondi, 2022).

Seen from a Global South perspective, the BRICS is the latest iteration of a much wider trend toward "South–South cooperation" (The South Commission, 1990). The concept of Global South entails complex layers of geographical, historical, cultural, political, and economic meanings (Lumumba-Kasongo, 2015). While "Global South" traditionally refers broadly to the regions of Africa, Asia, and Latin America as loci of underdevelopment and cultural primitivism in contrast to the "advanced" societies of North America and Europe in a postcolonial sense, the phrase has also signified over time "center-periphery" dynamics in geopolitical power relations (Dados & Connell, 2012). Historically, anticolonial movements have found expressions in the League Against Imperialism begun in 1928 as well as the Non-Aligned Movement started in the 1950s involving 120 countries to counterbalance the US and Soviet power blocs during the Cold War. It was from such historical lineages that one can trace the Group of 77 formed in the 1960s, Group of 15 in the aftermath of the Cold War, and the BRICS after the 2008 global financial crisis (Prashad, 2012). From a postcolonial perspective, BRICS symbolizes a continuation of a centuries' old attempt to challenge and change an unfair system that preserves former colonizers' interests and to gain independence.

Further, beyond the postcolonial lens, the emergence of the Global South, and BRICS in particular, signifies a "*post*global" moment when the world's subalterns recognize the US-led neoliberal globalization experiment as a failed master narrative (Lopez, 2007, p. 1). Instead of seeing globalization and trickle-down economics lift all boats, the last four decades saw the poor, the marginalized, and the disenfranchised bore the brunt of the suffering. Crisis after crisis – from the 1998 Asian financial crisis to the dot-com bubble, from 9/11 to the ensuing 20-year war on terror, from the 2008 financial crisis to the pandemic-induced global recession – traditional Western-led financial and governance institutions, notably the International Monetary Fund and World Bank, are often perceived in the Global South increasingly as barriers rather than propellers of economic and human development. While Russia is not typically considered part of the Global South given its previous super power status and its complicated relations with other developing countries, its membership in the BRICS bloc represents a repositioning of Russia's strategic interest and alliance vis-à-vis the West. It is within such historical contexts that the BRICS have led the search for a "post-Western" model of global governance.

Finally, whether "post-Western" or "non-Western," BRICS' default preference, unlike Russia's in retrospect, is evolutionary rather than revolutionary (Armijo & Roberts, 2014). As beneficiaries of the global system, BRICS members (China and India, in particular) may find it both hard and costly to abolish the existing global order and establish new ones. So, while the then President Trump attempted to weaken the existing rules and norms of the global system including the WTO and Paris climate accord, BRICS member countries have more invested interest in preserving them. Moreover, it seems that BRICS countries', especially China's, vision or capacity to create new systems and institutions such as the Belt and Road Initiative may not only lack intellectual foundation but also face mounting pushbacks and constraints from within the existing system between a rising power and a ruling one (Allison, 2017). Instead, BRICS countries have opted for a type of "competitive multilateralism" (Stuenkel, 2020) that allows them to flexibly choose political and collaborative frameworks to maximize their national interest. Even though BRICS countries may not speak for or represent the diverse voices and regions of the Global South, its emergence and heterogeneity do mark a crucial moment of international development that is worth unpacking and examining.

It is also worthwhile to emphasize the *emerging* nature of global power alliances that the BRICS represents. First, "emerging" suggests that the power alliances are still in the process of formation and there is an open-endedness to it. The BRICS+ model, for instance, developed quickly as six countries got admitted into this new alliance in 2023 with more countries to be added in the near future. Meanwhile, to counterbalance China in the Asia-Pacific, the US has been actively courting India, particularly by forming "the Quad" along with Japan and New Zealand in a new strategic alliance (White House, 2022).

Second, "emerging" indicates that these power alliances in development are relatively new, perhaps different from and not conforming to traditional conceptualizations of the Global South. In fact, scholars such as Acharya (2014) have argued that under the giant tent of the Global South, there are the "Power South" (e.g., China, India) and the "Poor South" (i.e., countries with few resources or little power) at various stages of economic and human development. Stuenkel (2014) also observed that unlike the more inclusive 1955 Bandung Conference or the Non-Aligned Movement that followed, the more powerful members of the Global South such as the BRICS, given their own ambitions for global influence, may not always recognize the challenges of small poor nations or represent their interests.

Should China and Russia be considered part of the Global South? One must admit there is an awkward "in-betweenness" about them. For some, much of China – beyond its first- and second-tier cities – and many of China's population may well qualify as part of the Global South. While China's economic development has lifted 800 million people out of extreme poverty in the last four decades (World Bank, 2022b), 600 million Chinese still live on incomes of barely 1,000 yuan (or $154) per month (BBC, 2021a), and 348 million Chinese on less than $6.85 a day (World Bank, 2022b). On the other hand, as the world's second largest economy with global ambitions, the collective might of China puts it in an emerging superpower category. In fact, the UN's Finance Center for South-South Cooperation (2023) includes 78 countries, but sometimes also label them as a "Group of 77 and China."

Further, Russia is a unique case on its own. Some (e.g., World Population Review, 2023) consider Russia part of the Global North. Others such as the World Bank (2022a) regard it as a mid-tier country between the Global North and the Global South in terms of per capita income. Still others think Russia now aligns itself with the Global South to address grievances with the Global North (Rizzi, 2023). "Emerging" captures the ambiguity of all this.

Finally, such "emerging" power alliances are also an outcome of continuously changing global geopolitics alignments, particularly in the midst of the Ukraine war and conflict over Gaza. The Ukraine war pits Russia against Europe that previously were on relatively cooperative terms over energy imports and exports. As the war unfolded, EU strengthened its transatlantic ties with the US. The Ukraine war also pushed Russia and China – two countries with a complicated history of distrust, competition, and even resentment (Maizland, 2022) – somehow together where the Ukraine war is perceived in both countries now as a proxy war between the US and its biggest rivals. When it comes to the Ukraine war, the Global South is reluctant to pick sides as this war is regarded as a European affair, but whose negative consequences (e.g., energy and food crises) they now must suffer (Tocci, 2023). Similarly, the Israeli-Gaza conflict had major BRICS powers, China and India in particular, gingerly navigate their relationships with Israel, Palestine, the Arab world, Iran, and the West (Burke, 2023). Crucially, some of the newly admitted BRICS countries, such as Egypt, Iran, and UAE, are playing a major role in these regional dynamics (The Economist, 2023). In this context, a multiplex of new global alliances is emerging to reshape the existing US-centric global order.

1.3 BUILDING DIGITAL SOVEREIGNTY "BRICS BY BRICS"

Just as the BRICS are the developing world's response to the instability and unfairness of a globalized economy, many of the BRICS "digital sovereignty" initiatives are also expressions of a strong inclination to build a multipolar world and seek independence from a US-centric model of digital development and governance, the latter perceived as unfair and unsustainable (Ebert & Maurer, 2013). While "digital sovereignty" is never explicitly mentioned in official BRICS documents, with 40% of the world's population and large sums of one of the world's most valuable resources – personal data (The Economist, 2017), BRICS countries are increasingly leveraging their positions to develop digital technologies, economies, and policies.

Although the "free-flow-of-information" narrative supported by Western countries and championed by the US is appealing, one must acknowledge that global data flows have grown in highly asymmetric fashions. Data has been extracted from Global South countries to generate value mainly in the US while simultaneously rendering the Global South increasingly dependent on technologies provided by a handful of typically US companies. In this context, joint partnerships and activities dedicated to digital affairs and technological cooperation started to appear in the BRICS grouping's strategic agenda over time. Post-Snowden, the 2015 BRICS Summit issued the *Ufa Declaration* to establish a working group on the security of ICT use with the aim "to develop practical cooperation with each other in order to address common security challenges in the use of ICTs" while "sharing information and case studies on ICT policies and programs" (Indian Ministry of External Affairs, 2015).

In the same year, BRICS ICT ministers signed the *Memorandum of Understanding on Cooperation in Science, Technology, and Innovation* to promote digital initiatives such as the BRICS Digital Partnership, the BRICS Partnership on New Industrial Revolution (PartNIR), and the Innovation BRICS Network (iBRICS Network). In 2021, the *New Delhi Declaration* jointly issued at the 13th BRICS explicitly called for – the first time in 15 years – the establishment of "legal frameworks of cooperation" on crucial issues such as "ICTs development and security" (Indian Ministry of External Affairs, 2021). Issues of data protection, cybercrime, content regulation, and e-commerce also received prominent attention.

BRICS's exploration of alternative modes of digital development, governance, and regulation is shaped by several epoch geopolitical events, chief among them: Snowden's 2013 revelations of NSA's global surveillance program, the vulnerability of democratic infrastructures to social media-enabled manipulation epitomized by the 2016 US presidential election, and Russia's invasions of Ukraine in 2014 and 2022 (and subsequent need to cope with Western-imposed sanctions). While China has been systematically grafting borders onto the internet for decades for fear of a "color revolution," many countries around the world were jolted by these events to move away from a "deterritorialized" view of the internet toward one that is "territorialized" and "sovereignty-minded." Russia's invasion of Ukraine has further prompted the creation of digital curtains on the internet, with the EU requesting to block Russian state media on TikTok, Facebook, and Microsoft (Bond, 2022), and Russia blocking access to Western social media.

As a result, we are witnessing strong currents of territorialization and renationalization of the internet, extending to infrastructure, data, hardware, software, platforms, and tech standards. BRICS countries are no exceptions, although their aims and strategies may be remarkably different. After Snowden revelations, Brazil passed the *Brazilian Civil Rights Framework for the Internet*, or *Marco Civil da Internet*, its first law to create rules and obligations in the internet environment. The Brazilian Central Bank also rolled out Pix quickly in 2020, an instant public payment infrastructure to spur domestic fintech innovations in anticipation of potential foreign dominance (see Doshi & Delgado's chapter). Here, asserting national digital sovereignty is not only compatible with human rights and rule of law but can also enhance participatory democracy. Russia, on the other hand, not only approved data localization in 2015 and the *Sovereign Internet Law* in 2019 but also developed infrastructural capabilities to disconnect the Russian segment of the internet "RuNet" from the global internet (see Chapter 8), which in retrospect appears to be a strategy to build resilience from Western sanctions and to maintain the Russian government's "sovereign" authority (Standnik, 2019).

Following an ambitious Digital India plan aimed at fostering digital inclusion and transformation, India banned zero-rating practices in 2016 on the ground of net neutrality to avoid what is perceived to be a disguised form of digital colonialism (Mukerjee, 2016). Moreover, after GDPR went into effect in 2018, India also passed its landmark Digital Personal Data Protection Bill in 2023 (Indian Ministry of Electronics & IT, 2023) modeled after GDPR and Singapore's data protection law with the intention to continue India's data trade with major countries including the US and Japan (Weymouth, 2023). On the other hand, China elevated "Internet sovereignty" and cybersecurity to a national priority. The Cyberspace Administration of China (CAC), headed by President Xi Jinping himself, was established in 2014. In the same year, CAC inaugurated the annual World Internet Conference held in Wuzhen, China to systematically promote its position of cyber sovereignty and develop international norms. Such high-flying state maneuverings were accompanied by legislative and policy efforts that saw the passage of numerous new Chinese legal regulations aimed at enhancing its cybersecurity and cyber independence (e.g., Jiang, 2021; Miao, Jiang, & Pang, 2021), including the *Cybersecurity Law* in 2017 as well as *Personal Information Protection Law* and *Data Security Law* in 2021 (Webster, 2023). South Africa, like many African countries, is not self-sufficient enough in technological development, which makes it reliant on US platforms, Chinese tech equipment, and EU digital legislation model, and it is nevertheless designing data protection policies with the unintended effect of increasing state control over private communication (see Chapter 4).

These state-led nation-building efforts, however, are not the only developments that define "digital sovereignty" in BRICS countries, for after all what is sovereignty without the autonomy, choice, or freedom of its own citizens (Fuchs, 2015)? Brazilian users' participation in Mastodon, a decentralized federated social media platform, points to the use of commons-inspired practices of digital sovereignty as an alternative to dominant, privatized, profit-oriented social media (see Chapter 9). In the Russian case, as intimidating as surveillance and censorship may seem, they are never complete with limited spaces for resistance and evasion (see Chapter 8). Often seen as totalitarian by Western observers, the Chinese internet is far from being uniform, obedient, or frictionless. In 2019, for example, a Chinese professor sued Hangzhou wildlife park over facial recognition data collection without his consent, for which the court ordered the park to delete his data and awarded him a partial compensation of $158 (Wu, 2021). Cases as such represent individual and community desires for privacy, autonomy, and self-determination that make up a key part of digital sovereignty discourses.

It is also widely recognized BRICS nations have a highly mixed record of digital authoritarianism and very heterogeneous use of offensive or defensive cyber capabilities to assert sovereignty. While Russia's RuNet goes to the far extreme of "digital isolation" (Sherman, 2021), the Chinese state is known to operate extensive domestic surveillance programs and is frequently cited as a likely originator of many cyberattacks on external targets (Arsène, 2016). Paradoxically, state's political priority mandating firms to maintain backdoors for government access to data for public security also weakens and compromises the development of robust commercial encryptions and data security (Laskai & Segal, 2021). New democracies such as Brazil and India have also experienced notable regress in civil liberties and restrictions of digital rights under Bolsonaro's and Modi's governments (see Chapter 2). South Africa's securitization discourse is similarly worrying for legitimizing state surveillance reminiscent of the apartheid police state (Kuehn, 2018). Far from being an immaculate source of inspiration and emulation, BRICS digital initiatives for online safety and cybersecurity can often seem as pretexts for surveillance and censorship.

Yet the tendency to lump BRICS nations into an authoritarian camp under a "democracy vs. authoritarianism" new Cold War framework is far too simplistic and conflict-prone by assuming Western countries are immune from surveillance or censorship. Rather, BRICS states' surveillance and censorship practices need to be held in juxtaposition to the grouping's legitimate anti-imperialist, anti-colonial desires, analyzed situationally. Dependence on foreign, especially US, digital technologies, platforms, and services can create and has created conditions of digital neo-colonialism that combines surveillance capitalism (Zuboff, 2019b) and data colonialism (Couldry & Mejias, 2019). The "free" addictive services offered by dominant US platforms are extractive instruments of data mining in building a new form of indentured labor that perpetuates economic and digital dependence (Avila Pinto, 2018). Overtime, "the BRICS grouping is increasingly aware of the economic opportunities brought by digital technology but also that 'free' digital services provided by foreign corporations are not free. They are paid with one of the most precious national assets – i.e. data – and, ultimately, with national sovereignty" (Belli, 2021a, p. 282). Such complex dynamics would not have been captured by an all-encompassing, categorical "democracy vs. authoritarianism" Cold War framework in the digital field.

To further complicate the anti-imperialist, anti-colonial narrative in the digital sovereignty debate are questionable digital practices within BRICS countries and conflicts between them (Fuchs, 2015). While US firms' extractive activities are the subject of postcolonial critique, there is no denial domestic BRICS companies have often benefited from the exclusion of foreign competitors. For instance, not only do large Indian tech companies such as telecom firm Reliance Jio gain valuable access to domestic user data, but data localization measures may well transfer power from foreign tech giants to domestic elites instead of instituting data policies that foster citizens' data sovereignty, as a public good of the people, by the people, for the people (Kovacs & Ranganathan, 2019). Tensions also exist between BRICS partners over their digital policies. China's neo-mercantilist expansion around the world, for instance, has met with both successes and failures (French, 2015). While Huawei and ZTE have offered low-cost, high-function handset solutions to many poor developing nations, Huawei's digital initiatives may well create new forms of digital dependence (see Chapter 7). In a more contentious episode, India banned 59 Chinese apps in 2021 following its border clash with China, with an additional 54 added to the list in 2022 (Reuters, 2022).

Aware of such complex and multifaceted contexts, we argue that the quest for digital sovereignty in BRICS countries to exercise agency, power, and control over digital infrastructure, data, services, and protocols is pursued by a plethora of actors beyond just the nation-states. They include empowered individuals, companies, communities, and even supranational alliances. Rather than following a linear inquiry on a topic as complex as digital sovereignty focused on nation-states only, it benefits to unpack its complexity that unfolds on different planes, in different domains, and across BRICS countries. Doing so will avoid making nation-states the default actors with the legitimacy or capacity to exercise digital power and control over citizens' data and digital lives. As judged by the short yet intense history of the internet, nation-states routinely fail to protect their citizens' digital rights and aspirations for self-determination. Questionable business players can also drive multi-stakeholder efforts in the name of human rights and democracy while stripping away human protection and dignity. Only by asking to who can (legitimately) wield agency, power, and control over digital infrastructure, data, services, and protocols; who ultimately defines "digital sovereignty" and for what purposes; and to what extent a particular form of "digital sovereignty" enhances or worsens the autonomy, choices, and protection of a country's citizens can we start to have a more meaningful debate of "digital sovereignty."

1.4 PERSPECTIVES ON DIGITAL SOVEREIGNTY

Given the plurality of discourses surrounding "digital sovereignty," we map out here seven major perspectives instead of assuming nation-states are the default and ultimate holders and arbiters of digital sovereignty. Not only does this approach acknowledge the important roles nation-states play in structuring digital infrastructure, data, services, and protocols within their borders, but it also recognizes the complicated realities in exercising digital sovereignty. We include in our conceptual mapping: state digital sovereignty, supranational digital sovereignty, network digital sovereignty, corporate digital sovereignty, personal digital sovereignty, postcolonial digital sovereignty, and commons digital sovereignty (see Table 1.2). We recognize various actors – policymakers, technologists, activists, and indigenous and local communities – approach "sovereignty" from highly diverse perspectives with unique assumptions about social justice, autonomy, and governance. In the following, we briefly explicate each perspective, related core concepts, their similarities, and differences as well as their applications in BRICS countries and beyond.

It is worth to note that the applications of these perspectives are highly contextual. For instance, while a BRICS or non-BRICS country's government can pursue state digital sovereignty, it can take different forms (Hong & Goodnight, 2019) – corporate, postcolonial, or commons – depending on the specific circumstances. The US government's laissez faire approach toward digital sovereignty, for example, favors its own tech giants, which in turn extends its structural power globally. While the Indian government initiated the ban of dozens of Chinese apps including TikTok to exercise its state sovereignty to protect domestic internet companies and the data sovereignty of its own citizens, it can also push for the creation and repository of digital public goods among BRICS and other developing countries, a move that aligns more with a commons digital sovereignty framework. Moreover, it is also possible that various civic groups may adopt any of the seven digital sovereignty perspectives outlined including the ones that support or oppose state regulation of cyberspace. In a word, various actors including nation-states may face and adopt different policy choices.

TABLE 1.2 *Perspectives and applications of digital sovereignty in BRICS countries*

BRICS	Theoretical Perspectives	Core Concepts	Applications
Brazil Russia India China South Africa	State Digital Sovereignty	State regulation of digital infrastructure, data, information flow, access, user rights; defense of cyber borders; digital independence; digital nationalism	Data, Algorithms, Undersea cable, Telecom networks (5G), Cloud services, Smart cities, Electronic payment systems, Digital currencies, Social media, Community networks, AI …
	Supranational Digital Sovereignty	Negotiated interdependence between states to assert digital agency, power, and control; framework of digital cooperation; collective state actions and digital cooperation bodies	
	Network Digital Sovereignty	Network interoperability; neutrality of networks; undesirability of state regulation; borderless cyberspace; cryptocurrency	
	Corporate Digital Sovereignty	Laissez-faire, private ordering, and tech giant self-regulation; government regulation as unwelcomed unless it supports tech giants' interests; surveillance capitalism	
	Personal Digital Sovereignty	Informational self-determination, autonomy; individual rights, digital personhood; self-sovereign identity; security and privacy by design	
	Postcolonial Digital Sovereignty	Voice and rights of indigenous peoples; post-colonialism, freedom from (neo)colonialism; access, possession, ownership, control of digital resources	
	Commons Digital Sovereignty	Network self-determination; free and open-source software (FOSS); freedom from corporate and state control; data cooperatives; digital public goods	

We envision the applications of digital sovereignty in multiple and proliferating domains given such domains spread across digital infrastructure, data, services, and protocols: data, algorithms, undersea cable, telecom networks (5G), cloud services, smart cities, electronic payment systems, digital currencies, social media, community networks, AI, and more. It is possible that particular actors may not consider certain domains digital sovereignty-pertinent (*emic* perspective), and scholars and researchers like ourselves may define them as such (*etic* perspective). For instance, we consider India's digital payment system UPI and Brazil's digital payment system Pix as DPIs that can greatly strengthen national digital sovereignty. Yet, they are not labeled as such in India or Brazil.

The application of digital sovereignty within specific domains ranging from data and algorithm to smart cities and community networks also often reflects specific digital sovereignty perspectives. For instance, it is possible to conceive of "data sovereignty" as a domain of national laws and governance structures (Lukings & Lashkari, 2022), thus grounding discussions of "data sovereignty" in a state-centric perspective. However, data can also be regarded as a sphere of individual freedom and personhood (Koopman, 2019) to be protected from state surveillance (Epstein, 2016), making discussions of "data sovereignty" comport with a personal digital sovereignty perspective. Similarly, "algorithmic sovereignty" may regard algorithms as scientific, neutral, and sovereign in their own right, which aligns with a network digital sovereignty perspective. Conversely, "algorithmic sovereignty" can also be positioned to wield corporate power (Jiang, 2014) or become an extension of state oversight of artificial intelligence in the case of China's new registry for recommendation algorithms (Sheehan & Du, 2022). Still others may argue that "algorithmic sovereignty" should be inclusive, transparent, bottom-up, and community-based, allowing communities to exercise agency, power, and control over fundamental digital protocols and infrastructures (Reviglio & Agosti, 2020; Roio, 2018). Given the proliferation of the discourse of sovereignty in many digital domains and applications, even in domains not traditionally thought to be relevant to digital sovereignty such as payment systems, it is key to recognize the particular theoretical perspectives from which actors and interlocutors evoke that carry unique assumptions, biases, and implications.

1.4.1 State Digital Sovereignty

Normative assumptions of sovereignty – territorial integrity, monopolistic use of force, legal equality, and noninterference in international affairs – have been seriously challenged by the advent of the cyberspace (Lessig, 1999a). Over time, however, many governments have reasserted their power (Goldsmith & Wu, 2006). Laws and policies regulating how digital technologies could be used at the national level have been passed since the mid-1990s, implemented through internet intermediaries who act as "points of control" (Zittrain, 2003) such as operators of national telecom infrastructure, hardware manufacturers, domain name systems, and cloud services. Overall, discourses of state digital sovereignty concern government authority and legitimacy as well as their ability to regulate and control digital infrastructure, data, and users to maintain national laws and achieve autonomy. Whether states can achieve popular sovereignty, or consent of the governed, in the digital realm is an open question (MacKinnon, 2012).

Over the past three decades, BRICS nations have been strong advocates of state digital sovereignty. China was among the first to graft borders back onto the internet in the 1990s through mechanisms such as the "Great Firewall" to filter content and maintain national ownership of digital infrastructure to achieve internet sovereignty (Jiang, 2010). Today, it has the only digital ecosystem that can rival Silicon Valley's, fueled by a degree of technological nationalism to produce indigenous technologies (Jiang & Fu, 2018). China's articulation of cyberspace sovereignty serves as a justification for rejecting foreign interference in its information environment as well as establishing the dominance of party-state ideology and indigenous capacity to innovate (Creemers, 2020; Fang, 2018). In the aftermath of Google's high-profile exit from China, "Internet sovereignty" was adopted as an official state policy by the Chinese government in 2010 to assert control over its infrastructures, information, and population (Jiang, 2021). This approach was further strengthened and promoted abroad by Xi's administration in response to the 2013 Snowden revelations. The "sovereignization" of the Russian internet leveraged the NSA scandal to legitimize the Kremlin's approach to controlling RuNet activities (Nocetii, 2015). Following the passage of *Sovereign Internet Law* in 2019, Russia developed its own technical work-around and alternative version of the domain name system (DNS) in a far more drastic step toward digital isolationism (Sherman, 2021). Brazil not only passed *Marco Civil da Internet* in 2014 and its general data protection law (known as "GDPL") in 2018 but also took concrete steps to construct undersea cable EllaLink connecting Brazil directly to Portugal and by proxy Latin America to Europe to bypass the US surveillance (Yahoo! News, 2022). India started to build a real-time payment system Unified Payments Interface since 2016 (see Chapter 5) to foster a thriving national e-payment ecosystem and has drafted or passed several important data legislations. Post-Snowden, South Africa's digital sovereignty agenda also emphasizes securitization and cyber defense, although such measures also raise concerns for state surveillance and censorship (see Chapter 4).

Besides legislative measures focused on data, state digital sovereignty is often expressed in discourses, projects, and actions of independence that blend into "postcolonial digital sovereignty" (see Section 1.4.5). The colonial legacy in the Global South leads BRICS nations to frequently do so, even though the "state digital sovereignty" perspective is applicable to developed countries too. For example, the Science Council of Canada advocated for "technological sovereignty" as early as 1967 (Globerman, 1978, p. 43). After Snowden revelations, Deutsche Telekom proposed a "national internet" to bolster Germany's digital independence (Deutsche Welle, 2013). As such, the assertion of state digital sovereignty through legislation, research, and development projects should not be deemed as negative or positive per se merely because it is branded as "digital sovereignty" and promoted by states. The past two decades demonstrate that both legitimate claims and abusive goals can underpin state assertion of digital sovereignty. Ironically, a global internet has not rendered the nation-state or its sovereignty obsolete. Instead, the pendulum is currently swinging toward de-globalization and renationalization of cyberspace.

1.4.2 Supranational Digital Sovereignty

The claim to digital sovereignty, as noted previously, is not limited to the nation-state. Small- and mid-sized countries, in particular, face the perennial challenge of navigating power imbalances (see Chapter 6). The European Council on Foreign Relations, for instance, has publicly endorsed a "sovereign Europe" and "digital sovereignty" strategy to enhance its capacity to act (Leonard & Shapiro, 2020). EU has not only embarked on a legislative restructuring of its digital policies to restrict the undue influence and abuse of dominance by US tech giants and in doing so setting global standards, but it has also teed digital sovereignty and technological strategic autonomy as top priorities (Michel, 2021; Obendiek, 2021).

This European desire harkens back to at least 2005 when a few European nations, led by France, proposed the creation of a Euro-centric search engine to compete against Google and Yahoo!. At the time, former French President Jacques Chirac promised to fund Project Quaero to counter the perceived "threat of Anglo-Saxon cultural imperialism" (Litterick, 2005), although after Germany withdrew in 2006, the project fell apart. Post-Snowden, EU strengthened its data protection by passing GDPR in 2016 and enacting it in 2018, starting to make the "Brussels Effect" (Bradford, 2020) felt around the world. Recently, perceiving EU's lag in advanced digital infrastructure development and deployment (e.g., China–US rivalry in 5G technologies) and digital market (e.g., US dominance in digital platforms and services in EU), EU has passed the Digital Markets Act and the Digital Services Act in 2022 in a bid to further beef up EU's control over its digital sovereignty. Despite national differences and bureaucratic burdens, EU seems committed to maintaining EU values and principles in deploying and creating digital technologies (Obendiek, 2021).

In addition, the world has also moved in a more multipolar direction with the creation of ASEAN in the 1960s, Mercosur in the 1990s, and Africa Continental Free Trade Area in 2019. Developing nations may desire to strengthen their digital policy alignment even though they may not achieve the same level of political coordination the EU seems to have maintained so far.

In contrast to EU's more uniform supranational stance of digital sovereignty as well as growing consensus in OECD countries (OECD, 2022) and ASEAN countries (ASEAN, 2012, 2022) in adopting data-related standards, BRICS nations have only taken initial steps to explore multilateral digital initiatives and cooperation while maintaining their state sovereignty stance. Previously, BRICS summits have issued declarations to address common security challenges in ICT use, promote the global cybersecurity rules within the UN, foster digital development initiatives, and even establish "intra-BRICS" legal frameworks of cooperation. However, concrete multilateral agreements are yet to be hammered out in many areas including tariffs, e-commerce, data protection, cross-border data transfer, technology transfer, cybersecurity, and knowledge sharing (Belli, 2021b; Observer Research Foundation, 2021). To what extent BRICS nations will negotiate between their state digital sovereignty and multilateral digital sovereignty in the bloc remains to be seen. However, should BRICS choose to adopt a set of binding digital agreements, the bloc would hold considerable sway in setting global digital standards and in conducting data trade and e-commerce given it represents more than 25% of global GDP and more than 40% of the world's population.

1.4.3 Network Digital Sovereignty

The romantic idea of cyberspace as a separate space exempted from traditional state jurisdiction, or even a sovereign in its own right, is best embodied in John Perry Barlow's popular manifesto *A Declaration of the Independence of Cyberspace* (1996). His proclamation asserts cyberspace's independence *from* nation-states:

> Governments of the Industrial World, you weary giants of flesh and steel, I come from Cyberspace, the new home of Mind. On behalf of the future, I ask you of the past to leave us alone. You are not welcome among us. You have no sovereignty where we gather (Barlow, 1996).

Bold or naïve, the manifesto taps into the public's yearning for freedom and aversion to state control of the new digital frontier. While Barlow seriously underestimated governments' persistent power, the utopian sentiment to reject nation-states in cyberspace lived on. In the essay *Against Sovereignty in Cyberspace*, Mueller (2019) maintains the importance of network interoperability, de-territorialized cyberspace as a global commons, and nonstate governance of the internet (e.g., ICANN) that prioritizes civil society and the private sector. While grounded in understandable and popular sentiments such individual freedom, mistrust of government, and preference for multi-stakeholderism, a weakness of this approach lies in the very flawed international system of asymmetrical power in which global digital governance is embedded. Realpolitik still favors powerful states and their capacity to enforce laws domestically and extend influence extraterritorially (e.g., GDPR's extraterritorial power and

US global dominance through the proxy of its private firms). In retrospect, the internet has long been treated as a medium to socialize, transact, and mobilize rather than as a by-product of a unique stage of capitalism (Cohen, 2019a; Zuboff, 2019a) where essentially a handful of global firms – aided by their governments, mostly the US and China – use it to deploy products and services to create profits and accrue power based on endless extraction, surveillance, and commodification of user data.

It is worth to note the meaning of "cyberspace sovereignty" or "Internet sovereignty" can vary. Barlow's or Mueller's approach evokes a global commons where "states cannot assert sovereignty over cyberspace" (Mueller, 2019, p. 790). The Chinese or Russian use of "Internet sovereignty" notably means exactly the opposite, more akin to the UN-based, state-centric, territorial model (Jiang, 2010) and the "state digital sovereignty" perspective outlined earlier. In theory, national authorities cannot extend control over users, services, applications, or devices outside of their national jurisdiction. In reality, however, state actors such as the NSA or data protection authorities of EU member states acting according to GDPR routinely assert extraterritorial influence. China's latest expansion of its extraterritorial reach through data laws, mirroring the EU policy, attempts the same as EU (see Chapter 3).

1.4.4 Corporate Digital Sovereignty

Exploited by market-centric neoliberalism, the turn from counterculture to cyberculture reimagined Cold War computers as tools for personal liberation, virtual communities as utopian communes, and the digital frontiers as realms of egalitarianism (Turner, 2006). The ascendance of US tech giants since the 1990s and their recent Chinese counterparts birthed a new class of outsized corporate sovereign powers in the digital age. Traditional sovereigns are marked by their authority, legitimacy based on God or law, and supreme power over a territory (Philpott, 2003). These new corporate digital sovereigns (MacKinnon, 2012) have amassed enormous power with little accountability in the digital spaces they create, deriving legitimacy to operate regionally or globally through intellectual property regimes and multilateral trade agreements to wield supreme power over cyberspace.

Tech companies exercise their corporate digital sovereignty through their "structural power" (Strange, 1988) by shaping the functioning of the societies, economies, and democracies through the technologies they provide. Hence, the technological architectures and contractual terms of service they unilaterally define can be seen as the regulatory tools allowing corporate entities to exercise and implement quasi-normative, quasi-executive, and quasi-judicial powers that underpin their corporate digital sovereignty (Belli, 2022).

Corporate digital sovereignty is the by-product of a new era of capitalism: "surveillance capitalism" (Zuboff, 2019a). Unlike industrial capitalism that made commodities out of nature (e.g., real estate), labor (e.g., salary), money (exchange) (Polanyi, 1980/1944), or post-industrial capitalism that commodified things such as risk (e.g., insurance) and reputation (e.g., PR), surveillance capitalism is based on the extraction, aggregation, and selling of behavioral data and human experiences, often without users' knowledge or against users' interest (Zuboff, 2019a). While corporate digital sovereigns have thrived in a neoliberal environment of free market, privatization, lax regulation, and weak industry self-regulation (Radu, 2019), the tides have turned following the crises of the NSA scandal, foreign interference in the 2016 US presidential election, the Facebook-Cambridge Analytica scandal, and COVID-19 misinformation spreads. US tech giants have been targeted by several regulatory probes (albeit with limited success) and Chinese tech titans have also faced increasing charges of neo-colonialism (French, 2015) and enormous pushbacks from the US amid trade wars and geopolitical rivalries between the world's two great powers.

While an increasing number of government initiatives aim at reigning in the excesses of tech giants, especially those based in the US (e.g., EU's GDPR, Digital Markets Act, Digital Services Act), the effectiveness of such initiatives is yet to be seen even though the negative externalities of such firms in multiple areas including taxation, personal data protection, and fair competition have long been well documented. For example, six Silicon Valley giants reportedly created a $100 billion global tax shortfall between 2010 and 2019 by shifting profits from higher-tax jurisdictions to lower-tax or no-tax jurisdictions (Fair Tax, 2019). Despite the recent agreement on a global minimum tax rate of roughly 15% to stop such practices, promoted by the OECD and adopted by the Group of 7 and the Group of 20, taxation of these tech giants has been limited by US government protectionism (Scott & Birnbaum, 2021).

1.4.5 Personal Digital Sovereignty

The claim to personal digital sovereignty – individual exercise of agency, power, and control over personal technologies, data, and personhood (Couture & Toupin, 2019) – has deep philosophical roots. Classical philosophies of individualism affirm the intrinsic value of the individual with precedence over the collective or the state in many modern democratic societies (Swart, 1962). Personal digital sovereignty is also associated with a broad set of civil and political liberties such as autonomy and self-determination that in turn have been appropriated by social and political movements on both the left and the right (Robinson et al., 2017). Moreover, the recent claim to personal digital sovereignty such as the case brought by data activist Maximilian Schrems in the European Court of Justice (Chander, 2020) reflects the backlash against the excesses of surveillance capitalism. Bulk collection of individual data, targeted political ads, and misinformation-amplifying algorithms have not only eroded individual and public trust in powerful states and tech giants but also exposed the limits of industry self-regulation (Cheung, 2023).

Ultimately, personal data – created, collected, and stored on an unprecedented scale in contemporary digitized societies – is always about someone, deeply connected to personhood (Koopman, 2019). Whether a Lacanian psychoanalytic subject or a Foucauldian political subject, the individual has both intrinsic needs and incentives to avoid the Other's excessive gaze to preserve one's privacy, personhood, and control over personal data (Epstein, 2016). This is precisely the rationale behind the formulation of a fundamental right to "informational self-determination" by the German Federal Constitutional Court (1983) in the landmark Census case, arguing this right must be considered an expression of the right to the free development of personality. In this perspective, every individual has not only a legitimate expectation but a constitutional right to exert control over personal data to know what information about him or her is collected, by whom, for what purposes, and with whom it will be shared. As such, any processing of personal data is in principle regarded as an interference with the right to informational self-determination, unless the data subject has consented or the law considers such processing as necessary and proportionate to achieve a legitimate aim.

Similar considerations led the Supreme Court of India to recognize the right to privacy in the landmark Puttaswamy case (Bhandari, Kak, Parsheera, & Rahman, 2017) and the Brazilian Supreme Court to enshrine "informational self-determination" as a grounding principle of the Brazilian data protection law (IAPP, 2020). However, the blurry boundaries between our physical and datafied bodies (van der Ploeg, 2012) as well as the surveillance capitalism logics increasingly jeopardize our autonomy and self-determination. In practice, widespread surveillance exposes the enormous distance between the ideal and the reality of informational self-determination. New discourses and practices of personal digital sovereignty now attempt to bridge the gap through the adoption of technologies, including encryption and free and open-source software and hardware, as alternatives to mainstream applications and services to minimize state or corporate surveillance and manipulation that limit individual choices, agencies, and freedoms (Benkler, 2006; Stallman, 2002).

Users in BRICS countries have been pushing back too, to varying degrees, on both excessive business and state intrusions in their informational self-determination. Whether it is a Chinese university professor suing a local wildlife park over facial recognition data collection without consent (Wu, 2021) or the retired Indian justice Puttaswamy challenging the constitutionality of the Indian electronic ID system "Aadhaar," individual users in the Global South are increasingly resorting to both legal and nonlegal recourses to raise public awareness, change social norms, if not seeking full-scale legislative intervention, to preserve personal digital sovereignty. The demand can also take collective forms as citizens in BRICS countries staged impressive resistance against censorship, surveillance, and shutdowns. Indian farmers protested against agriculture laws and severe internet shutdowns (BBC, 2021b) before winning concessions from Modi government. Chinese users also successfully pushed back Alibaba affiliate Ant Financial's unauthorized data sharing across Alibaba services and third parties (Wade, 2018).

1.4.6 Postcolonial Digital Sovereignty

Postcolonial thought and discourse have also informed various claims to digital sovereignty made by both indigenous populations and developing countries with colonial legacies. Previously, scholars have explored Australian indigenous data sovereignty (Kukutai & Taylor, 2016) and first-nation Indian network sovereignty (Duarte, 2017). Core issues of sovereignty involving data and network were raised by such works: Australian indigenous people's jurisdiction over data akin to the indigenous jurisdiction over territory, which would confer access, possession, control, and ownership of indigenous people's own data; the deficiency of American Indian tribes to exercise information and cultural sovereignty due to the lack of network infrastructure and indigenous digital content. Echoing the personal digital sovereignty perspective to some extent, this approach seeks a more independent, dignified, and affordable path for indigenous communities to achieve their sovereignty.

Beyond the calls to restore and enhance indigenous populations' agency, power, and control over their own data and networks, postcolonial digital sovereignty discourses also stem from the structural asymmetry and digital divide between developed and developing countries due in no small part to centuries of slavery, predatory practices, and unfair international norms. In various digital technology fields, the relationship between America and the rest of the world has often been viewed as one of center-periphery that replicates colonial relations (Garcia, 2022) through Silicon Valley's digital expansions and endless extractions of user data for profits that perpetuates economic and cultural dependencies. ICANN, initially contracted with the US Department of Commerce and eventually separated from it, was unanimously criticized as an instrument of US domination that often favored industrial and Western interests. While a private sector-led domain name system may seem neutral and convenient, it can continue to serve US interest and its global influence as the American private sector operates as de facto proxy to cultivate "the perception of market-based private ordering" (Bruner, 2008).

BRICS nations' claims to postcolonial digital sovereignty harken back to earlier times such as the Non-Aligned Movement in the 1950s, following decolonization and the New World Information and Communication Order (NWICO) movement in the 1970s and 1980s (see Chapter 2). In the Non-Aligned Movement, countries in Asia, Africa, and Latin America tried to abstain from alliance with either America or the USSR in support of self-determination against colonialism or imperialism. The NWICO debate led by the MacBride Commission was similarly concerned about economic, culture, and media inequality experienced by the Global South as a legacy of colonialism and imperialism (Fuchs, 2015). This form of international alliance of Postcolonial

Digital Sovereignty intersects with other types of anti-colonial efforts by states, individuals, and communities. In recent years, whether it's the Brazilian decision to adopt free and open software (adopted in 2003 by the Lula administration and later abandoned by the Temer administration in 2016), Russia's plan to build digital fences to protect the "RuNet," India's rejection of Facebook's zero-rating service Internet.org, China's adoption of a new Data Security Law, or community efforts in South Africa, India, or Brazil to create their own community networks, post-colonialism and anti-imperialism continue to find new expressions in current times.

1.4.7 Commons Digital Sovereignty

Beyond the postcolonial perspective, commons digital sovereignty – the idea of building digital public goods for digital commons such as FOSS and community networks – tries to transcend state and corporate limitations. In this approach, technologies are developed from and for civil society (Haché, 2017), driven largely not by bureaucratic power or profit but by social movements to create alternative forms of digital sovereignty (Couture & Toupin, 2019). The altruistic motivation draws inspirations from the hacker culture in the 1970s and the FOSS movement, epitomized by the GNU (2022) project launched by Richard Stallman in 1983. The popular Linux operating system, the success of Wikipedia, and growing adoption of Fediverse (Mastodon) for social media are examples of the potential of the FOSS movement (see Chapter 9).

The increasing development of community networks globally including in several BRICS countries – Brazil, India, and South Africa – highlights the evolving nature of new forms of Commons Digital Sovereignty. As crowdsourced collaborative digital infrastructure networks, community networks are quintessential expressions of Commons Digital Sovereignty. They are developed in a bottom-up fashion by groups of individuals, that is, communities that design, manage, and maintain the network infrastructure as a common resource. Thus, the communities and the Commons Digital Sovereignty of their members are the core elements of community networks as they are essential to initiate, maintain, and guarantee the success of such connectivity efforts (Belli, 2017). In fact, community networks are managed according to the governance models established by their community members in a democratic fashion and can be operated by groups of self-organized individuals or entities such as nongovernmental organizations (NGOs), local businesses, or public administrations.

Besides providing access to previously disconnected populations, these networks are particularly interesting as they give rise to an ample range of positive externalities to maximize the network self-determination of large groups of individuals (Belli, 2017). These positive external effects include the construction of new infrastructure with limited investment, the engagement of locals in the development of new self-governance models, the revitalization of social interactions among local community members and the emergence of new opportunities for accessing information, learning, and creating employment (Belli, 2017).

It is worth to note that the commons digital sovereignty approach – the collective production of digital public goods – is increasingly seen by small- and mid-sized countries as an important strategy to help ameliorate or overcome the dominance of digital superpowers of the US and China. Not only are countries such as France interested in creating new digital commons to avoid the "enclosure" and "exclusivity" of current commercial models (French Ministry of European and Foreign Affairs, 2020), BRICS countries such as India also invest in digital public goods to maximize their autonomy against structural dependence on great powers and their tech giants (see Chapter 6). For instance, starting from 2003, the Lula administration in Brazil forged an alliance with FOSS activists, adopting open-source software as a national policy as a path to digital sovereignty and digital common good (Kim, 2005). The Indian government has used open-source software and DPI in constructing the Indian payment system to leapfrog developed countries (see Chapter 5).

At the BRICS level, the *New Delhi Declaration* (2021), adopted at the 13th BRICS Summit, endorses a commons digital sovereignty approach. In principle, BRICS promotes the use of "innovative and inclusive solutions, including digital and technological tools to promote sustainable development and facilitate affordable and equitable access to global public goods for all" (BRICS, 2021, section 14). In implementation, BRICS line agencies are encouraged to develop a BRICS Platform on Digital Public Goods as a repository for all open-source technology applications created by BRICS members (BRICS, 2021, section 37). For smaller BRICS countries, the creation and repository of digital public goods contribute to "Sustainable Development Goals" that help BRICS and other developing countries to reap the benefit of global digital commons, all the more urgent as seen during the COVID-19 pandemic in distributing vaccines by the increasingly restrictive commercial intellectual property regimes.

The commons digital sovereignty approach may be particularly relevant in an era of billionaire ownership of public utilities, be it Bezos's ownership of Amazon, Zuckerberg's reign at Facebook, Brin's and Page's ownership of Google and Alphabet, or Musk's takeover of Twitter (now X). Overall, the commons digital sovereignty approach – developed by civil society or nation-states in support of this vision – allows for an alternative way to chart the digital future and its governance that is currently dominated by digital superpowers.

1.5 SUMMARY OF CONTRIBUTING CHAPTERS

The book is divided into three segments, bookended by an introductory chapter and a conclusion chapter. The introductory chapter lays the theoretical foundation for the book by disentangling the contesting discourses and interpretations of digital sovereignty informed by a wide range of literature. The concept of digital sovereignty itself is viewed as a site of power contestation and knowledge production rather than default acceptance. Specifically, seven major perspectives on digital sovereignty are identified from a complex discursive field (see Table 1.2): state digital sovereignty, supranational digital sovereignty, network digital sovereignty, corporate digital sovereignty, personal digital sovereignty, postcolonial digital sovereignty, and commons digital sovereignty. The chapter outlines who are actively shaping the definition of digital sovereignty and what perspectives and concepts inform the various discourses of digital sovereignty with what purposes. We also highlight affinities and overlaps as well as tensions and contradictions between these perspectives on digital sovereignty with brief illustrative examples from BRICS countries and beyond. While a state-centric perspective on digital sovereignty is traditionally more salient especially in BRICS contexts, increasing public concern over user privacy, state surveillance, corporate abuse, and digital colonialism has given ascendance to a wider array of alternative perspectives on digital sovereignty that emphasize individual autonomy, indigenous rights, community well-being, and sustainability.

The subsequent eight chapters form the main body of the book, divided into three parts. Part I "State-centric Formations of Digital Sovereignty" recognizes the popular and dominant discourses of digital sovereignty predicated on the nation-state in BRICS countries. This segment includes three chapters: Thumfart's contribution (Chapter 2) that traces the historical imaginaries of digital sovereignty by the Chinese, Russian, and Indian governments from NWICO and WSIS to SCO and BRICS; Cong's work (Chapter 3) that outlines the spatial expansion of China's digital sovereignty in its recent national digital legislations; and Calandro's summary (Chapter 4) of the South African approach toward digital sovereignty caught between securitization and development. Part II "Techno-economic Structurings of Digital Sovereignty" focuses on the implementation of digital sovereignty through technical and financial infrastructures in the BRICS: Hariharan and Natarajan's examination (Chapter 5) of Indian government's open-source digital payment system as an instrument of the country's digital sovereignty; Doshi and Delgado's investigation (Chapter 6) of India and Brazil as examples of "middle powers" with capacity to pursue autonomy and safeguard their digital sovereignty in technical and financial sectors; and Calzati's comparative work (Chapter 7) of Chinese tech giant Huawei's smart city initiatives in South Africa and Italy where corporate digital sovereignty intersects and negotiates with those of the states and local communities. Part III "Grassroots Contestations of Digital Sovereignty" features two chapters: Bronnikova et al.'s examination (Chapter 8) of the Russian public's resistance to the state-imposed "sovereignization" of the RuNet; and Tomaz's study (Chapter 9) of the Brazilian internet activists' discourses and practices in Mastodon, a commons-based alternative to commercial social media networks.

More specifically, Chapter 2 sets the historical context by outlining how China, Russia, and India – three member countries of BRICS and the SCO (Shanghai Cooperation Organization) – constructed imaginaries of "digital sovereignty" since the 1990s. Borrowing the concept of "sociotechnical imaginaries," this chapter examines the regulatory rhetorics, frameworks, and policies employed by the three countries from a state-centric perspective of digital sovereignty. Thumfart argues these sociotechnical imaginaries are centered on protecting national cultural identity, or "cultural sovereignty," against the "free flow of information," a motive that harkens back to the NWICO debates about the imbalance of media and information flows in the 1970s and 1980s as well as the WSIS discussions surrounding digital and knowledge divides in the information society in the 2000s. In particular, he traces the development of these three countries' "digital sovereignty" imaginaries from their unique histories, governing approaches, and global outlooks, whether it is grounded in the Chinese political philosophy of "tianxia" (under heaven), or the "Russian world" to restore Russia's traditional influence on the world stage, or India's anti-colonial tradition coupled with its recent drift toward digital authoritarianism. In the transnational evolution of digital sovereignty imaginaries, the SCO seems to have played a role in disseminating regulatory discourses, norms, and practices from China to Russia and India. Thumfart concludes if BRICS countries are to construct discourses and practices of digital sovereignty beyond US hegemony, they need to consider both the strengths and weaknesses of their approaches grounded often in state-centric and postcolonial claims to digital sovereignty.

Turning to China, Chapter 3 explores the Chinese government's legal strategies to counter EU's and US's regulatory reach and extend its digital sovereignty in cyberspace. Cong argues while China's reterritorialization of its cyberspace is well known, China's emerging tendency to claim extraterritoriality deserves more attention. By closely analyzing recent Chinese legislation – *Personal Information Protection Law, Data Security Law*, and the order by the Ministry of Commerce on blocking unjustified extraterritorial application of foreign legislation and measures, she detects a regulatory shift from territoriality to extraterritoriality. A more spatially expansive notion of "digital sovereignty," her chapter argues, is manifested in two approaches: expanding the territorial scope of application of new data governance legislation as well as blocking and countering foreign measures deemed discriminatory or restrictive against China. Emulating EU and US regulatory approaches, these new measures by the Chinese government either directly expand the legislative jurisdiction or produce extraterritorial effects to protect Chinese sovereignty and interest and to counterbalance the extraterritorial reach of foreign regulatory powers. Taken together, these measures reflect the intricate interaction between China's digital sovereignty and current geopolitical circumstances.

Discussing South Africa, the last country placed alphabetically in the BRICS grouping, Chapter 4 centers on South African digital sovereignty at the crossroad of securitization and ICT development. It explores South Africa's approach to digital sovereignty by analyzing its digital policies and regulations as well as its posture in the context of globalization. Calandro notes that like many other African countries, South Africa is crafting strategies, policies and rules to frame the increasingly essential role played by ICTs. This process is fraught with tension. On the one hand, South African authorities are struggling to cope with increasing responsibilities of state actors to protect citizens' rights while guaranteeing safety and security online. On the other hand, measures aimed at pursuing public-interest goals, such as data protection and cybersecurity, do not always protect citizens' fundamental rights. Instead, the increasing body of norms, rules, and regulations for the digital space risks expanding state control over private communications, facilitating surveillance and online censorship. In terms of digital sovereignty, he analyzes South African's priorities and positions within the global geopolitical governance of cyberspace, highlights the emergence of a securitization agenda in reaction of cyber threats, and interrogates how policy processes and citizens' rights are impacted by the South African position on digital sovereignty.

Turning attention to economic issues, Chapter 5 explores how the Indian state asserts its digital sovereignty by constructing the Unified Payment Interface (UPI) overseen by the National Payment Corporation of India (NPCI), the latter an entity regulated by the Reserve Bank of India. The case study of Hariharan and Natarajan demonstrates vividly how such indigenous digital payment design, architecture, and governance mechanisms allow for accessible, secure, and interoperable transactions in a mobile-first, open API-based payment network to increase financial inclusion. It also illustrates the need to reduce India's dependence on foreign financial systems, and thus better protected from the shocks that could result from sanctions imposed by foreign states. However, such a system, they argue, is not without potential drawbacks, some of which include the dominance of foreign entities (e.g., Google Pay and PhonePe owned by Walmart/Flipkart) on UPI as well as state-sanctioned monopoly that tends to minimize civil society participation or competition. Besides interoperability and risk mitigation, the authors also advocate a multi-stakeholder governance model for the national digital payment system that bolsters public ownership and institutional checks and balances, a potential model for creating global digital public goods.

Situating Doshi and Delgado's exploration of the digital sovereignty debate in a comparative framework, Chapter 6 considers India and Brazil as examples of "middle powers" and analyzes their capacity to pursue autonomy and safeguard their digital sovereignty. The authors seek to answer two broader questions. First, what agency do middle powers master to safeguard their digital sovereignty. Second, to what extent can domestic politics structure the outcome of this agency. This chapter focuses on the role firms play when great powers weaponize interdependence in finance and digital technology, and subsequently explore the variables along which middle powers can attain autonomy in the above two fields. The authors contend that middle powers have agency to seek autonomy for themselves and reinforce their digital sovereignty. In particular, data localization policies – structuring jurisdiction over data – play a major role in shaping a country's digital statecraft.

In another comparative chapter (Chapter 7), Stefano Calzati considers corporate digital sovereignty's entanglement with national, and local communities. His discourse analysis of Chinese tech giant Huawei's corporate approach to digital sovereignty in South Africa and Italy highlights its intersections with national (and supranational) digital sovereignty goals and local communities' desire to achieve autonomy and control. Two smart city initiatives – Huawei's OpenLab in Johannesburg and Huawei's Joint Innovation Center (JIC) in Italy – are analyzed to show how the posture of the Chinese corporation can vary according to the national context, thus modulating its impact on the construction of corporate digital sovereignty. The comparative case studies draw from not only the role of China in Africa's ICT development but also the competing visions of internet governance informed by "digital sovereignty" and "data colonialism." Taking a critical approach toward "smart cities," Calzati shows while Huawei partners with local private and public actors in Italy, its initiatives in Africa might frustrate South African authorities' hopes of strengthening national digital sovereignty through integrated local tech initiatives. His analysis reveals digital sovereignty is an increasingly entangled transnational geo-governance issue. Whether tech initiatives foster local digital ecosystems and strengthening local digital sovereignty, or end up creating, reproducing, or reinforcing power asymmetries depends on specific local, national, and international contexts.

In Chapter 8, Bronnikova et al. present the clash between two perspectives on digital sovereignty in the Russian context, namely state digital sovereignty and personal digital sovereignty. The evolution of the Russian government's efforts in implementing the nationalist vision of internet sovereignty runs against an impressive array of civic tactics of circumvention and evasion. Importantly, the chapter notes that the first decade of the twenty-first century has been characterized by relatively high levels of freedom in digital innovation in Russia. Since the early 2010s, regulations aimed at establishing internet sovereignty in Russia have increased as authority of Roskomnadzor, the regulatory body in charge of overseeing media and ICTs, has been substantially expanded. This chapter explores the core elements and limits of Russia's digital sovereignty strategy, which is centered on the "sovereignization" of the RuNet to limit the influence of foreign agents and technology through the implementation of internet sovereignty norms and technical tools. Despite Roskomnadzor's tactics of websites blocking and control of online content through a network of technical intermediaries, activists are continuously learning and using new techniques of circumvention. In the digital sovereignty debate, Russian is highly relevant as it is often deemed a "laboratory" of broader authoritarian internet "sovereignization" tendencies, thus allowing one to observe and conceptualize the changing patterns in digital policies and politics.

Grounded in a commons digital sovereignty perspective, Chapter 9 documents and critiques the Brazilian FOSS movement through a case study of Brazil's participation in Mastodon, a decentralized federated social media platform. This chapter invites readers to consider and imagine alternatives to corporate digital sovereignty, symbolized by the highly centralized and commercialized tech ecosystem concentrated in the hands of a few Silicon Valley monopolies. As the latest iteration of FOSS activism with regard to social media, Mastodon and the larger project of Fediverse present themselves not only as attempts to develop alternative software and tech ecosystems but also as ambitions to build social movements to transform regimes of intellectual property and surveillance capitalism. While Tomaz remains optimistic about a decentralized, community-driven, privacy-enhanced future, the chapter also cautions against potential pitfalls such as the critical mass needed in user adoption, control over digital infrastructure, persistent digital divide between central and peripheral countries, and power differentiations along racial, class, gender, and organizational dimensions.

The concluding chapter (Chapter 10) acknowledges both the fluidity and the complexity of the notion of digital sovereignty in the BRICS, while also highlighting the necessity of digital sovereignty strategies, policies, and governance mechanisms from a policymaking perspective. The chapter notes that digital sovereignty plays a pivotal role in fostering self-determination, while increasing cybersecurity and strengthening the control capabilities of the "digital sovereign." Importantly, depending on the policy or initiative at stake, the "sovereign" can be an individual, a community, a corporation, or a state. In such contexts, this chapter takes an agnostic approach to digital sovereignty, exploring a selection of practices and providing insight into what this fuzzy theoretical concept means in practical terms. Indeed, digital technologies can facilitate enormous advancements but can also be weaponized against individuals, corporations, and nation-states. BRICS countries' approaches offer some telling examples of how and why the need for digital sovereignty can emerge, but also how confused, and even dysfunctional the implementation of policies aimed at digital sovereignty may become. The heterogeneity and cultural richness of the BRICS is also visible in their approaches to digital sovereignty. Importantly, the differences in their approaches are partly explained by their political stances. Russia and China have played a traditionally antagonistic role to the main digital technology power, the US, and have more structured approaches to digital sovereignty, given the high risks they associate with the lack of such approaches. The other three members of the grouping have less antagonistic but strong historical reasons for being particularly attached to their (digital) sovereignty. These span from post-colonial sentiments to decades of engagement in the

Non-Aligned Movement, to sensitivities raised by recent US abuses of its dominance in digital technologies. Ultimately, BRICS instances illustrate that enhancing a digital sovereign's self-determination, cybersecurity, and control will inevitably reduce the those of other digital sovereigns, likely leading to conflict in the absence of shared and mutually accepted frameworks.

1.6 CONCLUSION

While once imagined as an instrument for a borderless "global village," the internet is currently undergoing complex processes of renationalization (e.g., China, Russia, India) and regionalization (e.g., EU). BRICS countries, like many others around the world, are grappling with conflicting sets of realities and desires: individual privacy and national security, data localization and cross-border data flows, digital independence and international technological trade, often driven by concurrent national priorities, international commitments, and ambitions for global expansion and influence.

This book volume focuses on the central idea of "digital sovereignty" in digital policymaking, disentangles the myriad discourses and interpretations of digital sovereignty, and views the idea itself as a site of power struggle and knowledge production. Toward this end, we mapped out seven theoretical perspectives on "digital sovereignty": beyond the traditional perspective of state digital sovereignty, we extended previous literature to also include supranational digital sovereignty, network digital sovereignty, corporate digital sovereignty, personal digital sovereignty, postcolonial digital sovereignty, and commons digital sovereignty. While the seven perspectives may not be entirely mutually exclusive, they offer analytical lenses to examine the different discourses and approaches toward "digital sovereignty." Rather than viewing digital sovereignty as a mere online extension of a nation-state's sovereignty narrowly defined, this introduction and the subsequent chapters demonstrate that digital sovereignty has become associated with multiple meanings accorded to different agents. It can be appropriated by an authoritarian state or designed for a protectionist agenda, but it can also be used to promote ideals and values rooted in human rights, national development, and community empowerment. The book's concluding chapter will offer more practical examples of and reflections on BRICS countries' digital sovereignty experiences to bookend the effort.

Collectively, we are fundamentally interested in who is actively shaping the definition of digital sovereignty, what perspectives and concepts inform the myriad interpretations of digital sovereignty with what purposes, and how they are applied in a wide range of areas in BRICS countries with what potential impact and challenges ahead. Not only does this collective effort draw on the experiences, practices, and reflections of digital sovereignty from the BRICS scholarly community that contributes to the global conversation on the subject, it also offers a forward-looking take on what a digital world less dependent on a handful of Silicon Valley or Chinese tech giants might look like in a post-Western world. We believe such an endeavor can help scholars, students, policymakers, businesses, and civil society groups gain interesting insights and perspectives on the conceptualizations, policies, and practices of digital sovereignty in Global South countries. Given BRICS countries' growing international relevance, we hope the perspectives and issues identified in the book project to be of great importance to the future shape and governance of the global digital world.

PART I

STATE-CENTRIC FORMATIONS OF DIGITAL SOVEREIGNTY

2

Digital Sovereignty in China, Russia, and India

From NWICO to SCO and BRICS

Johannes Thumfart

2.1 INTRODUCTION

This chapter investigates the sociotechnical imaginaries of digital sovereignty within the BRICS grouping and the Shanghai Cooperation Organization (SCO) with a focus on China, Russia, and India. Sociotechnical imaginaries include a complex network of regulatory, technological, cultural, and societal factors that characterize national approaches to technology (Jasanoff, 2015, p. 4). In addition to the analysis of national approaches, in this chapter, the concept of sociotechnical imaginaries is used to assess approaches characteristic to international organizations.

There is an essential difference between the BRICS and the SCO, the latter originally including Russia, China, and every Central Asian country except Turkmenistan (and today also Belarus, India, Pakistan, and Iran). Broadly speaking, the SCO is focused on regional security and development, whereas the BRICS is focused on global economy and trade. However, in terms of chronology, the SCO preceded the BRICS. When the dialogue between the BRIC countries began in 2006, the SCO had already existed for five years. And since India joined the SCO in 2017, the majority of the original BRICS countries and the most powerful of them are also members of the SCO.

With regard to digital sovereignty within the BRICS countries (Belli, 2021b), the SCO can be considered a forerunner. For instance, the SCO was one of the first international organizations to formulate a comprehensive agreement on information security – *Declaration of the Heads of the SCO Member States on International Information Security* (SCO, 2006). And in 2011 as in 2015, the SCO member states promoted the *International Code of Conduct for Information Security* at the UN General Assembly, which emphasized the "respect for the sovereignty, territorial integrity and political independence of all states, (...) the diversity of history, culture and social systems of all countries" (McKune, 2011). From a critical perspective, the SCO has been characterized as "perhaps one of the most successful examples of multilateral embrace of digital authoritarian norms and practices" (McKune & Ahmed, 2018, p. 3841). In order to conduct an informed debate regarding digital sovereignty within the BRICS, it is therefore highly relevant to analyze the position of the SCO and its leading nations: China, Russia and India.

This chapter demonstrates how the sociotechnical imaginaries of digital sovereignty in China, Russia, and India are related to the much earlier conception of "cultural sovereignty," which was developed at the New World Information and Communication Order (NWICO) debates at UNESCO in the 1970s and 1980s. This conception, in turn, influenced particularly the Chinese discourse of "information sovereignty" in the late 1990s, from where the idea spread to the SCO and to Russia and India.

Starting from this genealogy, this contribution makes the case that, intertwined with economic and geopolitical factors, the sociotechnical imaginaries of digital sovereignty in China, Russia, India, and within the SCO and later the BRICS are centered around the idea that it is necessary to protect national cultural identities against the "free flow of information" enabled by digital networks, which has both domestic and international aspects dimensions. This, of course, has problematic aspects. Although the tendencies of monopolization of global communication and the concomitant uniformization of global culture regularly draw criticism, these imaginaries of digital sovereignty often serve as a means to justify practices of censorship and, in particular, obstacles to transborder information access, which violate Article 19 of the *Universal Declaration of Human Rights* (UDHR) that includes the right to "receive and impart information and ideas through any media and regardless of frontiers" (Universal Declaration of Human Rights, Article 19).

Section 2.2 includes a brief definition of digital sovereignty. The subsequent sections follow a chronological order. Section 2.3 proceeds with an analysis of the paradigm of the free flow of information and the postcolonial NWICO debates at UNESCO (the late 1970s to the early 1980s). In Section 2.4, I will lay out how these debates influenced the Chinese imaginary of digital sovereignty in the late 1990s and how China promoted its ideas, for example, within the World Summit on the Information Society (WSIS) from 2002 to 2005. In Section 2.5, I will focus on the SCO itself, which appears to have served as one transmission belt to export the Chinese imaginary of digital sovereignty to other countries, most notably Russia. In Section 2.6, I will lay out how cultural issues matter to Russia's "sovereignization" of the internet from 2011 on and how the country's specific sociotechnical imaginary of the "sovereign internet" was constructed. In Section 2.7, I will show how the SCO-member India (since 2017) developed a semi-authoritarian imaginary of digital sovereignty closely related to cultural issues, most notably regarding the Hindu nationalist government's internet shutdowns. In the final part, I will discuss these findings in relation to BRICS.

2.2 DEFINITION OF DIGITAL SOVEREIGNTY: A NOT-SO-NEW ALIGNMENT

Concepts related to digital sovereignty are part of a whole group of comparable, yet not identical concepts: technological sovereignty, information sovereignty, cyber sovereignty, internet sovereignty, data sovereignty, souveraineté numérique, soberania digital, digitale Souveränität, 网络主权 ("network sovereignty"), 信息主权 ("information sovereignty") and Суверенный интернет ("sovereign internet") (Thumfart, 2022).

While these terms can, by no means, all simply be equated, they all can be used, often by national governments, to signify the idea of national control over digital phenomena. In almost every case, this includes the concept to "align" (Mueller, 2017) cyberspace with territorial borders, which has also been described as the "territorialization" (Lambach, 2020) or "sovereignization" (Shcherbovich, 2021) of cyberspace.

In the contemporary debate, digital sovereignty has become a buzzword. What distinguishes digital sovereignty in comparison to, for example, data sovereignty, information sovereignty, or cybersecurity, is its vast scope. Information ethicist Floridi (2020) defines the term as including control over data, software, standards, processes and protocols, hardware, services, and infrastructure. Corresponding to this wide scope, the agenda of digital sovereignty includes policies such as data localization, internet censorship, the nationalization of digital infrastructure, and the construction of cyber capacities. While Floridi and many others (including Jiang and Belli in this volume) make the case that digital sovereignty can also be attributed to individuals, companies, and supranational entities, I am focusing here on digital sovereignty understood as an attribute of nation-states.

From the perspective of the Global North's developed countries, the shift from the unregulated internet to digital sovereignty with increased state regulation of the digital has been primarily owed to the catalytic events of the 2013 Snowden revelations, the Facebook–Cambridge Analytica scandal during the US presidential election and Brexit in 2016, and the disinformation crisis during the Covid-pandemic in 2020 and 2021 (Thumfart, 2022).

However, as I have argued elsewhere, discourses related to digital sovereignty have a far older history outside of the West. Western conversion to this norm is a comparably recent phenomenon that rather universalizes digital sovereignty than constituting a new invention (Thumfart, 2022). In this sense, the discourse around digital sovereignty is exemplary for the dawn of a truly multipolar world, in which the developed countries of the Global North are no longer exclusively setting the agenda (Thumfart, 2024b). This contribution reconstructs the pre-history of the current debate about digital sovereignty from a decidedly non-Western perspective.

2.3 THE FREE FLOW OF INFORMATION AND NWICO (FROM 1944 ON)

The central idea opposing digital sovereignty is the paradigm of the free flow of information as institutionalized in the UNESCO constitution (UNESCO Constitution 1945, Article 1.2). This paradigm is particularly interesting within a BRICS context, because it is closely connected to the debate about access to colonial and postcolonial media markets. The origin of the free flow of information paradigm predates digital technologies. Around the end of WWII, US officials criticized European powers' grip on the informational infrastructure and markets in their colonies and demanded equal access (Schiller, 1975).

For example, in 1944, the chairman of the US Federal Communications Commission criticized that "Great Britain owns the major portion of the cables of the world" and condemned this "control of communication facilities by one country with preferential services and rates to its own nationals" (Schiller, 1975, p. 77).

In 1946, the US Assistant Secretary of State outlined the government's position, which was, at that time, not directed against dictatorships, but rather against European geopolitical competitors.

> The State Department (...) plans to do everything within its power along political or diplomatic lines to help break down the artificial barriers to the expansion of private American news agencies, magazines, motion pictures, and other media of communication throughout the world (...). Freedom of the press – and freedom of exchange of information generally – is an integral part of our foreign policy.

The US ambition was ultimately successful. The European powers were weakened by WWII and willing to cooperate due to their fear of the Soviet Union (Schiller, 1975). The US's position regarding information freedom influenced UNESCO's position on this matter, which included the free flow of information in its charter (Schiller, 1975, p. 79). As mentioned in the introduction, this is also backed by Article 19 of the UDHR, which includes the right to access information across borders through any media.

However, with decolonization movements from the 1970s to the 1980s, leading governments of the Non-Aligned Movement, India, Cuba, and Tunisia, supported by the Soviet Union and China, began to criticize the unidirectionality of the global information flow from the developed countries of the Global North to the rest of the world (Bhuiyan, 2014, p. 4). During the debates on the NWICO at UNESCO, these countries demanded restrictions to the free flow of information based on "cultural sovereignty," which is, in many ways, the origin of today's debate on digital sovereignty (Carlsson, 2003).

This agenda had clearly an economic aspect, as it was part of the wider concept of the New International Economic Order (NIEO). However, the main argument in the NWICO's conclusive report is that information cannot be a commodity as any other since it is the very foundation of society and, thus, inherently political: "Information is a service that must exist before commodities in general can be produced and exchanged. These considerations ought to act as a corrective to the transformation of information into a simple commodity" (MacBride & Commissioners, 1980, p. 153).

Further, the report argues that the diversity of cultures is threatened by global "assimilation" to a dominant global culture (MacBride & Commissioners, 1980, p. 31). The report sketches "cultural sovereignty" as a means to prevent such a decline of cultural diversity. However, the text also stresses that cultural sovereignty cannot be understood in a too simplistic, essentialist manner (MacBride & Commissioners, 1980, p. 161) and that it could be abused to justify the violation of human rights (MacBride & Commissioners, 1980, p. 189), for instance, regarding the freedom of expression and minority rights.

It is noteworthy that the NWICO debates included all of the original BRICS countries. However, the debates ended in the early 1980s due to, among other reasons, the fact that these proposals undermined the communication hegemony of both the United States and Great Britain who withdrew from UNESCO in 1984 and 1985 respectively.

Instead, the doctrine of the free flow of information prevailed. During the late 1980s, it became increasingly political. This was owed to the fall of the Soviet Bloc in 1989, during which the free distribution of information by dissidents played a crucial role. The experience of the end of the Cold War led the US to believe that the free flow of information was desirable because it inherently promoted democratization (McCarthy, 2015, p. 84). A particularly clear expression of this idea is an essay by Bill Clinton's foreign policy advisor Joseph Nye and US navy admiral William A. Owens from 1996, titled "America's Information Edge" published in *Foreign Affairs*. It reads:

> The beauty of information as a power resource is that, while it can enhance the effectiveness of raw military power, it ineluctably democratizes societies. The communist and authoritarian regimes that hoped to maintain their centralized authority while still reaping the economic and military benefits of information technologies discovered they had signed a Faustian bargain (Nye & Owens, 1996, p. 35).

The idea that the free flow of information inevitably democratizes societies corresponds to the "Internet dictator's dilemma" (Boas, 2000), which conceives of digital technologies as forcing authoritarian States into accepting freedom of expression and democratic participation. During Hillary Clinton's tenure as the US Secretary of State, this idea was reframed as the "Internet Freedom" agenda (Clinton, 2010a).

Although there were occasionally debates in the developed countries of the Global North regarding the harmful side of the free flow of information (e.g., on drug trade and child pornography), the issue of whether the free flow of information threatens national cultures and how this could be a political problem has rarely been addressed in the Global North. Different from a time when the Global North's hegemony was practically unchallenged, today's discursive landscape in the Global North includes extensive discussions of the problematic impact of disinformation on deliberative processes in liberal democracies, particularly disinformation that originates from hostile geopolitical rivals (Thumfart, 2022).

2.4 THE ORIGINS OF DIGITAL SOVEREIGNTY IN CHINA (1996–2015)

Inspired by the NWICO debates, the Chinese sociotechnical imaginary of digital sovereignty that focuses on national control over digital technologies first appeared during the 1990s (Cong & Thumfart, 2022). It is determined by five factors of cultural and political nature.

First, this development is owed to the fact that with the fall of the Soviet Union, China began to emerge as the US's main geostrategic and economic rival, a role that it even played in its domestic political imaginary before it was perceived as such in the West. In this context, the Chinese government was and is focused on defending itself against the possibility of regime change from abroad through the means of digital communication.

Second, this geostrategic rivalry is connected to a cultural and historical issue. Since China conceives of itself as a post- and anti-colonial power, it is, in principle, vigilant regarding any developments coming from the US as the global hegemon. This anti-colonialist national imaginary was particularly influential during the 1990s, which saw the return of Hong Kong (in 1997) and Macao (in 1999) and a popularization of anti-colonialism in computer games and movies (Sly, 1997).

Third, the non-liberal and socialist country knows no strict separation between the private and public sectors. Instead, it seems rather natural to put digital technologies under state control. This is informed by Marxist political economy, which prescribes an active role of the state in promoting and controlling new technologies.

Fourth, China's understanding of its sovereignty over digital communication is informed by Confucianism, which became very important with the rehabilitation of traditional Chinese culture under Deng Xiaoping (Jiang, 2010). In order to assess the impact of Confucianism, it is crucial to stress that China, although being officially atheist, cannot be considered a secular society according to European standards because secularization was a result of specific confessional conflicts in sixteenth- and seventeenth-century Europe. And, accordingly, Confucianism is neither a religion nor a secular philosophy in the Western sense. Rather than recognizing the independence of the religious or cultural sphere, Beijing understands religious and cultural traditions as means to achieve the wider aim of a Confucian "harmonious society." This is exemplified by Beijing's authority over the recognition of reincarnated Buddhist lamas (Szonyi, 2009). Accordingly, while imported from the modern Western legal tradition, the Chinese understanding of sovereignty is informed by a Confucian and imperial tradition that is characterized by a universal understanding of sovereignty according to a system 天下 (*Tianxia*, lit. "under heaven") (Coleman & Maogoto, 2013; Zhao, 2019). This holistic, all-encompassing understanding of the state is a crucial element of Chinese political ideology and leads to the idea that cultural issues are inherently political.

Last but not least, China's vigilant stance against US digital hegemony also stems from the fact that the domain name system, a core architecture of the internet based on the Roman alphabet, manifests Western cultural hegemony. It took until 2009 that the Internet Corporation for Assigned Names and Numbers (ICANN) globally approved the creation of internationalized country code top-level domains. In line with worldwide concerns regarding this issue (Baasanjav, 2014), Chinese scholars in the 1990s and early 2000s saw the predominance of the English language on the internet as a threat to their cultural identity (Gong, 1998; Han, 2000). The Chinese government was so concerned with this problem that it introduced domain names in Chinese characters independent from ICANN as early as 2000 (Baasanjav, 2014, p. 996).

The Chinese position on issues related to digital sovereignty was formulated by Chinese scholars from 1996 on (Cong & Thumfart, 2022). It was expressed in the most poignant way in an essay from 1998 written by Gong Wenxiang of the School of International Relations at Peking University on "information sovereignty" (信息主权) (Gong, 1998). First, the essay explicitly refers to the NWICO debates. Following the arguments employed there, it criticizes US cultural domination and argues for "the establishment of equal, just and mutually beneficial communication." Constructing a fundamental conflict between the notion of "information sovereignty" and the "globalization of communication and information," the essay states:

> The so-called 'Coca-Cola culture', symbolized by rock music, MTV etc., has long been popular all over the world, and several major news agencies, such as AP, Reuters, BBC and CNN, have dominated international news dissemination. In the last instance, cultural communication and journalism are all about values that affect and influence the lifestyles and ideologies of their audiences. National information sovereignty (信息主权) should include the right to develop and consolidate national ethos and national culture through national and international dissemination of information (Gong, 1998, 42f.).

Employing a more aggressive tone, the essay underlines the strategic origins of the internet itself in the US ARPANET. In this context, the essay highlights the tactical significance of IT infrastructure and refers to the US's use of EMP-warheads during the first gulf war in 1991. It concludes:

> From CNN's exclusive field reports to the use of advanced automated weapons, the United States presented the world with a new type of warfare, which foreign scholars called 'information media warfare.' According to experts, the important aspect of warfare in the next century will be information warfare: digital information weapons such as computer viruses, logic bombs, and long-distance telephone network jamming devices are the nuclear weapons of the 21st century (Gong, 1998, p. 44).

Drawing from the Confucian philosopher Mencius, reflecting on the Opium War and the Boxer Rebellion, the essay explicitly discredits the notion of the free flow of information as an ideology that serves the interests of Western "information superpowers": "Whilst the information superpowers sing the hymns of 'international freedom of communication' and 'information without borders,' many developing countries feel that their rights are being taken away and even their national security is being threatened" (Gong, 1998, p. 45).

Gong Wenxiang's (1998) essay and similar ones on 网络主权 ("network sovereignty") and 网络殖民主义 ("network colonialism") illustrate the intellectual historical background that predestinated China for being the first country to explicitly develop concepts related to digital sovereignty (Cong & Thumfart, 2022; Guan, 1997; Tang, 1998). On several occasions, the NWICO debates are explicitly cited as a blueprint for the Chinese approach of digital sovereignty (Cong & Thumfart, 2022).

The following practical and intellectual development of these ideas in China has three aspects: First, a cultural aspect; second, a security aspect; and third, an agenda related to global internet governance. The SCO, which will be discussed in Section 2.5, is part of all three aspects.

Cultural issues played a role both externally and internally. State control over internet content through censorship intensified in China in 1999 with the persecution of Falun Gong, which was considered a sect with political ambitions by the Chinese government. The group had been very active online, communicating through its international network, foreign servers and foreign websites to circumvent censorship by the Chinese government. In June 1999, the infamous 610 Office was established to crack down on this group through means including blocking access to the group's sites outside China, undertaking cyberattacks against the group's websites in the US, Canada, and Australia and requiring the registration of all encryption technology used by private entities and individuals (Chung, 2002, p. 96). This conflict acted as a crucial catalyst in the successive development of the "Great Firewall" that started to block content beyond Falun Gong, for example, the cause of Tibetans or Uyghurs or the events of June 1989 (Creemers, 2020, p. 13). It is obvious that the question of minorities within China is not only a political issue but also a cultural issue, particularly important from the perspective of the Chinese holistic and not necessarily secular (in the European sense) understanding of the state. These cultural aspects are not merely restrictive and top-down but have a productive and bottom-up element. They are reinforced by a form of "digital nationalism" in Chinese civil society (Schneider, 2018).

Beyond these cultural issues, security concerns played a role in the development of Chinese concepts related to digital sovereignty. One of the better-known outcomes of this discourse is an essay by the influential flight engineer Ji Zhaojun published in 2000. This essay "Network Security, Sovereignty, and Innovation" compared digital sovereignty to sovereignty over airspace and maritime space and promoted the idea that open digital networks further US dominance (McKune & Ahmed, 2018, p. 3838). In 2004, Chen Xueshi of the National University of Defense Technology affiliated to the People's Liberation Army defined national "information borders," which has since then been a characteristic feature of the Chinese discourse (McKune & Ahmed, 2018, p. 3838).

Third, China promoted concepts related to digital sovereignty in international fora of global internet governance, making it a prime norm entrepreneur in these contexts (McKune & Ahmed, 2018). Take as an example China's engagement in the World Summit on the Information Society (WSIS), ICANN and the International Telecommunication Union (ITU), the SCO, and the World Internet Conference (Negro, 2020).

China has had a presence at ICANN since 1999 and it demanded a reform of the ICANN multistakeholder system in favor of an UN-like, state-centric mode of control as early as 2002 (Arséne, 2015, p. 29). The country found its allies on internet governance in the first phase of WSIS that year (Negro, 2020, p. 8), when three countries of the Global South – Brazil, Cuba, and Iran – proposed to create an intergovernmental framework to replace the existing ICANN-led internet governance model (Bhuiyan, 2014, p. 51). In essence, these countries demanded "their sovereign right to make international public policy for the internet" (Mueller, 2020, p. 3).

In the second preparatory committee of the WSIS in Geneva in 2003, the head of the Chinese delegation criticized the status of internet governance as "monopolized by one state and one corporation that neither facilitate further growth of the internet, nor fully embody the principle of equity and full representation" (Negro, 2020, p. 10). During the WSIS, China's spokesperson tried to raise understanding for its restrictive approach to freedom of speech, calling the international community to "fully respect the differences in social systems and cultural diversity" (China, 2003). A key cultural issue discussed in WSIS was the question of domain names in non-Roman alphabets (Associated Press, 2005; Baasanjav, 2014).

Finally, the WSIS debates produced three opposing parties: Brazil, China, Russia, India, Pakistan, Iran, and Cuba, which advocated for governmental control of the internet within the UN; the US, which wanted to keep the status quo; and the EU, which initially supported the demand for governmental control over the internet, but then switched sides.

In the end, the resulting Tunis Agenda of 2005 recognized the call for digital sovereignty: "Policy authority for Internet-related public policy issues is the sovereign right of states" (WSIS, 2005). However, this declaration was not followed by real changes since the US put high diplomatic pressure on the EU to withdraw its support for the proposal to replace ICANN with a system of intergovernmental control over the global internet ("Letter by Gutierrez and Rice," 2005). An observer summarizes: "The irony is even though Europe has been critical of ICANN, they have given their blessing to it" (Associated Press, 2005). With the European retreat, the countries favoring governmental control of the internet were relatively isolated. In the developed countries of the Global North (with the notable exception of France), the issue did not appear in the debate any more during these years (Benhamou & Sorbier, 2006; Thumfart, 2022).

Conversely, China and Russia furthered the agenda between each other and several former central Asian Soviet Union states within the SCO. Hereby, China is clearly the most important actor. In 2008, China surpassed the US in the number of internet users and has since been the leading country in terms of internet users (Robson, 2017). Accordingly, Beijing intensified its ambitions to strengthen national sovereignty over digital technology and promote this approach through international organizations such as the SCO and the BRICS.

In addition to the SCO, which will be dealt with in detail in Section 2.5, the ITU is an important forum, of which the secretary-general was Chinese from 2015 to 2022. Another important forum is the Beijing-initiated and -controlled World Internet Conference (WIC), which started in 2014 and included representatives of SCO member states, observers, and the private sector, for instance, companies and organizations such as Baidu, Alibaba, Tencent, Apple, Amazon, Microsoft, Samsung, LinkedIn, and ICANN. Since 2014, China has been promoting a declaration regarding digital sovereignty that was officially presented to the participants of this conference in 2015 (Zeng, 2015).

2.5 DIGITAL SOVEREIGNTY IN THE SCO SINCE 2005

The SCO was founded in 2001 based on a treaty regarding central Asian border conflicts in 1996 that gave birth to the "Shanghai Five." Its original members were China, Russia, Kyrgyzstan, Kazakhstan, Tajikistan, and Uzbekistan. At first, Russia was its driving force with the two-fold strategic objective to prevent Western interventions following the wars in former Yugoslavia (1991–2001) and the "color revolutions" (2000–2005) as well as to combat Islamist extremism in the region that became a security threat with the conflicts in Chechnya and Dagestan and numerous terrorist attacks in the region (Souleimanov & Horák, 2006). The SCO's strategic goal against Western intervention and Islamic extremism connects cultural issues with security ones.

With a rising profile, China increasingly held more sway in the SCO. On issues concerning Xinjiang province, China shared the objective to combat Islamic separatists. The formation of the Regional Anti-Terrorist Structure

(RATS) in 2004 is the central pillar of the SCO and will be discussed later. In the context of its other objective, which is to strengthen state sovereignty against perceived Western interventions on issues such as human rights or popular consent, the SCO also served as a transmission belt for the Chinese imaginary of digital sovereignty to be exported to other member states. This applies foremost to Russia, which was concerned with Western interference but pursued a largely liberal approach to internet regulation until the Duma election protests of 2011 (see Section 2.6).

In 2005, the year of the Tunis Agenda of the WSIS, the SCO started to advance its strategic goals in digital sovereignty that bear resemblance to the NWICO or WSIS debates. The Astana Declaration of that year reads: "The world's diversity of cultures and civilizations is a universal human value. In an era of rapid development of information technologies and communications (...), the right of every nation to its own way of development should be fully guaranteed" (SCO, 2005).

The SCO's explicit demands for digital sovereignty fit well into this framework. These demands started with the *Declaration of the Heads of the SCO Member States on International Information Security* in 2006 that emphasized the willingness of the participants to collaborate. Although this declaration was explicitly following a recommendation included in the Resolution 60/45 passed at the 60th UN General Assembly on strengthening multilateral cooperation in matters of information security, it stands in evident contrast to the UN doctrine: The SCO member states emphasized a territorial understanding of sovereignty directly opposed to the global free flow of information. The signing member states stressed the need for international collaboration due to "the cross-border nature of ICT" but characterized ICTs as possibly contradicting the principles of "non-interference in the internal affairs of sovereign states" and "non-use of force" (SCO, 2006). Furthermore, the cultural aspect was explicitly stated in the SCO's 2006 declaration, particularly the "respect for religious feelings and traditions of nations, inter alia, within the Shanghai Cooperation Organization region."

Despite this rhetorical focus on territorial sovereignty, the SCO includes a significant degree of transnational cooperation in the service of preserving regime stability. In this sense, the SCO has been accurately labeled as "transnational authoritarianism" and criticized for being "a vehicle for human rights violations" (Tsourapas, 2020, p. 20). The SCO is built on the principle of mutual recognition within the Regional Anti-Terrorist Structure (RATS), which, for example, allows for the seamless extradition of individuals suspected of terrorism and the exchange of relevant information (International Federation for Human Rights, 2012, p. 5). In the language of the SCO, this is part of fighting the "three evils" of terrorism, separatism, and extremism. However, from a Western perspective, this constitutes transnational repression against individuals who can be regarded as dissidents, such as several Uyghur activists (International Federation for Human Rights, 2012, p. 16).

The SCO's Agreement on Cooperation in Ensuring International Information Security of 2009 was likewise a reaction to a UN resolution on multilateral cooperation in the field of information security. Outspoken about its fears of regime change orchestrated by the West, the agreement names what it considered "major threats in the field of international information security" including not only "information warfare," "information terrorism," cybercrime, but also the "use of a dominant position in the information space to the detriment of the interests and security of other states" and "dissemination of information prejudicial to the socio-political and socio-economic systems, spiritual, moral and cultural environment of other states" (SCO, 2009).

The Tashkent Declaration of 2010 clearly formulated the SCO project to create a normative order of cyberspace based on territorial sovereignty:

> Information security is closely linked to state sovereignty, national security, socio-economic stability and the interests of citizens. All countries are entitled to exercise control over the Internet in accordance with their domestic situation and laws, while expanding cooperation in a spirit of equality and mutual respect (SCO, 2010).

In 2011, the SCO member states submitted a Draft International Code of Conduct for Information Security to the UN General Assembly very much in line with China's position at the WSIS. The draft reaffirms that "policy authority for Internet-related public issues is the sovereign right of states" (McKune, 2011). The text also includes a condemnation of cyberwar. The drafters pledge "not to use information and communication technologies, including networks, to carry out hostile activities or acts of aggression." Furthermore, it includes a passage that, once more, directly links cultural issues to security issues, in which the drafters agree to combat the "use of information and communications technologies (...) that incites terrorism, secessionism or extremism or that undermines other countries' political, economic and social stability, as well as their spiritual and cultural environment." Little was changed in a new draft submitted to the UN General Assembly in 2015.

It is difficult to assess the impact of the SCO's rhetorical positions on existing policies. None of the regimes involved is particularly transparent, especially when it comes to security issues. In terms of the digital implications of the SCO, it is certain that the Regional Anti-Terrorist Structure (RATS) exists and that the SCO includes a regime of transborder exchange of e-evidence. But it is also likely that this organization is, in many aspects, a paper tiger. However, at the international level in particular where norms tend to be contested and permanently evolving, rhetoric can be extremely influential in the construction of sociotechnical imaginaries. In this sense, the declarations analyzed in this section demonstrate that the SCO served as a transmission belt for a sociotechnical imaginary of digital sovereignty that connects cultural issues with security issues in the digital realm.

2.6 DIGITAL SOVEREIGNTY IN RUSSIA SINCE 2011

Although the Soviet Union played a leading role in the NWICO debates and even criticized the NWICO for *not being focused enough* on sovereignty, the post-Soviet discourse on domestic sovereignty and digital technologies is not as elaborate as the Chinese discourse on this matter (MacBride & Commissioners, 1980, p. 280). An indicator for this is that Cyrillic domain names did not get introduced before 2010 (Radio Liberty Staff, 2010), while Chinese domain names were introduced independently from ICANN as early as 2000 (Arséne, 2015, p. 30; Baasanjav, 2014, p. 966). For a long time, Moscow even promoted a moderate form of freedom of speech on the internet since it regarded the digital public sphere as a "social decompression chamber" that would keep people out of real politics (Nocetti, 2017). Rather than censoring, the Russian government initially supported the development of a regime-friendly digital sphere including bloggers, influencers and institutions that would later become notorious as Russia's "troll factories" (Morozov, 2011, p. 126).

For this reason, China seems to have played the leading role in the propagation of more restrictive digital policies in the context of the SCO's early declarations. Around the year 2016 when the Chinese promotion of this matter within the ITU, SCO, and WIC reached a peak, Russia reportedly received surveillance and censorship technology from China (Soldatov & Borogan, 2016). Some suggested already earlier that Russia has been demoted from the leading force of the SCO to China's "junior partner" (Aris, 2008, p. 14).

However, the Chinese and Russian positions regarding digital sovereignty are complementary within the SCO and the BRICS contexts. While the Chinese discourse was from the start more focused on defensive sovereignty, the Russian one was more focused on aggressive digital sovereignty (Soldatov & Borogan, 2018). The first Russian (then still Soviet) cyberattack on the US happened as early as 1986 (Stoll, 1989). In 2007, the Kremlin's youth organization Nashi's attack on Estonia marked the beginning of the contemporary cyberwar discourse in the West by triggering the instalment of the NATO Cooperative Cyber Defence Centre of Excellence in Tallinn.

Then again, both China and Russia are subject to similar external drivers since they are geopolitically opposed to the cyber-hegemon USA and its actions, which became globally notorious with the Snowden revelations of 2013. The notion of "Суверенный интернет" ("Sovereign Internet") finds its origin in a column published some weeks after the Snowden revelations of 2013 by Sergei Zheleznyak, a leading politician for implementing Putin's authoritarian turn (Elder, 2013). Under the umbrella of digital sovereignty, Zheleznyak condemned the US, demanding a "national server network" and Russia's "own information products." Subsequently, in 2013, the *Internet Research Agency* was founded, which later influenced the US's 2016 election in an "attempt to duplicate what the Kremlin considered the West's unwarranted incursions into Russia's own political life" (Krastev & Holmes, 2019, p. 118). Furthermore, in 2016, the Yarovaya Laws on data localization have been passed, which require personal data from individuals located in Russia to be stored within Russian territory (Savelyev, 2016). Russia also pursued an infrastructural sovereignization of RuNet (Sivetc, 2021).

These measures of sovereignization are also the product of an earlier turning point than the Snowden revelations in 2013. In 2011, following the Arab Spring, Russia experienced the greatest wave of protests of its post-Soviet history, many organized through the internet (Asmolov, 2020, p. 243). Moscow believed these protests to have been orchestrated by the US (Snyder, 2018b), even though the main reasons for these protests were, in fact, domestic (Robertson, 2013). As a reaction, Moscow started to tighten political control of the internet (Harper, 2017), passing a "whole avalanche of new repressive laws" (Weiss, 2016, p. 289). In 2012, the state introduced Federal Law 139 FZ, which, at first, banned sites containing child pornography, information regarding suicide, and selling drugs, which would two years later, with the Law 398 FZ, also extend to political content (see Chapter 8). This form of internet censorship is, at least, rhetorically, closely related to cultural issues. The repressive laws crucial to internet censorship, all adopted around the year 2012, target blasphemy, obscene language and "propaganda of non-traditional sexual relations."

It is noteworthy that the cultural/religious turn marked by these laws was well understood in Russia, particularly the anti-blasphemy laws that triggered protest by the traditionally secular communists (Weiss, 2016, p. 290). In turn, the laws against obscene language produced less resistance and were accepted as a continuation of a Soviet tradition. However, here too a shift was visible. While the prohibition of obscenities in Soviet times was connected to insults and offenses, the new laws "are exclusively aimed at establishing and promoting language norms" (Kovalev, 2016, p. 339). The case of the so-called antigay laws is even more complex since they are based on irrational ideas. At least rhetorically, Moscow regards communication regarding homosexuality as part of Western information warfare with the objective to reduce low Russian birth rates even further (Mortensen, 2016, pp. 353–357). Overall, these concepts and laws are vague and it is exactly their vagueness and irrational nature that allows for the most repressive interpretations (Weiss, 2016, p. 289).

Some of the most notorious examples of these laws include investigations against a blogger who posed as a priest on Instagram and the forced psychiatric admission of a user of VKontakte who denied the existence of God (Weiss, 2016, p. 290). Another prominent example is the manager of a feminist website who was trialed for pornography and gay propaganda and put under house arrest (Amnesty International, 2019). Russia's internet laws have a strong chilling effect on civil society beyond these individual cases.

While it is relatively easy to connect the Chinese discourse on digital sovereignty to cultural and political specifics such as Confucianism and Marxism, this is much harder in the Russian case. As mentioned before, the incompatibility of the Cyrillic and the Roman alphabet plays a role in the Russian pursuit of digital sovereignty, and so does Moscow's involvement in conflicts with Islamist extremism in Chechnya and Dagestan.

However, the cultural conflict with Islamist extremism unfolds very differently in Russia since Moscow and the Orthodox church are sympathetic to the illiberal cultural claims of Islamism. For example, in contrast to Western European countries, the Russian government has banned Charlie Hebdo's satirical depictions of Mohammed for "inciting religious hatred" and the Orthodox church supported this step (Rainsford, 2015). On a number of occasions, Putin read from Quran, Bible, and Talmud at the same event, which expresses a close linkage between politics and religion (Black, 2021, p. 377).

These are examples of the inclusive, yet illiberal, imaginary of Русский мир (*russkii mir*) that undergirds Russian politics on many levels. The term "*russkii mir*" can be understood as "Russian World," which includes the canonic territory of the Orthodox Patriarchate, that is, Ukraine, Belarus, Moldova, Kazakhstan, and many other Slavic countries. The term can be also understood as "Russian Peace" in a sense of *Pax Russica* that constructs the notion of Russia's hegemony (Laruelle, 2015, p. 15) over a multicultural Eurasian space corresponding to the idea of Russia as a "Third Rome" (Poe, 2001). In addition to these rather conservative and expansive connotations, the idea of the "Russian World" includes the territory of the former Soviet Union.

Despite its baroque multiplicity of historical fields of resonance, this idea of the "Russian World" is extremely relevant politically. On March 18, 2014, Putin used it as a justification for Russia's annexation of Crimea (Laruelle, 2015, p. 15). Typical of imperial imaginaries, the lack of geographical precision makes the concept of the "Russian World" useful for the justification of any kind of territorial expansion.

The ultranationalist Russian think tank *Izborsk Club* close to Putin formulated a Russian messianic mission for Eurasia on these grounds, which includes combatting the cultural effects of informational globalization. Its manifesto from 2012 reads:

> The lethal ideological and informational "machine" that destroyed all the bases and values of the (...) Romanov empire and then destroyed all the foundations of the (...) Soviet empire is everywhere at work. The fall of these empires transformed the great Eurasian space into a chaos of warring peoples, faiths and cultures on fields of blood. (...) The Russian messianic consciousness, grounded (...) in the Orthodox dream of divine justice (...) summons the negation of Russia at the level of worldview, the attacks on her faith, culture, and historical codes (Snyder, 2018a, pp. 93–96).

From the point of view of the intellectual history of sovereignty, an interesting feature is Russian leadership's reference to German authoritarian legal theorist

Carl Schmitt's realist conception of international relations, which is widely shared among Eurasia ideologues (Snyder, 2018a, pp. 80–90). Schmitt's arguments against the illegality of wars of aggression partially explain Moscow's "hybrid warfare" of kinetic and cyber means (Renz & Smith, 2016; Snyder, 2018a, pp. 193–194). Of course, Moscow's stance is characterized by double standards. While promoting noninterference in the digital sector on a normative level, for example, within the SCO and the BRICS, it engages in using kinetic and cyber means for projecting power.

Schmitt's idea of sovereignty, namely its foundation in the state's monopoly of force and control and its emphasis on territoriality, is also a crucial feature of the Russian discourse on digital sovereignty. The "sovereign internet" (Суверенный интернет) grants the government far-reaching control, including deep-packet inspection of transnational data traffic. In 2019, Russia reportedly disconnected its internet from the global one, without ordinary citizens noticing it (Wakefield, 2019). Leonid Savin, a Eurasia political activist of the *Izborsk Club*, points out that sovereignty in the territorial Schmittian sense requires a realignment of cyberspace with territory, which must ultimately include the possibility to disconnect at will from global communication (Savin, 2019a, 2019b).

However, it should be noted that the Russian government's decidedly illiberal approach to digital sovereignty has its technological limits. For instance, Moscow's unsuccessful attempt to ban Telegram has shown that there is a merely rhetorical element to its claims of digital sovereignty (see Chapter 8). As of mid 2024, the jury is still out as to how the Russian army may perform on the kinetic battlefield and the cyber domain. So far, Moscow has not yet attempted the actual "disconnect" of RuNet from the global internet. However, it must be stressed that rhetoric matters when it comes to international norms and the construction of sociotechnical imaginaries.

2.7 DIGITAL SOVEREIGNTY IN INDIA SINCE 2017

India is the most complex of these three nations in terms of digital sovereignty formations. While India was a driving force behind the BRICS from the start with the creation of the BRIC in 2006, it is connected to the SCO in a loose way since it joined the SCO only in 2017. India was invited by Russia to join the SCO to counter China's invitation of India's archrival Pakistan. It is unclear to which extent previous declarations of the SCO will concern India as the country is a "digital decider" between liberal and non-liberal modes of digital governance (Basu, 2019). For instance, India joined the majority of the SCO and BRICS member states in backing the adoption of the UN resolution on *Countering the Use of Information and Communication Technologies for Criminal Purposes* (Sherman & Morgus, 2018).

India has a strong bipartisan anti-colonial tradition, which includes a general willingness to defend local cultures and economy against global hegemonic structures. Actors closer to the politically left promote a form of economic nationalism called *swadeshi* ("swa" = "self" and "desh" = "country"), while actors on the politically right promote *hindutva* ("Hindu-ness") (Prabhu, 2012). India has also been one of the leading forces of the Non-Aligned Movement, which was crucial to the NWICO debate in the 1970s and 1980s. During WSIS, too, India has been on the side of those nations who demanded more political oversight over internet governance (Vipin, 2011).

Comparable to China, the resistance against US-led digital colonialism is important to India, where a commentator labeled Google's crushing of the country's local search engines as "digital battle of Plassey" (Arya, 2020). Accordingly, India has implemented a relatively strict regime of data localization that is primarily focused on the idea that the data of Indian citizens (the second largest internet user base in the world) constitutes an economic resource that should belong exclusively to Indians. This perspective focused on the national economy is particularly convincing since the country maintains the world's largest digital biometrical ID program Aadhaar, which has been installed as early as 2009. This technological-demographical baseline situation also brought about a focus on privacy and national security (Kovacs & Ranganathan, 2019, p. 17).

However, the country's position is characterized by a double frontline. In addition to a guarded stance against Western digital hegemony, India seems to also fear the influence of China, with whom it forged an alliance through the BRIC grouping since 2006 and through the SCO since 2017. India and China also had a number of territorial disputes beyond the digital realm, for instance, the 2020–2021 border skirmishes. The ban of dozens of Chinese apps in June 2020 that resulted from these border conflicts also made clear that India's digital sovereignty can be in direct opposition to China from time to time (Al Jazeera, 2021). Due to diverging and converging interests on different issues and at different times, the SCO and the BRICS grouping can experience instability given their multipolarity.

Culturally, the notion of *hindutva* embodies a nationalist aspect that became increasingly important to Modi's Hindu nationalist government (Mohammed-Arif et al., 2020). However, today, the focus of this ideology lies not so much in its stance toward the West, with whom the Modi government maintains tight relations, but toward Pakistan and the approximately 200 million Indian Muslims (Tellis, 2018). Furthermore, in contrast to Russia and China and although Modi's government promotes the replacement of English by Hindi on all levels of Indian society, global Anglo-Saxon culture may not be regarded as an existential threat from an Indian point of view as a significant part of its population speaks English as a second language. Neither does India have only one non-Roman alphabet, which would produce a clear dichotomy. Since 2011,

ICANN has allowed for domain names in several regional languages: Hindi, Gujarati, Urdu, Punjabi, Bengali, and Telegu (Sengupta, 2011). Compared to China, the liberal Western idea of internet freedom poses no fundamental ideological problems to India since the country is constitutionally a democracy.

However, comparable to the domestic implications of the Russian and Chinese imaginaries of digital sovereignty, internet use in India can also be heavily restricted. This is largely owed to domestic security challenges related to religious issues. Already in the 2000s, the Indian government has shown a keen interest in cybersecurity due to Islamist terrorism (Kovacs, 2021, p. 134). Modi's Hindu nationalist government, in turn, stoked interreligious conflicts (Mohammed-Arif et al., 2020). In India's complex society full of inner tensions and anachronisms, such conflicts and conflicts of nonreligious nature can lead to violent online mobs, often fueled by disinformation. In August and September 2013, social media played a decisive role in stoking clashes between Muslims and Hindus in the state of Uttar Pradesh, which left 62 dead, 93 injured, and 50,000 displaced (Biju, 2019, p. 10). Also, following the anti-Muslim laws issued by the Hindu Nationalist government, the Delhi riots of 2020 killed 53. The riots were clearly of interreligious nature, stoked by hate spread through social media (Mehta, 2020). In another example from 2018, two young men were accused of being child kidnappers and were beaten to death on the grounds of a social media video (Deutsche Welle, 2018). Such lethal attacks on the basis of social media rumors occurred more frequently in India (Krishnan, 2018). In the first half of 2018 alone, more than two dozen people died related to rumors spread via WhatsApp (Samuels, 2020). In many cases, the perpetrators were "rightwing Hindu cow vigilantes" (Shah, 2021, p. 1932). However, in one of the latest such incidents – the 2020 Palghar mob lynching – two men were killed on the grounds of WhatsApp rumors, and both the perpetrators and the victims were Hindu.

Such incidents, which the Hindu nationalist government partly stoked, serve as the justification for the government's more expansive control over web content. For instance, the Indian government has requested Twitter (now X), Google, and YouTube to remove posts considered blasphemous or inciting communal violence (Segal, 2017). In 2019, Netflix agreed to delete all content that disrespects the country's flag, hurts religious sentiments, or promotes terrorism (Dixit, 2019). After the Indian government waged a "war with Twitter" (Biswas, 2021), Twitter too agreed to delete 90–95% of accounts requested for removal by the Indian government (Business Insider India, 2021). However, since the removal requests concerned mostly the accounts of anti-government protesters, it is obvious that the Indian state's actions do not exclusively serve security purposes, but also the government's own interest.

Since the Temporary Suspension of Telecom Services Rules came into force in 2017, the Indian government also frequently uses these rules to enact local "internet shutdowns." Although this practice also exists in Western democracies (De Gregorio & Stremlau, 2020), India is, by far, the number one country in enacting such shutdowns. Of the 155 internet shutdowns imposed globally in 2020, a staggering 109 occurred in India, which means that the country is even more authoritarian on this issue than other SCO member states (Chakravarti, 2021).

India has also enacted one of the world's longest and most far-reaching internet shutdown so far, lasting from August 4th, 2019 to March 4th, 2020 affecting the former Muslim-majority state of Jammu and Kashmir with 12.5 million inhabitants (Internet shutdowns in India, n.d.). The toll on the local economy and on civil society, particularly the work of journalists, is high (Sarkar et al., 2020). An analysis from 2019 has shown that shutdown orders mostly do not require suspension of internet services in their entirety, but rather a direct blocking of specific mass messaging platforms such as Facebook, Twitter, and WhatsApp (Internet Freedom Foundation, 2019). Furthermore, internet shutdowns became so common in India that they are not always seen as political or security issues. In widely criticized displays of local authoritarianism, local governments regularly suspend internet connectivity to ensure that no cheating takes place during civil service exams (Sanzgiri, 2023). This is to be understood not only as a display of authoritarianism but also as an expression of the "heavy emphasis on education in the country, where for many, proper schooling could be the key out of poverty" (Yeung et al., 2021).

Also beyond the measures mentioned earlier, the current Hindu nationalist government promoted digital authoritarianism (Sherman, 2019). It has extended the use of artificial intelligence-enabled facial recognition in urban centers and successively transformed the country's digital biometrical ID program Aadhaar from a voluntary to a de facto compulsory ID since it is needed for a great number of governmental services. This, too, has been raising fears of governmental surveillance (Khera, 2019). This top-down authoritarian turn is worsened by increasing digital vigilantism in the Indian civil society of the so-called "cyber Hindus" (Biju, 2019, p. 10).

In summary, the Indian concept of digital sovereignty includes highly authoritarian aspects, most notably censorship and internet shutdowns, which are partly connected to complex authoritarian strategies of the Hindu nationalist government but the concept has also to be understood within India's complex cultural contexts. While the Russian notion of a disconnectable "sovereign" internet explicitly refers to Schmitt's understanding of sovereignty against foreign powers, the Indian concept of digital sovereignty realizes the Schmittian principle on the domestic level as Schmitt defined sovereignty as the power to declare the state of exception, and internet shutdowns are an expression of such a "liminal" understanding of sovereignty in the digital realm (Thumfart, 2024a).

It is important to note here that such dramatic authoritarian approaches include a great degree of make-belief. It is more than questionable whether internet shutdowns actually achieve their security goals since they have been found to be combined with governmental inaction in critical situations of civil unrest (Ruijgrok, 2021, p. 32). Furthermore, it is not possible to shut down the internet in a country completely (Shah, 2021, p. 2696). However, there is no doubt that internet shutdowns represent an impressive staging of the nation-state as "taking back control" over digital networks. And such staging of governmental power matters, particularly regarding sociotechnical imaginaries.

2.8 CONCLUSION: DIGITAL SOVEREIGNTY FOR GLOBAL CULTURAL DIVERSITY?

Digital communication has become a decisive factor in the economy and politics of all countries. A critical understanding of the global digital infrastructure and economy as enabling "digital colonialism" is not entirely unjustified even for authoritarian countries (Avila Pinto, 2018; Hicks, 2019). Neither are fears that democratization campaigns based on social media might lead to regime change – regardless of whether this regime change might be desirable from a human rights perspective or not. Developing nations with non-liberal traits, as in the cases of China, Russia, and India, have constructed imaginaries of digital sovereignty that can be evoked to implement economic protectionism and political censorship. Such obstacles to the domestic and transnational free flow of information often include violations of article 19 of the UDHR.

Beyond political and economic aspects that influence the imaginaries of digital sovereignty promoted within the SCO and the BRICS by China, Russia, and India, it is crucial to consider cultural factors. Although threats to national cultural identities are often exaggerated and politically exploited, governments and civil societies of all three nations do have reason to believe that their traditional culture can be threatened by the free flow of information enabled by global digital hegemons. As a matter of simple fact, ICANN for a long time allowed only top-level domains in the Roman alphabet. Additionally, all of these immensely diverse countries hardly fit the idea of consolidated nation-states following the European pattern of development for they are often confronted with significant internal cultural conflicts. Whether perceived or real, internal cultural challenges and external cultural threats have informed these countries' non-liberal or authoritarian positions on domestic digital sovereignty in the form of censorship and on external digital sovereignty in the form of protectionist policies, and in the case of Russia, also aggressive cyber operations.

This chapter highlights the relationship between digital sovereignty and cultural identity. It does so by tracing the historical narrative that informed the development of the notion of "cultural sovereignty" during the NWICO debates in the 1970s and 1980s, the digital sovereignty discourse that emerged in China in the 1990s, and the subsequent spread of an extreme form of state-centric digital sovereignty to Russia since 2011 and the embrace of it by a nationalist Indian government from 2017 on. In these processes, the multilateral forums of the SCO, and to a lesser extent the BRICS, served as a transmission belt in proliferating state-centric imaginaries of digital sovereignty. It is a central finding that in all three of the examined countries, imaginaries of digital sovereignty are related to a non-secular understanding of the state that merges politics and religion (Russia and India) and traditions that are neither secular nor religious (Chinese Confucianism). And since 2006, SCO statements routinely connected religious issues, information technologies, and security concerns. In this sense, the global emergence of digital sovereignty can be compared to the evolution of state sovereignty from the confessional wars and the connected development of the printing press in sixteenth- and seventeenth-century Europe. On a methodological level, this chapter demonstrates that, similar to this more or less well-fitting historical comparison, the construction of state-centric digital sovereignty can only be understood considering a complex entanglement of domestic social, economic, political, and cultural dispositions, power dynamics in international relations, and the development of concrete technological capacities (see also: Thumfart 2024b).

As of 2024, it is difficult to speak in positive terms of a common future of the BRICS or SCO that includes a militaristic Russia, as doing so may normalize Russia's aggressive authoritarianism that is not shared by China or India. However, a more hopeful long-term outlook for the BRICS beyond Russia's war of aggression in Ukraine and Putin's misrule could emphasize cooperation between BRICS nations to realize the objectives set by NWICO and WSIS by making the digital world less one-dimensional or monopolistic (see Chapter 1). One does not need to be a right-wing nationalist to regard global cultural assimilation as a problem. If one takes the impact of digital communication on the development of human civilizations seriously, then US-led standardization and destruction of cultural diversity by Googleization, Facebookization, Twitterization, and Uberization could constitute a threat to human civilizations severe enough to warrant a serious response. Due to prejudices incurred by biased algorithms and faulty AI, cultural diversity is more than a nice-to-have luxury, but of vital importance to adequately represent the full scope and complexity of human social and intellectual capacities. Digital sovereignty grounded in legitimate reasons and proportionate actions can be a crucial means to protect cultural diversity across the globe and harvest its potential.

If one assumes that regulation of digital content and services to preserve cultural diversity around the globe is legitimate, where does the legitimate interest in preserving one's own culture end and where does the persecution of religious and other minorities begin, as this is the case of Muslims, dissidents and members of the LGBTQ+-community in China, Russia, and India? What about respecting citizens' privacy and right to communicate freely across borders and conduct business online when doing so contradicts the interest of the state? These are difficult questions. Decolonization and authoritarianism converged historically in their shared resistance against Western norms, which are frequently thought of as including human rights such as the freedom of speech and the right to privacy (Watson, 2021). An informed debate on digital sovereignty has to consider both: the dangers of digital authoritarianism and the productive potential of digital decolonization.

Funding acknowledgement: During this research, Johannes Thumfart received funding from *Gerda Henkel Stiftung's special programme Security, Society, and the State* (2020–2022) *and the European Union Horizon 2020 research programme under MSCA COFUND grant agreement 101034352 with co-funding from the VUB-Industrial Research Fund* (2022–2024).

3

The Spatial Expansion of China's Digital Sovereignty

Extraterritoriality and Geopolitics

Wanshu Cong

3.1 INTRODUCTION

For various historical and political reasons, the idea of digital sovereignty, and the concept of sovereignty more broadly, is largely a state-centric one in China, revolving around the discourse, policies, and practices of the Chinese government. Within the history of the internet, China has a relatively long tradition of proclaiming cyber sovereignty and establishing state control over the cyberspace and digital infrastructures. Various practices of China bordering or "re-territorializing" the cyberspace (Kettemann, 2020) demonstrate this sovereigntist approach of governing the internet, such as the Great Firewall that censors the transmission of information to China, and the rule of data localization prescribed by Article 37 of China's *Cyber Security Law* (CSL). Deep political and ideological reasons make it unlikely for China to depart from its adherence to the sovereigntist approach for governing the internet. However, the application of strict territoriality principle to the governance of the internet has indeed been challenged by its high economic costs and lack of efficacy to protect the expanding market and interest of Chinese tech and digital companies overseas. These challenges called for new ways of understanding the scope and substance of state digital sovereignty and of exercising its sovereign power over the internet and data. The Chinese regulatory evolution appears to be a gradual spatial expansion of its regulatory power beyond the physical borders, reflecting an emerging tendency from territoriality to extraterritoriality in the conception and practice of China's digital sovereignty. This tendency is what this chapter inquires.

Of course, one may ask whether there is really a shift from territoriality to extraterritoriality in the cyber context.[1] In addition, despite its attempts of grafting borders onto the internet, China is no less reluctant to undertake

[1] Notes: See discussions about the extraterritorial effect of territorial control of the internet, for example (Hildebrandt, 2013; Mueller, 2010).

extraterritorial measures against dissidents, and, therefore, its seemingly territorial approach does not reflect the complexity of actual practices. The chapter does not present this tendency as a sudden new phenomenon. What is interesting, however, is that the mismatch between China's official stance and actual practice may become less stark due to the emerging change of regulatory philosophy: the regulatory tendency toward extraterritoriality can be identified explicitly in recent initiatives as well as scholarly discussions. They differ from previous practices of which extraterritoriality is rather implicit and barely gets clear legal justifications.

This chapter, adopting a state-centric perspective of digital sovereignty (see Chapter 1), draws attention to China's three recent regulatory instruments, which most remarkably demonstrate the direction toward the spatial expansion of China's digital sovereignty: China's Personal Information Protection Law ("the PIPL"),[2] Data Security Law ("the DSL"),[3] and the order by the Ministry of Commerce on blocking unjustified extraterritorial application of foreign legislation and measures ("the Blocking Rules"). In Section 3.2, I discuss two approaches of broadening the spatial dimension of China's state digital sovereignty, which can be identified in these three instruments. The first one is to include extraterritorial rules in data governance legislation, making such legislation applicable beyond China's territory or produce extraterritorial impacts. The other approach is to resort to blocking or countering measures against certain foreign measures related to data that China deem illegitimate. While their practical effects need more time to manifest, they demonstrate a clear intention of the Chinese government to regulate extraterritorially data, data activities (such as data collection, processing, and transfer) and data-related activities (such as trade and investment in relation to data), and hence to expand the spatial scope of China's digital sovereignty. International environment is indispensable to understanding this regulatory and conceptual evolution. Accordingly, given the current, increasingly confrontational international context, I argue in Section 3.3 that this regulatory evolution represents a greater incorporation of geostrategic interests in China's conception and practice of digital sovereignty, as a response to the geopolitical challenges that China is facing.

While the term "digital sovereignty" may be intuitively related to having and exercising control over data and digital infrastructures (Floridi, 2020), it remains highly controversial and has varied meanings for different societies (see Chapter 1).[4] For this chapter, as it analyzes and interprets recent

[2] The law was passed on August 20, 2021 and entered into force on November 1, 2021.

[3] The law was passed on June 10, 2021 and entered into force on September 1, 2021.

[4] Highly contestable issues include, for example, who is endowed with digital sovereignty, how does different actors' control relate to each other, whether "digital sovereignty" necessarily lead to trade protectionism and restrictions of individual rights and whether "digital sovereignty" can empower countries to resist the domination of foreign tech giants and lead to a more just redistribution of power and resources.

legislative and policy initiatives, it pays less attention to theorizing what "digital sovereignty" means. Instead, I use "digital sovereignty" as a composite term to refer to state authority over digital technologies and their social, political, and economic impacts. To justify this broad use of the term within the state-centric perspective, it suffices to say that in the Chinese context, as data is deemed as "fundamental strategic resources" since the thirteenth five-year plan (NPC & Central Committee of the CPC, 2016) and an important factor of production (Huang et al., 2020; Shi, 2018), digital sovereignty is as much about infrastructural and technological sovereignty as about economic sovereignty and hence is inherently multidimensional. As will be seen, this imbrication of the digital with the material is reflected by the way how the notion of digital sovereignty incorporates both geostrategic interests of the state and private economic interests. Given changes in these two interests in the current international environment, the spatial expansion of China's digital sovereignty should not be surprising.

3.2 TWO APPROACHES TOWARD EXTRATERRITORIALITY

Two approaches toward the spatial expansion of China's digital sovereignty can be identified in the three instruments. The first and the most straightforward approach is to explicitly adopt extraterritorial rules in the PIPL and the DSL. The second approach, present in all three instruments, is to block or counter certain foreign measures deemed discriminatory or restrictive against China.

3.2.1 Extraterritoriality in Data Governance Legislation

The attempts of re-territorializing the cyberspace and data flows by the CSL, reflecting a more exclusive and territorialized conception of cyber sovereignty and greater securitization of the internet, have been criticized widely both inside and outside of China. In terms of the territorial scope of application, the CSL applies only to the construction, operation, maintenance and use of network, and cybersecurity supervision and management within the territory of the People's Republic of China.[5] Regarding cross-border data transfer, the default rule in the CSL is for critical information infrastructure operators to store personal information and important data that they collect within China.[6] The PIPL and DSL differ considerably from the CSL in both aspects. With respect to extraterritorial application, the PIPL applies to the following situations where activities of handling personal information of natural persons in China take place outside of China:

[5] CSL, Article 2.
[6] CSL, Article 37.

1. When the purpose of such activity is to provide products or services to natural persons within China,
2. When analyzing or assessing activities of natural persons within China, and
3. Other circumstances provided by laws or administrative regulations.

To give teeth to the extraterritorial scope of this law, Article 42 of the PIPL addresses enforcement issues. It authorizes the Chinese cybersecurity and informatization department to impose administrative sanctions on foreign organizations or individuals whose personal information handling activities create harms on the rights and interests of Chinese citizens or on China's national security or public interest.[7]

As for the DSL, apart from data activities carried out within China, Article 2(2) sets out that "data processing activities outside China which harm China's national security, public interest or lawful rights and interests of citizens and organizations, are to be pursued for legal responsibility in accordance with the law." These provisions of extraterritorial application in these two instruments illustrate an exercise of legislative jurisdiction that combines the principle of territoriality and the effects doctrine, making the location of the effect of data activities a crucial factor for re-territorializing the cyberspace.

With respect to cross-border data flows, Article 38 of the PIPL sets out four options for transferring personal information abroad, easing the data localization rule in CSL:[8]

1. passing a security assessment organized by the State cybersecurity and informatization department,
2. obtaining personal information protection certification conducted by a specialized body according to provisions by the State cybersecurity and informatization department,
3. concluding an agreement with a foreign receiving party according to the standard contract formulated by the State cybersecurity and informatization departments, which sets out the rights and obligations of the parties,
4. other conditions provided by the State cybersecurity and informatization department in laws or administrative regulations.

In addition to these options, personal information handlers are required to ensure that the treatment of personal information transferred abroad is up to the standard of this law.[9] Furthermore, these options are followed by

[7] The sanctions include putting such organizations or individuals on a list that would limit or prohibit the provision of personal information to them, issuing a warning, or limiting or prohibiting the provision of personal information to them.

[8] These conditions do not apply to international agreements or treaties that China joins which contains requirements for sending personal information outside China. See, PIPL, Article 38, para 2.

[9] PIPL, Article 38, para 3.

the obligations of individual notification, obtaining individual consent,[10] and conducting risk assessments by those who seek to export personal information.[11] A default data localization requirement still exists in the PIPL and applies to critical information infrastructure operators and those entities who process personal information up to certain quantities determined by the State cybersecurity and informatization department. For these two categories of data collecting/processing entities, only the first option in Article 38 is available.[12]

The DSL introduces a single article addressing the export of data upon requests by foreign governmental authorities.[13] According to this provision, such requests shall be dealt with in accordance with relevant laws and international agreements and conventions to which China is a party, or according to the principle of equality and reciprocity; without the approval of relevant competent departments of China, no data stored within China shall be transferred abroad upon such requests. Organizations or individuals within China that violate this provision will face administrative sanctions.[14] A similar provision also exists in the PIPL.[15] Beyond this particular scenario, the DSL does not say much about cross-border data transfers. Article 31 specifies that the CSL shall be applied to important data collected and produced by operators of critical information infrastructure within China, and that for important data collected and produced by other data processors within China, special rules shall be made by the State cybersecurity and informatization department with relevant departments in the State Council. Therefore, data localization remains the default rule for the former category of data. For the latter category, the possibility of cross-border transfer needs to be decided and formulated in future rule-making processes. Despite the lack of more concrete mechanisms for data cross-border transfer, the DSL pledges the Chinese government to "ensure the lawful, orderly and free flow of data"[16] and to "promote the safe and free flow of data across borders" by actively participating in international exchanges and cooperation for the making of international rules and standards on data security.[17] Such undertakings, although largely political rather than legal, suggest a cautiously positive attitude of China toward cross-border data transfers and a more proactive approach to their regulation. Accordingly, China's stance on data localization seems to be more restrained.

[10] PIPL, Article 39.
[11] PIPL, Article 55 (4).
[12] PIPL, Article 40.
[13] DSL, Article 36. The draft version of this provision formulated differently, starting with the requirement of approval and making obligations under international agreements and conventions as exceptions. See Article 33 of the first draft and Article 35 of the second draft.
[14] DSL, Article 48.
[15] PIPL, Article 41.
[16] DSL, Article 7.
[17] DSL, Article 11.

These two legislative moves – i.e., the extraterritorial application of laws and the rules for cross-border data transfers – are indicative of the spatial expansion of China's digital sovereignty, and reflect a nascent, post-CSL regulatory tendency as a result of multiple internal and external factors. To begin with, the data localization rule of the CSL has encountered various criticisms inside and outside of China. Some Chinese scholars comment that the Article 37 of CSL lacks distinction between different data subjects (Cao, 2018, pp. 99–100), fails to meet the requirement of proportionality (Hong, 2017, pp. 59–60), and is unable to balance the two equally important objectives – security and development (X. Zhu & Dai, 2020, p. 87). In the business sector, foreign companies have considered the CSL as a step toward greater trade protectionism and warned the Chinese government that the CSL could further isolate China from the global digital trade (Donnan & Mitchell, 2016). Chinese companies were much less outspoken about their concerns, but it has been pointed out that such strict data localization requirement may trigger protective measures by other countries, impeding the "going-out" of Chinese companies (Liu & Cui, 2020, p. 103). Facing these criticisms, even the Chinese government seemed less ascertain about data localization. Right before the CSL entered into force on June 1, 2017, the Cyberspace Administration of China (CAC) told journalists in a press conference that the objective of the CSL was neither to restrict foreign companies from entering the Chinese market nor to restrict lawful, orderly, and free flows of data. The CAC acknowledged that cross-border data flows had become a precondition for economic globalization and for China's Belt and Road Initiative (Cyberspace Administration of China, 2017). Nevertheless, the blackletter law of the CSL has retained its broad and sweeping phrasing, which continues to be a source of concern for Chinese and foreign companies. The problem of the CSL is partly because the CSL only provides the general structure of cybersecurity, leaving many specific requirements to be fleshed out by complementary laws and regulations in its implementation. However, subsequent implementation and specification of the CSL rules were largely unsuccessful in resolving those concerns and criticisms.[18]

Despite the CSL's formulation, parallel and subsequent regulatory initiatives already pointed toward the direction of extraterritoriality. For example, the Chinese government released several draft guidelines and regulations related to the export of data since the CSL's adoption.[19] In particular, the 2017

[18] For example, in December 2017, the inspection group of law enforcement of the NPG Standing Committee published a report where it admitted that no consensus had been reached regarding the meaning, standard, and determining procedure of critical information infrastructure (S. Wang, 2017).

[19] For example, Measures for the Security Assessment for Cross-border Transfer of Personal Information and Important Data (draft for public comments) was released in April 2017; information security – guidelines for data cross-border transfer security assessment (draft for comments) was released in August 2017; Measures for the Security Assessment for Cross-border Transfer of Personal Information (draft for public comment) was released in June 2019.

draft Guidelines for Data Cross-Border Transfer Security Assessment clearly incorporates extraterritorial application, making, inter alia, "accessibility" of data rather than its physical location the trigger for its application.[20] Considering these pre-existing attempts, the PIPL and DSL exemplify the most recent legislative moves toward extraterritoriality.

Externally, the impact of the US's and EU's regulatory power is undeniable, and superficially, the PIPL and the DSL can be seen as China's emulation of their regulatory models. The US is well known for its extraterritorial laws and the long-arm jurisdiction of its courts (e.g., Putnam, 2016). Its 2018 Clarifying Lawful Overseas Use of Data Act ("CLOUD Act") is an exemplar of the global reach of its sovereign power over data.[21] As for the EU, the General Data Protection Regulation ("GDPR") has become a global model for regulating personal data. China's two legislative moves, particularly with the PIPL, which resembles the GDPR in many respects, may be considered a manifestation of the so-called "Brussels effect" (Bradford, 2020). Indeed, many Chinese scholars recommended to follow the footstep of the GDPR (Shi, 2018; K. Xu, 2019) and legislators admitted that they closely studied foreign and international experiences on data protection when drafting the PIP bill (N. Zhu, 2020). However, China's shift toward gradual extraterritoriality is not a unidirectional imitation of foreign regulatory models; as will be discussed later, this shift will produce geostrategic implications on the emulated regulatory models as well. It suffices to mention here that the emulation of the GDPR by the PIPL is accompanied with caution, especially with respect to the negative effects of extraterritoriality (e.g., the potential trade barriers that other states may put in place in response) and the practical difficulties of enforcement (Liu & Cui, 2020, p. 107). In turn, the PIPL seems to be slightly more restrained than the GDPR regarding extraterritoriality. As we can see, the text of the PIPL makes the intention (i.e., "purpose") of offering products or services to persons in China an explicit criterion for triggering the law's extraterritorial application, whereas the requirement of intention is only mentioned in the GDPR's Recital 23.

In addition to the modeling influence of US's and EU's extraterritorial legislation, it is impossible to overlook the impact of recent mega trade and investment agreements that China has joined. The most notable one is the Regional Comprehensive and Economic Partnership ("RCEP"), which was signed in November 2020 and has accounted for over a third of China's foreign trade in its first year since entry into force (China SCIO, 2023). The RCEP provides a templet of international data governance that contains rules to promote data flows among its members. For example, Article 12.15 of the E-commerce Chapter obliges states not to prevent cross-border transfers of information by

[20] Article 3.7(b).

[21] On this front, it can be argued that the provisions of the PIPL and the DSL on cross-border transfer of data upon foreign authorities' requests are part of the Chinese responses to the US CLOUD Act.

electronic means (Regional Comprehensive Economic Partnership Agreement, 2020). It is true that this rule is followed by a significant list of exceptions, and that compared to the US-led model of digital trade (such as the Trans-Pacific Partnership), the RCEP looks rather unambitious. However, the RCEP remains to be the first significant international agreement that commits China to enhance data mobility across borders. While China's commitment has been interpreted as more symbolic than substantive (Cory, 2021, p. 26), it can still create considerable motivation to speed up domestic legislative process addressing transborder data flows (Li, 2016, p. 781; Gao, 2022). Moreover, China applied to join the Compressive and Progressive Agreement for Trans-Pacific Partnership (CPTPP) in September 2021 (Xinhua News Agency, 2021) and has started adopting CPTPP rules in pilot free trade zones and ports in 2023 (K. Wang, 2023). As the CPTPP has far more stringent rules ensuring cross-border data transfers than those in the RCEP,[22] Xi's gesture may indicate China's moving toward a greater degree of data liberalization, although such liberalization only concerns data related to trade (Gao, 2022). This prospect of greater and freer data flows, however, should not be deemed as a waning of the state's regulatory sovereignty. The deepening of trade liberalization effectively depends on the state's capacity of creating and enforcing legal infrastructures to support and guarantee the operation of the market (Slobodian, 2020; Tzouvala, 2020). Therefore, what may appear to be a retreat of the state's sovereign power is in fact its transformation. When it comes to China, the political will to enhance data mobility goes together with the increased flexibility of the ambit of China's regulatory power over data.

In brief, the recent legislative development in China suggests a revision of the CSL's stricter territoriality. Partially, such a revision is compelled by the economic impracticality of the CSL's sweeping data localization and its enforcement difficulties. It is also caused by a convergence of internal and external incentives pushing for greater data mobility. This revision, however, should not be understood as the weakening of China's digital sovereignty, but rather its adaptation to emerging challenges. The CSL and China's National Security Law remain the basic reference point of recent regulatory instruments, suggesting that the notion of sovereignty is not stepping back but is reinforced through its spatial expansion. As discussed in Section 3.1, such metamorphosis of digital sovereignty is also driven by geostrategic considerations and accordingly will likely have important implications globally.

3.2.2 Blocking and Countering Measures and Their Extraterritorial Effects

The second approach, that is, to block or even counter certain foreign measures deemed discriminatory or restrictive against China, can also be found in the PIPL and the DSL. Article 43 of the PIPL provides: "Where any country or

[22] See, CPTPP Articles 14.11 and 14.13 (Government of New Zealand, n.d.).

region adopts discriminatory prohibitions, limitations or other similar measures against the People's Republic of China in the area of personal information protection, the People's Republic of China may adopt retaliatory measures against said country or region on the basis of actual circumstances." Similarly, the DSL proclaims that when any nation or region employs "discriminatory, restrictive, or other similar measures" against China "in areas of investment or trade in data and technology for the exploitation and development of data," China may employ "reciprocal measures" against that nation or region based on the actual circumstances.[23] Such provisions certainly make the two instruments an outlier case in current major data regulatory regimes globally. Again, like many Chinese laws, the phrasing remains highly abstract and broad, and relevant guidelines for implementation would be needed to specify key issues, such as how to decide whether a particular measure adopted by another country is discriminatory against China, what "retaliatory" or "reciprocal" measures would be envisaged, or how to determine the target, scope, or severity of such measures.

Irrespective of these details, the two provisions send a clear political signal about China's reaction to the global reach of regulatory powers such as the US and the EU. For instance, with respect to personal data, as the EU has not granted China an adequacy decision, it is fair to ask whether this could be deemed by China as "discriminatory" against China and trigger "retaliatory measures" (Cerulus, 2019). The possibility of retaliation, such as more restrictive market access and data export, could reduce the PIPL's limited liberating effects of cross-border data transfer. While these potentially restricting consequences may lead to data localization or China's self-isolation, such revert is not incompatible with the idea of China's spatial expansion of digital sovereignty, but only one dimension of China's evolving digital sovereignty. In the case of the EU's non-adequacy decision, the potential "retaliatory measures" adopted by China, such as prohibiting data transfers to the EU, would effectively regulate EU-based companies who operate business in China or with Chinese companies, thereby stretching China's sovereign power to what is under the EU's territorial jurisdiction. Hence, the undermining of cross-border data transfers, a form of negative externality, can also be a net result of China's extraterritorial regulatory power.

Compared with the PIPL, the provision in the DSL covers a broader range of measures by foreign countries or regions that could face China's countermeasures, that is, foreign measures regarding investment or trade in data and technology for the exploitation and development of data. This recalls the blacklisting of Chinese tech and telecom companies (e.g., Huawei, ZET, and China Telecom) and sanctions imposed by the US government since the US–China trade war. Elsewhere, India banned Chinese apps including the TikTok for national security reasons. The EU has also begun imposing greater

[23] DSL, Article 26. It's the same wording as Article 25 of the second draft version, which slightly changed the phrasing in the first version from "corresponding measures" to "reciprocal measures."

screening requirements on investments by the Chinese tech companies in the EU market on security ground. In short, all these measures based on national security could possibly be judged by China as discriminatory or restrictive and be responded by "reciprocal measures." An example would be blacklisting certain American or Indian companies to the Unreliable Entity List, which imposes a series of restrictive measures.[24]

Another possible reciprocal measure is provided by Article 25 of the DSL, which says that the state shall implement export controls on data of controlled items for the purpose of protecting national security and interests and fulfilling international obligations. This provision brings to mind the Catalogue of Technologies Prohibited or Restricted from Export, published jointly by the Ministry of Commerce and the Ministry of Science and Technology in August 2020 (PRC Ministry of Commerce & PRC Ministry of Science and Technology, 2020). The Catalogue that includes technologies related to artificial intelligence and data analytics has been widely regarded as a countermeasure to the Trump Administration's TikTok ban by effectively prohibiting TikTok from selling itself to a US company. Again, the negative consequences of such reciprocal measures, such as potential disruptions of global trade and investment that the blacklisting and export control can create, do not necessarily suggest a return to bordered sovereignty based on physical territoriality. Instead, the "other-oriented" character of such tit-for-tat restrictions, based on the self-judgment of whether China is the victim of someone else's wrongdoings, produces extraterritorial consequences affecting foreign actors, effectively subjecting them to China's regulatory power.

In addition to the two laws, the Blocking Rules published by the Chinese Ministry of Commerce on January 9, 2021 is of particular interest. The Blocking Rules applies to

> situations where the extra-territorial application of foreign legislation and other measures, in violation of international law and the basic principles of international relations, unjustifiably prohibits or restricts the citizens, legal persons or other organizations of China from engaging in normal economic, trade and related activities with a third State (or region) or its citizens, legal persons or other organizations (Article 2).

"Blocking" in this document refers to both judicial and political measures, that is, nonrecognition, nonexecution, and noncompliance of foreign legislation or measures identified by the blocking decision made by the Ministry of Commerce.

According to the mainstream interpretation in China, Article 2 means that the Blocking Rules essentially responses to the so-called secondary sanctions of the US (Miao, 2021; Shang, 2021; W. Xu, 2021). In contrast to primary sanctions that prohibit US companies or citizens from doing business with

[24] See, Article 10 of the Provisions on the Unreliable Entity List, released by the Ministry of Commerce on September 19, 2020 (PRC Ministry of Commerce, 2020).

those being sanctioned,[25] secondary sanctions have a much broader scope, covering non-US subjects as well, deterring them from having economic engagements with the sanctioned entities or individuals and therefore are highly controversial (Lowe, 1997; Meagher, 2020, pp. 1005–1006; Meyer, 2008, pp. 926–930). It has been responded to by various third countries adopting blocking statutes to counteract the effects of secondary sanctions. Among them, the EU's Regulation 2018/1100, which was passed after the resumption of the US sanctions against Iran in 2018, has been closely studied in China. Although China's Blocking Rules does not explicitly mention the US, its political gesture is, conceivably, to question the legitimacy of unilateral and extraterritorial economic sanctions imposed by the latter, while providing legal tools for Chinese companies that might be affected by those sanctions.

By opposing the US secondary sanctions, the Blocking Rules also produces extraterritorial effects. Article 2 quoted earlier covers the following two scenarios. First, when China (or specific Chinese companies or individuals) is the target of US economic sanctions (as with the recent Hong Kong Autonomy Act), companies of a third country may decide to cut economic relations with certain Chinese companies in or outside China. Second, when a country other than China (e.g., Iran) is targeted by the US sanctions that apply to non-US companies, Chinese companies may decide to close their business in Iran or terminate contracts with certain Iranian entities in China. In both scenarios, transnational business activities are disrupted by secondary sanctions, and if the Chinese government deems the sanctions as violating international law and basic principles of international relations, the blocking measures could be activated to preserve or restore those business activities between Chinese and foreign companies within or outside the Chinese market.

According to the current texts of the Blocking Rules, we can roughly envisage its operationalization in the following way. For example, the US government decides to impose sanctions on Huawei, prohibiting both US companies (e.g., Qualcomm) and non-US companies (e.g., TSMC, which is Taiwanese) from selling semiconductor chips to Huawei. Facing such sanctions, Huawei reports them to a special working body setup by the Chinese government that would assess the relevant sanctions and decide whether to issue a prohibition order of nonrecognition, nonexecution, and noncompliance. Once the prohibition order is issued, TSMC would be prohibited from complying with the US sanctions and hence should continue selling semiconductor chips to Huawei (while Qualcomm would not be impacted by the prohibition order). If TSMC, caught between the US sanctions and the Chinese prohibition order, decides to comply with the former, Huawei can bring a civil lawsuit before a Chinese court against TSMC for compensation, and the Chinese Ministry of Commerce may also issue TSMC a warning or a fine.

[25] By contrast, the Anti-Foreign Sanctions Law, adopted on June 10, 2021, provides measures countering primary sanctions that directly target China.

In addition to the extraterritorial effects created by "blocking" the extraterritorial reach of foreign legislation or measures, the Blocking Rules has left room for more direct, extraterritorial exercise of the state's sovereign power. According to Article 12, "necessary countermeasures" could be also taken to respond to "unjustified" extraterritorial application of foreign legislation or measures. This reads similar to provisions in the PIPL and the DSL mentioned earlier. The examples of blacklisting "unreliable entities" and adding technologies to the export control catalog are equally relevant here.

It remains to be seen whether "necessary countermeasures" under the Blocking Rules may also take the form of unilateral sanctions by China against a foreign companies or political regime and whether those sanctions may concern companies or individuals of third countries.[26] Similarly, the adoption of the blocking measures provided in the Blocking Rules needs to be specified in practice. Furthermore, given the limited practical effect of the EU's blocking statutes, one may also wonder if the Chinese Blocking Rules would have real consequences on transnational economic activities and on countries imposing unilateral sanctions. Nevertheless, it suffices to say that at this stage, the Chinese government has demonstrated a clear objective of counterbalancing the extraterritorial reach of foreign regulatory powers through the extension of its own. This objective of counterbalancing, also taking into account the provisions in the PIPL and the DSL discussed earlier, is intrinsically tied to the spatial expansion of China's cyber sovereignty.

3.3 ANALYSIS: THE INTEGRATION OF GEOSTRATEGIC INTERESTS INTO CHINESE CYBER SOVEREIGNTY

3.3.1 An Increasing Integration between Digital Sovereignty and China's Geostrategic Interests

The metamorphosis of China's digital sovereignty can be regarded as both conditioned by and contributing to the so-called "cyber-geopolitics" (An, 2020; Gómez, 2014), by which geopolitical games take a specifically technological turn and data become the main strategic focus. The geopolitical stakes of having extraterritorial power over data and data-related activities and entities become increasingly clear. The examples of countermeasures such as blacklisting foreign companies or imposing export bans discussed earlier demonstrate how the extraterritorial exercise of state power is closely tied to the state's geostrategic interests in an increasingly hostile international

[26] China has adopted the Counter Foreign Sanctions Law on June 10, 2021 (effective on the same day). The two questions, i.e., whether "necessary countermeasures" would involve unilateral sanctions by China and whether such sanctions may concern companies or individuals of third countries, are likely to be answered affirmatively according to this law. Discussing this law is, however, beyond the scope of this chapter.

environment. In addition, the conclusion of the RCEP has been widely interpreted through the geopolitical lens as bringing China enormous geopolitical advantages vis-à-vis the US (Carrai, 2021; Gao & Shaffer, 2021). As these (and future) mega trade and investment agreements create pressure for China to develop regulatory frameworks to enhance the global digital economy, they are also geostrategic drivers shaping the evolution of China's digital sovereignty.

The current cyber-geopolitics that largely started by the trade war with the US has turned into a competition for technological supremacy, as the Huawei sanctions show. The competition for technological supremacy is as much about China's national pride as about the global market share of Chinese tech companies, for dominating the global market help to guarantee a leading role in technological standard-setting that would in turn reinforce the dominance of Chinese companies and technologies in foreign markets. Insofar as the two approaches toward extraterritoriality discussed earlier can be regarded as tools to facilitate the "going-out" of Chinese companies, we can identify a symbiotic relationship emerging between China's digital sovereignty and economic interests of Chinese tech companies: the spatial scope of the former is stretched along with where the latter lies.

This connection between the enlargement of private companies' market share and profits and the extraterritorial spillover of state sovereignty has been examined closely by the scholarship of Marxist and Third World approaches to international law (Anghie, 2007; Chimni, 2017; Parfitt, 2019). From a Marxist perspective, in particular, capital exports are accompanied by capitalist countries' projection of political and military powers overseas; economic competitions between capitalist countries can therefore lead to political competitions, clashes of spheres of interests, and eventually interimperial rivalries (Knox, 2016, pp. 312–315; Miéville, 2006, pp. 227–230). In this sense, the spatial expansion of China's digital sovereignty and regulatory power, as both compelled by and supportive of the market growth of Chinese companies abroad (see Chapter 7), can be seen as demonstrating a rising interimperial rivalry of our time.[27]

Meanwhile, the connection between private economic interests and state sovereignty is particularly pertinent to the Chinese context due to the character of state capitalism that deliberately blurs the line between the public and

[27] One may ask, since data may be argued as "non-rivalrous" (Jones & Tonetti, 2020) and hence fundamentally different from other resources, such as oil, that were objects of historical interimperialist conflicts, whether we can speak about data imperialism and digital interimperialist rivalry. A full explanation would need a separate chapter. It suffices to make two points here: first, the notion of data as non-rivalrous goods is controversial (Rinehart, 2020); second, we may observe both continuities and discontinuities in the transformation of imperialism. What remains central is unequal capacities and distribution of resources to convert data to power (both economic and political) globally. The power dimension of data would make the lens of imperialism highly relevant.

the private interests. This more explicit merge between the public and the private also makes the notion of "digital sovereignty" intrinsically elastic. This elasticity is further reinforced by President Xi's holistic approach to national security, pronounced since 2014 (Xi, 2014). According to this holistic notion, national security integrates multiple elements including "political, homeland, military, economic, cultural, social, science and technology, information, ecological, resource and nuclear security," and has internal and external dimensions. Internally, national security refers to the promotion of development, reform, stability, and safety in China; externally, it refers to the pursuit of peace, cooperation, and mutual benefits with others to build a harmonious world. This all-encompassing notion of national security absorbs China's geopolitical and geo-economic interests, which are by no means purely external – they are intimately tied to domestic factors and produce enormous impact on the domestic economy and politics (Shang, 2021, p. 76). Under this holistic framework of national security, extraterritoriality has been mobilized to stabilize domestic situations (Y. Wang, 2016, pp. 57–58), to empower Chinese tech companies doing business abroad, and to gain China an upper hand in current geopolitical struggles (He, 2019, p. 95; Shang, 2021, p. 76). Either from a Marxist theoretical perspective of interimperial rivalry or focusing on Chinese characteristics of state capitalism and national security, it is not surprising that the notion of digital sovereignty can evolve in a way that blurs the distinction between not only the public and the private but also the domestic and external, projecting China's regulatory power outwardly.

3.3.2 Competition and Confrontation through Regulatory Emulation

This spatial expansion of China's digital sovereignty is obviously conditioned by the international environment that China is subject to. In this respect, it is remarkable that the ongoing "cyber-geopolitics" that China is involved in is partly unfolding through regulatory emulation: as discussed previously, both approaches toward extraterritoriality are considerably influenced by the EU's and US's extraterritorial regulations. The connection between geopolitical competition and regulatory emulation is however neither straightforward nor necessary. Putting aside the geopolitical dimension, a more common view in regulation literature is that regulatory emulation can remove regulatory conflicts and contribute to the harmonization of laws (Enriques & Gatti, 2006, p. 961; Lazer, 2006, pp. 460–462; Szyszczak, 2006). For example, the US and the EU, being hegemonic regulatory powers, have created modeling effects that led to a significant degree of global regulatory convergence in many fields, for example, intellectual property, financial regulation, labor, and environment (Braithwaite & Drahos, 2000). Conversely, when sovereigns have "competing regulatory philosophies" (Koh, 2008, p. 16), it has been argued that they can bring about clashes between sovereigns that call for judicial and political solutions. In other words, tensions between regulatory sovereigns are more often associated with regulatory divergence, and emulation is often seen as one way to resolve regulatory conflicts.

However, the above observation gets much more complicated when (geo) political factors come into play. What China's move toward extraterritoriality by learning from the EU and the US demonstrates is how, in the current geopolitical circumstances, regulatory emulation regarding extraterritoriality can potentially become a tactic by which one polity empowers itself through imitating others to challenge its rivals. This form of regulatory emulation does not solve but rather is likely to perpetuate competitions and even conflicts.

More precisely, the first approach of China's spatial expansion of digital sovereignty may appear as following and contributing to a nascent trend of global convergence for data regulation – convergence in the sense that more and more states (e.g., Brazil, Australia, Canada) start to legislate extraterritorially and design rules for data transfers while strengthening data protection. However, this ostensible trend of regulatory convergence is not just a positive result of "trading up" by competing regulatory sovereigns (Bradford, 2020, pp. 5–6; Vogel, 1995). Rather, such convergence can also be a form of contestation. Take the example of the GDPR, which is often depicted as bringing the "first mover advantage" to the EU in the global regulatory race on the protection of personal data (Smuha, 2021, p. 74), the dynamics of its Brussels effect is not a unidirectional reception of the GDPR's model elsewhere that leads to global regulatory harmonization. The fact that other countries are inspired by and draw upon the GDPR at different degrees can be regarded as precisely the way to mitigate the unilateral global reach of the GDPR. Similarly, the PIPL (together with preceding regulatory instruments on personal data protection) can be considered counterbalancing the EU's role as a global regulatory hegemon.[28]

As for the second approach, contestations caused by regulatory emulation can be much more serious. China's emulation, using mainly the EU's blocking statutes as a model, addresses a particularly confrontational situation, such as secondary sanctions by the US, by reacting with an equally confrontational stance of blocking or retaliation (Huang, Yuan & Hu, 2020). Compared to the contestation in the first approach that still takes place in the broader trend of regulatory convergence, the second approach is explicitly adversarial and may lead to conflict escalation. Given the current international context, the difference between contestations in the first approach and confrontations in the second may likely be more a matter of degree than kind. The slippage between the two situations is reflected by the fact that the PIPL and the DSL contain both approaches. For instance, the respective extraterritorial scopes of the PIPL and the GDPR can create jurisdictional overlaps, which lead to a

[28] Similarly, Chinese scholars have also suggested that the DSL should emulate the extraterritorial scope of the GDPR, shifting the defensive stance of digital sovereignty to a more offensive stance (K. Xu, 2019, p. 59).

regulatory contest; this contest may then be turned into a confrontation where both China and the EU pass normative judgments on each other, leading to the adoption of "retaliatory measures" by China.

In brief, regulatory tensions driven by economic interests (or other normative principles) can slip into geopolitical confrontations, and the likelihood of this slippage is significantly amplified by the emerging cyber-geopolitics, especially since the US–China trade war and the COVID-19 outbreak. In turn, the unfolding of geopolitics can involve the instrumentalization of regulations and regulatory emulations by sovereigns. A common call in China for an extraterritorial regulatory regime for data is precisely based on an acknowledgement that such a regime is necessary to support China in the current geopolitical game where cyber/data security and transnational data mobility are two important levers (e.g., Huang, Yuan, & Hu, 2020).

That regulatory emulation may lead to geopolitical competition is discussed in the general context of tensions China has with the West. Outside this particular rubric of "interimperialst rivalry," what the spatial expansion of China's digital sovereignty can lead to and how "elastic" the spatial scope of China's digital sovereignty can be remain open questions. From a normative perspective that values peaceful coexistence of sovereigns, the openness of these questions leaves room for states' self-restraint and mutual respect and helps to avoid a vortex of tit for tat between rivals. From China's own perspective, the openness of these questions about sovereignty is related to the difficulties peculiar to China that perceives itself as anti-imperial. More specifically, the spatial expansion of China's digital sovereignty, accompanied by the development of extraterritorial legal frameworks, stands in ostensible contrast to China's traditional adherence to the principle of noninterference. The extraterritorial application of Chinese laws necessarily overlaps with and even suspends the jurisdiction of the territorial state. However, given the history of extraterritoriality in China, China has been particularly careful with the wording, avoiding any mention to "治外法权" (the Chinese term for the extraterritorial system created by colonial powers in China since the First Opium War) and sticking to "域外适用" (extraterritorial application, which may sound more technical). This terminological distinction is important for China to not present its expanding regulatory power as imperialist. In addition to the historical factor, there are more practical problems with noninterference. China's extraterritorial jurisdiction over data or data-related entities abroad may trigger objections based on the principle of noninterference by the territorial state. Conversely, if China conceives of certain exogenous economic interests as part of its sovereignty, as the holistic understanding of national security seems to entail, China will logically have no objection for other states to do the same. This means that in cases such as the US applying the effect doctrine to enforce its antitrust law against Chinese companies, China's noninterference claims may be undermined by its own exercise of extraterritorial jurisdiction. Essentially, there will be a growing tension between the principle of noninterference and

China's move toward extraterritoriality to regulate data and data-related entities and activities, both deriving from and justified by the idea of state sovereignty. How to make the two mutually compatible is one of the crucial tasks of defining China's digital sovereignty in an anti-imperialist way. This tension is already displayed in the PIPL and the DSL: while introducing the idea of countering or blocking measures, the two also commit China to international cooperation on data regulation while providing.[29]

3.4 CONCLUSIONS

Focusing on three recent regulatory instruments, this chapter identifies an emerging shift toward increasing extraterritoriality in China's approach to governing the cyberspace, data, and data-related activities. This shift is more specifically manifested in two ways: first, introducing extraterritorial rules in data-related legislation and second, authorizing counter or blocking measures against extraterritorial legislation or measures of others. This regulatory tendency indicates a more spatially expansive notion of China's digital sovereignty that evolves in tandem with the growth of profits and global market share of Chinese companies. This more spatially expansive notion also shows the integration of China's geostrategic interests into the notion of digital sovereignty in current international contexts. Furthermore, this tendency is to a certain degree a result of regulatory emulation with the purpose to counterbalance the unilateral global reach of the EU's and the US's regulatory powers.

This tendency toward extraterritoriality is by no means specific to the issue of data governance, since digital sovereignty is closely related to other dimensions of state sovereignty in the Chinese context (keeping in mind also Xi's holistic notion of national security). Therefore, it is not surprising that a more general move toward extraterritorial governing is being conceived of by the Chinese government. Since 2019, the Chinese government started pushing for the establishment of extraterritorial legal frameworks to expand Chinese law's applicability through both extraterritorial legislative and enforcement jurisdictions (Xinhua News Agency, 2019, 2020). The intention, therefore, seems to be not only to facilitate the export of Chinese economy but to export Chinese law more specifically. As a Chinese scholar commented, "the export of Chinese capital will lead the export of Chinese law as a soft power" (Shang, 2021, p. 77). This process of projecting a kind of "Beijing Effect" (Erie & Streinz, 2022) is considered mutually supportive with China's other strategies, such as the Belt and Road Initiative (Shang, 2021, p. 77; K. Xu, 2019, p. 59; Ye, 2020, p. 62).

Despite the increasing motivation and push for extraterritoriality, the expansive notion of digital sovereignty has its own contradictions. As discussed, although China's shift toward spatial expansion is partly conditioned

[29] PIPL, Article 12; DSL, Article 11.

by current geopolitical relations with its competitors, it remains that this shift is at odds with China's traditional anti-imperial and anti-hegemonic posture and its emphasis on sovereign equality. This oddity is also seen in the "Chinese approach" to global internet governance. Termed as "building a community with a shared future in cyberspace" (Xi, 2019), the Chinese approach seems to have a universal pitch, but it reaffirms the principle of respecting sovereignty in cyberspace and condemns "cyber hegemony" (Chinese Academy of Social Science et al., 2020, p. 12). How to have *a* community that is decentered and pluralist is an age-old question, and in the context of this book, this question also involves how to approach diverse, nonstate-centric understandings of digital sovereignty and plural actors claiming digital sovereignty. Yet, a more immediate and practical difficulty for China would be from its own commitment to respecting the sovereignty of other states. As China has traditionally been against the long-arm jurisdiction and unilateralism, how to adapt digital sovereignty to contemporary needs while maintaining internal normative coherence would be a key question.

4

South African Digital Sovereignty at the Crossroad of Securitization and Development

Enrico Calandro

4.1 INTRODUCTION

Like many other African countries, South African authorities are designing strategies, policies, and rules and assigning responsibilities to the existing and new agencies to govern emerging digital technologies. Nevertheless, national policy and regulatory directions for the governance of the digital economy and society, on the one hand, are struggling to cope with increasing responsibilities of state actors to protect citizens' rights to data protection and safety and security online. On the other hand, data protection and cybersecurity measures do not always protect citizens' rights to privacy, confidentiality, and freedom of expression. Instead, the increasing body of norms, rules, and regulation on the digital space might increase state control over private communications and online censorship. State and nonstate actors are also conscious of the manipulative power of digital communications and have used various digital platforms to launch sophisticated disinformation and misinformation campaigns to manipulate public opinion (Pretorius, 2021). It exposes the many conflicts that arise when different forms of digital sovereignty analyzed in this book – especially state-led, corporate, postcolonial, and individual digital sovereignty – enter in contact.

To anchor the concept of digital sovereignty in South Africa, the study seeks to answer to the following questions: what are South Africa's national priorities regarding the governance of the digital space? What digital (and offline) processes are impacted? Moreover, to what extent are citizens' rights to privacy and freedom of expression at risk?

To explore the emerging policy position on digital sovereignty in South Africa within the global geopolitical theater on the governance of cyberspace, the chapter first reviews international processes relevant to understanding digital sovereignty positions of South Africa. It reviews the participation of the country in multilateral organizations, including the UN Group of Governmental Experts (GGE) and the Open-Ended Working Group (OEWG) on ICT state security; Third Committee Resolution on Countering the Use of Information and Communications Technologies for Criminal Purposes; the United Nations Office for Disarmament Affairs (UNODA); Intergovernmental Group of Experts (IGE) on Cybercrime; the World Trade Organization (WTO) processes on e-commerce; and the Moratorium on Customs Duties on Electronic Transmissions. By looking at international multilateral processes, South African stance on digital sovereignty and its quest to construct a state-led form of digital sovereignty are explored as a reaction to power dynamics in the international system of the governance of the internet. Nevertheless, the study looks inward to reflect on the national posture of digital sovereignty by highlighting national positions in international *fora* dealing with digital policies.[1] More specifically, at a national level, the policy and regulatory response to the *platformization* of the digital economy (Poell et al., 2019), techno-authoritarianism, and the increase of digital regulation of cyberspace is explored through a critical review of digital policy and regulatory processes related to online content regulation, regulation of bulk surveillance, data policy, and cybercrime. In Section 4.9, the emerging stance of South Africa on digital sovereignty is discussed through the lens of securitization and development.

4.2 SOUTH AFRICA'S ROLE AS A "DIGITAL SWING STATE" IN GLOBAL GEOPOLITICAL LANDSCAPE

Generally speaking, a state-centric approach to digital sovereignty focuses on states' capacity to exert control on digital infrastructures in their territories and datasets relating to their citizens (Couture & Toupin, 2019). Although it is a broad concept, digital sovereignty can be defined as "the right of a state to govern its network to serve its national interests, the most important of which are security, privacy and commerce" (Lewis, 2020). This definition may not seem too problematic when applied to mature economies and democratic countries capable of boosting their economies through competition policy and economic regulation while upholding human rights online. However, serving national interests and governing national networks might have different connotations in small and emerging economies for many reasons. Although developing countries share similar security, privacy, and economic growth objectives, state organizations in emerging economies are poorly resourced to put in place the necessary policy and regulatory mechanisms to effectively

[1] South African statements during the meetings until end of 2021 of the UN OEWG were reviewed. The statements were reviewed across the main themes of the OEWG: International law, cyber norms, confidence building measures, cyber capacity building, and emerging threats in cyberspace. A summary of the statements is available from the Global Partners Digital's Africa OEWG Positions Tracker, available at the following link: https://africa-oewg.org/.

counterbalance anticompetitive behavior in digital markets, predatory data extraction practices, and various cyber risks and cyber threats. Besides, democratic assumptions of freedom of expression[2] are often perceived as a threat of established political orders. Lastly, digitalization may result in state control over digital lives and citizens' political positions through misinformation (Pretorius, 2021) and mass surveillance.

In his 1996 *Declaration of the Independence of Cyberspace*, John Perry Barlow, a proponent of a *laissez-faire* approach to the internet's governance, asserted that cyberspace was a new territory that governments should not regulate. Since then, many things have changed. The number of policies and regulatory and legislative initiatives on the governance of the internet has increased dramatically. Different countries and regions have adopted diverging approaches to digital space governance. States have gained greater control of how the internet is used within their borders as a result of growing risks to security and privacy, combined with the erosion of national sovereignty from global connectivity (Lewis, 2020).

Interventions to spur digital competitiveness go beyond regulatory interventions, which can also take the form of new technological standards for digital infrastructure. A growing number of countries discuss plans to recreate national boundaries in cyberspace (Shcherbovich, 2021) through national Domain Name Systems or data localization laws (Lambach, 2019) or by exerting control over their citizens through technology (Shahbaz, 2018). For instance, contrary to the libertarian point of view of Barlow and the multi-stakeholder approach to internet policymaking, there is the recent Chinese proposal to redesign the TCP/IP protocol stack to allow for centralized government control over authentication and internet communication (Gross & Murgia, 2020). Another form of state control over the internet within national borders is shutting down the internet during political elections,[3] a practice implemented by authoritarian or even democratic countries.

[2] Democratic freedom of expression recognizes that everyone's human rights are the same and therefore must be given similar consideration. In a democratic society, the right of freedom of expression is equal for everyone and it comes with the responsibility of respecting everybody else rights. In such a democratic system, the liberty is not arbitrary power, but it is based on accountability. If freedom of expression becomes an act of domination, it infringes the rights of others and therefore a system of justice should hold agents responsible. In this governing system, a democratic state is considered an effective instrument to protect human rights and abolish domination.

[3] In 2019, Access Now documented cases of partial or total internet shutdowns in 25 African countries, compared with 20 in 2018 and 12 in 2017. In October 2020, Tanzania restricted access to the internet and social media during elections. In June 2020, after unrest following the killing of a famous Oromo singer and activist Hachalu Hundessa, Ethiopia forced an internet shutdown that lasted for almost a month. Access Now also documented that Burundi, Chad, Guinea, Mali, Togo, and Zimbabwe also restricted access to the internet or social media at some point in 2020. More recently, in the run-up to the presidential election on January 14, Uganda shut down the internet.

Politically driven by digital sovereignty and strategic autonomy (Timmers 2020), Europe has found its digital "third way" (Siebert, 2021) by placing itself as a regulatory superpower by setting rules underpinned by civil rights and self-determination, in opposition to the Chinese techno-authoritarianism (Polyakova & Meserole, 2019; Wang, 2021) and the US surveillance capitalism (Zuboff, 2019b). At the end of 2020, the EU launched a significant regulatory initiative (i.e., the Digital Services Act package) and in November 2022, the Digital Services Act and the Digital Markets Act were adopted by the Council of the European Union, intending to increase innovation, growth, and competitiveness in digital markets (European Commission, 2021). As part of its digital strategy, EU is investing in the "development of digital standards and promot[ing] them internationally" (Aggad, 2021). The new Africa–Europe digital economy partnership of the EU–AU digital economy task force, now advocates for the development of "policies and regulation in areas such as telecom[munications], data economy, data protection and privacy, start-up laws, e-commerce and e-government" (Aggad, 2021). Therefore, regulatory convergence on data use is already quietly happening under the umbrella of "technical assistance," which might have important repercussions on African citizens' privacy (Aggad, 2021). On the other hand, the US has gained an undisputed leadership over operating systems, social media, and cloud computing platforms, posing regulatory challenges to ownership and control of data and related commercial value (Roberts, 2020). Furthermore, as part of a broader US stated effort to address concerns about cybersecurity and data privacy, particularly regarding China's role in the global technology and telecommunications industry, the 2017–2021 US Secretary of State Mike Pompeo's "Clean Network"[4] program aimed to create a more secure and trusted environment for US technology and data with a particular emphasis on countering perceived threats from the Chinese Communist Party.

In response to the Trump administration's position against Chinese tech firms defined as national security threats, in September 2020, China announced its most ambitious contribution to international lawmaking on data governance with the Global Initiative on Data Security (WSJ, 2020). This was done on the one hand to attempt to shift control of the data security narrative away from the US, which, according to China's Foreign Minister Wang Yi, made "groundless accusations" against Chinese tech firms as national security threats and "used security as a pretext to prey on enterprises of other countries who have a competitive edge" (Wang Yi, 2020); and on the other, to set global standards on data security at a multilateral level (Tiezzi, 2020). The Global Initiative on Data Security invites countries to handle data security in a "comprehensive, objective, and evidence-based manner" while emphasizing the importance of a stable supply chain for

[4] The initiative, announced by the UN Secretary of State Mike Pompeo, goes under the name of The Clean Network. See https://2017-2021.state.gov/the-clean-network/index.html.

information, technology, and services. This initiative is also an invitation to all countries to consider other countries' approaches in managing their data and internet sovereignty (WSJ, 2020). Considering that affordable devices and networking infrastructures with increased accessibility for the majority of Africans are largely sourced from China (Cascais, 2019; Wilson, 2019), it is expected that national technological standards will be anchored in these suppliers that are supporting the closure of the usage gap. These standards will certainly shape African countries industrial policy and, as a result, its capacity of self-determination on digital sovereignty.

In this virtual space of competing positions on regulatory, technological, and industrial standards, many African governments' plans on digital transformation or on the ambitious Fourth Industrial Revolution (4IR) might increase the reliance of Africa on the US platforms, on regulations modeled after EU, and Chinese networking technologies. African countries are not self-sufficient in terms of technological innovation and development and, like many countries, import a considerable (if not all) portion of these technologies. This high dependence on technological innovation and digital transformation on global powers presents diplomatic challenges (Ndzendze, 2021) for digital sovereignty and self-determination in cyberspace.

Nevertheless, South Africa, as one of the pivotal middle powers in the Global South – together with Brazil, India, Indonesia, Saudi Arabia, and Turkey – stands out as a "swing state" within the BRICS alliance (Kupchan, 2023). This designation positions South Africa in a unique position where it maintains a degree of autonomy and the flexibility to craft its digital policies and navigate complex geopolitical landscapes independently. Unlike nations fully aligned with superpowers, as a "swing state," South Africa straddles the middle ground, allowing it to influence and even reshape emerging power dynamics (Fontaine & Kliman, 2013). As a middle power, South Africa has seized this opportunity to assert its influence in international relations (Kupchan, 2023). One defining feature of the group of "swing states" is the absence of strong ideological affiliations, setting them apart from previous groupings in the Global South, such as the BRICS. This lack of ideological bonds allows these states to adopt a pragmatic, transactional approach to foreign policy, amplifying their collective impact on the global stage. The intensifying rivalry between the United States and China offers a "swing state" like South Africa opportunities to leverage its positions, as both superpowers seek their alignment. This strategic positioning grants South Africa bargaining power with both the US and China vying for their support. However, digitalization might be an exception, particularly when it comes to foundational technologies such as semiconductors, artificial intelligence, quantum technology, 5G telecommunications, and cloud computing. South Africa is primarily a user of such technologies and therefore may need to make strategic choices between trading with the United States or China, as these domains are subject to rigid competition (Kupchan, 2023).

The following sections explore the South African approach to digital sovereignty and its evolving digital policy posture. I consider its positions in international processes related to cybersecurity and national development with regard to digital policymaking.

4.3 ICT FOR DEVELOPMENT NARRATIVE IN NATIONAL DIGITAL CONNECTIVITY POLICY

A state-centric approach to digital sovereignty focuses primarily on government strategies and actions to govern digital infrastructures and datasets in their territories. Like many other countries, South African authorities are designing strategies, policies, and rules and assigning responsibilities to the existing and new agencies to govern emerging digital technologies nationally. Differently from mature economies, the international stance of South Africa in the governance of cyberspace does not seem concerned about how to wield cyber power against its rivals (Dunn Cavelty & Egloff, 2019). On the contrary, the country's political priorities and policy objectives related to the governance of digital infrastructures, at least on official papers, emphasize leveraging digitalization to overcome some of the pressing national challenges such as poverty, unemployment, and inequality. Considering that the narrative on ICT development is predominant across all South Africa's main digital policy documents, the emerging model of digital sovereignty needs to be understood within the context of the ICT for development narrative.

There is almost undisputed and general understanding that improving connectivity will facilitate growth and development (UNDP 2015; World Bank 2016; WSIS 2018 in Roberts, 2021). The sustainable development goals (SDGs) include a focused approach for increasing use (target 17.8) and access to ICT; provide affordable and universal access to internet in least developed countries (SDG 9c); enhance regional and international cooperation and access to technology and innovation (SDG 17.6); and promote women's use of ICT for empowerment (target 5b). At an international level and a technical cooperation level, improving internet access and use in Africa[5] has been one of the main priorities of various UN agencies, whose objectives and goals have been translated in digital policy documents at regional and national levels (Calandro, 2015).

Nationally, the 2013 national broadband policy South Africa Connect (SA Connect) was designed to integrate supply- and demand-side approaches to foster a "dynamic and connected information society and a vibrant knowledge economy that is more inclusive and prosperous." South Africa Connect gives expression to South Africa's vision in the National Development Plan (NDP)

[5] Although internet usage figures in Africa are rising, they remain behind world figures. On average, in 2019, only 28.6 individuals out of 100 were using the internet in Africa, according to the ITU (2020).

of eliminating income poverty, decreasing inequality, and enhancing employment opportunities. In the problem statement presented in the broadband policy, reference was made regarding proven relationships between investment in the digital infrastructure and improvements in the overall economy. Furthermore, the document describes how making broadband available at competitive rates fosters an increase in broadband penetration, subsequently linked with job creation and overall economic growth.

Comparable goals are outlined in the National Integrated ICT Policy White Paper, which highlights how ICTs play a fundamental role in enabling the National Development Plan to achieve its goal of constructing a more inclusive society that reduces poverty and inequality. In this regard, ICTs play a transformative role, which is acknowledged in the Vision and Principles Chapter of the ICT White Paper. It emphasizes that "the main purpose of this White Paper is to unlock the potential of ICTs to eliminate poverty and reduce inequality in the country by 2030" (DTPS, 2016, p. 10).

More recently, also the 4IR plan expressed similar ambitions to those expressed in SA Connect and in the ICT White Paper. In the Summary Report & Recommendations presented by the Presidential Commission (January 2020), the South African "triple scourge," that is, unemployment, poverty, and inequality, are the unequal outcomes of a history of exploitation and exclusion and are recognized as the "Grand Challenges" that the 4IR Commission, the State, and all institutional actors and citizens, in their capacity, have to overcome (Presidential Commission on the Fourth Industrial Revolution, 2020, p. 11). The 4IR and the related institutional arrangements, therefore, are about "contemplating solutions to South Africa's development challenges" (Presidential Commission on the Fourth Industrial Revolution, 2020, p. 14).

Despite good intentions, policy and regulatory outcomes have been suboptimal. The national telecommunications market remains structured around integrated network and service operators, with two incumbents MTN and Vodacom dominating the mobile telecommunications market with a combined market share of 78% (Research ICT Africa, 2020). Many rural areas are still served by one or both incumbent operators where populations remain unable to benefit from the lower prices of smaller operators. Besides, the fiber-optic market has significantly penetrated only urban areas and the main transmission routes, leaving other areas poorly covered. Therefore, while the top-end market is well served, people with low incomes are paying a premium for low-value products. In addition, the proposed strategy of SA Connect to leverage private and public investments to provide connectivity to public buildings in under-serviced areas failed (Research ICT Africa, 2020). Lastly, the inability to release high-demand spectrum, compounded with the separation of the Ministry of Communications into two in 2014, severely undermined digital policy action and operationalization (Research ICT Africa, 2020).

All in all, while developmental aspirations underpin these national policy documents, they run short in terms of implementation. From a digital sovereignty perspective, there is little recognition of high dependency on digital supply chain and technological standards. Moreover, risks to human security might jeopardize developmental aspirations. The misuse of digital technology as a weapon, compounded with the risk of escalation of developing cyber offensive capabilities in the absence of shared regulation of how states should behave in cyberspace, could have unintended consequences for human security in South Africa (Allen, 2019).

4.4 A SECURITIZATION AGENDA IN REACTION TO CYBER THREATS

It is well known that in the past few years, and specifically after Snowden's revelations, digital security has received prominence in political security agendas worldwide (Dunn Cavelty & Egloff, 2021), including Africa. In these agendas, online risks become a security issue not always because threats are objectively measurable as such, but because actors define them as threats in political processes (Buzan et al. 1998, Dunn Cavelty & Egloff, 2021) by using the language as a performative act. The narrative of existential risks, sometimes put forward to justify increasing policy and regulatory measures on cybercrime, is often linked to high political stakes and it is a powerful mobilizer to legitimize extraordinary responses and undemocratic procedures (Dunn Cavelty & Egloff, 2021).

In this sense, cybersecurity measures have increased parallel to growing threats and risks emerging from access and use of digital technologies (Dunn Cavelty & Egloff, 2021). Different actors have used different representations of danger to create or change political, private, social, and commercial understandings of security in selected public spheres (Dunn Cavelty & Egloff, 2021). Within this political arena of problems, risks, and threats, cybersecurity policy is shaped at the intersection of "hypersecuritization," "everyday security practices," and "technification" (Dunn Cavelty & Egloff, 2021; Hansen & Nissenbaum, 2009). They do not exclude each other, but they are all present at different times in the cyber-insecurity discourse.

While hypersecuritization refers to the invoking of an imminent status of destruction and existential threats often without linkages to the historical incidents of similar scope, everyday security practices refer to the practice of creating a feeling of insecurity by connecting the hypersecuritization scenarios to the life and experiences of individuals, primarily to ensure compliance and partnership (Dunn Cavelty & Egloff, 2021; Hansen & Nissenbaum 2009). In the technification logic, the technical construction of the cybersecurity discourse is molded by technical knowledge and expert positions that are used to serve a political and normatively neutral agenda (Dunn Cavelty & Egloff, 2021).

In its submission on the Cybercrime and Cybersecurity Bill, Research ICT Africa[6] (2015) observed that draconian restrictions and regulations on the internet might be the result also of lack of empirical measurements and assessments of cyber threats and cybercrime. Research ICT Africa (2015) noted that to ensure the penalties are aligned with the crime, it is imperative that cyber-threat representations are fully documented as a means of preventing any (over)reactions that are linked with excessive implementation costs and lack of clarity in terms of the benefits (Research ICT Africa, 2015).

Within the South African context, the country adopted a human-centered approach to national security in its 1996 Constitution, distinguishing it from the conventional state-centered approach. As Duncan (2018) observed, in light of South Africa's history of apartheid, a more refined definition that treats state protection as a higher priority over citizens could lead to a situation in which the government can abuse its power and shield itself from any criticism while simultaneously failing in its objective to address the underlying issues that put society at risk. A human security approach, on the other hand, deals with seven fundamental security threat domains[7]: food security, economic security, health security, personal security, environmental security, political security, and community security (UNDP, 1994). This human-centered approach to national security is perceived to be more democratic than a state-focused approach. However, Duncan highlights the need to put checks and balances in place to prevent excessive levels of scrutiny in aspects of public and private lives (Duncan, 2021). If national security achieves a "freedom from fear and want" (UNDP, 1994), such a broad framework might entail a strategic and operational expansion of intelligence (and, thereby, surveillance) to increasing "insecurities" and risks. As observed in South Africa, discourses related to securitization can serve to legitimize surveillance in ways not unlike the apartheid police state that preceded it (Kuehn, 2018).

4.5 SOUTH AFRICAN POSITIONS ON ICT STATE SECURITY IN UN PROCESSES

South Africa has been involved with the UN GGE on advancing responsible state behavior in cyberspace in the context of international security since the beginning in 2004 and 2005, although that process failed to produce a consensus report. Subsequently, it served as the only African representative in the second GGE in 2009 and 2010, and the result of which was a consensus report A/65/201 (2010). It did not take part in the third, fourth, and fifth GGE, but it had a seat in the recently concluded sixth GGE together with

6 Research ICT Africa is a digital policy and regulation think tank based in Cape Town, South Africa. The author of this chapter is a senior research associate with the think tank.

7 The seven threats to security are based on those identified by the 1994 UNDP Human Development Report.

Kenya, Mauritius, and Morocco from Africa, and with all BRICS countries, which were all represented in the recent GGE. South Africa has been not only an active member of the GGE but also one of the most active African countries during the substantive meetings of the OEWG, sponsored by the Russian Federation and established with resolution A/RES/73/27 in December 2018.

During these meetings, South Africa suggested several inputs including the consideration of gender disparities in ICT access and use and the recommendation of conceptual and practical clarification on the notion of a "human-centric approach." It also suggested that exchanges within the Southern African Development Community (SADC) and the AU could effectively function as Confidence Building Measures[8]. In its comments to the predraft of the UN OEWG report, South Africa has expressed concerns about stockpiling of ICT-related vulnerabilities by state actors[9] and has also called for a "long-term view" that includes binding instruments of international law "to hold Member states accountable and assist in the arbitration of grievances." In May 2020, at the United Nations Security Council (UNSC) held in an Arria-formula meeting[10] to discuss "cyber stability, conflict prevention, and capacity building," South Africa expressed concerns about malicious cyber acts aiming at damage or impairing health infrastructure or responses to the COVID-19 crisis (Pytlak, 2020b). Lastly, South Africa abstained on the UN L.8/Rev.1 (UNGA, 2020) on the extension of the mandate of the OEWG for another five years, tabled by Russia at the end of October 2020. During the meeting, South Africa stressed that although it supports the idea of extending the OEWG in general by two years, it would like to focus on the implementation of existing norms instead of developing new ones (Pytlak, 2020a).

From its statements, it is clear South African positions on international law are leaning toward the support for the creation of a new instrument in international law in the form of legally and politically binding norms under the aegis of the UN.[11] This is also quite clear in the BRICS context, considering that since the *eThekwini Declaration* (2013) on Partnership for Development,

[8] https://front.un-arm.org/wp-content/uploads/2020/04/south-africa-inputs-of-oewg-predraft.pdf

[9] A similar position was expressed by Digital Europe (2017), when it shared its concerns of governments exploiting vulnerabilities instead of reporting them to be fixed.

[10] An Arria-Formula Meeting is an informal meeting of the UN Security Council that is convened at the initiative of member or of a group of members of the Security Council to discuss various issues within the competence of the Security Council. The Arria-Formula Meeting mentioned in this chapter took place online under the presidency of Estonia to discuss issues related to cyber stability, conflict prevention, and capacity building.

[11] This might be also one of the reasons why in the United Nations General Assembly subsidiary committees, South Africa through the UN Third Committee that deals with human rights, humanitarian affairs, and social matters, voted in support of a resolution on countering the use of ICT for criminal purposes that will elaborate a comprehensive international convention on countering the use of information and communications technologies for criminal purposes.

Integration and Industrialisation, the discussions and initiatives on cyber-BRICS have intensified. BRICS countries have shared common interests and enhanced cooperation in the area of science, technology, and innovation, with the aim of designing a legal framework within which the various areas of this cooperation and partnership can grow and develop (Belli, 2021b). More recently, in September 2021, cybersecurity was a priority at the 13th BRICS summit, when BRICS leaders reiterated their willingness of "advancing practical intra-BRICS cooperation in this domain, including through the implementation of the BRICS Roadmap of Practical Cooperation on ensuring Security in the Use of ICTs and the activities of the BRICS Working Group on Security in the use of ICTs" (BRICS India, 2021, p. 7).

At the same time, during the third substantial meeting of the UN OEWG, South Africa stressed the importance of reaffirming that a universal cybersecurity framework can only be grounded in the existing international law, including the *Charter of the United Nations* in its entirety, and respect for human rights and fundamental freedoms (DigWatch, 2019). Therefore, it seems that South Africa is cognizant that despite the intention to work (also with BRICS) toward a UN cybersecurity framework, the country is already a signatory of a binding instrument of international law on cybercrime: *The Convention on Cybercrime of the Council of Europe* (better known as the Budapest Convention). While the two international efforts are not mutually exclusive, the envisaged UN Treaty on cybercrime probably will not create a different framework than the one already established under the Budapest Convention (for South Africa and for any other Budapest Convention's signatory).

The importance of addressing developmental issues has emerged when South Africa voiced the concern of developing states related to the increasing sophistication of malicious ICTs and the need to bridge the digital and gender divides. South Africa has stated the need to implement existing norms and their role in identifying capacity building and warned of strain on resources (DigWatch, 2021).

The commitment of South Africa in international cybersecurity is evident not only at the UN First level but also at the UNODC level, in particular with the open-ended intergovernmental expert group (IEG) to conduct a comprehensive study on cybercrime.[12] The IEG is a process particularly relevant for South Africa, considering that it has played a diplomatic role as Chair of the Bureau of the IEG. The country has occupied this role since 2011, making its most significant diplomatic stance in 2017 when it facilitated the adoption of a multi-year plan for delegations to interrogate the findings of the draft report on cybercrime matters affecting UNODC Member States.

[12] The UN Commission on Crime Prevention and Criminal Justice (CCPCJ) has been the main venue for discussing cybercrime within the UN context. The CCPCJ established an IEG based in Vienna, tasked with conducting a Comprehensive Draft Study on Cybercrime. The study, presented in 2013, is still subject of discussion among states (EU Cyber Direct (2021)).

In 2020, South Africa chaired the sixth session of the IEG on Cybercrime that deliberated on two important issues namely: (1) international cooperation and (2) prevention (UNODC, 2020). This was the last substantive meeting of the IEG, followed by a stocktaking exercise in April 2021 aimed at putting together a list of recommendations for submission to the CCPCJ. This session was also a platform for delegations from the United States (Nemroff, 2018) and its allies to contest Russia-led third committee resolution.[13] The contestation was to preempt the call of the IEG[14] on active participation of all Member States in the work of the ad hoc committee[15] to develop a new cybercrime convention (UNODC, 2021).

4.6 PROMOTING INCLUSIVE DEVELOPMENT IN WTO PROCESSES ON ELECTRONIC TRANSMISSION

Another perspective worth to explore to understand South Africa's approach to digital sovereignty is the country's position on electronic international trade. At that level, South Africa and India have argued in favor of suspension of the WTO Moratorium on Electronic Transmission.[16] Both countries have suggested a multilateral dialogue to promote an inclusive development-oriented approach to e-commerce. Such a dialogue, they argue, should include the examination of the challenges experienced by developing countries and least developed countries (LDCs) in relation to e-commerce and explore ways of enhancing the participation of such countries in digital transmissions. They have argued that the Moratorium has several implications for developing countries, including tariff revenue losses, and it has impacts on industrialization, the use of digital technologies such as 3D printing in manufacturing, and the losses of other duties and charges (IISD, 2020).

Since 1998, this Moratorium has been renewed biannually (except for 2003–2005 when the members failed to reach consensus in Cancun). The debate however on whether this Moratorium on custom duties on electronic

[13] Ad hoc committee established by General Assembly resolution 74/247.

[14] Concept note, Seminar on International Cybersecurity, cohosted by DIRCO and Research ICT Africa, January 2020.

[15] In December 2019, a significant development took place within the United Nations General Assembly when resolution A/RES/74/247 was adopted. This resolution set in motion a parallel process with the mandate to create an Open-ended Ad Hoc Intergovernmental Committee of Experts, comprising representatives from all regions. The primary objective of this committee was to work on the development of a comprehensive international convention aimed at addressing "the misuse of information and communications technologies for criminal purposes." This process commenced in August 2020.

[16] The WTO moratorium bans countries from imposing customs duties on electronic transmissions. It was adopted in 1998 during the Second Ministerial Conference that ended with the Declaration on Global Electronic Commerce. Since then, at every Ministerial Conference, WTO members have agreed "to maintain the current practice of not imposing customs duties on electronic transmissions."

transmissions should be done away with or made permanent has not been decided upon yet even after 20 years of discussions in the WTO (Roberts, 2020). Tariff revenue losses for South Africa are estimated at USD 37 million using bounded or most favored nation (MFN) duties and USD 25 million when using effectively applied duties (UNCTAD, 2019 in Roberts, 2020). This is due to the fact that South Africa and other developing countries and emerging economies (with the exception of China) are highly dependent on foreign digital networks and services such as telecommunications networks, cloud computing, social networks, and data centers. The bounded duties equal Rand 542 million or 1% of South Africa's tax revenue in 2017 (Roberts, 2020). Although these might not seem big amounts, the proportion of electronic transmissions in trade is expected to increase with the growth of the digital economy. Therefore, according to Roberts (2020), a permanent moratorium on customs duties essentially means an increasing loss of customs revenue for developing countries because of their position as large and growing net importers of electronic transmissions in trade. Further, the moratorium makes it virtually impossible to rebalance the current dependency on foreign services. Lastly, the Moratorium may impede countries from adopting rules for the access to data and appropriate incentives for transnational investments in local capabilities.

4.7 EMERGING NATIONAL REGULATION ON DIGITAL SOVEREIGNTY

Before delving into some of the policy and regulatory measures adopted to secure network infrastructures and citizens' data, it is important to contextualize these measures in the worrisome reality of increasing national vulnerability in cyberspace.

4.7.1 Cyber Vulnerabilities

Recent cyber incidents make it clear that South Africa is facing an undoubtedly real wave of unrelenting cyberattacks and incidents, which is affecting many economic sectors. Kaspersky (2023a) has reported that ransomware attacks in South Africa increased by 10% in the second quarter of 2023 in comparison to the first quarter of the same year, as well as phishing attacks, which grew by 7% between 2022 and 2023 (Kaspersky, 2023b). Not only do individuals and consumers fall victims of cybercrimes, but also public and private organizations alike. In the past few years, South Africa experienced a sharp increase in cyberattacks on all fronts that hit banks, internet service providers (ISPs),[17] utilities, and e-commerce platforms (Accenture, 2020), with smaller and less

[17] See, for instance, the cyberattack that in February 2023 hit RSAWEB, a nation-wide ISP (Smith, 2023).

resourced actors being the most vulnerable (Calandro & Berglund, 2021). According to SEACOM (2023), a private operator of Africa's first broadband submarine cable system along the continent's Eastern and Southern coasts, South Africa has the highest number of ransomware and email attacks in Africa, with over 220 million email threats detected in 2021, costing the country billions in losses. In 2022, there was a surge in ransomware attacks, including a particularly damaging form of malware called "Agenda," which targeted healthcare and educational institutions, while the average ransom payout for South African institutions is estimated to be around R3.2 million. Regarding attacks to critical infrastructures, in May 2023, the Development Bank of Southern Africa (DBSA) experienced a ransomware attack by a threat actor believed to be the Russian group Akira (DBSA, 2023). While the extent of the breach is still under investigation, DBSA reported that servers, logfiles, and documents were encrypted and suspects that various categories of stakeholders' personal information may have been unlawfully accessed or acquired (DBSA, 2023). In 2021, two incidents were particularly concerning. First, in September 2021, the Department of Justice and Constitutional Development's IT system was interrupted due to a security breach through a ransomware. While all information systems were encrypted and unavailable to the Department's employees and member of the public, the Office indicated that data was not compromised (Ngqakamba, 2021). Second, Transnet SOC Ltd., South Africa's port and rail company was attacked with a ransomware that encrypted terabyte of personal data, company files, financial reports, and other documents, forcing the operation to switch to manual processing of cargo (Gallagher & Burkhardt, 2021).

There are many interconnected factors that make South Africa an attractive target by cyber-threat actors. First, many South African internet users are novices and therefore inexperienced and less digitally literate than users in other more developed nations. A significant portion of the South African population is not always able to recognize different kinds of cyberattacks and may unintentionally fall victim of cybercrime. Second, lack of investment in cybersecurity inhibits South Africa's ability to put in place measures to prevent and mitigate advanced threats. Third, the development, implementation, and adoption processes of policies and mechanisms that combat cybercrimes are lengthy. Fourth, the South African Police Service (SAPS), which is now legally mandated to act against such crimes, lacks cybercrime training and is not knowledgeable in handling cybercrime-related cases (Dlamini & Mbambo, 2019) in addition to not having adequate resources to investigate, detect, and combat cybercrime. Finally, cybersecurity awareness is a challenge as well, increasing the risk of negligent use of ICT among citizens, consumers, public officials, and small and medium enterprises (Dlamini & Mbambo, 2019). These factors do not affect only South Africa, but are common to most countries and are particularly evident in most developing countries.

4.7.2 Data and Cloud Policy

To respond to increasing threats and risks to data security, one of the most significant policy developments indicating a possible emerging approach of South Africa on digital sovereignty is the Draft National Policy on Data and Cloud, published on April 1, 2021 by the Minister of Communications and Digital Technologies. The Draft Policy covers a number of areas such as access to data and cloud services, data protection, localization and cross-border data transfers, and cybersecurity measures. The Draft policy seeks to promote "data sovereignty"[18] and recognizes data as a "tradable commodity" (DCDT, 2021, p. 29) and a critical element for the digital economy, although it does not clearly define what these terms mean. Additionally, while the developmental spirit of the data and cloud policy is clear from its key objectives,[19] the document seems more concerned with how to address the lack of data ownership and control. According to the Draft Policy, most of the data centers and cloud computing infrastructure hosting data generated in South Africa are under foreign ownership.

The developmental spirit of the Draft policy is evident in the inception as it aims at enabling South Africans "to realise the socio-economic value of data" (Department of Communications and Digital Technologies, 2021, p. 13) and to ensure socioeconomic development for inclusiveness. The policy aspires to foster a digital economy that is data driven and data intensive. Explicitly, the Draft Policy places attention on leveraging the socioeconomic value of data through relevant policies and law that support access, reuse, and publication of data while also ensuring adequate privacy, protection, security, and confidentiality in line with the South African Constitution.

From the perspective of securitization, one of the biggest issues associated with this policy concerns the nationalistic elements and government's heavy control over data. Specifically, the Draft policy attempts to position the government at the center of data ownership,[20] control, and distribution in South Africa (Cohen, 2021). It states that "data generated in South Africa shall be the property of South Africa, regardless of where the technology company is domiciled. Government shall act as a trustee for all government data generated within the borders of South Africa." The plan contains clear characteristics of a state-led approach that will ultimately serve to establish

[18] The Policy explicitly refers to data sovereignty and its connection to security: "The Data and Cloud Policy seeks to strengthen the capacity of the State to deliver services to its citizens, ensure informed policy development based on data analytics, as well as promote South Africa's data sovereignty and the security thereof." Draft National Policy on Data and Cloud, p. 11.

[19] Some of the objectives of the draft data policy include "to ensure socio-economic development for inclusivity, promote connectivity and access to data and cloud computing, remove regulatory barriers and enable competition, and ensure the implementation of effective cybersecurity, privacy, data and cloud infrastructure protection measures," among others.

[20] Although ownership is not explicitly defined in the policy, the document refers to data ownership in a few sections in relation to data control (p. 30), to localized data storage and acquisition (p. 9) and to data ownership as a critical element for the digital economy (p. 20).

a High-Performance Computing and Data Processing Centre, which will act as a repository for "[all] data generated from South African natural resources [which] shall be co-owned by government and the private sector participant/s whose private funds were used to generate such."

In its written submission in the response to the draft policy, Research ICT Africa (2021) warned on the positions on sovereignty and localization of the Draft policy, stating that this does not support data flows required to increase trade under the African Continental Free Trade Agreement (AfCFTA),[21] arguing that in its current form the Draft policy prevents cross-border data flows. The document adopts a Russian approach to data storage in that it describes that a copy has to be maintained within South African borders in addition to storing copies for law enforcement purposes. Nevertheless, it states that citizen data[22] may be kept outside South Africa and cross-border transfer can be executed in line with the Protection of Personal Information (POPI) Act. This is markedly distinct from the European Union's General Data Protection Regulation, which emphasizes the need to maintain data security regardless of where it is stored (Cohen, 2021).

As such, to some extent, the Draft National Policy on Data and Cloud appears to adopt an approach that is relatively different to South Africa's POPI Act 4 of 2013, which is based on the EU's personal data protection model, specifically Directive 95/46/EC of the European Parliament and the Council of October 24, 1995. For example, cross-border transfers are not forbidden in South Africa unless they are not aligned with certain requirements, emphasizing the need for adequate legal protection, consent, performance of a contract, or the data subject's interests or benefit.[23] In this sense, adequacy

[21] The Agreement establishing the African Continental Free Trade Area (CFTA) was signed in March 2018 by the 54 Member States of the AU. Since then, 30 countries have deposited their instruments of ratification with the AU Commission. The Agreement lays the foundations for the future establishment of a Continental Common Market. Trading under the CFTA started on January 1, 2021.

[22] The Draft Policy refers to citizen's data in the section related to localization and cross-border data transfers. Nevertheless, it does not provide a clear definition of the term "citizen data."

[23] Regarding "data sovereignty," section 72 of POPI Act provides that:

(1) A responsible party in the Republic may not transfer personal information about a data subject to a third party who is in a foreign country unless any ONE of the following conditions/considerations exist –
   (a) the third party who is the recipient of the information is subject to a law, binding corporate rules or binding agreement that provide an adequate level of protection that reflects the principles of POPI;
   (b) the data subject consents to the transfer;
   (c) the transfer is necessary for the performance of a contract between the data subject and the responsible party;
   (d) the transfer is necessary for the conclusion or performance of a contract concluded in the interest of the data subject; or
   (e) the transfer is for the benefit of the data subject.

mechanisms can be seen as a form of data sovereignty that does not preclude cross-border data flow. A data sovereignty's approach that recognizes adequacy mechanisms does not evoke necessarily data localization, but rather the possibility to transfer personal data freely as long as equivalent jurisdictional guarantees are applied.

4.7.3 Online Content Classification and Emergency Regulation against Disinformation

In the review of the policy posture of South Africa with regard to digital sovereignty, online content regulation provides an example on how state-centric and securitization trends are emerging in the governance of the digital space nationally. The Films and Publications Amendment Act 11 of 2019 (FPAA)[24] was highly criticized by human rights observers and termed as the "Internet Censorship Bill" (Mungadze, 2019) as it is overhauled for infringing on freedom of speech. While the objective of the law is to regulate the development, ownership, creation, and distribution of films, publications, and games with the underlying objective of protecting young people from any harmful material, the underlying definition of what is harmful and disturbing is somewhat vague. Its broad lexicon may engender a situation in which constitutional rights to privacy and freedom of expression are infringed (Mungadze, 2019).

In summary, while the Act appears to protect people against revenge porn or fake news and enables them to consult the Film and Publication Board (FPB) for remedy (ITweb, 2017), the Act requires ISPs[25] to block access to any sites that host repudiated classification content. After it has been enacted, the FPAA will give the FPB the power to demand that any content that is deemed to be prohibited is taken down. However, the Association of ISP (ISPA) has criticized the amendment on the basis that it goes beyond the FPB's mandate and creates an environment in which the FPB can censor content as a quasi-governmental department. This would be contrary to the existing arrangements, which give the courts the power to adjudicate defensible limitations to the freedom of expression (Freedom House, 2020).

A further regulation that could impede the rights of freedom of expression is intermediary liability. ISP's liability was limited by the Electronic Communications Act 2002, which required them to cooperate with takedown notices. However, the existing provisions fail to provide immunity to

[24] The Act was signed into law by the President and published in the Government Gazette on October 3, 2019.

[25] The FPB published draft regulations to implement the Act in 2020. Within these regulations, website owners are classified as "internet service providers." This significantly increases the costs associated with hosting websites and mandates that all online content providers submit content to the FPB for its oversight (Freedom House, 2020).

all forms of communications providers. The takedown process does not provide the individual who uploaded the material the right to argue against any claims. Nor does it allow people to seek recourse for false claims (Comninos, 2012, in Razzano et al., 2020). As such, in practice, the takedown process may represent an indefensible infringement of people's rights to freedom of expression. One proposed modification, which was designed to address the current lack of appeal process, did not improve the situation; it gave the complainant the right to decide on the validity of the response to the complaint. According to Rens (in Razzano et al., 2020), a notice process may address many issues that arise on notice and takedown. This process would give the intermediary the obligation to share the notice that was received with the subscriber to attempt to strike a balance between the competing interests (Razzano et al., 2020).

In more recent times, false information about COVID-19 spread throughout South Africa via the internet. This false information has impeded the nation's COVID-19 response (Kazeem, 2020) and provoked the government to put in place emergency regulations in an attempt to fight the "infodemic" (WHO, 2021). Essentially, spreading any false information[26] related to COVID-19 became a criminal offense.[27] Although the enactment of the regulation resulted in multiple arrests in the early stages of the pandemic, there was no evidence of government abuse of this power (Wild, 2020). Rather, the state collaborated with technology companies and fact-checkers to diminish any proliferation of false information (South African Government, n.d.). The strong response may have helped reduce the spread of hoaxes and rumors concerning COVID-19.

4.7.4 Downsized Mass Surveillance

To supplement the evolving national approach to the regulation of online content, the national regulation of surveillance provides a further case of securitization in the governance of the digital sphere. Surveillance is perceived to be illegitimate or unconstitutional if it fails to sufficiently delineate the process by which an individual is informed that their information has been intercepted or fails to make it clear what processes need to be followed by officials who examine, replicate, share, or sort any data that they access as a result of intercepting communications. In South Africa, the Regulation of Interception of Communications and Provision of Communication Related Information Act (RICA) outlines the legal requirements associated with the interception

[26] The focus is on information that is purposefully rather than unconsciously false – disinformation, not misinformation.

[27] See COVID-19 regulations issued in terms of Section 27(2) of the disaster management act, 2002 (https://cdn.24.co.za/files/Cms/General/d/8296/998082c0829846979a52f11933b621bd .pdf). Specifically, "any statement, through any medium, including social media, with the intention to deceive any other person about COVID-19; COVID-19 infection status of any person; or any measure taken by the Government to address COVID-19."

of communications. Regulation of Interception of Communications and Provision of Communication Related Information Act mandates that communication companies provide interception-capable networks. It also demands that intelligence agencies seek an interception direction (or warrant) from a certified judge prior to performing any type of communication surveillance. However, the Act was endorsed in a rushed response to the global panic observed in the aftermath of the September 11, 2001, terrorist attacks (Duncan, 2021). It has not undergone any modification since that period and has fallen behind any international developments on democratic oversight. The South African Constitutional Court questioned the constitutionality of the RICA in 2019 when it issued a judgment that temporarily halted the country's foreign signals intelligence (SIGINT) capabilities (Duncan, 2021). In the case of *AmaBhungane Centre for Investigative Journalism NPC and Another* v *Minister of Justice and Correctional Services and Others* [2019], the Court, after being informed of mass surveillance by state security entities, ordered: "It is declared that the bulk surveillance activities and foreign signals interception undertaken by the National Communications Centre are unlawful and invalid." This emerged in the absence of any express empowering legislation to do so. Legislation for mass surveillance needs to take into consideration necessity and proportionality of such a law. However, in light of the nature of proportionality requirements within international law, it is challenging to delineate what is a justifiable and lawful permission for this type of activity (Razzano et al., 2020).

4.7.5 Cybercrime Legislation

From a cybercrime perspective, as observed earlier, it is undisputed that cyberattacks have costed South Africa billions of Rands and that they have posed real risks to the well-functioning of governments, critical infrastructures, and affected confidentiality, integrity, and availability of individuals' data. That might be the reason why Hlase (2018) observed that due to the need of putting in place appropriate measures to protect information systems and critical infrastructures otherwise vulnerable to infiltration and sabotage, "securitization may be unavoidable" in South Africa (2018, p. 62).

The protracted process associated with establishing jurisdictional clarity on cybercrime concluded in June 2021 when it was passed as law. The President proclaimed that certain sections of the law to commence on December 1, 2021 (Sheik, 2021). As a result of the Cybercrimes Act 19 of 2020, the relationship between law enforcement bodies and electronic communications service providers (ECSPs) has been revamped, leading to the introduction of several new mechanisms for the SAPS to access and to maintain the preservation of any evidence held by ECSPs.

Particularly, Section 54 outlines several reporting obligations and the maintenance of evidence to be imposed on ECSPs and financial institutions, which may help SAPS during the process of any investigations of an offense. However, the Act also specifies that these measures must not be misused to enforce obligations on electronic service providers or financial institutions to monitor any data that the ECSP or financial institution stores or transmits; or proactively seek circumstances or facts that are indicative of unlawful activity.

Despite these positive developments, a challenge associated with the Cybercrime Act concerns the operationalization of the law because resource limitations and competing policy priorities have culminated in a serious lack of personnel who have the skills required to establish defense against cybercrimes (Allen, 2019).

4.8 DISCUSSION

Based on the earlier discussions, it is possible to argue that national policy and regulatory directions for exerting sovereignty in the digital domain in South Africa are informed by developmental aspiration linking digital transformation to socioeconomic development. However, institutional failures due to the delayed implementation of digital policies extensively undermined policy and regulation actions on improving digital connectivity. Besides, existing and newly established state entities are struggling to cope with increasing responsibilities to protect citizens' rights to privacy, safety, and security online.[28] On the other hand, the country is facing an unprecedented wave of cyberattacks and incidents resulting from competing policy priorities and inadequate investment in cybersecurity and, more recently, from criminals capitalizing on COVID-19, which is affecting many economic sectors. From a geopolitical point of view, the high dependence on digital services from the US, technological equipment from China, and regulatory standards from the EU (McKenzie Baker, 2022) place the country also in a position of diplomatic pressure from diverging global powers and different approaches in the governance of the digital realm, undermining self-determination on digital sovereignty.

As a result, securitization trends are permeating an increasing number of areas of digital governance. It can be understood almost as a protectionist reaction to the fear of losing control over national digital assets and the benefits of digitalization. At the same time, however, the increasing use of surveillance and the use of social media for disinformation and misinformation campaigns are expression of the need of exerting control through manipulation of information.

Internationally, at the UN First Committee level, developmental ambitions are expressed in several inputs at the OEWG, those for instance related to the consideration of the digital divide and gender disparities in ICT access and

[28] On this note, South Africa's information regulator is struggling with lack of funding while it is battling to cope with rising incidents of data breaches (eNCA, 2020).

use amid a securitization agenda spurred by increasing threats of cybercrime. The position of vulnerability in cyberspace of South Africa emerged from its concerns on stockpiling of ICT-related vulnerabilities by capable state actors and not by the country's concerns with growing cyber offensive and defensive capabilities of adversary states.

At the level of international digital trade, South Africa has advocated for an inclusive and development-oriented approach to transnational e-commerce in the WTO process related to the moratorium on electronic transmission. While the ban from imposing customs duties on electronic transmission is perceived as a loss of tariff revenue and duties, in an international digital trade system, developing countries might become rent seekers considering that most of e-commerce would be incoming. Therefore, in addition to advocating for the removal of the ban on tariffs, a bigger effort should be placed on creating favorable conditions for outgoing e-commerce to grow.

Nationally, with the recent Draft National Policy on Data and Cloud, the country took a predominantly state-centric position on data sovereignty, stating that data generated in South Africa shall be the property of South Africa, with the government acting as a trustee for all government data generated within the borders of South Africa. While the ambition of the policy document is to realize the socioeconomic value of data and to ensure socioeconomic development for inclusiveness, the outcome may restrict data flows necessary to increase trade under the AfCFTA. Similarly, the approach to online content regulation is shaped by securitization forces through a state-centric vetting approach for the classification of digitally distributed content. On the other hand, the takedown procedure that gives expression to limited liability for ISPs (Parliament of the Republic of South Africa, 2022) has an impact on the rights of freedom of expression, because it does not provide a right to respond to claims made by a complainant, nor imposes adequate penalties for false claims. More recently, as a result of the infodemic related to disinformation on COVID-19, alongside emerging regulation to fight against the pandemic, disinformation on COVID-19 became a criminal offence. Lastly, practices of mass surveillance by state security agencies have been fought in court, which acknowledged them as unlawful and invalid.

4.9 CONCLUDING POLICY OBSERVATIONS

The South African state stance to digital sovereignty is at the intersection of a digital transformation for development and securitization agenda. Nevertheless, in a national context of cyber vulnerability, institutional failure to effectively implement inclusive digital connectivity and transformation policies and lack of personnel, skills, and capacity to deal with increasing cyber threats and cyber risks, balancing the need to securitize elements of the critical infrastructures and to protect data while respecting fundamental rights of privacy and freedom of expression is a major challenge for South African policy makers.

In South Africa, cyber threats and vulnerabilities are growing in parallel with responsibilities of state actors to protect citizens' rights to privacy, safety, and security online. The public sector response is putting human and constitutional rights under pressure with increasing government control over various elements of the digital infrastructure. To improve developmental outcomes of digitalization while protecting privacy, safety and security online of South Africa citizens, policy options for digital sovereignty should consider elements of proportionality as the most important requirement that must be satisfied in the limitation of human rights. The four major elements of this principle are legitimacy, adequacy, necessity, and proportionality *stricto sensu* (Anđelković, 2017). At the same time, emerging digital policy regimes on data, cybersecurity, and online content governance should be human-centric to deal with the underlying factors that make society vulnerable, instead of abusing national security narratives to protect state actors from criticism. In this way, self-determination in cyberspace would respect human rights and would promote the human security approach to national security as enshrined in the 1996 Constitution. Lastly, in order to implement a positive digital sovereignty agenda for South Africa, existing digital policy regimes and legislation on data protection and cybercrime should be effectively implemented. This can be done only if the necessary skills and capacity in public sector institutions are in place, so that public authorities can tackle emerging threats and risks, leverage digital transformation for socioeconomic development, while protecting citizens' rights to privacy and freedom of expression.

PART II

TECHNO-ECONOMIC STRUCTURINGS OF DIGITAL SOVEREIGNTY

5

Digital Sovereignty and Payments

A Case Study of the National Payments Corporation of India

Venkatesh Hariharan and Sarayu Natarajan

5.1 INTRODUCTION

In early 2014, the United States imposed economic sanctions prohibiting the export of American goods to Russia (Borger, Lewis, & Mason, 2014). MasterCard and Visa, credit card providers, rushed to comply, leaving millions of Russians without access to their credit accounts and several hundred billion dollars of assets frozen (BBC, 2014). At the time, these two American corporations controlled over 90% of the Russian credit card market. While services were restored within days, the situation prompted Russia to issue an alternative credit card – MIR. Since payments are the lifeblood of an economy, Russia also contemplated a law that will require payments providers to register in-country within a stipulated time or exit the country (Dettmer, 2019).

This incident in Russia and the US consideration in prohibiting Visa and MasterCard from operating in Venezuela as financial sanctions (Mason, 2019) raise questions about the value of sovereignty over fundamental digital infrastructures and the need to reclaim these in the public interest (Stanford PACS, 2020). In this chapter, we examine the intersection of India's indigenous payments system, the Unified Payment Interface (UPI) and the National Payments Corporation of India (NPCI), a special purpose vehicle set up to manage payments and strengthen India's digital sovereignty.

With this chapter, we wish to add to the growing literature on digital sovereignty. A non-Western view of sovereignty may add to the growing voices on policy and design around digital infrastructures in the Global South, applicable to digital infrastructures in other domains of state activity (e.g., technology used to access judicial services). We hope to inform policymakers, think tanks, and citizens of the trade-offs in building digital infrastructures for payments. Our chapter aims to highlight, through the study of the NPCI and analysis, the key parameters and choices that policymakers, designers, and researchers might consider in evaluating investments in digital infrastructure. We do not aim to prescribe any course of action but merely demonstrate the choices available.

We find that, in India, the NPCI and the UPI are instruments that advance digital sovereignty. Following Pohle & Thiel (2020), we interpret digital sovereignty as combining the protection of infrastructure, enablement of market competition, and the enhancement of individual self-determination. We argue that technological, institutional, regulatory, and programmatic efforts are needed to enhance digital sovereignty, and these are the approaches policymakers globally may consider examining. The idea that digital infrastructures advance sovereignty finds articulation in the New Delhi Leaders' Declaration (2023, p. 22).

For this chapter, we select the UPI and the NPCI for analysis. The case study method allows us to surface structural characteristics that are worthy of study (Tillin, 2013). In this case, we explore those characteristics and approaches that have been important in the trajectory of the NPCI. We chose the NPCI because it speaks to emerging concerns around digital economies, payments, and sovereignty. This is additionally contextualized in the growing conversations around Digital Public Infrastructure (DPI) and Digital Public Goods (DPGs).[1] The NPCI's existence for nearly a decade now as well as India's experience with indigenous DPI development and governance have useful lessons to offer in terms of building flexibility and resilience into a country's digital ecosystems.

Methodologically, we combine a theoretical treatment of sovereignty with an empirical and practical understanding of the experiences and concerns of lawmakers and practitioners globally along with the performance of the NPCI itself. This effort looks at both the NPCI and the underlying technological architecture, the UPI. This empirical approach allows us to have a real sense of the efforts and trade-offs involved in building, deploying, and managing digital infrastructures while protecting citizens' interests. For this study, in addition to desk research, we conducted ten interviews with policymakers, practitioners, and experts in India and globally. Interviews were analyzed interpretatively by the researchers together.

We believe our work and approach and this analysis are significant for two reasons. First, we build on the emerging literature on digital sovereignty to emphasize the concerns and constraints of price-taker states, which have lesser bargaining power in negotiations. These states far outnumber powerful states but may lack similar bargaining power due to a host of economic and historical reasons. Understanding the parameters for consideration in building out digital infrastructures is significant for such states. Second, we examine the implications of sovereignty in the context of

[1] For more information on DPGs, see http://digitalpublicgoods.net.

digital infrastructure guaranteed by the state (payments). Unlike sovereignty debates in the context of creative services (e.g., applications, software) that may concern issues such as monopoly, data protection, or abuse of power, payments are intimately linked to state function. Thus, interpretations of sovereignty need to additionally engage with the denial-of-service issues and their catastrophic implications for the economy.

This chapter is structured as follows: Section 5.2, following the introduction, builds a working definition of sovereignty. This definition relies on a broad interpretation of sovereignty and considers some of the critiques of such expansion. Section 5.3 describes the structure and operations of the NPCI in brief. Section 5.4 explores the workings of the NPCI through the framework and approach described in Section 5.2 and examines its successes and failures. Section 5.5 conducts a broad assessment of the working of the NPCI. A concluding section follows Section 5.6, providing possible avenues to address some of the concerns described in earlier sections, and explores some meta issues in the context of payments.

5.2 BRINGING THE STATE BACK INTO DIGITAL: BUILDING A WORKING UNDERSTANDING OF SOVEREIGNTY

In this section, we take a brief look at digital sovereignty and arrive at an operational frame for analysis. We follow Pohle and Thiel (2020) to unpack sovereignty as control over critical infrastructure, economic freedom, and individual agency. We then examine the threats to sovereignty and the mechanisms available to exercise sovereignty. Our analysis is underpinned by Floridi's approach of seeing *power as control* (Floridi, 2020). We argue that a sovereign state needs to control and protect digital infrastructures against state and nonstate and domestic and foreign threats through legitimate means available to it.

Sovereignty is the ability of a nation to make not only its own laws but also the ability to protect itself and its citizens from harm, achieve policy objectives, and enhance citizen well-being. The core meaning – sovereignty as the supreme authority over territory – emerges from the Westphalian notion of sovereignty, which bases state sovereignty on territoriality and the absence of a role for external agents in domestic structures. This definition of sovereignty places the state, whether liberal democratic or not, and its physical territory at the center of the imagination (Philpott, 2020).

In the digital realm, two main challenges to territorial notions of sovereignty have arisen: the ideas of cyber exceptionalism and multi-stakeholder governance (Pohle & Thiel, 2020). Cyber-exceptionalism sees cyberspace as exceptional and therefore contends that traditional frames of reference are not adequate (Pohle & Thiel, 2020). This has been articulated in multiple ways, starting with John Perry Barlow's 1996 declaration:

> "Governments of the Industrial World, you weary giants of flesh and steel, I come from Cyberspace, the new home of Mind. On behalf of the future, I ask you of the past to leave us alone. You are not welcome among us. You have no sovereignty where we gather." (Barlow, 1996)

Cyber exceptionalism is based on the premise that the rise of the internet implies the demise of state sovereignty and that national borders are rendered irrelevant. Multi-stakeholder governance is closely related to the ideas of cyber exceptionalism, which focuses on the roles played by various actors toward the development of shared norms and rules in the regulation and development of the internet. The ideas of multi-stakeholder governance emphasize open, consultative, and bottom-up decision making, involving those who are affected by decisions (Hoffman, 2016; Raymond & DeNardis, 2015).

Both cyber exceptionalism and multi-stakeholder governance are not a part of prominent narratives of digital governance. Instead, nations across the world are increasingly using the vocabulary of digital sovereignty to assert control over digital infrastructures within their borders. The term has become a way to bring back the state, as well as ideas of nationhood, economy, and citizenship, into debates around governance of digital infrastructures (Pohle & Thiel, 2020). There is a robust literature in the context of the European Union (EU) as the EU and its member states grapple with the emergence of technology giants who possess significant amounts of data as well as well as vast networks from which to mine data (Couture & Toupin, 2019; Gueham, 2017; Pohle & Thiel, 2020; Ruohonen, 2020).

In a context of increasing datafication of our lives, it is critical to examine conceptions of sovereignty and the role of the state. The state is relevant to examine for two reasons. First, individuals are increasingly engaging with the state through digital means across many arenas and domains. Several aspects of state functions such as welfare and government services are increasingly digitally mediated. Additionally, as Marianna Mazzucato (2018) has demonstrated, the state is central in framing and enabling the digital world. Her book, *The Entrepreneurial State*, demonstrates how the state does so through policies, subsidies, and infrastructure, playing a role in "making" the digital (Mazzucato, 2013). In that sense, the digital and the state cannot be parsed from each other. Importantly, digital goods and services are deeply connected with conceptions of liberty, rights, and norms, many of which are articulated through constitutional and legal frameworks at a national level. Accordingly, it is critical to center the state.

Second, the state is important in the imagination of digital infrastructures for the public. Many critical digital infrastructures are built using public funds and offer public services that emerge from statute or law, to which the principles of nondiscrimination and equal access apply. Nondiscrimination and access are enforceable in that citizens may bring claims in a court of law. Accordingly, the role of the state in ensuring this access for all necessitates an examination of state sovereignty and a deeper engagement with the state.

To analyze relationships between the state and digital infrastructure and the functioning of the NPCI, we adopt the framing in Pohle and Thiel (2020). Their paper suggests that the reemergence of sovereignty in digital debates is founded in three strands of thinking: (1) state autonomy and the security of national infrastructures; (2) economic autonomy and competition for market actors within the territory, and (3) autonomy and individual self-determination for citizens. Of these three, only the first argument refers to a territorial sense of the state and the need to protect infrastructure. This is akin to the need for the state to protect digital infrastructures such as physical infrastructure. The other two aspects of sovereignty relate to state goals of protecting indigenous market actors to enable a fair and free market economy to flourish and supporting citizens' aspirations of self-determination (Pohle & Thiel, 2020). The second strand also speaks to emergent literature in the context of the EU that frames sovereignty as the need for the state to protect the interests of citizens and the ideals of a free and fair internet and to enable a free market and level playing field (Gueham, 2017).

Understanding sovereignty as autonomy and individual self-determination requires some thought to operationalize. We use the language of agency to unpack autonomy and individual self-determination. The work of Sharma and Natarajan (2020) suggests that agency is fundamental to individual self-determination. However, agency is a complex concept and needs to be seen near ideas of inclusion and equal access. Sharma and Natarajan argue that for technologies that arise from one's rights under constitutional or legal frameworks, the onus is placed on the state to ensure that all individuals have access, and therefore agency. Agency can be dimensionalized to include concepts such as choice (among alternatives) and ability (to make choices and bargain). Agency must additionally be framed within a language of rights, aspects of access that relate to individuals' rights under the constitution (specifically, Articles 19(1)(g) and 21[2]) (Sharma & Natarajan, 2020).

In our exploration in this chapter, we consider challenges to sovereignty from both state and nonstate actors. First, we consider state actors. States are sovereign entities themselves, subject to international law, agreements, and norms. Second, we consider nonstate actors. While nonstate actors may include legally established and recognized entities (e.g., corporations, both domestic and foreign) and unrecognized entities, we focus on the former category. We exclude bad actors such as hackers from the scope of this chapter. Indeed, all our interviewees concurred with the view that sovereignty must consider state and nonstate actors as oppositional forces that might undermine sovereignty.

We also need to address the question of how sovereignty is exercised, that is, what modes and mechanisms are available to the state and what the ultimate outcome of this exercise must be. Floridi (2019) articulates the latter through

[2] Article 19(1)(g) of the Constitution guarantees the freedom "to practise any profession, or to carry on any occupation, trade or business." Article 21 states that "No person shall be deprived of his life or personal liberty except according to procedure established by law."

the language of "control," that is, that power is control. Fioridi describes power as being both poietic (creative control, vesting with companies) and cybernetic (the ability to regulate or steer, vesting with the state). This framing and the delineation between creative control and cybernetic/regulatory control offer a way to think about the goals of the sovereign exercise of power, and the means available to the state. The goal of cybernetic control is attained through regulation and policies (Floridi, 2020). The cybernetic power is the control we attempt to assess through this chapter.

In this assessment, we must be careful not to depoliticize the idea of sovereignty and grant it only a functional and utilitarian character. A widened interpretation of digital sovereignty comes with simultaneous concerns about the expanded role of the state in business (Kelkar & Shah, 2019) and the enablement of a surveillance state (Srnicek, 2016). The availability of vast data to the state can enable large-scale violations of individual privacy. When combined with state power sans adequate data protection frameworks or procedural safeguards, individual liberties are at risk.

Sovereignty must not be seen as a frame to empower an already powerful state. Particularly, they must not enable ways to erode judicial and legislative checks and balances over executive power. The inadequacies of legal frameworks in the face of authoritarian governments' inclination to override them cannot be ignored. Equally, choices and practices of defending and defining sovereignty, particularly the ways in which questions relating to the individual are handled, are political in themselves as they are likely to privilege certain viewpoints and identities.

5.3 UNDERSTANDING THE NPCI AND UPI

NPCI, a nonprofit company regulated by the Reserve Bank of India (RBI), was set up as a DPI that manages the payment backbone of India. NPCI's majority shareholding is held by public sector banks and offers utility pricing for its services. For this chapter and analysis alone, we define DPIs as *technology infrastructures built/managed by the state for universal use and availability, and upon which innovation can occur.*

NPCI operates India's ATM networks, National Automated Clearing House to facilitate interbank transactions, the RuPay credit and debit card network and other payments infrastructures. In 2016, NPCI launched a new generation payment network called the Unified Payments Network (UPI), a mobile-first, open API-based, instantaneous payment network. While card networks have been around in India for decades, their penetration has been low. UPI enabled India to leapfrog to a mobile-first era of digital payments, similar to how countries leapfrogged the landline era and went straight to the mobile phone era. Countries that do not have card networks but have growing telecom and smartphone penetration have the potential to leapfrog the cards era straight into a mobile-first, UPI-like ecosystem.

5.3.1 Understanding the UPI

India has built three key digital infrastructures: Aadhaar, UPI, and the Data Empowerment and Protection Architecture (DEPA). These three layers come together to form India Stack (n.d.) and provide identity, payments, and data as services. The payments layer of India Stack, which forms the subject of this chapter, has been housed within the NPCI, which is an umbrella organization for operating retail payments and settlement systems in India. It is an initiative of the RBI and Indian Banks' Association (IBA) under the provisions of the *Payment and Settlement Systems Act*, 2007, for creating a payment and settlement infrastructure in India (NPCI, n.d. -a). The NPCI has been set up as a non-for-profit company, with the goal of providing physical and electronic payment and settlement systems in India. Six public sectors, two private sectors, and two foreign banks were the ten core promoters. In 2016, the shareholding contained 56 members.

NPCI operates an array of infrastructures such as the RuPay debit, credit, and prepaid cards; the UPI, which is a mobile-first, interoperable payments network; and the Immediate Payment Service (IMPS). Launched in April 2016, the UPI has been the biggest success in NPCI's portfolio, achieving 2.5 billion transactions in January 2021 (NPCI, n.d. -b). UPI enables anyone with a mobile app from one of the 224 participating banks, or Third-Party Service Providers (TPSPs) such as Google Pay or PhonePe to make payments within the UPI network using QR codes or virtual Payment Addresses like abc@xyzbank.

Worldwide, payment networks have evolved as monopolies or duopolies, due to network effects. Consumers flock to the networks that have the widest acceptance, while merchants flock to the networks that have the most customers. In contrast, NPCI built UPI as a relatively open payment rails upon which banks can become payment service providers (PSPs), to their own customers, and to third-party apps such as Google Pay, PhonePe, and WhatsApp. The design of UPI and the institutional architecture of NPCI have many implications for digital sovereignty. This chapter will take a deeper look into them. Figures 5.1 and 5.2 explain the difference between card networks and the UPI network.

5.3.2 Cards, UPI, and NPCI

Traditional card networks are a three-party model with transactions routed from the payer's card to the switch, which sends the money to the payee's bank account. The switch is at the heart of the network, which is why when sanctions were imposed on Russia with which MasterCard and Visa complied, the lifeblood of payments came to a halt. Since 90% of card payments in Russia were routed through MasterCard and Visa, this had a very disruptive impact, leading Russia to create an indigenous payment system MIR.

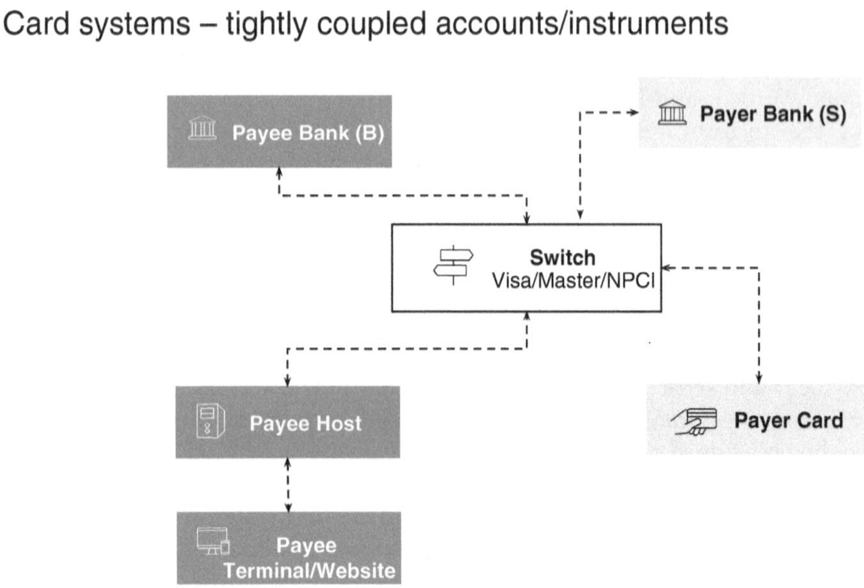

FIGURE 5.1 Schematic description of card systems[3]
Source: iSPIRT, Sanjay Swamy

In India, NPCI operates its own card network called RuPay, which has 60% share of the cards issued. In terms of value, MasterCard and Visa cards have a higher share because of incentives and cash backs. All three networks operate in parallel, and the existence of RuPay means that if MasterCard and Visa were to stop working, Indians have another network to switch over to.

RuPay also has a lower cost structure. Therefore, the Indian government has issued RuPay cards along with its financial inclusion initiative, the Jan-Dhan bank accounts. Over 424 million bank accounts were opened as part of an initiative to provide minimum balance bank accounts to the poor, so that money from welfare schemes can be transferred directly into the recipients' Jan-Dhan accounts. Of these 424 million accounts, 310 million users were issued RuPay cards (PMJDY, 2023).

5.3.3 UPI

In contrast to the card networks, UPI has been set up as a four-party model. The payer uses an app, which could belong to a bank or a TPSP. The key innovation in UPI was decoupling permissions from the payment instruments such as online banking. The UPI app acts as a permission collector and the user approves a payment through the app. This approval is sent to the payer's

[3] This figure is adapted, with permission from Sanjay Swamy, based on his presentation "Payments4G" at iSPIRT's Fintech Leapfrog Council on September 6, 2016 in Mumbai, India.

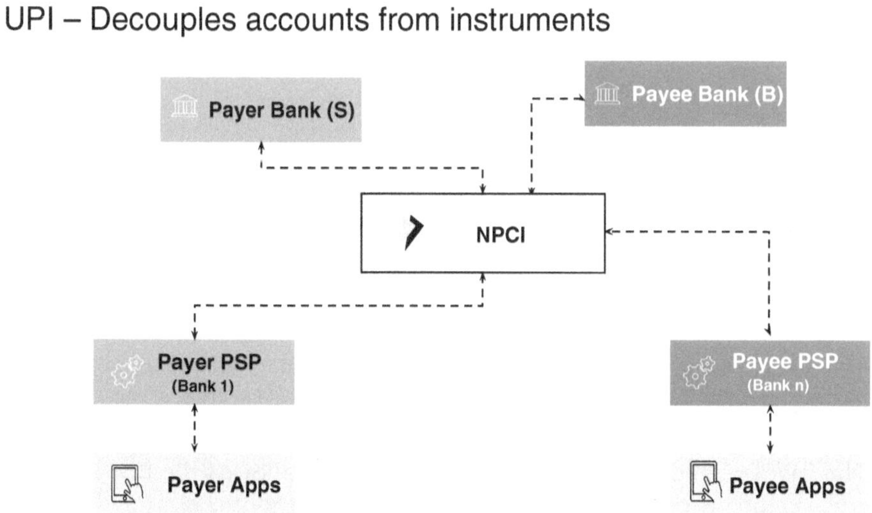

FIGURE 5.2 Schematic depiction of UPI[4]
Source: iSPIRT, Sanjay Swamy

bank account through the UPI switch controlled by NPCI and the payer's account is debited and the payee's account is credited.

Since the UPI switch is housed within NPCI, which is run as DPI and all UPI players have to connect to this switch, it is difficult for network monopolies to emerge. Interviewees suggested that TPSPs such as Google Pay and PhonePe have acquired a sizable market share of UPI transactions because of the incentives and cashbacks they offer, but not through network effects.

5.3.4 Understanding the Structure of the NPCI

The NPCI is the institution that houses the payments protocol, the UPI. Marianna Mazzucato (2013) has argued against the idea of the state as a collection of static bureaucratic organizations needed only to "fix" market failures, leaving dynamic entrepreneurship and innovation to the private sector. She has instead worked to reshape the narrative of the state's role in the economy to one of creating and shaping new markets.

In their working paper on the NPCI, William Cook and Anand Raman of the Consultative Group to Assist the Poor (CGAP) sketch out the history of NPCI where Indian regulators actively shaped its formation (Cook & Raman, 2019). In 1996, Y. V. Reddy (the then deputy governor of the RBI and later its governor) asked, "How far are we from global standards?" In the early 2000s when India's GDP grew at 7.3%, the country's payment systems were not keeping pace. The RBI's Vision Document for 2005–2008 scanned fourteen

[4] This figure is adapted, with permission from Sanjay Swamy, based on his presentation "Payments4G" at iSPIRT's Fintech Leapfrog Council on September 6, 2016 in Mumbai, India.

leading markets and found that very few central banks operate retail payment systems. In the Vision Document, RBI stated:

> The primary goal of any national payment system is to enable the circulation of money in its economy. It is recognised worldwide that an efficient and secure payment system is an enabler of economic activity. It provides the conduit essential for effecting payments and transmission of monetary policy. Payment systems have encountered many challenges and are constantly adapting to the rapidly changing payments landscape. More recently, the proliferation of electronic payment mechanisms, the increase in the number of players in the financial arena and the payment crises in quite a few countries and regions in the 1990s have focused attention on public policy issues related to the organization and operation of payment systems. Three main areas of public policy have guided payments system development and reform: protecting the rights of users of payment systems, enhancing efficiency and competition, and ensuring a safe, secure and sound payments system (Reserve Bank of India, 2005).

The Payment and Settlement Systems Act in 2007 allowed the RBI to authorize a company or a corporation to operate or regulate the clearing houses of banks, provided that at least 51% shares of such an organization are held by public sector banks.

All of this paved the way for the creation of NPCI. The body was set up as a nonprofit company that would answer to the RBI, but was operationally independent. The decision to structure as a nonprofit underscored the NPCI's utility nature from the outset. NPCI follows the principle of cost-plus pricing, and this enables financial inclusion and penetration across the country. Furthermore, NPCI is not driven by considerations of valuation and going public as are private corporations (Ramesh, Jangid, Sivamalai, & Rebelly, 2020). The nonprofit company status also allows the NPCI to be an agile organization that could hire the best talent available in the market.

Globally, payment systems have been privately owned duopolies because of the very nature of the business. Due to network effects, merchants and customers gravitate to the largest payment platforms, resulting in a few large players dominating the market. UPI was set up as a comparatively open, interoperable payment platform. Any bank can plug into the NPCI's backend system and offer UPI as a service to their own customers or to Third-Party App Providers (TPAPs) such as Google Pay and PhonePe. For customers, this means that they have a choice of more than a hundred UPI apps to choose from.

As of June 5, 2021, more than 224 banks were providing UPI transactions as a service by plugging into NPCI's UPI backend (NPCI, n.d. -c). Sixteen TPAPs such as Google Pay, the Walmart-owned PhonePe, and WhatsApp ride on top of banks who offer UPI services as registered PSPs of NPCI (NPCI, n.d. -d). These TPAPs collectively account for more than 90% of total UPI transactions by offering cashbacks and incentives with PhonePe accounting for 48.73% and Google Pay accounting for 37.31% of total UPI volumes in May 2021 (NCPI, n.d. -e). Since banking is a highly regulated sector, these TPAPs have to have an arrangement with one or multiple banks that provide UPI as a service.

UPI is also a policy innovation because it was designed to be interoperable from the start. In many countries, payment networks have grown rapidly, and regulators have tried to enable interoperability in hindsight. For example, it is only after the rapid growth of Alipay and WeChat that China made them connect to Nets Union Clearing Corporation (NUCC), a public clearing and settlement institution for online payments.

The interoperability of the UPI platform means that, once a user has downloaded and signed up on UPI, they can instantaneously send money to anyone else on the UPI system. It must be noted that very few countries, including the US, have a mobile-first, interoperable national payment network that enables instant settlement. Enabling interoperability post-facto is often hard because the dominant players will always resist opening up their networks to other players.

5.4 NPCI AND SOVEREIGNTY

In this section, we explore the workings of the NPCI and the UPI (NPCI, n.d. -b) through the framework proposed in Section 5.2. We attempt to uncover the functioning and the performance of the UPI with respect to the three elements of sovereignty and then examine what states might do to respond to nonstate and other state actors. In doing so, we look at both technological approaches and institutional mechanisms.

5.4.1 State Autonomy and Security of Digital Infrastructure

The security of digital services from denial of technology remains the primary articulation of state sovereignty. As discussed earlier, situations such as the MasterCard, Visa, and SWIFT sanctions of Russia can be a threat to a given nation-state and the primary entry point for framing inquiries into state sovereignty. Policy shifts in other nations and insidious and criminal threats from malicious nonstate actors can heavily undermine the functioning of elements of the digital economy such as payments in this case.

This is articulated in two ways. First, the effects of geopolitical actions such as economic sanctions or war may result in private service providers having to comply with orders. This was demonstrated in the case of Visa and Mastercard in suspending their operations in Russia (Dettmer, 2019). Second, nations might want greater control over the payments infrastructure to achieve policy goals such as financial inclusion and regulatory oversight to accelerate a shift from cash to digital transactions, encourage competition and innovation, and prevent monopolies or duopolies.

Introduced in 2016, UPI has become the fastest growing payment network in India, achieving 2.5 billion transactions in May 2021 (NPCI, n.d. -b). Since the UPI switch is controlled by NPCI, which is an organization incorporated in India, UPI is relatively immune to sanctions. In the case of card networks, if sanctions cut off access to MasterCard and Visa networks in India, customers will be able to switch over to the indigenous RuPay card network with relative ease. Therefore, UPI and RuPay networks insulate the country from sanctions that could lead to denial of technology.

5.4.2 Economic Autonomy and Competition

Economic autonomy, and the ability to foster self-reliance, innovation ecosystems, and sustained local businesses, is another articulation of sovereignty. The provision of a technical "infrastructure" and open[5] APIs lower the cost of innovation for local entities through lower barriers to entry. The NPCI structure and the open APIs under the UPI system theoretically enable innovation. Additionally, the NPCI has also made significant efforts in helping local businesses to innovate through hackathons.

However, the ability to leverage this infrastructure remains with corporate players. Large corporations have access to capital, data, networks, technical skills, and resources to develop and deploy a range of services very quickly. Despite the relatively open payment rails, October 2020 figures reveal that two US-owned entities – PhonePe (Walmart) and Google Pay – had 83% of the total volume of UPI transactions. This has prompted NPCI to issue a circular that no TPAPs can exceed more than 30% of the total volume of UPI transactions to curb the risk of a few parties dominating the UPI ecosystem.

Some of our interviewees highlighted the risk that by offering savings, investments, and a basket of financial services, TPAPs could control the consumer interface and reduce banks to back-end service providers. At a later stage, if they acquire a banking license, the need to rely on banks as PSP will also be eliminated. Therefore, there needs to be a deeper assessment of the risks involved in the consumer interface of UPI residing in two foreign-owned entities. If nothing else, the dominance of foreign-owned TPAPs on top of the UPI platform indicates that the task of protecting a country's digital sovereignty is not a static task but a dynamic one that involves technological, institutional, regulatory, and programmatic efforts.

Shifting from Cash to Digital: Cash is the most widely accepted form of payment. If an economy wants to move people from cash to digital, ensuring that digital modes of payment are widely accepted is absolutely essential. If a payer on network X is not able to pay a merchant on network Y, the utility of each network is greatly diminished for the payer and the merchant.

For merchants, cost is another factor that impedes adoption of digital modes of payment. Card networks entail a one-time payment for the point-of-sale terminal and minimum monthly transaction fee guaranteed by the

[5] NPCI code is not open source. It offers open APIs for innovation. See https://partners.apisetu.gov.in/directory/api/npci?ref=blog.quickwork.co. Accessed June 11, 2024.

merchant, apart from relatively high transaction costs. With UPI, merchants need to set up a QR code connected to their bank accounts to start accepting payments. UPI transactions are free so there are no set-up or recurring fees. Merchants also like the fact that the money is credited immediately into their accounts. This has brought many new merchants into the ambit of digital payments.

For users, a high credit score is required to get a credit card, which restricts its reach to the relatively well-off section of Indian society. Since UPI (like debit cards) is attached to the bank account, there are no additional know-your-client (KYC) requirements to establish a customer's identity and identify risk factors. It is also easier to use since payments can be made and received using virtual payment addresses (similar to email addresses) or QR codes. This has helped take digital payments beyond the major metros in India to tier 2 and tier 3 cities in India.

Therefore, the UPI network has accelerated the shift from cash to digital by virtue of ease of use, interoperability, and lower transaction costs. The incentives and cashbacks offered by UPI players have also helped speed up adoption by consumers and merchants.

Encouraging Competition and Innovation: NPCI has conducted many hackathons to encourage innovations on top of the UPI platform. NPCI has also made it easier for small banks and third parties to provide payments as a service. Once an organization connects to the UPI switch, their customers can make payments to anyone else within the UPI network. This open-loop architecture enables firms to direct their energies to providing customer-facing innovations, instead of negotiating interoperability agreements and other related tasks that closed-loop networks would have to undertake.

UPI is also a payment system that has been built with open application programming interfaces (APIs) at the core. This has enabled players to build their customer-facing and merchant-facing apps on top of these APIs.

Preventing Monopolies and Duopolies: Policymakers have found it very difficult to regulate the winner-take-all model that results from network effects in the areas such as payments. Classical competition theory states that one should not regulate monopolies, but the *abuse* of such monopolies. However, this is easier said than done. Competition theory has not kept pace with the exponential growth of digital networks and their winner-take-all nature. China, which started with a light-touch regulatory regime, has moved to create NUCC, an NPCI-like organization, in response to concerns that capital flows through direct payment tools could be misused for money laundering and other illicit activities. NUCC allows the government to ensure interoperability among payment instruments and provides greater oversight of the payments ecosystem. In Kenya, mobile money interoperability became a reality eleven years after M-Pesa was introduced (Mburu, 2018) but reports indicate that such interoperability is quite cumbersome for consumers (Cook, 2018).

Payment networks can easily function as quasi-regulators. This helps the state keep direct control over the playground and its participants, as well as keep a check on monopolies. In the hands of a well-intentioned state, this can be a boon and in the hands of an ill-intentioned state, it can be a bane. However, the scope of this chapter centers around a state's *capacity* to maintain digital sovereignty, and not so much state *intent*, which could be the subject of a separate paper.

Interestingly, the rapid growth of UPI has also raised concerns within RBI that NPCI has become too big to fail. RBI therefore issued a policy paper on Authorisation of New Retail Payment Systems (Reserve Bank of India, 2019). Subsequently, RBI invited bids from organizations wishing to operate NUEs and seven consortia applied for the NUE license. This included a consortium led by a leading telco, Reliance Jio, which had members such as Facebook and Google, while another consortium was led by Amazon. Hariharan (2021) has criticized this move as it is likely to fundamentally alter the nonprofit, utility-pricing, and Indian-banks-owned nature of India's payments infrastructure. In August 2021, RBI put the plans for issuing the NUE licenses on hold. A MINT news report cited RBI's concerns over data security and compliance with its data localization norms as the reasons for this freeze (Gopakumar, 2021).

5.4.3 Individual Self-Determination and Inclusion

A third component of digital sovereignty is the ability to foster individual self-determination and inclusion. In countries such as India, social structures intersect with economic conditions to mediate vulnerable populations' access to technologies. This is increasingly being demonstrated in the context of areas such as payments (Borgonovi et al., 2018; Demtschenko, 2020) and governance technologies (Sharma, Natarajan, & Udhayakumar, 2020). These barriers are being observed across geographies as well. The literature suggests that across contexts, the already disadvantaged, and those who are on the vulnerable side of the digital divide are doubly disadvantaged when systems shift toward digital ones (Sharma, et al., 2020). The digital gender divide, for example, hinders the ability of women to participate freely in the economy. This circumscribes opportunities for economic development, including by limiting access to markets, or worse, to entitlements and welfare from the state.

Examining the accessibility of the NPCI in this context and the ways in which its design and implementation encourage inclusion and agency is the third element of sovereignty. The structure of the UPI that fosters interoperability across different payments systems is a critical element of this accessibility. M-Pesa, another digital payment system, is similarly interoperable, though it is far less so than the UPI. This type of technological interoperability lowers the barriers to entry as all banks can "communicate" with each other. Interviewees identified interoperability as a critical element in driving inclusion and agency for users. Interoperability encourages firms to innovate and reduces friction and risk in everyday transactions. Together, these enable inclusion and agency.

Interoperability also allows firms to develop applications to service preferred market segments, distributing the costs of widening reach and allowing the development of innovative methods. For instance, Google has developed Google Pay/Tez to provide a payments interface application to its users; PhonePe and Paytm operate on a similar premise. Our interviewees pointed out that this offers significant advantages in that firms are then incentivized to innovate in order to make payments available to wider segments of the population and expand their customer bases. This widens the choices available to individuals, in turn supporting agency and inclusion.

Additionally, interoperability also reduces friction in everyday payments transactions. An example of this is the reduction in the need for communicating bank account numbers. Payments are immediately credited, reducing the latency between the issue and receipt of payments. This allows for reduction risk in the payments process.

However, as our interviewees pointed out, neither increased agency (as choice) nor reduced friction are adequate for inclusion. Nor are they addressable through technology alone. Indeed, as established earlier, there are profound challenges of inclusion and these fault lines map onto existing social cleavages of gender and geography in the Indian context. This requires institutional structure and programmatic efforts to be critical elements of this process. In this regard, the NPCI's structure as a not-for-profit and its programmatic efforts are noteworthy.

The NPCI is structured as a nonprofit entity. The multi-stakeholder governance approach (representation from stakeholders) ensures that the NPCI represents diverse voices (NPCI, n.d. -f). The involvement of public sector banks also carries connotations of stakeholder engagement. However, the NPCI may additionally need to make efforts to make the process of governance itself inclusive. For example, the structure imagines the inclusion of civil society. In reality, no civil society organization is a part of the NPCI's formal governance. Nor is there any subcommittee of the board or formal mechanism to consider financial inclusion.

Additionally, programmatic efforts are also an important component of inclusion. Given the difficulties in developing an application that is widely available and accessible, the NPCI developed the BHIM application.[6] This is a reference application to work in low resource settings, available in multiple languages. The design and maintenance of BHIM by the NPCI ensure that it continues to be available to those who need it. This programmatic effort is valuable

[6] BHIM is a low-frill app provided by the government that leverages the UPI.

for inclusion. However, the NPCI needs to be mandated and incentivized to continue engagement with voices and actors who may further widen reach and address problems of ability and access to infrastructure on the ground.

5.5 DISCUSSION: ASSESSING THE NPCI

In this section, we assess the impact and effectiveness of the NPCI from a state digital sovereignty perspective. The empirical evidence and the interviews gathered so far suggest that the NPCI addresses some aspects of digital sovereignty. The fact that the UPI payment rails are hosted and governed within the territory of India offers insulation against denial of technology regimes. However, the fact that the dominant entities on the UPI rails are foreign entities who might leverage their hegemony to enter adjacent areas such as savings, insurance, and loans opens up a new set of challenges from a digital sovereignty perspective for regulators.

An additional concern is that the character of the NPCI, which can be classified as a state-sanctioned monopoly, may result in institutional capture. The NPCI structure has representation from a range of actors. However, over time, representation may exclude those entities (e.g., civil society) that lack the capacity to participate and engage in national-level institutions.

Equally, corporate power may impact the process of inclusion. To address this, RBI has proposed the setting up of New Umbrella Entities (NUEs) for retail payments, which would compete with NPCI, while interoperating with it. If Big Tech companies win the NUE licenses, it might invert the power relationship between banks and Big Tech. Currently, Big Tech companies operate as Over the Top (OTT) players on top of UPI Payment Services provided by banks. If Big Tech NUEs become a reality, banks will become OTT players on Big Tech payment platforms. Concerns have been expressed that since the bidders for NUEs include telecom giant Reliance Jio and firms such as Facebook, Amazon, and Google, the NUEs might undo the work of NPCI in ring-fencing India's digital sovereignty and keeping the power of Big Tech in check (Hariharan, 2021).

In addition, since the NPCI is a government-regulated entity, fears of government surveillance remain. Threats from bad actors should not be leveraged by the state to acquire more power to the detriment of citizens. In particular, executive actions without judicial scrutiny must be guarded against.

Insulating the economy from state sanctions: NPCI controls the switch that routes the vast majority of payments within India. The major foreign payment players in India are the card networks, MasterCard and Visa. If US sanctions pull the plug on these card networks, it would immediately benefit the indigenous RuPay network that is the dominant network with 60% of credit and debit cards issued in India. On UPI, the biggest players are foreign-owned entities such as Google Pay and PhonePe (owned by Walmart), which collectively operate 80% of the UPI transactions. In a worst-case scenario, if they were to be switched off, it would not impact the underlying UPI network, which is controlled by NPCI. Given that UPI is an interoperable network, the cost of switching from one UPI app to another is negligible for customers. It is likely that they will switch to NPCI's BHIM app or one of the 200 plus banks that offer UPI as part of their mobile banking services.

India's ATM networks, Real Time Gross Settlement (RTGS), Immediate Payment System (IMPS), National Automated Clearing House (NACH), and others are also operated by NPCI. Therefore, India is well protected from shocks that might result from sanctions imposed by foreign states.

Deepening Digital Payments: Having control over the payment infrastructure can be helpful for attaining policy goals. A major policy goal in India has been to move the economy away from cash to digital, as this reduces black money transactions and encourages better tax compliance and financial inclusion. High Merchant Discount Rates (MDR), which is the transaction fee that merchants pay to the card networks, has been one of the factors that hindered the growth of digital payment networks. With retailers usually operating on a 5% margin, an MDR of 2–2.5% can cut into their profits. Therefore, retailers would sometimes include this fee in their total bill, which incentivized customers to pay in cash instead of card. Regulatory intervention in 2012 brought down MDR on debit cards from 2.5% to between 0.75 and 1% since debit card transactions are directly debited from users' bank accounts and carry no credit risks (Reserve Bank of India, 2012). MDR on debit cards was further reduced (Reserve Bank of India, 2017). Similarly, NPCI trimmed the ATM interconnect fee in 2012 from INR 8 (0.11 USD) charged by MNC networks to INR 0.45 (0.0061 USD), which enabled greater debit card usage (Baruah, 2016).

Reducing the cost of cash: RBI estimates that the net cost of cash amounts to 1.7% of the GDP, compounded by the possibility of abnormal losses of cash via accidents.

Regulating the domestic payments ecosystem: For context, the Chinese government pulled the plug on Alibaba's IPO because it had become too big to fail (Salmon, 2020). Beijing also tried to bring in interoperability among domestic payment systems through NUCC (Knowledge at Wharton, 2018). Imposing interoperability post-facto is difficult unless the regulator brings a strong hand to bear on the implementation because dominant players have every incentive to thwart its success and retain customers within a closed-loop, non-interoperable network. By design, UPI has avoided this problem. Once a bank connects to the NPCI's UPI backbone, its users could make payments to anyone else on the UPI network. To reduce the systemic risk of any one TPSP becoming too big to fail, NPCI issued a volume cap of 30% for each TPSP (NPCI, 2021) on January 1, 2021 and gave organizations two years to comply. Implementing such rules might have been difficult if NPCI was not run and operated as a DPI.

5.6 RECOMMENDATIONS

Besides sovereign "control," a well-implemented payments infrastructure can have a multiplier effect on an economy and help achieve policy goals such as financial inclusion, better regulation of an economy, and transfer of benefits directly to citizens' bank accounts during pandemics such as COVID-19. Therefore, policymakers may consider implementing a UPI-like payment network, keeping the following factors in mind:

Interoperability: If the policy objective is to give citizens an alternative to cash, interoperability must be strictly enforced. An open-loop network such as UPI, with regulatory oversight and strict action against bad actors, can help countries provide their citizens with an attractive alternative to cash. This involves significant investments in technology, regulatory capacity, branding, marketing, and enforcement.

Multi-stakeholder governance: Interoperability has to work hand in hand with sovereign control over core elements of the stack (e.g., registries and API design) and robust governance of private parties. While the government manages and regulates the payment network, private sector players who build on top of this network need a stable policy regime to enable their investments to be amortized over a reasonable period. Voices of civil society, privacy advocates, and financial inclusion activists must also be factored into the network's roadmap. This includes establishing robust integrity measures and checks as well as feedback loops.

Ownership: The consortium model followed by India (NPCI) with majority of the ownership of the infrastructure company being held by Public Sector Banks is one model that can be considered. In this model, the infrastructure company offers utility pricing and is run as a nonprofit. For-profit entities such as banks and TPAPs operate on top of this network. This enables regulatory oversight and prevention of money laundering and other illegal activities that would be hard to trace in a closed-loop network. If the infrastructure layer is operated by for-profit companies, countries must invest in significant regulatory capacity to ensure speedy dispute resolution and smooth functioning of the network.

Institutional checks and balances: A critical element of sovereign function, especially in the liberal democratic construct, is the requirement to serve and be available to all citizens. Access to payments can be interpreted as a component of life and liberty. Moreover, the unregulated institutions can end up amplifying powerful voices at the expense of others, causing harm in the process. Since payment is a sovereign function and norms of inclusion and access are central to sovereignty, exploring some measure of judicial scrutiny and review of actions may be useful. This may be done through the power of writ in the hands of citizens or widened applicability of legal frameworks.

Risk mitigation: Policymakers must conduct periodic risk assessments of the payment network from technology changes such as crypto currencies and cybersecurity risks.

5.7 CONCLUSION

As a DPI, India's UPI has succeeded beyond most expectations. UPI, which is housed inside the NPCI and governed by the RBI, operates as a nonprofit utility. In the month of August 2021, UPI recorded 3.5 billion transactions worth Rs 639,116 billion (or USD $86 billion). India has the technological, institutional, and regulatory capacity to pull this off with a sizeable domestic market that supports such a massive scale of transactions.

However, many countries might lack such deep state capacities. Such countries could consider a variety of other options. Open-source DPGs such as the MojaLoop project could provide some technological infrastructure. Multilateral agencies could also support the deployment of these infrastructures for specific contexts, and the creation of regulatory capacity. For countries that do not have populations to support large-scale transactions, technology service providers could support cloud-based deployments. These deployments could be based on open standards and APIs that allow payment networks in different countries to work with each other.

India's UPI and NPCI offer a case study that demonstrates that a DPI-based approach can provide a viable alternative to private sector-payment networks. More work is needed to understand the different ways in which countries with and without the capacity to build digital payment systems might need to grapple with these issues of sovereignty. There are emergent efforts to promote DPGs in payments and other areas (Digital Public Goods Alliance, 2021), which may become available. Indeed, the New Delhi Leaders' Declaration acknowledges India's commitment to establish the One Future Alliance, which aims to bring financial and technological capability to countries in need (G20 New Delhi Leaders' Declaration, 2023, p. 22). The hope is that these efforts, in addition to driving resources, can foster a culture of inquiry and engagement.

6

Digital Statecraft of Middle Powers

Tech Landscape and Digital Sovereignty in Brazil and India

Vashishtha Doshi* and Henrique Estides Delgado

6.1 INTRODUCTION

Power, in international relations, comprises autonomy and influence. Influence is the ability to affect others, while autonomy is the ability to prevent others' actions to affect oneself. As argued by Benjamin Cohen, "power must begin with autonomy, which generates a potential for leverage. Influence – the deliberate activation of leverage – should then be thought of as functionally derivative" (2019a, p. 23). In this logic, states must possess autonomy before they can influence those outside their borders. This materializes in the ability to enact policy at home without outside constraint or preserve and enhance a policy space. Autonomy then becomes a necessary, but not sufficient, condition for influence (Cohen, 2019a, p. 23). Great powers such as the US possess both autonomy and influence. However, middle powers such as Brazil and India do not possess both. Rather, they are seeking to enhance autonomy.

In this chapter, we argue that autonomy is a foundational element of digital sovereignty. Autonomy is important to preserve democracy and state security as well as to protect and advance local innovation and economic interests. This chapter argues that in a world of weaponized interdependence, middle powers such as Brazil and India have policy choices that can enhance their autonomy. However, having this policy space is not enough. In order to turn the potential for policy space into policy enactment, domestic politics has to align in a particular way. In this chapter, we argue that when the independence of institutions' interests are taken into or not usurped by the parliamentary process, we observe autonomy inducing policy enactment. We try to explain this using the case study of data localization policy in Brazil and India.

* Vashishtha Doshi would like to thank Henrique Estides Delgado, Aaron Schneider, and SUNY Press for graciously allowing parts of the chapter titled "Building Digital Sovereignty in Middle Powers: The Role of Intended and Spillover Effects" by Vashishtha Doshi from the edited book Popular Sovereignty in the Digital Age (2024) to be reprinted in this chapter.

Farrell and Newman (2019) describe weaponized interdependence as an influence on the entire network of interdependence, arguing that it works through two mechanisms: panopticon effect and chokepoint effect. They classify panopticon effect as such where "states[1] that have physical access to or jurisdiction over hub nodes can use this influence to obtain information passing through the hub," while chokepoint effect involves "states'[2] capacity to limit or penalize use of hubs by third parties" (p. 56).

Middle powers,[3] with mid-level international power, capacity, and influence in the international system (Jordaan, 2003), do not enjoy the systemic ranges of action achieved and maintained by great powers; however, they still have the wherewithal to pursue autonomy and safeguard their sovereignty in narrower measures and fields. The paradigm of economic statecraft has largely focused on the actions, institutional setups, and structural asymmetries enjoyed by the great powers who utilize them for their own foreign policy goals (Narlikar, 2021). Much less attention is given to the role of middle powers such as Brazil and India.

This chapter seeks to answer two broader questions: (1) what agency do middle powers have in a world marked by weaponized interdependence to safeguard their digital sovereignty[4] and (2) how does domestic politics structure the outcome of this agency?

We seek to answer these two global questions using the case studies of India and Brazil. In the realm of technology, both countries are similar in the way their domestic industry is structured, yet we have observed key differences in policy outcomes. This chapter is an example of the agency and policy space middle powers such as Brazil and India have but the enactment is mediated by domestic politics. In short, this study provides an example of the missing link between capability and outcomes in middle powers policy, and how they can achieve autonomy even under conditions of weaponized interdependence.

To answer the above questions, first, we discuss the role of firms in weaponize interdependence by great powers, using the fields of finance and

[1] As of now, according to Farrell and Newman (2019), only the United States possesses both these capacities in the realm of finance and technology.

[2] For example, global financial interbank messaging occurs through the SWIFT network. Due to the preponderance of dollar in the world economy, only the United States can weaponize SWIFT messaging for its own foreign policy goals cutting the target country's access to the entire world's financial network as Iran found out in 2012. Thus, a multimember global organization can be utilized for US foreign policy goals.

[3] We define middle powers using Jordaan's (2003) definition as "states that are neither great nor small in terms of international power, capacity and influence, and demonstrate a propensity to promote cohesion and stability in the world system." We argue, according the framework of Cooper, Higgot, and Nossal (1993) and Holbraad (1986), that middle powers policy behavior is a product of their contextually located deliberate action emanating from their position in the world order.

[4] Utilizing Pohle and Thiel's (2020, p. 8) framework, we define the concept of "digital sovereignty" as the "idea that a nation or region should be able to take autonomous actions and decisions regarding its digital infrastructures and technology deployment."

digital technology as examples. Second, we examine the variables along which middle powers can attain autonomy in the above two fields, thus strengthening their digital sovereignty. Third, we explore how the range of policy outcomes varies among middles powers due to the constraints and opportunities emanating from domestic politics.

Utilizing the framework set forth by Farrell and Newman (2019) and Cartwright (2020), we argue that great powers weaponize interdependence through their firms. They internationalize state power by exercising jurisdictional authority over their market-dominant firms. Within this overarching architecture, middle powers have agency to seek autonomy for themselves along a set of variables that helps block the most adverse effect of weaponized interdependence, that is, the chokepoint effect. We argue that data localization is one such policy through which middle powers can achieve autonomy from weaponized interdependence. Data localization policies help eliminate the chokepoint effect by keeping the jurisdiction over the stock of data at home. We argue that data localization then becomes a necessary but not sufficient condition on the path to state-led digital sovereignty. In this chapter, we inquire the reason for observed variation in data localization policy in India and Brazil despite similar domestic interests.

We define data localization as "mandatory requirements of local storage of data, whether exclusively or in the form of mirror data copies, thus fundamentally steering, and altering, data flows" (Bailey & Parsheera, 2018).[5] Brazil has no data localization policies, whereas India has a fractured outcome with sectoral data localization (Burman & Sharma, 2021).

In August 2023, India passed its Digital Personal Data Protection Act (DPDP Act). Through this act, India cemented the debate on data localization in the country. This act allows for cross-border transfers of data to all countries unless specifically restricted by the Indian government. Thus, India's data protection bill is now in line with Brazil's in removing almost all barriers to free cross-border flow of data. However, the key difference that remains and reinforces this paper's argument is that in passing the Bill, the Indian government did not usurp the data localization mandates set by sectoral regulators.[6] Section 16 (2) of the DPDP Act states, "Nothing contained in this section

[5] In practice, policies with regards to data localization differ widely. For example, China's data localization policies require Apple to store all iCloud data not only in China but on servers run by Chinese state-owned entities (Nicas et al., 2021). In Russia, data localization in practice means storing of Russians' data on servers located in Russia, but not necessarily on servers owned and operated by Russian state-owned enterprises (SOEs) as in China (Reuters, 2021). India's data localization mandates require only certain forms of data to be stored within India; however, the data is allowed to be transferred abroad for processing (Burman & Sharma, 2021).

[6] The DPDP Act continues to uphold sectoral data localization mandates set forth by the Reserve Bank of India (RBI), Securities and Exchange Bureau of India (SEBI), Insurance Regulatory and Development Authority of India (IRDAI), Ministry of Consumer Affairs (MCA), and the Department of Telecommunications (DoT).

shall restrict the applicability of any law for the time being in force in India that provides for a higher degree of protection for or restriction on transfer of personal data by a Data Fiduciary outside India in relation to any personal data or Data Fiduciary or class thereof." Industrial sectors can still maintain their own sectoral data localization mandates.

We argue that these divergent outcomes in data localization policies between Brazil and India stem from the difference in whether the interest of independent institutions was incorporated into the decision-making process. India's sectoral data localization stems from independent institutions allowed to exercise their jurisdictional authority without explicit interference from the political process. However, in Brazil, independent institutions' sectoral interests were subordinated to those of the Brazilian congress.

In this chapter, we argue that data localization is one such autonomy-inducing policy choice to enhance digital sovereignty. However, the availability of data localization policy is not enough. Domestic politics must align in a particular way to enact them through meaningful digital statecraft. The novelty of our argument is that we examine the role of middle powers in the world under weaponized interdependence. We argue that middle powers face two sets of constraints – the international sphere and domestic sphere (politics and institutional design) – that eventually determine the outcomes of their sovereignty enhancing policies.

6.2 US HEGEMONY IN FINANCE AND TECHNOLOGY

Our theoretical argument begins with an emphasis on the role of US hegemony. This hegemony is manifested here as extraterritorial exercise of digital sovereignty at global scale. In this section, we argue that the US – and as of now only it[7] – exercises hegemony in fields of finance and technology that are analogous and important for comparison. Section 6.3 will address how to limit this in order to build up the digital sovereignty of Brazil and India. We begin this section by listing the variables and mechanisms through which the US exercises power in the field of finance benefiting from the centrality

[7] Even though China is to some extent replicating the US strategy and challenging the latter's monopoly in these areas, the very consternation provoked by Chinese incursions is an example of an exception that proves the rule. China has reached autonomy and has different tools of influence, but the US still is in a different level in the fields of finance and technology. The other great power, the mighty political and economic network that is the European Union (EU), also has some important firms that serve as tools to project influence, but is still having to deal with the fact that European states, firms, and citizens are "gradually losing control over their data, over their capacity for innovation, and over their ability to shape and enforce legislation in the digital environment" (European Parliament, 2020, p. 1). The EU is still trying to secure "strategic autonomy in the digital field," something discussed around three building blocks: "(i) building a data framework; (ii) promoting a trustworthy environment, and (iii) adapting competition and regulatory rules" (p. 5).

of US firms in the global financial system, which may end up enjoying what this book considers as a form of corporate digital sovereignty or even acting as proxies for state digital sovereigns (Belli, 2022). The discussion on finance will be brief as finance is not the core topic of this chapter but a useful comparison. We then discuss the variable through which power resides in the technology industry and the centrality of US firms within it. Finally, we discuss how the US externalizes its power through the centrality of US technology firms.

The US can exercise influence through the networks that have been formed because of the dominant role of its firms in fields of both finance and technology (Babic et al., 2017; Birch et al., 2021; Farrell & Newman, 2019; Starrs, 2013). There is now substantial research on how the US is able to exercise influence over the international financial system through two distinct actors: public institutions (de Goede, 2021; Helleiner, 2019; Murau et al., 2021; Schwartz, 2019) and private activity (Fichtner, 2016, Fichtner & Heemskerk, 2020; Petry et al., 2019; Winecoff, 2015).[8] US centrality in both is reinforcing. For the purposes of our study, we highlight how the US is able to exert influence through the activities of its firms. The international financial system is a complex network that is hierarchical in nature, with the only core nodes being the US and UK (Fichtner, 2016; Oatley et al., 2013; Winecoff, 2015). This high level of international market dominance coupled with US authority over domestic firms allows the US to internationalize state influence through its firms (Cartwright, 2020).

Centrality of US firms exists in the technology sector as well (Starrs, 2013, p. 822). Out of the top 100 technology companies in the world, 35 are US firms (Forbes, 2019). Further, out of the top 100 websites visited in the world 60 of them are US firms' websites (Routley, 2019). None are Brazilian or Indian firms (Jawaid, 2023). "A huge fraction of the global data traffic is channeled through the servers of a handful of US companies" (Farrell & Newman, 2019, p. 64). Some estimates suggest that up to 70% of global web traffic passes through servers in Northern Virginia (Mekouar, 2020). Similarly, Google dominates worldwide search engine market share (over 85% market share). Facebook and other US firms dominate social

[8] It is interesting to note here that another kind of authority is emerging through the creation of private standardization bodies that regulate by proxy entire sectors (Belli, 2022; Bruner, 2008). The global regulation of credit risk through the creation of private credit rating agencies and the regulation of the domain name industry through the creation of the Internet Corporation for Assigned Names and Numbers (ICANN) are just some of the examples (Sinclair, 2008; Bruner, 2008). However, it is important to note that home states of these private bodies can and do utilize the centrality of these private actors' regulatory position to satisfy state goals. For example, despite ICANN's removal from under the aegis of US Department of Commerce, it is still subject to regulation by the California attorney general's office and all federal laws that apply to nonprofit entities registered in the US. Should there be a need, it is not inconceivable to imagine US government mandating ICANN to deregister an enemy country's websites.

media market share. Further, as these firms grow bigger, they will funnel more global data within their ambit. Majority of these firms' business model is dependent on extraction of value from personal data processing (Birch et al., 2021; Zuboff, 2019a). This requires the immense collection and storage of personal data, and then the ability to monetize it for profits (Birch et al., 2021, p. 9).

The global dependence on US technology firms, their need to accumulate data, coupled with US legal framework – which includes the lack of a general data protection law matched with legislation allowing both international surveillance and access of data treated or stored domestically and abroad by US firms – allows the US government to create a panopticon effect on global information flows.[9] As stated by General Hayden, former CIA director, "because of the nature of global communications, we are playing with a tremendous home field advantage, and we need to exploit this edge. We also need to protect this edge and those who provide it." (Hayden, 2006).

The Snowden leaks revealed how the US utilizes the dominant position of its internet firms to conduct mass surveillance in the world. At the time, there was an upheaval in Brazilian politics and diplomacy. In wake of the Snowden leaks, President Dilma Rousseff wanted all internet companies operating in Brazil to store data of Brazilian clients in the country (i.e., data localization) (Douglas, 2013). Cartwright (2020) provides many examples of how the US government has utilized the dominant position of its technology companies to create a panopticon effect. For some analysts, unless there is a decline in the usage of US digital technology companies for most of the global internet traffic and personal data, it seems highly unlikely that US's panopticon effects can be curtailed in any meaningful way. There is also the pathway for different jurisdictions to design stronger and better enforced regulation on local data, matched with enhanced investments in cybersecurity that curtail data leaks and cyberespionage. As Farrell and Newman (2019) describe – for reasons of the US's own industrial policy goals together with specificities of history and context – the US government has not yet turned this advantage of panopticon effect into more than small-scale chokepoint effect. However, it is not an inconceivable scenario where one day the US could order its firms to exercise a chokepoint effect on the data of extraterritorial entities (whether it be public or private).[10] As discussed earlier, the requisite recipe – concentration of data on US soil, US firm's market dominance, and legal framework – is in place to exercise this option at large scale with the potential of major disruption to others' national security, as well as economic and human rights.

[9] See Stored Wire and Electronic Communications and Transactional Records Access, 18 U.S.C. § 2701 (1986) and FISA Amendments Act Reauthorization Act of 2012.

[10] This scenario is actually not very far from what happened when Android was prohibited from supplying software to Huawei in 2019 (Quinn, 2019).

While we are not arguing that data in the possession of or passing through US technology firms is the sole basis of US's ability to weaponize interdependence, we believe that having US technology firms at the core of the global data economy – some providing services presented as "free" but in reality paid with data – is one of the ways in which the US maintains the upper hand in the digital age. Moreover, data concentration follows from such centrality and makes it impossible for other firms to compete.[11] Through a combination of centrality of US firms, provisions (and practice) for US government agencies to access data that flows within the ambit of these firms and willingness of the US to utilize this privilege to achieve state goals has meant that the US enjoys extraterritorial projection of its digital hegemony while other countries face constraints on their digital sovereignty stemming from this. Moreover, the levels of data concentration in a few US tech giants are such unsurmountable barriers to entry that even in US home markets other firms find it hard to compete. Hence, awareness about the importance to break these barriers and level the playing field are behind the efforts to enact data localization measures.

Currently, we can think of several other ways through which the US can weaponize interdependence.[12] For example, most of the world's location-based devices are connected to the US's GPS system. It is not inconceivable that the US can block a country's access to the GPS system.[13] Another variable is undersea cables. A significant amount of data that passes through US firms' servers in the US goes through undersea cables. It is possible that the US can utilize this privileged position to block access to these cables for certain entities. Protection of undersea cable is such a significant part of US geopolitical strategy that the country even forced a joint Facebook–Google undersea cable to not have a landing site in Hong Kong. The US State Department's Clean Network, an initiative publicly delineated in 2020, provides insight into the technology industry variables that the US considers geopolitically relevant. In short, there exists *potentiality* for the US to weaponize interdependence along other variables of the technology industry as well.

The above discussion delineates how the US exercises both forms of power – autonomy and influence – in the fields of finance and technology. And, in turn, middle powers have responded with measures to counter some

[11] See reasoning behind EU efforts to "open" access to US tech giants' data bases via the Digital Service Act and Digital Markets Act.

[12] Middle powers have instituted measures ranging from data localization to nationalizing the cloud to GPS alternatives (see footnote 14) to creating alternatives to SWIFT (such as China's CIPS and Russia's SPFS).

[13] In order to minimize the potentiality of weaponization of interdependence by the US, countries such as Russia (GLONASS), China (BeiDou), and India (NavIC) have deployed their own global navigation satellite system (GNSS) analogous to the US's GPS system and mandate that mobile phones sold in the country either have to run on their GNSS or both GPS and domestic GNSS. Russia ("GLONASS to be," 2013); China (Global Times, 2020).

of these variables of hegemony such as developing their own alternatives to GPS, nationalizing the cloud, developing more subsea cables, and promoting data localization measures. In this section, we have focused on the role of US firms as conduits through which the US state can exercise power and highlighted some of the measures undertaken by middle powers. Combining the concepts of Farrell and Newman (2019) and Cartwright (2020), we argue that the high international market dominance of US firms in finance and technology combined with US jurisdictional authority over them allows the US to weaponize interdependence (both panopticon and chokepoint effects) over the entire network. In Section 6.3, we begin to look at how middle powers operate under this environment.

6.3 CONSTRAINTS AND OPPORTUNITIES FOR MIDDLE POWERS

In this section, utilizing the "dual faced nature of power" framework, we discuss the opportunities and constraints faced by middle powers as it relates to US hegemony. We briefly discuss the strategies middle powers utilized in the field of finance. Then, we argue middle powers have similar opportunities in the field of technology. Finally, we look at one such opportunity – data localization – and how it can enhance the autonomy of middle powers.

Power hierarchies pervade the international system (Lake, 2011), in which a set of countries are engaged in subordinate relationships with the hegemon (Lake, 2007). International hierarchies exist in various facets of the international economic system as well (Cohen, 2000). If hierarchy was a pyramid with the US at its apex, the countries that occupy space between the apex and bottom would classify as middle powers. Our understanding of middle powers is not that dissimilar to how semi-peripheries are described in world systems theory (Wallerstein, 1976). Middle powers are still engaged in a subordinate relationship with the hegemon but have significant market dominance in their home countries and presence in the countries surrounding them (Wallerstein, 1976, p. 464). The difference is that instead of deterministic outcomes – derived from an "antipossibilist" policy orientation as once criticized by Hirschman (1980) – we emphasize further possibility of agency and statecraft as able to create apertures and innovation in the system.

Considering the dual faced nature of power – autonomy and influence – these countries certainly cannot exercise influence in fields of finance and technology like the hegemon. However, due to their large internal markets, relevant levels of human capital, and financial capacity they are not completely subordinated either.[14] They still retain a modicum of agency

[14] Countries such as Mexico, Brazil, India, and Indonesia would be perfect example of such middle powers. They each have over $1 trillion in GDP, a large population, the requisite technical know-how, and large internal markets.

(Narlikar, 2021). This means that middle powers can ward off potentially adverse effects emanating from the panopticon and chokepoint effects exercised by the hegemon on the network. However, they are not able to influence the entire network as the hegemon does. Their power is thus only limited to autonomy and not influence, that is, middle powers can carve out policy spaces in a world of weaponized interdependence should they want to bear the costs. In essence, they have the potential to safeguard their sovereignty but not have the ability to undermine the sovereignty of others by influencing the network.

Middle powers have utilized defensive financial statecraft to shield the domestic economy from external financial pressure (Armijo & Katada, 2014a, p. 8). They have utilized the strategies of capital controls, state-owned banks, and foreign currency reserve accumulation "to shield their country not against a particular foreign state but rather against systemic influences, whether coming from global markets or from the rules and institutions of global financial governance" (Armijo & Katada, 2014a, p. 169). The authors label this as "defensive but systemic financial statecraft" (Armijo & Katada, 2014b). As we have seen before, US financial institutions are central to the global financial system, and US interests are executed through them. Thus, even if the actions (under the measures that constituted systemic but defensive financial statecraft) were not targeted against a particular government, they amounted to carving out policy space (autonomy) from the weaponized interdependence effects of the US.

In the technology industry, some of the most prominent variables through which countries have sought to limit the effect of US's weaponized interdependence include: promoting data localization (Burman & Sharma, 2021), developing other GNSS, blocking access to US firms in the home market, indigenizing the cloud, and developing an entire tech ecosystem largely independent of the US system as in the case of China. Among middle powers, Brazil partnered with Europe to create the subsea cable connection for internet traffic called EllaLink that connects the two continents directly to bypass US surveillance (González, 2017). The list of variables is by no means exhaustive, but indicative of how countries have sought to undermine the effects of US's weaponized interdependence in digital technologies.

For the purposes of this chapter, we are looking at one variable – data localization – and how it connects to US's weaponized interdependence.[15] Countries that enact data localization policies can jurisdictionally assert control of the data stored within the country, which means that the access to and processing of data would be governed by local laws. The physical and legal

[15] The US is used here as an example, but the same set of weaponization of interdependence dynamics can be potentially enacted by other foreign powers. China is the closest that comes to US's example, but certainly there can be more.

shifting of jurisdiction of the data from the US to the home country allows for the minimization of US extraterritorial reach.

Data localization would severely limit or remove the ability of foreign states to block access to data generated by the countries themselves.[16] Key mechanism through which the chokepoint effect works – states' capacity to limit or penalize use of hubs by third parties (Farrell & Newman, 2019) – would be limited as the jurisdictional control over hubs of information would become either transient or nullified. If the dominant internet firms in the concerned countries are still US firms, data localization policies would largely limit although perhaps not block entirely the panopticon effect as the US can still conduct surveillance operations through these firms. Putting this in generalized economic terms, the US would still be able to access the flow of data (panopticon effect), but data localization policies would limit access to the stock of data, thus curtailing the chokepoint effect. But, if the dominant internet firms in the concerned countries are national champions, then both the chokepoint effect and the panopticon effect would be curtailed or eliminated as hubs of information flow would be outside of US jurisdiction and so will be the storage of the stock of information.

The physical location of where data is stored is so important that in fact there are proposals in the US congress pushing for the US to follow explicit data localization strategies while using US economic diplomacy to advocate for the opposite abroad. Thus, access to global personal data is important not only for US industrial policy but also for the exercise of weaponized interdependence over the network. Hence, data localization has become the heart of global information geopolitics. Thus, we argue that attaining digital sovereignty for middle powers would be impossible without the curtailment or elimination of the most basic exposure to weaponized interdependence, that is, the chokepoint effect. Data localization policies then become necessary but not sufficient conditions to attain digital sovereignty for nation-states.

[16] From an economic point of view, data localization would help ameliorate some of the inequity that is generated due to the enormous value captured within servers located in the US servers while not paying any taxes in the countries where data is extracted. However, it seems that countries such as India who are putting in mixed data localization measures are not intent on forcing foreign cloud companies (who host would most of the data on their servers located in India) to share their data with local market players, so that the local players are able to extract value and grow. But, rather, they are mandating localization because of lack of access to data (if needed) in criminal investigations (since the US MLAT process is very arduous) and for national security rationales. For countries such as India, it is more about ease of access (a national security concern) than an economic value extraction concern. Please see page 41–42, Report of the Joint Committee on the Personal Data Protection Bill, 2019 published in December 2021. In all, in both India and Brazil, the institutional framework of data privacy would need to be reviewed for a further step of creating data pools to be accessible and commercially exploitable for the advancement of local firms, as well as research and policy institutions.

6.4 OVERVIEW OF DIGITAL TECHNOLOGY INDUSTRIES IN INDIA AND BRAZIL

In the area of digital technologies, a characteristic of middle powers is manifested by the presence of relevant domestic players in a given industry. These countries can carve out some space for their firms at the frontier of the expanding digital economy. A closer look at the landscape reveals how a pattern of partial autonomy emerges, one in which business sectoral interests are essentially similar between India and Brazil.

Tech landscape in any country can be analyzed at three levels: infrastructure, multi-sector platforms, and single-sector platforms. While this classification is not perfect, it does allow us to group services provided by different internet companies into relevant and comparable bins across countries. Before beginning the discussion of these three layers, it is important to note that the boundaries between these layers are distinct but porous, activities of firms can often include functions in all three layers. For example, in general, there has been trend toward vertical integration between access providers and content and app providers at least since the late 2000s (Guo, et al., 2010).

Infrastructure refers to the core of technology, the backbone on which other services rest. This includes not only telecom providers but also core operating system providers, cloud service providers, and logistical providers (UNCTAD, 2019). It also includes the "under the hood rails" of certain key economic activities such as payments. The middle level is what we colloquially think of as multi-sector platforms. They provide a sort of virtual meeting place (or marketplace) for actors to interact and conduct commerce (Belli, 2019). Finally, the outer layer is composed of other consumer facing digital services that are single-sector platforms.

Some key roles of platforms are: the ability to create and shape markets, benefit from "network effects" (where the value of the service increases with the number of users), and capturing and monetizing value through data accumulation (Belli, 2022). Using this standard definition of platforms begs for further explanation about the distinction between our usage of the term "multi-sector platforms," and "single-sector platforms." After all, both are consumer facing. However, there are distinct analytical differences. In this chapter, we refer to multi-sector platforms as the (i) e-commerce companies involved in the transaction of a wide range of products and services and (ii) platforms of digital banking, financing, and instant payment. Often (i) has (ii) as an important and growing part of their business. Platforms – both the internationally established large ones such as Walmart and Mercado Libre and the rising ones still inscribed to a domestic market such as Magalu – are either actually or potentially at a higher level of data-driven power than other consumer facing applications and websites that are single-sector platforms.

Moreover, platforms are at a lower level than core infrastructure, even though some players at the core also occupy multi-sector platforms and single-sector platforms services. For example, there is certain level of irreplaceability that happens due to positive feedback loops between organization of consumer behavioral data across different sectors on the one hand and data accumulation and targeting on the other by Amazon that is not replicated by Uber or Lyft. Khan (2017) argues that Amazon's structural dominance stems from, inter alia, expansion into multiple business lines (p. 754), its logistics dominance and leveraging of that to disadvantage rivals (p. 774),[17] and premature acquisition of rival firms (p. 768). Further, regulators have found that once Amazon moves into a particular business line it disadvantages sellers on its platform and organizes consumer behavior toward its own product by gleaning off consumer data on their rivals' products, eventually leading to rivals leaving that business (Mattioli, 2020). This entire hydra-like business strategy is cemented by accumulation and targeting of data that organizes consumer behavior in ever more sectors on Amazon's platform, further entrenching the irreplaceability of Amazon. Nothing of this sort exists with, say, a company like Uber.

Uber is a single-sector platform. Consumers are able to switch out of Uber relatively easily, should they want to, into a rival service without facing significant and sometimes irreplaceable switching costs that they would with Amazon. Thus, in our classification, Amazon is a multi-sector platform, whereas services such as Uber are single-sector platforms. This distinction between the traditional broader definition of platforms and how we outline their functioning is important to keep in mind as it highlights an essential difference between digital market players in India and Brazil, which we will outline in the following sections.

6.4.1 India's Tech Landscape

India's tech landscape is populated with a collection of US big tech firms, Indian conglomerates, a vibrant start-up ecosystem, and digital public infrastructures (DPIs).[18] DPIs, as the term suggests, represent the digital variant of nonexcludable and non-rivalrous public infrastructures (Sukumar, 2021). Like other infrastructures, DPIs are the tools and systems required to make digital life function. US big tech firms are the only ones that span all three layers of the tech landscape in India.

6.4.1.1 *Infrastructure Level*

Three US tech giants dominate in India: Google, Facebook, and Amazon. They provide cloud infrastructure for businesses and the government. Google Cloud and Amazon Web Services (AWS) dominate India's cloud market.

[17] The EU and Italian regulators judge this practice anticompetitive and hit Amazon with massive fines for this precise reason (Bodoni et al., 2021).

[18] We define infrastructures as the technologies and systems necessary for society to function. Infrastructures are backbones on top of which other services can be provided.

Cloud, despite the oxymoronic name, is located in a physical environment. It requires servers, coolers, and an entire industrial setup. Without cloud services, it would be impossible to imagine a networked tech economy where even small players can rent space on these servers to start their online presence. AWS has the largest contract with Indian governmental agencies.

Finally, Google's Android is the dominant mobile operating system in India. Most Indians who have a connection to the internet do so through their mobile phones. Google's Android has a 96% market share. This means that Indian businesses must continuously monitor their compliance with Google's standards, which indirectly allows Google to play the standard-setting role within India's technology industry. Furthermore, this dominance in operating system deployment allows Google to exclusively deploy its platforms.

The only Indian companies that possess infrastructural roles in the technology sector are telecom operators Reliance Jio and Bharti Airtel. The third telecommunications company – Vodafone Idea – is still majorly owned by UK's Vodafone. These three telecom operators deliver internet connection to most Indians. In fact, Reliance Jio has been credited for single handedly bringing 400 million previously disconnected Indians online in a span of two years and for dropping India data charges to the lowest in the world (Purnell, 2018).

However, such achievements are not enough and do not cover enough issue areas to really propel the vision of Digital India. This ambitious agenda stands on three legs: Jan Dhan (roughly translated to mass financial inclusion), Aadhaar (unique identity provision to every Indian to avail of government services), and Mobile. India calls this the JAM trinity (Ravi, 2018). To provide infrastructural support for the J & A aspect of the JAM trinity, the government decided to step in with the provision of DPI. This is also colloquially referred to as the India Stack.[19]

6.4.1.2 *Multi-Sector Platform Level*

The second layer of the tech landscape is populated by multi-sector platforms. The whole idea of an internet platform is to provide centralized spaces for multiple parties to interact in a trusting manner. However, platforms do not act in a neutral manner (Mattioli, 2020). Platform power rests on *data-centric models* and *network effects* (Rolf & Schindler, 2023). Even if they are providing a

[19] "IndiaStack is a set of APIs that allows governments, businesses, startups and developers to utilize an unique digital infrastructure to solve India's hard problems towards presence-less, paperless, and cashless service delivery. It consists of 4 layers: presenceless layer, paperless layer, cashless layer, and consent layer. Presenceless layer is where a universal biometric digital identity allows people to participate in any service from anywhere in the country. The paperless layer is where digital records move with an individual's digital identity, eliminating the need for massive amount of paper collection and storage. Cashless layer is where a single interface to all the country's bank accounts and wallets to democratize payments. Consent layer allows data to move freely and securely to democratize the market for data." For more on India Stack, please see www.indiastack.org/.

service presented as free, multi-sector platform companies collect vast troves of data on the user, the access to which they sell to third parties and use for many purposes. The more users utilize a multi-sector platform, the more data a multi-sector platform collects, which in turn allows it to outcompete rivals through better product design and more efficient operations. Network effects boosted by 'first-scaler advantage' propel market dominance (Khan, 2017). Once achieved in one sector, market dominance enables companies to influence other sectors through vertical and horizontal integrations. They can leverage their existing user base and accumulated data intelligence to enter new markets. This market power is further entrenched if multi-sector platforms end up providing infrastructural services. As noted earlier, four US firms occupy both spaces in India. However, Indian players do not have a significant presence at the platform level of the tech landscape.

Facebook and its subsidiary WhatsApp's largest user base is in India. This means most Indians converge on a singular digital interface daily and communicate with each other. If users want to switch to another messaging platform, it becomes harder as they would lose access to all their centralized spaces for connections. This captive audience in India and elsewhere gives FB immense user data and an attractive centralized portal for other service providers to link up. Similarly, Amazon and Walmart not only connect buyers with sellers on their portals, but they are able to offer other services that keep users engaged on their respective multi-sector platforms. "Currently, Walmart-owned Flipkart and Amazon dominate the Indian ecommerce space with around 60% share between them. Reliance is a distant third" (The Economic Times, 2023).

Finally, even when these multi-sector platforms allow third-party business to link and do commerce, the multi-sector platforms eventually learn enough about their third-party sellers' services and mimic to undercut them (Mattioli, 2020). This centralizes consumer behavior toward the multi-sector platform. For example, in India, Amazon offers payment services (Amazon Pay), operates an ecommerce platform (Amazon.in), is one of the largest players in the cloud (AWS), offers insurance (Amazon Insurance), operates a digital banking platform, offers a food service delivery, and so on. All these services are then discounted for its Indian Prime subscribers. Thus, once an Indian user enters the Amazon ecosystem, it would be harder for them to escape for Amazon has now become their banker, payment processor, insurer, food deliverer, grocer, and shopper.

Similarly, Google's infrastructural dominance through the Android operating system allows it to nudge users toward using Google Suite of services and the Google Play Store. All Android phones come preloaded with apps ranging from the functional (such as Gmail, Google Drive, and Google Calendar) to the financial (such as Google Pay). Further, to utilize an Android phone, users must create a Google Play account to download other apps. This gives Google immense leverage over consumers and businesses (obey Google mandates or face being deplatformed). In this way, Google gets to set the terms of access and exclusion to most internet-connected Indians and Indian businesses (Kalra & Bhattacharjee, 2020). Without access to Google Play Store, app-based businesses cannot function, and most Indians are only connected to the internet through mobile phones and their apps.

6.4.1.3 *Single-Sector Platform Level*

At the single-sector platforms level, except for the payment space, India's technological landscape resembles a vibrant competitive market. As one journalist remarked, "this is Indian tech's Belle Epoque." There are homegrown apps in fierce competition with foreign customer-facing apps.

For example, while Netflix and Disney's Hotstar are dominant in the streaming services, Indian players such as Eros with their extensive library of local content have begun to carve out space for themselves. In the education technology sector, homegrown, venture-capital backed BYJU'S is one of the most valued firms in the world. Similarly, the music streaming service provider Gaana now has more listeners than Spotify. At this level of tech landscape, some Indian firms are not just dominating the local market but are competing with Silicon Valley and Chinese behemoths in overseas markets. For example, OLA, a ride sharing app, is now available in Australia, New Zealand, and the United Kingdom. Similarly, OYO rooms, a hotels-aggregator, has successfully expanded in the US.

Just by looking at market share, this space looks like a competitive environment between homegrown startups and American tech giants. Finally, the Indian state does not have any DPI at this level.

6.4.2 Brazil's Tech Landscape

This section overviews the industrial organization of the data economy in Brazil and traces the relationship between economic statecraft and the structure of domestic capital as this relationship evolves and carves out some room for market participation in Brazil's dependent development model–that is, one that is dependent on foreign players. Special attention is given to businesses to which data localization is potentially relevant, as is the case of digital financial transactions and e-commerce in Brazil.

6.4.2.1 *Infrastructure Level*

Brazil is highly reliant on US and EU core-level providers. In cloud computing, the demand for cloud services rose significantly due to the COVID-19 pandemic, speeding up a trajectory where key players are well positioned to turn products into services, create revenue, and further feed the data economy with granular information. The threefold basic division of cloud computing is represented by the provision of Infrastructure as a Service (IaaS), Platform as a Service (PaaS), and Software as a Service (SaaS). The five largest players in the world include four US companies – Amazon (through AWS),

Microsoft (through Azure), Google Cloud, and IBM – and the Chinese firm Alibaba Cloud. Together, these five are reported to have two-thirds of the world's cloud infrastructure services market.[20] While Amazon dominates IaaS by far – and IaaS is often regarded as the core of cloud and its most promising part – Microsoft is the leader in SaaS, where it is followed by a group of the traditional Silicon Valley players plus Germany's SAP. The main players of cloud computing in Brazil are the same.

While in Europe there is some action to promote local players in cloud computing, that understanding was not reached in Brazil yet. In Europe, the Gaia-X project seemed to add a twist in the EU's long-lasting strategy to simply regulate the digital world. With Gaia-X, the EU affirms that valuable cloud contracts and data should remain within the bloc for both security and economic reasons. Even though the pursuit of data sovereignty through the networked system of cloud providers envisioned by Gaia-X extends participation to players from outside Europe, it is carving out some space for local players, including European players active in the telecom sector in Brazil. Telecom providers such as TIM (from Italy) and network infrastructure providers such as Ericsson (from Sweden) are involved with Gaia-X. They are also involved with the implementation of 5G, which has a cloud-native architecture. TIM for instance is migrating all content from its Brazilian data centers to cloud operated by Oracle and Microsoft.

In all, EU's General Data Protection Regulation (GDPR) and Gaia-X initiatives have a demonstration effect on digital policies in Brazil, not only serving as an inspiration for different actors interested in strengthening the Brazilian digital economy, but also allowing normative diffusion to occur through market leaders operating in both EU and Brazilian markets. In addition, EU's global digital footprint is also enhanced by norm-building exercises such as the "EU-Brazil Digital Economy Dialogue" (European Commission, n. d.). In practical terms, EU's digital sovereignty practices have considerable influence in Brazil. There is also infrastructure underway to serve this influence strategy. In 2021, the submarine cable EllaLink – financed by the EU with the explicit purpose to link the bloc with Brazil to bypass US surveillance – was inaugurated. This new network connects, among other things, cloud services on both sides of the Atlantic.

In the area of mobile operating systems, similar to India, Google's Android is the dominant player in Brazil with 81% of market share. The remaining market share is mostly controlled by Apple's iOS. In 2022, 62% of Brazilians access the internet exclusively through their mobile phones (CGI, 2023). This means Brazilian app providers must continuously monitor their compliance with the standard-setter Google. This is exacerbated by the zero-rating practice that provides free internet access to users under the condition of limited access to a small number of websites or subsidy via ads. The main player is

[20] Microsoft, Salesforce, and Adobe are leading the SaaS (Software as a Service) cloud market.

Facebook, which attempts to set the standard for communication in a country while collecting personal data from zero-rating users. While India promotes a stronger defense of network neutrality on the basis of which Facebook's zero-rating service has been rejected, Brazilian regulators have been adopting the controversial rationale that zero-rating does not imply a violation of network neutrality (see Belli, 2019).

Finally, nowadays Brazilian telecom has three large players at the national level: they are subsidiaries of Italian (TIM), Spanish (Telefónica), and Mexican (América Móvil) multinationals.

6.4.2.2 *Multi-Sector Platform Level*

While Brazil is not an exception to foreign dominance in the infrastructure area, local platforms associated with big tech players have carved out some space for themselves in e-commerce and fintech. For example, Magazine Luiza, a retailer with a much bigger market share than Amazon in Brazil, uses Google Cloud technologies to boost its e-commerce platform.

Fintech is advancing in Brazil under the guidance of the Central Bank of Brazil. While the country's central bank allowed Facebook's WhatsApp to initiate financial transactions, it granted permission only after the creation of the Brazilian central bank's own instant-payment system Pix. Recognizing WhatsApp's largest user bases are located in India and Brazil, where WhatsApp's first-mover advantage could potentially lead to its dominance in fintech, the Central Bank of Brazil helped promote broader competition in this area by launching Pix first.

In terms of access to bank accounts, most providers are local. Although fintech expanded in Brazil, 40% of its economically active population still did not have a bank account before the 2020 pandemic. That was drastically changed during the COVID-19 pandemic when welfare payments were attached to the creation of a digital bank account in a state-owned bank CAIXA. It remains to be seen if such digital bank accounts will be used in the future as a comprehensive move toward digital banking and financing in the country.

The Central Bank of Brazil is overseeing three important developments in the country's financial system: the creation of Pix, the issuance of digital currency by 2024, and the Open Banking environment. The latter is another pro-competitive policy reform to reduce information asymmetry among market participants through the sharing of data, thus facilitating innovative digital financial services.

Brazilian platforms differ from their Indian counterparts in certain aspects. For instance, although the supermarket/grocery side of retail is controlled by French players Carrefour and Casino, both online retail and delivery services are dominated by Brazilian players. Firms such as Magazine Luiza, Via (through brands such as Casas Bahia), B2W (through brands such as Americanas and Submarino), and the Argentine Mercado Libre are competitive, even though Amazon arrives with a capitalization that only the world's largest retailer has. However, these online retailors all rely on US technologies to structure their e-commerce platforms. In all, local firms are once more trading "the rents associated with state protection of the local market for those associated with their transnational corporate allies' proprietary technology and global market power" (Evans, 1995, p. 16). However, this time, instead of the state offering protection in the local market, what local firms have to offer is their market shares based on a history of accumulating data and information about the local consumer base.

In the immediate post-WWII era, the Brazilian government deliberately aligned domestic policies with international capital within a growing neoliberal context, allowing Brazilian private capital to associate with leading transnational corporations that would retain the lion's share. Even though this association is once more marked by imbalance, it allows these local businesses to flourish into the next phase of capitalism, evolving into a full-fledged digital economy. What were automotive products in the 1950s and 1960s,[21] now is the data-driven and ICT-controlled knowledge economy in which finance and digital technologies are increasingly merging.

Brazil and India remain *intermediate* cases between predatory states and efficacious developmental states as studied by Evans (1995). They are *intermediate* cases because some "examples of successful intervention could be found even if the broader state apparatus did not approximate the developmental state model" (Haggard, 2018, p. 42).

6.4.2.3 *Single-Sector Platform Level*

At this level, Brazil's situation is similar to India's in terms of the local competitiveness and greater margin for innovation. Customer-facing apps are created on a competitive basis both to reach niche markets and to compete in larger ones. Even though the most used apps belong or end up being purchased by big techs, venture capital still boosts some local apps. However, different from India, fewer apps have reached one billion dollars in value in Brazil. Among those that do, there is one for general delivery (Loggi), one specifically for food delivery (iFood), one for car hailing (99), which was acquired by the Chinese vehicle-for-hire company Didi in 2018, and one fintech (Nubank). Nubank, which is mainly owned by international investors, is the most valuable unicorn with headquarters in Brazil and has disrupted the very profitable banking establishment.

Google's YouTube is the number one platform to watch videos online in Brazil. In terms of paid streaming services, local player Globoplay has the most subscribers; Netflix comes in second. Globoplay, however, faces limitations to expand to international markets because most of its content is not in English.

[21] Automotive industry was at the core of Brazilian industrialization strategy. The arrangement that would be called the triple alliance (see Evans, 1979) would coordinate state capital and private domestic capital with foreign direct investment (FDI). In this alliance, SOEs produced the heavy inputs necessary to the foreign-owned automotive plants, while the domestic private sector would provide downstream services as well as a network of component suppliers for the factories ran by the multinationals.

6.5 DATA LOCALIZATION IN INDIA AND BRAZIL

In the digital technology landscape, access to stock and flow of data is of the utmost importance. The stock of data allows technology firms to create better suited products toward consumers, which then creates a network effect of consumer behavior on that platform – the flow part. These two aspects of data work in positive feedback loop that entrenches bigger players at the expense of smaller ones. Beyond high-quality and creative engineering and programming, there is a *quantitative* aspect moving the mechanisms of the digital economy, which gain and sustain advantage through a series of tipping points and accelerating feedback loops (Lee 2018). Complementary, contextual, tailored data is also important. If one wants to put in place microlending apps in Rio de Janeiro or self-driving cars in Bengaluru, specific data from these places will always be superior to all possible data from the rest of the world (Lee, 2018). Accessing and amassing data, both in quantity and in quality, is thus the essence of platform and customer-facing dominance in technology.

Accessing and amassing data acquired new importance for statecraft as well. Beyond the idea that "war made the state, and the state made war" (Tilly, 1975, p. 42), the formation of states is also intrinsically linked to administrative institutions such as the *census* and other myriad of data-driven decision-making mechanisms, which serve as *precondition*s for the Weberian state (Gerth & Mills, 2009). It is no surprise why great powers such as the US and aspiring great powers such as China adamantly defend their advantage in ICT and digital technologies given what is at stake.

Data localization requirements have now appeared in the government's toolkit of actions to boost a country's tech landscape while guaranteeing levels of data sovereignty that serve goals ranging from security to guardrails for local business and economic interests (Cory & Dascoli, 2021). By itself, data localization does not guarantee an upgrade for the tech sector. However, determining that certain data generated in these countries should be stored domestically – even if some could be replicated abroad – can be part of digital policies that seek to enhance both cybersecurity and data sovereignty (Cory & Dascoli, 2021). Sections 6.5.1 and 6.5.2 explain data localization (or lack thereof) policies in both India and Brazil, and the reason for observed variation.

6.5.1 Data Localization in India: A Fractured Outcome

Countries such as India that do not have any domestic multi-sectoral platforms are placed at a disadvantage. Once a foreign multi-sectoral platform becomes relatively successful, the onset of network effects will privilege it over other domestic entities. Birch et al. (2021, pp. 5–6) explain how network effects coupled with exploitation of data allows for a "winner takes all" market. Multi-sectoral platforms combine network effects with exploitation of ever-expanding data within their ambit to utilize advantages from one aspect of their business to entrench consumer behavior in another aspect of their business. For example, Walmart's Flipkart had such a dominance in e-commerce in India that because of network effects on its platform it was able to leapfrog an Indian payments player like Paytm to quickly become the top three payments processors in the country. This bleeding and spreading of dominance into more and more sectors of the economy is what has alarmed India.

India has pursued to limit this loop and privilege of big foreign platforms and thereby limiting the chokepoint effect of US's weaponized interdependence by undertaking data localization policies. India is accused of using "data localization to merely entail a transfer of power to domestic elites and contribute to strengthening India's profile and power in the community of nations" (Kovacs & Ranganathan, 2019, p. 20). The authors argue that policymakers in India "have constructed data as a primarily economic resource to be used in the service of economic enrichment of the country" (Kovacs & Ranganathan, 2019, p. 21).

Despite the overwhelming desire to be a technological powerhouse and limit the chokepoint effect of the US's weaponized interdependence, India has avoided undertaking sweeping data localization measures. What has led the Indian government to make this policy choice?

Before we begin the analysis, it is important to see how India's data storage landscape is governed. As discussed earlier, in August 2023, India passed the DPDP Act. This Act removes all constraints on the free flow of data across boundaries (bar some countries). However, as noted earlier, Section 16 (2) of the DPDP Act allows for independent regulators to enact data localization mandates and cements the mandates already put in place by sectoral regulators. Thus, the main characteristic of India's data localization landscape is sectoral fragmentation. India already has data localization requirements placed through a number of sector-specific measures. Burman and Sharma (2021) compile ten sectoral data localization initiatives in place. They include "payment systems data (Reserve Bank of India (RBI), 2019), subscriber data in the broadcasting sector (Department of Communications & Digital Technologies, 2021), and insurance policyholder data (Insurance Regulatory and Development Authority of India (IRDAI), 2017)" (Kovacs & Ranganathan, 2019, p. 16). Policies that mandate data localization are underpinned by two main considerations: one is Criminal Investigation and Prevention and the other is Economic Gains. But, their effect is in limiting US's weaponized interdependence effects.[22]

So how did this fractured landscape come about? If the Indian government has been aware of the monopolization of data on foreign platforms entrenching their dominance, why did it not pursue a full-scale data localization? In our view, the Indian government tries to strike a balance between appealing to the desires of its own population with demand to access global

[22] We have explained how data localization would amount to limiting of US's weaponized interdependence effects earlier in this chapter.

standards of tech lifestyle and safeguarding against punitive measures from external actors, chiefly the US.

The interests of domestic conglomerates and government that tend to be in favor of data localization and American tech giants that assume an anti-data localization stance interact through India's institutions. For instance, the Indian supreme court's judgment in *Puttaswamy* v *Union of India* (2017) enshrined that every Indian has the right to privacy. This has meant that interests of both these domestic conglomerates and American tech giants must fit within the framework of privacy. Further, a few independent institutions in India took cue from the judgment to pass their own data localization mandates, namely RBI, SEBI, IRDAI, MCA, and the DoT. This is a key difference vis-à-vis the Brazilian case. In the Brazilian case, the enactment of the data protection bill by the Brazilian congress subsumed the interests and mandates of sectoral regulatory agencies within it; however, in India, the interests of independent regulatory agencies were not subsumed under the DPDP Act. Furthermore, a plan was in the works for localization of health sector data as well, but the proposal has now been withdrawn since the health sector does not have an independent regulatory body like finance or insurance does (Bailey & Parsheera, 2021, p. 139).[23]

So, as we proceed with the complex nature of interactions, we see that the interests of the foreign businesses are getting more and more constrained by the effect of exogenous institutional diktats informed by macropolitical constraints. On the other hand, the need to access funding for elections by political parties from domestic conglomerates (Bardhan, 2023) further fractures this dichotomy (Indian institutions' independent interests and the need to carve out spaces where domestic conglomerates are able to garner some of the user-generated data to compete with American Big Tech). The promotion of India's Reliance Jio into e-commerce and associated IT services can be well understood as a state strategy to promote national champions (and compete against foreign companies) (Subramanian & Felman, 2022).

Further, the impetus behind creating the Data Empowerment and Protection Architecture framework[24] can be viewed through the lens of protection of privacy as guaranteed by the Supreme Court of India, but also as a way to create business sector development opportunities for local firms by carving out lakes of data for them. Regardless of the impetus, the effect of such data localization policies would be the limitation of US's weaponized interdependence effects. While we use this as an example in one issue area,

[23] "The draft Digital Information Security in Healthcare Act, 2018 (DISHA), a now withdrawn proposal, this bill sought to create scope for the proposed National Electronic Health Authority to impose localization requirements with respect to digital health data" (Bailey & Parsheera, 2021, p. 139).

[24] It is a consent-based sharing that reduces the possibility of firms to create walled gardens of data. It allows for individual to permit sharing of their own data held by one firm to another one. One can think of it as a UPI-style infrastructure layer that will facilitate consent-based sharing of personal data.

such a framework can be applied to other areas of the technology landscape in India to trace how a particular outcome has come about.

6.5.2 Data Localization in Brazil: A Dependent Outcome

The debate about whether Brazil should move toward requiring internet-transacted data related to Brazilian citizens to be stored in the country gained momentum following the Snowden revelations in 2013 about spying activities pursued by the US National Security Agency (NSA). Whether characterized as a whistleblowing about uncivil and undiplomatic panopticon activities or as a treason promoted by a contracted agent against the principal, it is clear that an US agency was dedicated precisely to achieving panopticon advantage. Snowden revelations not only demonstrated the US will and technological capabilities to collect intelligence globally but also ignited recalculations regarding (inter)national security by national governments around the world.

The Brazilian Civil Framework of the Internet, or Marco Civil da Internet, was a bill proposed to the Brazilian Congress by the executive branch of the government in 2011 after extensive multistakeholder discussions held since 2009 under the Ministry of Justice's coordination. When the bill began to be considered in the Chamber of Deputies – the lower house of Brazil's Congress – 36 other projects were attached to it, including some that had been pending in the Chamber since 2001. Following the 2013 Snowden incident, the executive branch used a legal device to request urgency in the appreciation of the bill by the legislature, while legislators close to the executive branch included in the bill a data localization mandate. That was a clear turning point whose impacts will likely go beyond the mere Brazilian Civil Framework of the Internet and all other internet-related legislations that have been approved since then.

At the time, the representative serving as bill's rapporteur considered the data localization rule as a "political answer against a political act that violated our sovereignty" (Israel & Soto, 2013). Perhaps because it was framed primarily as a "political answer" without further strategic considerations of economic interest, the data localization part of the bill did not gather enough support to move forward. Symptomatically, what moved forward became just as quickly undone when there was a change in government. An executive decision in 2013 to transfer to the Federal Data Processing Service (Serpro) the contracts that were with Microsoft was reversed in 2016. Among other services that it was already used to and able to provide, Serpro was commissioned with launching a cloud with IaaS, PaaS, and SaaS facilities, a move that did not receive either macropolitical or material support, thus was short lived.

Arguably, the way that data localization was dealt with as haphazard politics without seeking consensus with clear explanation about its importance to local actors shrunk the margin of maneuverability of the groups supporting the mandate. The entire process lacked a well-designed strategy for achieving data localization while managing the negative reactions from international business lobbies. Originally supporters of data localization included telecom companies, broadcasters, and other domestic copyright holders, together with governmental, judicial, and police authorities. The main and most cohesive opposition was from foreign content and services providers, aided by fractured opinion and interests among representatives of civil society and national content providers (Chamber of Deputies, 2016). In the end, data localization was defeated.

Inspired by the European GDPR, Brazil passed its General Data Protection Law (LGPD) in 2018, which became effective in 2020. Regarding the lack of data localization requirements, the current LGPD is a compromise. At this point, Brazil basically affirms its right to extraterritorial reach to the data in case of domestic contestation of something related to the data, its treatment, and storage, that is, violation on national data protection law by foreign actors. While defeated sectors in Brazil wanted data to be stored in the country at least for some categories of data, a compromise was designed by a winning coalition[25] in which data would be allowed to be stored anywhere. The text of the compromise affirms that Brazil would have extraterritorial reach to its national data stored abroad, as well as the right to define what foreign system is to be considered "adequate" in terms of data protection, that is, to what country Brazil's data can flow freely. Nonetheless, it is clear that this purported extraterritorial reach lacks enforcement power. As for Serpro – the one that was commissioned in 2013 with launching a cloud with IaaS, PaaS, and SaaS facilities and was being privatized in the early 2020s – in 2020, it hired Amazon's AWS directly without a public bidding process to be in charge of those facilities.

Since this issue is being addressed in the Brazilian legislature rather than by independent agencies as in India, interest groups were unable to form a coalition that sees data localization as beneficial and desirable. So far, groups in favor of data localization policies were not able to articulate arguments to either convince the legislator or create a competitive coalition to support policies that would foment a feasible technological upgrading that would address data sovereignty concerns and generate more gains and maneuverability for domestic actors in areas such as artificial intelligence, cloud computation and storage, internet of things, and machine learning. If well explained, this action can arguably be performed hand in hand with some sort of understanding with established (international) interests.

Current Brazilian framework does not limit at all the chokepoint effect of US's or any other eventual superpower's weaponization of interdependence in the digital sector. Given current winning coalitions in Brazil, curtailed sovereignty and economic dependence tend to be embraced as paths of least resistance, differentiating Brazil from India, the latter restricting cross-border flow for certain data as well as defining categories of data that can cross India's border as long as a copy of it is kept in a data center in the country.

[25] See Chamber of Deputies (2016) for a detailed account of these negotiations in Congress between different groups of interest.

6.6 CONCLUDING REMARKS

In this chapter, we surveyed the digital technology landscapes of Brazil and India, especially their data localization policies. To a large extent, both middle powers are interdependent on the US-led digitalization of socioeconomic processes. We present support for the idea that data localization is a necessary, but not sufficient, condition on the path to digital sovereignty, and that it can be designed to diminish US chokepoint effects under weaponized interdependence.

We have observed that in both countries, a fractured, technological landscape exists, albeit differently assembled. In India, the core of the technological landscape represents a healthy mix of foreign tech giants, domestic conglomerates, and independent governmental entities. In the Brazilian case, a similarly fractured outcome exists at the infrastructural level. However, at the intermediary level (such as large retail and finance platforms), Brazil's landscape is dominated by local conglomerate players, whereas India's landscape is completely dominated by American tech giants. Finally, at the single-sector level, both India and Brazil represent a vibrant competitive market with a healthy mix of domestic private-sector players and foreign players (including both tech giants and single-sector players); however, with the caveat, India has an advantage due to broader human capital dedicated to these industries.

In general, our note on fractured outcomes fits in well with the existing developmental politics literature on Brazil and India (Evans, 1995). However, when each country's digital technology landscape interacts with other political institutional designs and macropolitical arrangements, such as the US hegemony in digital technologies, different outcomes result, especially in terms of data localization policies. While India reaffirms a fractured outcome, Brazil moves to a more dependent one.

Thus, reiterating our central argument: data localization policies help countries avoid chokepoint effects under weaponized interdependence; however, the enactment of these policies is dependent on domestic politics. The two case studies discussed earlier highlight how countries that are similar in the hierarchy of international relations – middle powers – can have varied outcomes when it comes to critical policies that may enhance their autonomy under weaponized interdependence. We argue that the observed variation in these policies occurs because of a variation in authority of a country's independent institutions. The two case studies of India and Brazil are emblematic of a wider argument about middle powers, autonomy under weaponized interdependence, and domestic institutional authority.

7

A Modulated Approach to Digital Sovereignty

Exploring Huawei-Led Smart City Initiatives in South Africa and Italy

Stefano Calzati

7.1 INTRODUCTION

This chapter is framed within the broad and multilayered issue of China–Africa relations in connection with Information and Communication Technologies (ICTs). At such a juncture, it becomes particularly relevant to unpack the geopolitical and tech-dependent power relations between two BRICS countries – China and South Africa – in the context of smart city initiatives. The Huawei OpenLab in Johannesburg is chosen for the study, with a similar initiative from Cagliari – the capital of Sardinia, Italy – used as a comparison. The goal is to explore the extent to which bilateral cooperation between China and South Africa in constructing smart cities can be said to empower all actors involved, especially South African actors and citizens, rather than (re)producing power asymmetries within a South–South geopolitical scenario. Further, the chapter offers a better understanding of how Huawei-led smart city initiatives are conceived by scrutinizing their discursive framing, exploring the extent to which the tech giant actions can be deemed as an example of corporate digital sovereignty (see Chapter 1). The chapter also sheds light on the governance model of these smart city initiatives, with particular attention paid to Huawei's partnerships and the management of data lifecycle.

Today, South Africa has one of the most advanced ICT markets in the African continent, largely due to interventions and investments by foreign partners, both Western and Chinese. Chinese tech giant Huawei, in this regard, represents a key actor. Huawei has entered South Africa's ICT market since early 2000s and gained an increasing centrality over the years. In this context, Huawei OpenLab is a paradigmatic example of Chinese-led multi-stakeholder tech initiative whose goal is to conceive, develop, and implement smart city solutions (e.g., face recognition, mobility sensors, diffused Internet of Things (IoTs) for pollutions monitoring, traffic management, and building energy savings) in and for the city of Johannesburg. For comparison, this initiative is juxtaposed to a similar one, the Joint Innovation Center (JIC) in Sardinia, Italy, of which Huawei is also a key stakeholder. This comparison highlights the similarities and differences between the two initiatives in discourse and governance.

The chapter is structured as follows. First, it briefly discusses methodology and the documents reviewed for the study, followed by an outline of the theoretical framework along three main axes: (1) the role of China in Africa in the context of ICT development; (2) current competing visions about internet (geo) governance through the lenses of "digital sovereignty" and "data colonialism"; and (3) a critical review of the concept of "smart city." Then, the author introduces the two case studies: Huawei OpenLab in Johannesburg and the JIC in Italy, highlighting major discursive and governance-related similarities and differences. Lastly, the chapter draws some conclusions, linking the major findings from the case studies to the theoretical framework (see Chapter 1), highlighting the strains and exchanges when different forms of digital sovereignty – especially state and corporate ones – may clash or converge.

7.2 METHODOLOGY

Huawei OpenLab in Johannesburg and the JIC in Cagliari were chosen as case studies due to three considerations. First, Huawei played a key role in both initiatives as a main actor and provider of technological support. Second, these two initiatives aim to achieve similar goals in smart city solutions. Third, the comparison offers an interesting opportunity to triangulate and explore the activities of Huawei in different settings, notably in a country part of the BRICS and in a country of the "Global North." The study examines a series of documents, reports, and press releases to provide valuable insights into the inner workings of these two initiatives as well as the development models they represent. The analysis helps unveil the discourses surrounding the two Huawei-led initiatives as well as the management of data lifecycle and the smart solutions developed. It should be noted that the analysis here does not draw from direct feedback from Huawei. Despite the author's attempts to interview Huawei representatives for the two smart city projects, the Chinese company did not provide a response.

7.3 THE ROLE OF CHINA IN AFRICA'S ICTS AMONG SOFT POWER, DIGITAL SOVEREIGNTY, AND "SMART" DEVELOPMENT

7.3.1 China in Sub-Saharan Africa

Currently, Africa is the continent with the strongest growth in digital connectivity worldwide: more than 5.2% of annual growth rate in mobile subscriptions and 8.7% in internet users between 2018 and 2019 (We Are Social, 2019). Despite the remarkable advancement, internet penetration in the continent remains uneven across regions. In North and South Africa, at least 50% of the population have access to the internet. However, in East and West Africa, the percentages of penetration are lower, at 32% and 41% respectively, with Central Africa reaching only 12%.

Sub-Saharan Africa (SSA) represents a crucial crossroad along the New Maritime Silk Road. A set of major techno-infrastructural investments, the New Maritime Silk Road is part of the Belt and Road Initiative, and it aims at connecting Mainland China to Europe via Hong Kong, India, and Africa. Chinese ICT-related investments in SSA span across all African regions (Oreglia, 2012): eastern (e.g., Kenya, Ethiopia, and Zimbabwe), western (e.g., Ghana and Nigeria), central (e.g., Cameroon), and southern (mainly in South Africa). These investments, often in the form of financial loans, have initially focused on infrastructures (backbone and last-mile cabling), while over the last decade, they have shifted toward knowledge transfer, cloud computing, artificial intelligence solutions, and smart city projects.

Different from Western powers, China has been said to exert "soft power"[1] on the African continent by promoting investments "with no strings attached" (Gagliardone, 2019). At least in rhetoric, China is committed to developing African infrastructures and services by fostering agreements that keep African business partners, local authorities, and workers involved, tailoring investments for their needs. In various international documents, China's relationships with SSA countries are discursively shaped as peer-to-peer forms of collaboration rather than top-down aids (King, 2013). However, the extent to which China's and Chinese companies' commitment to fostering vibrant ICT markets in SSA aims to empower African actors instead of subjecting these actors to forms of soft colonization is still being debated. For instance, not only do Chinese individuals tend to occupy managerial roles in Chinese–African partnerships, but knowledge transfer to Africa is also contested (Makundi, Huib, & Develtere, 2016). Some scholars have found that effective cooperation on a peer-to-peer basis is limited (Cheru & Obi, 2010; Gagliardone, 2019; Shen, 2013; Taylor, 2006). On the other hand, it is also recognized that China's involvement in Africa does produce sharing and collaboration with local communities, helping to foster a positive perception of Chinese expats by locals (Agbebi, 2018; Anshan, 2007; Musyimi, Malechwanzi, & Luo, 2018). In a more balanced summary, King (2010) notes that "there is recognition by Chinese officials that the transfer of Chinese labor practices can lead to friction, and they provide advice about this. On the other hand, there seems to be a good deal of admiration for the Chinese determination to start and finish a job on time and on budget" (p. 494).

[1] "Soft power" is the term that Chinese authorities adopt when describing their engagement with and in foreign countries, especially low-to-middle-income countries (LMICs). It is a broadly conceived form of power based not much on military force or economic agreements (although economy does play a role), but on diplomacy and culture as keys to establish relations across the world (see, for instance, Bodomo, 2009; Fijalkowski, 2011).

Hence, the idea of a homogenizing "soft power" exerted by China on Africa calls for contextualization. In fact, such label can hardly account for the variety and complexity of Chinese investments in the African continent. It would be too simplistic to consider Chinese companies as the *longa manus* of the Chinese government in Africa, insofar as the diverse, multilayered initiatives put forth by various Chinese actors – diplomats, private companies, state-led companies, trade intermediaries, and so on – can often have competing agendas. For instance, Xu's research (2014) shows that the Chinese Ministry of Commerce and Ministry of Foreign Affairs tend to have different approaches toward their foreign partners. Gu and colleagues (2016), in turn, observe that "the Chinese state has engaged in unprecedented economic diplomacy in Africa" (p. 25), implying a flexible approach of Chinese authorities to African economies and societies, instead of presupposing a uniform top-down relationship. This is in line with Li's argument (2008) that China's paradigmatic approach to Africa has shifted from "economy serving diplomacy" to "diplomacy serving economy," manifest of China's soft power in developing regions of the world.

Besides a pan-Africa diplomacy framework, China is increasingly committed to fostering bilateral agreements with individual African states. Gu and colleagues (2016) note:

> this [diplomacy] has two aspects: multilateral (pan-African) and bilateral (state-to-state) diplomacy. The former is driven through the FOCAC [Forum on China-Africa Cooperation] framework, a dialog and institutionalized process for cooperation established in 2000. The latter is driven by extensive tours of African states by Chinese state and party officials and bilateral cooperation agreements (p. 25).

From a Chinese perspective, the goal is to adapt to each context without imposing an agenda, while seeking a convergence between China's own interests and those of local actors. On this point, Gagliardone (2019) claims that "a continental overview of China's engagement (...) corroborates the impression that China is not trying to impose a blueprint (...) Rather, [it] has produced specific and individual responses in different African countries" (p. 56). For this study, the involvement of the Chinese tech giant Huawei in South Africa is of special interest.

Huawei is the major Chinese ICT actor in South Africa. It entered the country in 1999, just one year after its arrival in Kenya, which marked the beginning of Chinese investments in SSA's ICTs. Huawei's presence in South Africa has grown considerably over the years. Huawei's sales in Africa reached $4 billion in 2012. As for June 2021, Huawei compete with Samsung to be the leading mobile phone provider, after having already overtaken Apple (Statista, 2021). In addition, Huawei has also committed to delivering ICT training through its Huawei Authorized Information and Network Academy (HAINA), which has so far mentored more than 50,000 graduates.

In early 2019, Huawei played a crucial role in the rollout of the first 5G commercial network in South Africa, together with Rain, the country's mobile data-only network operator. In 2020, following the US ban of Huawei, South Africa's government confirmed its support to the Chinese company. Currently, Huawei is at the center of a project of techno-renovation of the city of Rustenburg, near Pretoria. Famous for its mines, the city has been identified as the target of major investments and deployment of smart city solutions.

7.3.2 Unpacking (Cyber) Power Relations

The genealogy of China–Africa relations in the ICT realm can date back to the 1970s. Riding on the wave of Third-Worldism, commercial and political partnerships between China and states of the Non-Aligned Movement, that is, countries not directly subsumed under either of the two superpower blocs centered around the United States and USSR, thrived. Half a century later, the geopolitical scenario has radically changed, with the eclipse and metamorphosis of the former Soviet Union into Russia and China's rise on the global stage as a leading commercial, technological, and political power. On the other hand, African countries experienced substantial demographical and technology-led economic growth, although uneven across the continent. Today, China, Russia, and South Africa – the most economically developed African country – together with Brazil and India, are part of the BRICS alliance composed of some of the largest emerging economies of the world.

The rise of China and the emergence of the BRICS bloc challenge conceptual frameworks and theories of the Global North and Global South as well as of a world system divided into "the first world," "the second world," and "the third world." It has been contested that such epistemological categories have their limitations and even harmfulness vis-à-vis the goal to account for and put forth a truly inclusive internationalist perspective in which all actors – nations, public institutions, private companies, and people – are granted a proactive (and not only reactive) agency. While such categories might be useful for identifying patterns of socioeconomic imbalances, they nonetheless tend to oversimplify stratifications and tensions cutting through these geographies, thus fundamentally overlooking the unique histories, internal and external power relations, and cultural differences affecting the involved countries. This has become more pronounced in global trade and ICT infrastructures, consolidated around China and the US. For instance, China's involvement in Africa and Europe, via the proxy of Huawei's investments in both continents, requires not only a contextual assessment of technological and geopolitical power relations between the "superior" and the "subaltern" actors but also a paradigmatic rethinking of the theoretical basis of such assessments. As Wen (2021) writes in his book *Huawei's Model*, "the development of the global economy has been characterized by the transition toward transnationalized digital capitalism, within which information and communications technologies have increasingly played a pivotal role in restructuring the global capitalist system" (p. 12). To foster generative discussions and debates and institute practical policies, it is important to subject the new global map of power relations to a critical examination.

This entails the undoing of dichotomies such as global–local, especially when it comes to issues of "data colonialism" (Couldry & Mejias, 2019) and "digital sovereignty" (Belli, 2017) as well as conceptual binaries such as "multi-stakeholderism–multilateralism" (Nonnecke, 2016) in the realm of internet governance. In this respect, Wasserman (2018) observes that what is at stake is the remaking of global power relations that "have prompted different ways of thinking about categories such as the 'South,' the 'global,' the 'local' and the 'transnational' in communications" (p. 448). What has emerged bears resemblance of federated forms of technological globalization – contested internally as much as externally – in which the circulation of data, tech expertise, innovation, and policies can be prompted or hindered by competing discourses, actors, and agendas part of different ecologies *at once*.

Elsewhere (Calzati, 2020a), I have noted that any discussion on data colonialism can be fruitful only to the extent it is contextualized and historically thickened. Otherwise, the risk lies in reifying the same power asymmetries that the notion of data colonialism aims to uncover. For instance, while US corporations tend to dominate internet services and software, the "ownership" of the internet infrastructure's components sees an imbrication of actors. A case in point is the transpacific FASTER cable system between the United States and several cities in Japan, China, and Korea. This is a major infrastructure jointly developed by Chinese, American, and South Asian private companies, including Google, China Mobile, China Telecom, SingTel, KDDI, and Global Transit. It is evident that within such a multilayered, entangled scenario, the very concept of digital sovereignty risks losing its epistemological validity if it is not anchored to the ground: each "North" contains its "South," each node exists as an extension of its edges, each network is traversed and repeatedly remolded by contingent (data) interests.

When ICTs are framed within a geopolitical North–South perspective, the risk of new forms of power asymmetry emerges. Studies have shown the "misalignment" between the internet as a commons infrastructure and the legitimacy of sovereign powers (Mueller, 2019) as well as the shifting toward a multipolar scenario (Winseck, 2017) in internet governance. Traditional categories such as "market" and "state," "national" and "international," and multi-stakeholderism vs. multilateralism may no longer be sufficient to account for such changing and complex realities. For instance, as Yu and Goodnight (2020) note with specific regard to China: "cast in light of the cybersphere, China's so-called Intranet also reveals entanglements with foreign capital, foreign technology, foreign markets, and foreign labor" (p. 13). Hence, digital sovereignty, data colonialism, and also digital self-determination can be best regarded as macro-entangled dimensions that contest and resist linear (agent-structure) readings.

SSA's digital transformation is increasingly associated with a new "scramble for Africa" (Taylor, 2013) aimed at controlling the deluge of

ICT-derived data from the continent. There exists a grave risk due to the lack of agency provided to African institutions and African peoples when it comes to their own digital transformations. Studies have shown a colonially tainted asymmetry between Africa and the developed countries (Mohan & Lampert, 2013; Taylor & Broeders, 2015), which relegates African countries and people to a subaltern role. Given the power asymmetry, scholars have emphasized the urgent need to "Africanize technology" (Mutsvairo & Ragnedda, 2019, p. 22) to empower African actors and ICT users. However, it remains to be seen whether such asymmetry also affects South–South power relations, such as those among BRICS countries. Thus, this study seeks to investigate the tensions informing the smart city initiatives led by Huawei in Johannesburg and compare them with similar projects developed in the Global North, of which Italy is part traditionally. More broadly, the study assesses the indigenous *and* transnational entanglement of digital sovereignty and data colonialism and how such double-sided articulation impacts an effective emancipation of African (and Italian) actors.

This brings us to explore the concept of "digital sovereignty," deeply intertwined with "data colonialism." Historically, the notion of sovereignty emerges at the intersection of exclusive authority and territoriality. This chapter will show that, when contextualized, the concept can be usefully adopted to understand Huawei's initiatives across the globe.

According to Kushwaha and colleagues (2020), "digital sovereignty" is a concept that is midway between the broad idea of "technological sovereignty" and the narrow idea of "data sovereignty." In her speech in February 2020, the President of the European Commission Ursula von der Leyen defined digital sovereignty as the capability "to make its own choices, based on its own values, respecting its own rules" in the field of tech (von der Leyen, 2020). At the heart of the matter is control over data and/or tech infrastructures (Hummel et al., 2021). More concretely, to assess the soundness of the concept, it is necessary to put it in context. Apart from those countries able to chart their own course of economic and technological developments – those which can "consider creating a national programme to foster and promote nationally headquartered companies to invest in creating and offering CSP services within their country" (Kushwaha, Roguski, & Watson, 2020, p. 60) – for the majority of countries around the world, especially LMICs, the risk of being co-opted by major global powers, private or public, in their infrastructures and services is extremely high. As de Nardis (2014) pointed out, technology governance becomes part and parcel of geopolitics when power relations heavily influence how a technology is developed, implemented, controlled, shared, and used. Such technology, in turn, impact people's lives – both individually and collectively – in creating or eroding values at social, economic, cultural, environmental, and institutional levels (Cardullo & Kitchin, 2019; Micheli et al., 2020).

This type of cyber-geo-governance has peculiar features. One such feature is the increasingly federated forms of transnational technologization, with China gaining a central role in shifting global power relations. Thus, it should not surprise anyone that the European Union (2019) warned against the "digital dependency on non-European providers and the lack of a well-performing cloud infrastructure respecting European norms and values." This also means that "states will increasingly face difficult policy decisions with regard to deciding how best to balance competing sovereign interests" (Kushwaha, Roguski, & Watson, 2020, p. 58). For instance, Wu (2021) notes that the US *Cloud Act*, passed after China's adoption of its *Cybersecurity Law*, is a typical example of a law that, under the guise of data localization and protection, has an eminently transnational character. Yet, such a law might also have undesirable commercial repercussions, especially for the US's European allies.

Given such scenario, it is certainly insightful to examine the power relations binding two BRICS countries – China and South Africa – through the lens of digital sovereignty (and colonialism), as applied in studying a smart city project in Johannesburg (and one in Cagliari for comparison). The way in which the Chinese tech giant Huawei approaches different contexts and fosters multi-stakeholder partnerships for developing smart city solutions sheds light onto how the concept of digital sovereignty gets challenged and rearticulated differently in reality.

7.3.3 Smart Cities: A Critical Review

Despite the fuzziness, multiple interpretations, and sometimes abuses of the term "smart cities," the notion has come to signify primarily the fostering of highly efficient urban spaces based on ICTs and the gathering of IoT-related data. Plus, the development of smart cities has occurred at a time of increasing responsiveness to the need for sustainability of the whole built environment. The International Telecommunication Union (ITU)'s Focus Group on Smart Sustainable Cities (FG-SSC 2016) defines smart cities as follows: "A smart sustainable city is an innovative city that uses ICTs and other means to improve the quality of life, efficiency of urban operation and services, and competitiveness, while ensuring that it meets the needs of present and future generations with respect to economic, social and environmental aspects."

With nuances from report to report, such a definition has become the standardly accepted idea of what a smart city should be and do, ideally. However, what counts as "quality of life," "efficiency," and "competitiveness" and whether such features are desirable, compatible, and truly beneficial to citizens remain open questions. Many smart city initiatives have increasingly been shaped by a techno-optimism ethos that tends to overlook the realpolitik behind the implementation of tech-based solutions in the urban environment. As Angelidou (2017) notes in her critical review of several case studies, "most smart city strategies fail to incorporate bottom-up approaches, are poorly adapted to accommodate the local needs of their area, and consider issues of privacy and security inadequately."

The hyperefficiency that the smart city is meant to realize conflates "easiness of use" with "living wellbeing." The idea that a city is good to live in when it is easy to navigate betrays the underlying technological rationale of an urban space "founded on the basis of utopian 'clean and orderly' pervasive computing" (Viitanen & Kingston, 2014, p. 807). Things, however, are more complex. Oftentimes, how, where, and what smart technology is deployed contributes to widening socioeconomic disparity, precisely because technology is already epistemologically loaded with the same principles and rationalistic logics that guide its development and which, in turn, technology reinforces.

Secondly, the idea of a city's smartness often conceals economic drives and interests. Turning a city into a clean and orderly space on the ground of an accrued attention to citizens' needs also implies shaping the city as a space to be *used*. The smart solutions adopted in cities are often offered by private companies and co-opted by market forces (Mann, Mitchell, Foth, & Anastasiu, 2020), which then take the lead in defining the normative ideas of what counts as "smart," that is, something that they can profit from. It is no surprise that given tech innovation is primarily led by private firms, the underlying business model of today's smart cities is one that produces power asymmetries at various levels: not only does it subordinate public spaces and actors to private ones, but it also turns citizens into consumers.

Thirdly, it is not rare to find the concept of smart city coupled with that of "safe city," via the creation of a network of diffused technological solutions, among which video cloud, facial recognition, and tracking sensors, which overlaps to the citizen's being-in-the-city as a ghostly shadow. A safe city, then, can be realized above all as a "monitored city" in which technology can be used in exploitative (and often lucrative) terms. In this sense, "safe city" is to be found somewhat in the middle between "care" and "control" (Lyon 2007): the extent to which safety morphs into surveillance rather than enhances people's wellbeing is an economic-political matter closely linked to how smart technologies are developed, deployed, by whom and for which purposes. As Deleuze (1992) acutely points out by distinguishing between an old "disciplinary" city governance from a new "control" one: "the disciplinary man was a discontinuous producer of energy, but the man of control is undulatory, in orbit, in a continuous network" (p. 4). The citizen of smart cities is metamorphosed into a trace-leaver. "Any one of us," Bratton writes (2016), "is (or could be, or should be) less a political subject of this one city – London, Mumbai, Shanghai – but of the City, of the globally uneven mesh of amalgamated infrastructures and delaminated jurisdictions" (p. 152). The smart city is an agglomeration that transcends borders and specificities to impose a new layer of global technologized living space that demands to be unpacked in all its internal complexities.

7.4 HUAWEI OPENLABS IN SOUTH AFRICA AND THE JOINT INNOVATION CENTER IN ITALY

Over the last few years, Huawei has launched a number of OpenLabs around the world. Except the OpenLab in Suzhou, Mainland China, which opened in 2012, the others are all abroad, for example, in Johannesburg (April 2017),

Istanbul (December 2017), Paris (April 2018), Moscow (April 2018), and New Delhi (October 2018).

These initiatives are conceived as hubs where, based on shared infrastructures and facilities provided by Huawei, various stakeholders can converge for developing and testing innovative technological solutions for the "smartening" of the urban environment. It is significant to delve into the governance model that regulates the relations among the OpenLab's stakeholders in order to understand how data are put to use, by whom, for whom, and for which purposes.

More specifically, while the vision of sharing hardware, software, and tech know-how is clear, it is worth exploring how the data lifecycle is managed as well as how the tech solutions developed address issues of cybersecurity and local actors' empowerment. This same approach also applies to the second case study – the JIC in Cagliari, Italy – of which Huawei is also one of the leading actors in constructing tech infrastructures, facilities, and know-how.

7.4.1 The OpenLab in Johannesburg

The OpenLab in Johannesburg is interesting as it was one of the first hubs to be opened by Huawei outside Mainland China and it remains the only one of its kind in SSA. The initiative hopes to bring together various stakeholders to create a synergic model of tech innovation with an impact at the urban level.

As stated in the press release published at the occasion of the launch of the OpenLab (Huawei, 2017), "Huawei will provide the data centre facility, hardware and software infrastructure and technical team while the partners will contribute ideas, products and human resources" with the goal to "test and customise a broad range of solutions under the umbrella of safe cities and smart grids." Here the equation of smart city *as* safe city returns, a *leitmotif* in Huawei's discourses on technological solutions applied to urban environments.[2] On its website,[3] Huawei elaborates:

> The center focuses on four capacities: joint innovation, partner development, solution development, and industry experience. Johannesburg OpenLab works together with global, regional, and local partners, concentrating on Safe City, Smart Grid, and

[2] In a 2020 white paper issued by Huawei specifically dedicated to smart cities, the term "safe city" appears seventeen times over nineteen pages. The concept is deeply entrenched with that of "smart city" and is considered de facto as a driver to realizing the latter. More to the point, the document unfolds an all-monitoring characterization of "safe city" as that which "uses ICT to predict, prevent, and reduce crime; address new and emerging threats; improve emergency/disaster planning and response. (...) Safe Cities us[e] a variety of tools such as advanced analytics, social media, collaboration and information sharing tools, and mobile technologies to support (...) local law enforcement and policing, and the justice and corrections system including local courts, locally operated jails and prisons, probation, community corrections, and parole." The wide and diverse application of smart solutions raise concerns over their impact on individual rights and freedoms, especially when the "implementer" is a private company in a foreign context.

[3] See https://e.huawei.com/en/partner/openlab/johannesburg.

Smart City solution [sic] to develop competitive solutions for industrial customers. Johannesburg OpenLab supports the demonstration of Safe City converged command, video cloud, and facial recognition scenario.

Overall, the presentation of the OpenLab is rather minimal and factual. The description of the smart city projects is kept at a high level of abstraction and any form of qualitative assessment is avoided. While the Lab is open for "cooperation/consultation," Huawei's representatives declined to respond to this researcher's request for interviews. Such an approach seems symptomatic of a corporate strategy that, while leaving the doors open to a wide spectrum of partnerships, remains problematically vague over the concrete projects and the effective results of the Lab toward a broader audience. In fact, the stress on "industrial customers" is indicative that the smart city's solutions developed, albeit having an immediate impact on the local communities, are kept among a small cohort of actors.

Further, the concept of "safe city" is projected to be realized through a network of tech solutions that include video cloud and facial recognition. "Safe city," therefore, can be intended above all as "control city" to the extent to which the restriction of access to the OpenLab mainly to industrial customers and lack of community presence cast doubt on the public agency and publicly beneficial impact of the solutions developed by the Lab.

After operating in Johannesburg for six years, the OpenLab provides few details about the extent tech solutions developed within the Lab have been deployed. Nor has it openly addressed concomitant issues of privacy and data protection as well as other potential unintended consequences such as different forms of bias and discrimination. While there is no legal obligation for any private tech company to explore and account for these concerns outright, from a cyber-geopolitical perspective, these issues remain front and center of large-scale public projects and beg for more transparency.[4]

Such technological side effects are of particular relevance in a multiracial context such as South Africa, to the point that Kwet (2019) speaks of the risk of "AI-powered apartheid." Yet, Huawei does not openly address such concerns related to the activities and solutions of its OpenLab. Instead, it tends to favor a purely technically optimistic presentation of the smart city initiative, seemingly oblivious to the intrinsic social facets of technology and its governance. In the words of Arsène (2018), "the very sensitive character of these technologies and the geopolitical stakes paradoxically lead to a certain level of secrecy around the technologies that are supposed to bring more transparency" (p. 58).

More information on the smart city solutions envisioned and developed by Huawei can be found in its 2018 Corporate and Social Responsibility

[4] Not rarely, Corporate Social Responsibility initiatives are adopted by companies as brand-enhancing strategies for compensating the lack of approach to the development of on these issues and present the companies' goodwill to the population see (King, 2013; Makundi, Huib, & Develtere, 2016).

(CSR) report, which describes the ambitious project in the mining city of Rustenburg to be turned into a smart city:

> A world-class city where all communities enjoy a high quality of life, and one that is interconnected, energetic, healthy, green, friendly, secure, smart, prosperous, efficient, and sustainable. (...) To efficiently implement this project and build a smarter Rustenburg, the municipal government has picked a number of partners, including South Africa's ICT and financial technology company Electronic Connect, Sanchuan Water Meter Co., Ltd., intelligent transportation system provider Xiamen Lenz Communication Inc., and Huawei (p. 34).

Unlike the limited information about such smart city projects made available on its OpenLab's website, Huawei's CSR report puts forth an overinflated discourse on smart cities. It presents the upcoming renovation of the city of Rustenburg as an all-encompassing masterplan that will significantly uplift the quality of citizens' life, characterizing the "smart city" as the "optimal city" with such intrinsic qualities as "security," "interconnectedness," "prosperity," and "sustainability." Yet, no further insights are provided in support of these projected values or how they are realized through specific technological solutions.

To put things into perspective to assess a smart city's socioeconomic-ethical implications, it is worth looking at a similar project initiated in 2015 by the Chinese Development Group Zendai, which proposed a plan to turn the neighborhood of Modderfontein (east of Johannesburg) into a smart city. After two years, the project fell into disgrace due to the conflicting visions between the company and the municipality of Johannesburg. The city required at least 5,000 affordable homes to be included in the plan, while Zendai insisted on building luxurious housing, offices, and venues.

This case pulls aside the curtains, allowing a glimpse into the realpolitik behind smart cities. The label of "smart city" often conceals rather than reveals how the smartening of a city can lead to diverging interests among the actors involved, thus raising concerns about the socioeconomical sustainability of the solutions proposed. In other words, the benchmark against which to assess smart city solutions cannot be solely their tech feasibility or efficiency, but also their concrete economic, cultural, and social impacts on the local communities. The Modderfontein case epitomizes the extent to which smart initiatives, especially those led by private companies only, risk reinforcing or exacerbating existing socioeconomic inequalities and demand a thoughtful assessment involving all parties before being implemented.

One further aspect to be stressed is that both cases – Modderfontein and Rustenburg – entail a synergy of local and foreign actors, both public and private, concretizing the idea of cooperation among Chinese and African actors discussed earlier. However, the scenario is much different when it comes to Huawei OpenLab that provides few details about its "global, regional, and local partners." Among the publicly listed partners involved in the OpenLab are[5]: (1) a French and a Chinese company focused on railways infrastructures, (2) a UK firm that offers consulting digital services (both business-to-consumer and public-to citizens), (3) three Chinese tech companies focused on smart city solutions and smart grids for energy efficiency and facial recognition; (4) a German and a Danish company in the field of surveillance and tech safety solutions; (5) a Swedish IT company that provides smart city solutions; (6) two US tech companies; and (7) a French company involved in digital identity and security solutions.

On the one hand, the OpenLab clearly can attract an array of private partners. On the other, the glaring absence of South African partners, either public or private, is significant. This is particularly striking because the focus of the Lab on smart city solutions by default bears a local outreach. The lack of local community representation is thrown into sharp contradiction considering South Africa's Minister of Communications and Digital Technologies, Stella Ndabeni-Abrahams' recent remarks: "South African initiatives are likely to be successful only if they happen in an integrated manner" (SA News, 2019). Lacking integration with local stakeholders, Huawei OpenLab risks compromising the digital sovereignty of South Africa and its citizens, severely limiting the potential beneficial effects of its tech solutions.

Overall, it is possible to identify four major actors leading tech innovation initiatives in South Africa: (1) foreign ICT companies (mainly Western and Chinese); (2) South African ICT companies; (3) South African governmental bodies; and (4) South African universities. While a number of tech hubs and incubators witness the collaborations among these four types of actors (e.g., The Innovation Hub in Pretoria and Thsimologong Precint in Johannesburg), Huawei has favored a proprietary, corporate approach to the development of the OpenLab, which makes the development of the solutions potentially disempowering for South African actors.

7.4.2 The Joint Innovation Center in Cagliari

For comparison, this chapter also examines the JIC launched in Cagliari, the capital of Sardinia, at the end of 2019. A comparative analysis aims to produce more insight into the governance models of Huawei's smart cities initiative around the world. Similar to the OpenLab, the JIC focuses on the collaborative development of tech solutions to turn the Italian city of Cagliari into a smart city. In this case, too, Huawei is the leader of the initiative, together with CSR4, the Centre for Advanced Studies, Research and Development of Sardinia, which is an interdisciplinary pole of technological innovation whose sole public shareholder is the regional agency Sardegna Ricerche. In this case, Huawei joins forces with the main public actor in the region in technological R&D. Beyond that, other partners of the JIC include:

[5] https://openlab.huawei.com/portal/en-us/pages/earth/johannesburg.html.

(1) an Italian company that develops core IT infrastructures through cloud computing; (2) an Italian company that offers hardware and software solutions for the IoTs including cybersecurity services; (3) an Italian company that develops network and connectivity solutions; and (4) an Italian firm focused on IT projects and installations.

Although neither Huawei Italy nor CSR4 were available for interviews before the end of the partnership (expected at the end of 2021), on the JIC's (2020) website,[6] the media section provides valuable information from the stakeholders involved in the initiative. As Massimo Carboni, coordinator of the JIC for Sardegna Ricerche, states: "the project is a collaborative venture of three main actors: CSR4, which provides skills and know-how, Regione Sardegna, which defined the vision and mission of the initiative, and ICTs companies, among which Huawei is the main partner, plus other six SMEs." From this perspective, the initiative has a "indigenous" component, especially in comparison with Huawei OpenLab in Johannesburg. This, however, does not provide a clear indication of the governance behind the initiative, that is, the power relations among the actors when it comes to the data lifecycle's management. The JIC website states:

> The objective of the project is the realization of an experimental infrastructure with which new technologies will be developed for widespread connectivity on a metropolitan scale (...) aimed at solving problems related to smart cities, the experimentation of widespread sensors for the acquisition of large amounts of data that will be managed through the development of architectures for Open Data and Big Data, the testing of systems for city safety (safe city) and the study of new generation e-LTE systems.

Resonating with the mission of Huawei OpenLab in Johannesburg, here too the stress is on "smart city" as "safe city." Mentioned on the JIC's website is the development of an array of sensors for vast collections of data: video cameras and distributed urban tracking systems such as "face recognition, plate recognition, intrusion detection, behavioural analysis, etc." The idea of amassing large amounts of data by means of innovative tech solutions is again framed within a techno-optimistic discourse of "improvement of citizens' quality of life" and even of "increase [of] both cultural and educational mutual knowledge" for all the companies involved. Hence, the discourse supporting the initiative tends to present a win-win situation, which echoes the idea of peer-to-peer cooperation typical of Chinese companies' "going out" efforts. As Lidia Leoni in charge of strategic partnerships at CSR4 points out, what counts the most is the ultimate goal rather than the means: "it is extremely important to have an idea of what is happening everywhere (...) by connecting data which would remain otherwise unrelated." While such a functionalistic approach of the tech cooperation between Huawei and CSR4

[6] www.jicsardegna.it/en/. If not differently specified, all subsequent quotes are taken from the website.

adheres to an understanding of the city as a space to be mapped in real time for increased control and efficiency, overlooked are issues of realpolitik and people's safety and security behind data lifecycle. Missing from JIC's public discourse is clear communication of which actors and under which obligations are responsible for the management and security of data and potential data breaches.[7]

What we do know, via the media releases, is that through the deployment of these smart city solutions, the JIC aims to build an intelligent operation center (IOC), that is, a centralized platform on which all data converge for the formation of what is called the "data lake." Vincenzo Strangis, director of smart cities and innovation at Huawei, defines the IOC by resorting to the human–machine metaphor: "the IOC is like the brain of the human body connected to the nervous system, for us the nervous system is that which comes from all the sensors that are present in the city." The platform is based on open-source technologies on which vertical applications can then be implemented. The open-source choice favors the potential arrival of (new) partners by lowering barriers to access and enhancing interoperability. Namely, the IOC is based on a logic of federation of the data, which maximizes data's capitalization through the creation of the data lake by an array of different actors. On this point, Strangis specifies that "the infrastructure gravitates around the data center, that is, the storage technology that allows for the emergence of the data lake, to which all the various stakeholders will contribute by making available *to us* the data coming from their applications [emphasis added]."

The fact that the JIC is led by a public stakeholder should prioritize, in principle, the public interest in using data to tackle social and environmental issues in the urban context instead of profit-only objectives. In a way, data are expected to be repurposed for the benefit of the local community. On the other hand, however, the network through which these data run is owned by Huawei, making the Chinese company an inalienable actor of the whole initiative (the "us" used by Strangis is emblematic). And this does raise concerns over the risk of tech dependency voiced by the European Union recently. To borrow the well-established and somewhat questionable metaphor of data as "the new oil," the IOC could be seen as the public-led data refinery and Huawei as the owner of the pipeline through which the oil runs. On the JIC's website, it is also reported that the goals of the initiative are:

[7] On this point, it is worth highlighting the results of a longitudinal qualitative analysis about Huawei's communication on social medial platforms (Calzati, 2020b). From the study, it emerges that the company's lack of responsiveness to users' comments on Facebook and Twitter is the results of a precise communicative strategy rather than the lack of monitoring of interactions. In fact, once the company feels the need to rectify/preserve its online image (such as when accused of being owned by the Chinese's government), it shows a very proactive attitude in creating online interactions.

To experiment and demonstrate on the field the effectiveness in the implementation of a private network, which exploiting a high data transmission capacity, allows the study of new solution for the benefit of the city community and of public and private institutions. We will then proceed with the experimentation of sensors able to detect data that will be processed by other parts of the project. Prototypes of mobile devices operating on the frequencies of the private e-LTE network provided by Huawei will be tested in the field.

E-LTE networks are also at the core of the OpenLab initiative in Johannesburg. The corporate-based conception of the "pipeline," which makes the collection of data possible, puts Huawei in a privileged position, whether the solutions developed will concretely and beneficially impact on the community and/or other partners or not. At stake, it is not to contest such conception – these solutions might really improve the quality of citizens' life – but rather to shed light on the trade-offs in terms of digital sovereignty that the governance model of these initiatives entail. Notably, compared to the South African case where the joint venture capitalized exclusively on foreign actors, the JIC enacts a multinational approach that sees Huawei establishing not only commercial ties but also institutional partnerships (e.g., the CSR4) with local actors. However, such multinational approach should be dutifully scrutinized from a cyber-geopolitical perspective, considering that, as Wen (2021, p. 31) notes, Huawei's activity "has been closely entangled with the Chinese government's (...) attempt to extend China's control over transnational network infrastructures." The stake is eminently sociopolitical, that is, accountability of the extent to which technology and data use/ownership create socioeconomic value and for whom.

7.5 CONCLUSION

By comparing Huawei's OpenLab in Johannesburg and the JIC in Cagliari, the chapter scrutinized the discursive framings of these initiatives with regard to the normative tech-centered conception of smart city solutions, and assessed the different governance models and partnerships supporting the initiatives in terms of their potential (dis)empowerment for local actors and citizens.

Both initiatives put forth a techno-optimistic vision that presents them as win-for-all projects. This framing avoids an in-depth characterization of actual implementations of smart city solutions and their impact on local communities. In this regard, the discourses surrounding both initiatives adhere to the normative understanding of smart city solutions as ICT-based endeavors to enhance decision-making efficiency and quality of life, by default rather than proven. Of particular significance is the coupling of smart city with the concept of safe city, that is, increasingly controlled spaces. From this perspective, socioeconomic considerations are eschewed as if the smartening of the city were an inevitable tide uplifting all actors involved. The analysis also revealed differences in the ways in which these initiatives have been publicly communicated.

While there is more publicly available information in the Italian case, very minimal exists in the case of Johannesburg's OpenLab. In both cases, however, Huawei refrained from delivering any statements upon request about the workings and outcomes of its initiatives.

In terms of governance, the OpenLab is heavily based on foreign private stakeholders. In fact, no South African stakeholders, either private or public, are officially part of the Lab. Instead, the OpenLab includes Western and Chinese private ICT companies alike. Running against the call by South African authorities to fuel tech initiatives in an integrated manner, the foreign-led nature of the OpenLab frustrates the development of local stakeholders and hinders the emergence of South Africa's digital sovereignty. This unbalance emerges even more vividly when comparing the OpenLab with the JIC in Italy. Although Huawei is the main private stakeholder, the JIC is nonetheless led by CSR4, an Italian public research center. However, in this case too, the cyber-geopolitical tensions surrounding the technology governance of the initiative cannot be overlook in that they do represent a potential threat to digital sovereignty as underscored by the European Union.

To an extent, Huawei shows high contextual flexibility when establishing its investments and partnerships abroad. The proprietary approach Huawei favors in South Africa undoubtedly gives the company more discretion with regard to the type of projects developed. The diversity of stakeholders with whom Huawei partners, particularly in Italy, does highlight the extent to which its smart city initiatives rework the concept of digital sovereignty and how, beyond theory, such diversity fosters a *certain* real-political form of digital sovereignty based on contextual opportunities. Beyond a domestic and foreign dichotomy, these smart city initiatives rearticulate the concept of digital sovereignty according to a transnational approach, underscoring Huawei's modulated interventions across the globe.

For both case studies, further field research is needed to substantiate the discursive analysis with ethnographic findings. Indeed, the assessment of the extent to which digital sovereignty is a contested arena along the Global North–Global South axis, *as much as* the South–South axis cannot do without the direct engagement with stakeholders. This, in turn, requires putting pressure on all ICT actors for demanding a more transparent and accountable communication concerning how the data fueling their smart city projects are managed, especially considering that digital sovereignty is an increasingly entangled transnational geo-governance issue.

PART III

GRASSROOTS CONTESTATIONS OF DIGITAL SOVEREIGNTY

8

Circumventing the "Sovereignization" of the Russian Internet

Toward an Infrastructure-Based Sociology of Digital Sovereignty and Its Resistances in Russia

Olga Bronnikova, Françoise Daucé, Ksenia Ermoshina, Valéry Kossov, Benjamin Loveluck, Francesca Musiani, Bella Ostromooukhova, Perrine Poupin, and Anna Zaytseva

8.1 INTRODUCTION

In the first decade of the twenty-first century, characterized by relatively high levels of freedom in digital innovation, the technical constraints on the construction of the Russian Internet (RuNet) have remained mostly invisible to its users (Deibert & Rohozinski, 2010). However, since the early 2010s, the increasingly strict regulations imposed by the government have made these aspects more evident (Oates, 2013; Soldatov & Borogan, 2015; Gritsenko, Wijermars, & Kopotev, 2021). In particular, Roskomnadzor (RKN), the federal government communications control body,[1] has seen its jurisdiction and reach rapidly extended to domains as varied as the control of online content, the right to block websites, and the registering of blocked websites, with a substantially increased possibility of censorship. RKN's control relies on its important nexus of relations and collaborations with actors that maintain and keep the internet operational and propose connectivity solutions to users including access providers and owners of digital businesses.

This scenario has led to a particular and Russia-specific instantiation of the "digital sovereignty" label, which has taken hold in the past decade, not only offering a telling example of how state-centric formations of digital sovereignty may be structured, but also highlighting the limits of such model, showing how it might be challenged by grassroot initiatives. In this regard, the Russian context illustrates the tension between two types of digital sovereignty as outlined in the introduction to this book: state-centered digital sovereignty and "personal" digital sovereignty struggles as a response to the increasing constraints on digital and civil liberties imposed by the State. Indeed, Russian

[1] RKN is also the data protection regulator in the country; it is not an independent authority, but a governmental agency (federal service) established under the Ministry of ICTs and Media.

authorities are actively pursuing a digital sovereignty strategy that focuses on an autonomization and "sovereignization" of the RuNet through the adoption of new laws to counter foreign influences and agents, as well as their devices and applications. Exemplars of this tendency are what have become known as the *Sovereign Internet Law*, adopted in 2019 with the official aim of protecting the country from cyberattacks, and the *law against Apple*, passed in 2020 with the objective of having all smartphone devices in Russia to preload a host of "Russian-made" applications (Musiani et al., 2019).

In this context, since 2018, the *ResisTIC (Criticism and circumvention of digital borders in Russia)*[2] project team endeavors to analyze how different actors of the RuNet resist and adapt to the recent wave of the so-called authoritarian and centralizing regulations, with a particular focus on online resistance that reveals so far lesser-known social practices and techniques for circumventing online constraints. These circumventions expose the limits of what the introductory chapter to this volume considers as state digital sovereignty and the underlying tensions that this type of digital sovereignty inevitably unleashes against competing forms of individual digital sovereignty, echoing a long history of social inventiveness in the last decades of the Soviet period when many Soviet citizens routinely transgressed and reinterpreted the norms and rules of the socialist state (Yurchak, 2013). These "arts de faire" were notably visible in their use of communication infrastructures (Zakharova, 2020).[3] They are also in line with the protests that emerged after the demise of the USSR. Since the 1990s, Russian society has been neither apathetic nor resigned, as shown by the local mobilizations contributing to the development of citizen activism (Kleman, et al., 2010) or the large demonstrations against electoral fraud in 2011 and 2012 (Gabowitsch, 2016).

One of the project's primary objectives is to explore the extent to which control and circumvention strategies are embedded in and conducted by means of the infrastructure of the RuNet; our aim has been to shed light on the complex relationship between technical devices and algorithms (Brousseau, Marzouki, & Méadel, 2012; Musiani, 2013) in the Russian digital sphere, and the politics and markets taking shape in the country. As the project moves toward its conclusion (June 2022), this chapter proposes to take stock of the project's different fieldworks and insights concerning the theme of this book, at the crossroads of digital sovereignty, data, and infrastructure – both its development and its uses, oftentimes very creative and subversive. Beyond the Russian case,

[2] Our project website is www.resistic.fr.

[3] Zakharova (2020) recalls that postal mail in the USSR was the dominant mode of communication in Soviet society until the late 1970s. However, letters were heavily monitored and censorship agents enforced random checking of mail as well as the control of foreign correspondence. The population adapted by moderating its speech, but also by developing parallel distribution channels, through railway employees for example, or by using diplomatic mail from foreign states to contact relatives outside the Soviet borders.

understood as a "laboratory" of broader tendencies in internet governance worldwide, the project seeks to contribute to a conceptualization of the changing patterns in politics as it is exposed to information and communication technology (ICT) in the modern world.

The chapter undertakes an infrastructure-based sociology of the RuNet, focusing on the technical devices and assets involved in surveillance and censorship, and on the strategies of resistance and circumvention "by infrastructure" that follow. In the tradition of Science and Technology Studies (STS), we understand the "infrastructural" quality of the network of networks, and its multitude of physical and logical apparatuses, as relational and conditional; infrastructures can be more usefully understood in terms of function than form. Thus, beyond objects whose infrastructural aspect is immediately obvious, such as bridges or pipes, a number of artifacts and entities that populate and shape the network of networks could be described as infrastructure because they have an infrastructural *function* – because they help to structure, shape, enable, or constrain our "being-together" on and with the internet. In this sense, internet infrastructures include physical objects, for example, submarine cables that carry global telecommunications or data centers that host our digital content, and objects that are a priori much less concrete, such as internet protocols, applications, and software (see, e.g., Musiani, 2018 for further discussion of this point).

The analyses presented in the chapter are based on original data, both quantitative and qualitative (interviews and observations on the field). In addition to the presentation of the case studies, a recurring point of interest is a reflexive assessment of our methods, in particular those related to field survey, which can be problematic and sensitive in Russia because of the constraints on researchers and the protection of interviewees, but is extremely useful as it allows to question the preconceptions attached to the RuNet and renew our understanding of the role of infrastructure in digital control and circumvention.

The empirical core of the chapter will provide an overview of a number of studies undertaken by the ResisTIC project team in the past few years. While the presentation of the case studies will, by necessity, be relatively brief, presenting them together will allow to draw some general conclusions about the state of infrastructure-based digital sovereignization in Russia; interested readers will be able to delve deeper into the case studies by means of a special issue of the open access First Monday journal (Daucé & Musiani, 2021).

Before we delve into the case studies, however, we seek to outline the particular relationship that exists in Russia between law and infrastructure as means of control, as it has taken shape in the past few years. In response to the Russian government's increasingly coercive grip, direct political confrontation is difficult and risky; thus, we argue that the use of infrastructure is a way to indirectly bypass constraints and coercion. A number of dynamic behaviors, which can be qualified as infrastructure-based ruse and resistance, have emerged in close response to legislation. Russian "digital resisters" adapt to new laws and invent new techno-legal tweaks that challenge the Russian lawmaker. Understanding this dialectic is of vital importance to understand the context in which the initiatives described below, between promotion of and resistance to digital sovereignty by means of infrastructure, take place.

8.2 THE RELATIONSHIP BETWEEN LAW AND INFRASTRUCTURE IN RUSSIAN DIGITAL SOVEREIGNTY STRATEGIES

The regulation of internet infrastructure began in a firm manner since 2012 with new laws such as 139 FZ,[4] which establishes a legal framework for the system of filtering websites included in the "blacklist" of digital resources, whose illicit nature may be defined by various state institutions. This law introduces a new relationship between the infrastructure providers and the state. Indeed, the law obliges internet service providers (ISPs) to inform site owners of the need to remove pages with illegal information or to block access to sites listed in the register prepared by RKN. Initially, the law prohibits content relating to child pornography, suicide, or drug use. However, the new Law 398 FZ extends blocking practices to the sites calling for unauthorized public protest actions considered "acts of extremism"[5]; for example, media such as Grani.org were banned on Russian territory for their publications dedicated to actions in support of the people prosecuted for participating in political protests on Bolotnaya Square in 2012. The prosecutor's office also deemed Kasparov.ru's website as "extremist," in an article related to the annexation of Crimea. Since March 2014, "nonsystem" political opposition sites[6] have been blocked under the law.

These blocking attempts, as well as RKN's "manual" control of ISPs – that is, the case-by-case verification of the blocking of prohibited sites – have proven to be ineffective. From 2015, RKN is therefore imposing Revizor boxes on operators, which automatically check whether prohibited resources have been blocked by ISPs. The new monitoring system entails additional costs for ISPs due to installation of hardware and software components and the high fines for noncompliance to the law (Stadnik, 2021). The web community is responding to blocking practices with the increasingly common use of virtual private networks (VPNs) or Tor software, dynamic IP addresses, and mirror sites.

[4] Federal Law 139-FZ of July 28, 2012 "On Amendments to the Federal Law on the Protection of Children from Information Harmful to Their Health and Development and to Certain Legislative Acts of the Russian Federation."

[5] Federal Law 398-FZ of December 28, 2013 "On Amendments to the Federal Law on Information, Information Technology and Information Protection."

[6] A variety of political groups dissatisfied with the actual regime, and not represented in official bodies at the federal and regional levels.

In parallel with these information control practices, the Russian authorities are attempting to regulate the RuNet by law, targeting its infrastructure more directly. On July 21, 2014, the President signed Law 242 FZ,[7] which requires private internet players to store the personal data of Russian users on servers physically located on Russian territory. The Law 531 FZ[8] prescribes the hosting on Russian territory of all sites of Russian public authorities. These measures are justified by the need for data security for the population and the State in a tense international context linked, *inter alia*, to the conflict with Ukraine, and to a broader context in which cyberattacks from Russia to US, and vice-versa, happen on a regular basis (Sanger & Perlroth, 2019) and, to some extent, the need for a RuNet is seen by the Russian government as a cybersecurity strategy. Ultimately, the application of the law 242 FZ has been postponed until October 30, 2022.

The trend of repatriation of digital resources and data continues with the so-called Yarovaya Law 374 FZ.[9] This time the legislator modifies the nature and quantity of data that would be controlled by the state in the context of the fight against terrorism. Indeed, the law obliges operators to store telephone conversations, SMS, videos, and emails of users for a period ranging from 30 days to 6 months. The encryption keys must be made available to security services upon request. Given the significant cost to operators, it was expected that their storage capacity would increase by 15% annually. However, the application of this rule was temporarily suspended in 2020 because of the pandemic, which caused an explosion in the number of video and other content exchanges, making it impossible to store such a large volume of data (Peškova, 2020).

All this legislation aimed at territorializing infrastructure of the RuNet finds a general framework in the Doctrine of Information Security (Presidency of the Russian Federation, 2016). This document provides definitions of critical infrastructures, emphasizing the territorial anchoring of information systems and communication networks.

The Doctrine gave rise to the Law 90 FZ called "on the Sovereign Internet," which came into force on November 1, 2019. Indeed, it takes up the notion of sovereignty of the Russian digital space and tasks the government with ensuring the stable functioning of its critical infrastructure by taking control

[7] Federal Law Concerning the Introduction of Amendments to Certain Legislative Acts of the Russian Federation to Clarify the Procedure for Processing Personal Data in Information and Telecommunication Networks.

[8] Federal Law 531-FZ of December 31, 2014 "On Amendments to Articles 13 and 14 of the Federal Law on Information, Information Technologies and Information Protection and to the Code of Administrative Offences of the Russian Federation."

[9] Federal Law 374-FZ of July 6, 2016 "On Amendments to the Federal Law 'On Combating Terrorism' and to Certain Legislative Acts of the Russian Federation with Regard to Establishing Additional Measures to Counter Terrorism and Ensure Public Safety." The law borrows the name of its sponsor, Russian MP Irina Yarovaya.

of the traffic exchange points, all autonomous systems and the system of national domains ru. and рф. The law also provides for the establishment of state control over cross-border traffic by the infrastructure that will ensure network routing in case of the impossibility of connection to foreign servers. In addition, it requires ISPs to install Deep Packet Inspection (DPI) filtering equipment. RKN has been given the power to set routing policy for ISPs and to ensure centralized network management. To this end, tests were planned to simulate the situation where RuNet would be disconnected from the external network. However, after a first test in December 2019, others were canceled in 2020, officially due to the pandemic. In January 2021, the Ministry of Digital Development announced that the final plan for the exercises would be decided after the end of the pandemic (Pâtin, 2021). In contrast, COVID-19 did not become an obstacle for Twitter throttling in 2021,[10] which was done with the use of DPI equipment. Furthermore, the pandemic did not prevent the passage of Law 19 FZ, which holds operators accountable for not installing DPI equipment.[11]

The process of RuNet sovereignization continues to develop according to the guidelines of the Information Security Doctrine, with Law 425 FZ mandating foreign hardware manufacturers to preinstall Russian software on electronic devices sold in Russia from April 1, 2021 (Presidency of the Russian Federation, 2016, art. IV, sect. 23, par. 3). The so-called "anti-Apple" law has been met with an unfavorable response from other major computer brands including Microsoft and Intel. However, even the most resistant, such as Apple, have found a compromise with the government: Russian applications are proposed as opt-in mechanism for the device buyer, without the device manufacturer preinstalling them (Kodačigov, 2021).

The adoption of new laws regulating the internet infrastructure reduces opportunities of circumvention for digital companies, the media, NGOs, and simple users. However, the digital ecosystem is organizing itself to cope with the constraints of the legislation. First, there are legal means such as appeals against court decisions or even legal recourse against RKN decisions. Second, the RuNet community continues to seek for technical solutions to adapt to restrictive rules. Finally, the proliferation of punitive laws and the high rate of their adoption are turning against the state, which is failing to enforce them in a regular and systematic manner throughout the Russian territory. This diminishes the effectiveness of the law and leads to the slowing down of the sovereignization process.

[10] RKN started throttling Twitter in Russia on March 10, 2021. The agency explained it by the fact that the social network does not respond to requests to remove "illegal content": appeals to suicide, extremist materials, child pornography, information about drugs. On May 17, RKN decided to remove access restrictions on desktop terminals, keeping Twitter traffic slowed down on mobile devices. See Roskomnadzor (2021).

[11] Federal Law 19-FZ of February 24, 2021 "On Amendments to the Code of Administrative Offences of the Russian Federation."

8.3 SOVEREIGNIZATION AND RESISTANCE "BY INFRASTRUCTURE" IN THE RUNET: INSIGHTS FROM THE FIELD

We now turn to the empirical core of the chapter, which provides an overview of a number of studies undertaken by the ResisTIC project team in the past few years. We focus on both the technical devices and assets involved in sovereignization processes, and the strategies of resistance and circumvention "by infrastructure" that follow.

8.3.1 "Black Boxes" and Strategies of Internet Service Providers

One of the key levers of control over the RuNet is the legal framework targeting ISPs. These private technical intermediaries ensure the routing of internet traffic toward end users, and in Russia, they represent a vibrant and diverse market with many actors of different sizes, providing an overall good quality of service. Digital sovereignty policies regarding ISPs seek to achieve two main objectives: enabling surveillance of the traffic and ensuring compliance with censorship regulation. Moreover, the technical solutions to cater for these regulations need to be "made in Russia." A domestic industry of surveillance and censorship has thus flourished, which affects the ISP market in different ways.

We explored this industry through a two-year fieldwork in 2017–2019, including in-depth interviews with ISP representatives, a web-ethnography of ISP forums and chats, and a content analysis of professional documentation (Ermoshina, Loveluck, & Musiani, 2022). Our research focused on the vendors of surveillance and censorship solutions and on the "black boxes" known as "middleboxes," which ISPs must implement on their infrastructures: actual physical boxes that are plugged on the network, but also software solutions and distributed technical devices and equipment. By drawing on both STS and the political economy of information and communication networks, we sought to understand their functioning and the ambiguities and controversies they generate, as well as assessing the liabilities, technical impediments, and economic costs that weigh on ISPs, and the strategies they devise in order to circumvent them or negotiate compromises.

We focused on two types of "black boxes" that ISPs need to embed within their infrastructure. The first one is known as SORM (System for Operative Investigative Activities), and it is used to collect and store metadata and internet traffic, which must be made available to the authorities upon request as lawful interception. Though SORM must be installed at the ISP's expense, it is controlled by the FSB (the Russian Federal Security Service) via a terminal and can be accessed by other agencies and police departments (tax, customs, border police, etc.). SORM-1 was set up in 1995 for wiretapping and phone surveillance, before adapting to the internet in 1998 as SORM-2, and it has evolved several times since then. The latest iteration was defined by the "Yarovaya" 374-FZ4 and 375-FZ laws passed in 2016 (and somewhat loosened in 2018): the law now requires all telecom providers to store metadata for 3 years and content such as data, voice calls, images, and text messages for 30 days. The hefty costs of this system and the long delays in specifying the certifications have drawn criticism on the part of ISPs – who must choose between various expensive solutions, are never completely sure they are complying with the regulation, and may also face legal responsibilities in the case of data breaches. Indeed, not only are there different ways of conforming to the regulation, but misconfigurations of SORM are also common. Moreover, requirements are different according to ISP size and to mitigate these different risks, various strategies are adopted such as sharing solutions between ISPs or even buying already "SORMed" traffic from bigger actors. Finally, SORM is contested not only because it is costly but also because it involves cumbersome compatibility issues with existing ISP infrastructures, because most of the stored traffic is encrypted and therefore unusable, and because the FSB often uses other ways to access specific information. It is said to mainly benefit a small number of firms who have gained quasi-monopolistic positions on the market, and who benefit from existing ties with the Defense sector.

The second type of "black box" we focused on is the solution needed to filter the traffic and make it "RKN-compliant" – blocking any website that RKN (Roskomnadzor, the Russian federal executive body responsible for media and telecommunications) has added to its "black list" of banned websites. Although ISPs previously received blocking requests on a case-by-case basis, a centralized list was set up in 2012 after the protests against electoral fraud, and was further expanded especially after the Ukrainian crisis in 2014. There is no unique "law on censorship" however, but many existing laws that have been amended to include responsibility for publishing "illegal" content. This category is only vaguely defined and decisions to ban content are made with no oversight, paving the way for politically motivated suppressions.[12] Moreover, precise requirements such as standardized "blockpages" and guidelines for traffic filtering were only issued in 2018. Prior to that, vulnerabilities in the mechanism meant that activists could leverage DNS-based "guerilla" tactics to block other websites – including at one point the Ministry of Justice main website – as a sign of protest. With no standardized blockpages, these could also be used by ISPs to criticize censorship and promote circumvention tools such as VPNs. Today, there are still different available methods for blocking websites, which range from homemade scripts to hardware devices, cloud-based solutions, and DPI-blocking software, but attempts have been made to standardize the blocking procedures. And with an increasingly voluminous

[12] In June 2020, the European Court of Human Rights has delivered multiple judgments stressing the incompatibility of the Russia take-down system with the ECHR. See, for example, Grover and Thomas (2021).

blocklist, cobbled-up solutions have gradually become increasingly difficult to maintain. Nevertheless, ISPs still actively seek to avoid complying completely with censorship – in order to reduce their costs but also to remain attractive to their clients. Some even engage in selective censorship or try to fool the system in various ways, such as blockpages or the so-called "DNS guerillas" (see Ermoshina, Loveluck, & Musiani, 2022).

Both SORM and RKN-compliance must be implemented if ISPs want to avoid being fined. However, none of them are standardized and the certification processes are lengthy. ISPs therefore often find themselves in uncharted waters, where they must *interpret* these requirements and often experiment in order to find a balance among imprecise (yet strict) rules, technical feasibility, and economic costs. These gray areas present strong uncertainties for ISPs but also opportunities. Our research shows that along with ethical and political concerns, Russian surveillance and censorship policies generate inefficiency and potential corruption of the market and affect the overall topology of the RuNet. However, we also highlight that ISPs develop different forms of technical, legal, economic, and sometimes political resistance. Far from a vertical, centralized, and all-powerful model of State control, the regulation of surveillance and censorship shows that control – though burdensome – is only partial, often inefficient and fraught with contradictions, opening up spaces for resistance and evasion.

8.3.2 The "Telegram Ban": RuNet between Infrastructural Dependency and Resistance

These resistance tactics of both technical experts and users have become especially visible through the case of the "Telegram ban," a two-year long attempt by RKN to block one of the most famous messaging applications in Russia. The "Telegram ban" should be approached as a sociotechnical controversy that unveils the close dependencies of RuNet *vis-à-vis* global internet infrastructures. Indeed, this case questions both technical and geopolitical boundaries as it opposes the strong government-originated discourse on the Russian "Sovereign Internet" (Freiberg, 2014) and the transnational character of material internet infrastructures. This "Telegram ban" favors a better understanding of both the threat of balkanization of the internet and the "turn to infrastructure" (Musiani et al., 2016) in RuNet governance, as it makes visible the ensemble of sociotechnical and legal mechanisms used to exercise control over RuNet.

Created in 2013 by the Durov brothers, Telegram fell under scrutiny of the Russian political police in the space of a few years: on July 14, 2017, the Russian FSB requested decryption keys for all messages sent and received via Telegram, in accordance with the 2016-approved Yarovaya Law. Telegram did not satisfy the FSB's request, and after a second request to provide the keys in March 2018, Telegram's lawyers explained that it was cryptographically impossible because of the way in which encryption works in Telegram. In response, on April 16, 2018, Telegram was officially blocked by RKN. However, Telegram was never completely blocked on the territory of the Russian Federation. Users could access all of its services rather easily – sometimes even without any circumvention tools because small and medium ISPs did not always comply with RKN's requirements to block the app. This inability of governmental agencies to successfully block Telegram raised concerns as to the efficiency of RKN and technical expertise of its employees.

This trust in Telegram, according to our interviews (see also Maréchal, 2018), lies not so much with the technology, but with its main developer, Pavel Durov, his reputation, and his political position. Indeed, Telegram became so influential in Russia that governmental institutions kept maintaining their own official Telegram channels, probably so as to maintain some kind of influence within this platform. Interestingly, and ironically, the Russian government itself kept on using Telegram as one of its primary means for official communications during the COVID-19 pandemic, despite the fact that the tool was still officially blocked until June 2020. As the official Telegram statistics show, Telegram's Russian audience has doubled since 2018 and the ban did not impact this growth.

Telegram has attracted tech user communities that have chosen it as their primary messenger, not only for daily one-to-one communication but also for professional chats. Telegram's API has engendered a dynamic user-driven development of the bot and bridge ecosystem that made Telegram something "bigger than just a messenger, a new kind of social network" – as one of our respondents puts it. Telegram has evolved into a hybrid network with multiple functions and purposes, offering shelter to censored media using Telegram as a circumvention tool to deliver content to their audiences, allowing public group chats and proposing tools to promote cultural and political events and gatherings, organize surveys, create and distribute cultural and artistic content, generate stickers, and process payments.

There is no single history of the Telegram ban, but several ways to tell this story, competing chronologies and narratives that trace it back to different moments in the history of the RuNet – itself a rather controversial one. The defenders of Telegram do not interpret the ban as an isolated case but analyze it in a broader context of "the war on RuNet," while pro-governmental media, on their end, frame the Telegram ban as "the (legitimate) war on terrorism." The difference in framing strategies unveils how an instant messenger becomes in itself an instrument used to build and distribute concurrent political narratives about what RuNet has been and how it should function in the future. The Telegram ban crystallizes two competing paradigms: the one mourning RuNet's "Golden Age," based on free competition and cooperation between tech professionals, absence of censorship and centralized regulation, transnational circulation of tools, services, and people; and the other that affirms the necessity of stronger, infrastructure-driven control of RuNet's "borders" and content production and circulation. Both paradigms include a third party: the complex network of foreign, mostly US-made, services such as Google or Amazon Web Servers that actually become crucial for the functioning and well-being of RuNet. While the Telegram ban unveils these fundamental dependencies on foreign infrastructures, it paradoxically becomes the trigger for faster "sovereignization" – the relocalization of servers, data, and services – of the Russian segment of the global network.

Indeed, the very circumvention mechanisms used by Telegram (such as IP hopping) relied on Amazon and Google Web servers to temporarily host the elusive messenger. Access restrictions to Telegram were extended to all third parties providing infrastructural support for the infamous messenger. In April 2018, eighteen million IP addresses were blocked, including hundreds of IPs of Amazon, Google, and other major web services. This method, dubbed by Telegram defenders as "carpet blocking," turned out to be quite inefficient: only 18 IP addresses out of three million blocked Amazon addresses were actually used by Telegram.

Collateral damages caused by these blockings had an important effect on the politicization of particular segments of RuNet users (e.g., small entrepreneurs whose websites were accidentally blocked). These new "concerned publics" (Geiger et al., 2014) were either involved into collective action or engaged into usage and understanding of circumvention technologies. Researchers have observed a wider adoption of privacy-enhancing technologies and circumvention tools such as VPN and Tor. A vibrant market of proxies for Telegram developed, while popular opposition media helped raise user awareness about internet censorship and circumvention.

During the first months of The Telegram ban, tech activists developed a new repertoire of contention (Tilly, 2002) ranging from disobedience (ISPs using various tricks to avoid blocking Telegram) to hacktivist actions. The Telegram ban also led to a rise of offline activism focused on internet freedom. A wave of demonstrations "For Telegram" took place across the country. The instant messenger became, at least for Spring and Summer 2018, a contextual point of unity for various anti-governmental movements.

Telegram was officially unbanned in June 2020, for two main reasons explained by the Ministry of Communication: first, the "technical impossibility" to effectively block it, and second, because Telegram has agreed to block specific channels related to drug sale or terrorism; a less-official but no less important reason was the need to share information via governmental channels during the COVID-19 pandemic. While the outcome of the battle for Telegram shows the inefficiency of the infrastructural apparatus and of the censorship methods used by RKN, there are indications that the Russian authorities, RKN in particular, may also have learned some lessons from the case, in terms of how they could adapt their "sovereignization" strategies by being more "hybrid" and acting at both the infrastructure and content governance levels (buying popular Telegram channels, sponsoring ideological content by their means).

8.3.3 Yandex.News, "Official" News Ratings, and Their Circumvention

Russia is one of the very few countries where search is not monopolized by Google, with Yandex owning a share of over 45% – thus making it a prized national champion of the Russian digital economy. Yandex has also developed other services such as Yandex.News, which presents a selection of topics and articles to reflect the themes most widely covered by the media at a given moment. The algorithms deployed by Yandex.News and Google.news can be perceived as an "invisible hand" deciding which topics will be singled out as relevant and which news outlets will be pushed on the forefront according to sometimes unfathomable criteria (Brake, 2017).

The controversies that arose after 2012 in Russia put an end to the belief in the objectivity of the aggregator. Control over the public sphere stepped up again in 2014, during the conflict with Ukraine and the occupation of Crimea. Yandex.News was accused of partiality by the authorities for providing visibility to information that didn't align with the official narrative. This led to the adoption in 2016 of a law on news aggregators, designed to extend control to such intermediaries and specifically targeting Yandex. News. It became legally responsible for any content published in its results (and at risk of heavy fines in case of violations), unless the selected media are officially registered with RKN. As a consequence all non-registered media as well as all foreign media (such as the BBC in Russian, as well as exiled media such as Meduza) disappeared from the Top 5 results. An audit of the aggregation algorithm we conducted in 2020 (Daucé & Loveluck, 2021) strikingly shows the concentration of information on Yandex.News among 14 large media players: public press agencies, state-funded media, leading newspapers, and mainstream online publications. This is a much narrower range than the results observed by Nechushtai and Lewis (2019) in the case of Google News in the US for instance where, although a small selection of 14 outlets also dominated the aggregator, a long tail of other publications also figured in the results.

Media players and news professionals, along with the new hurdles they face, are gradually developing critical views of the role and functioning of platforms and their algorithms – uncovering the political stakes of these key infrastructures. Controversies, regulations, and concentration of information lead to a delegitimation of the algorithm in the eyes of journalists, as well as web professionals and programmers who seek ways to bypass it. Some of them consider the service to be useless. As Lev Gershenzon, the former head of Yandex.News, remarked in 2016: "Aggregators make sense (...) only when there is something to aggregate. If all independent, interesting, professional publications on a federal scale can be counted on the fingers of one hand, rocket technology for their aggregation and processing is not needed – you can simply add them to your bookmarks" (Gershenzon, 2016). The idea of closing the service seems to have been considered by Yandex executives themselves. According to well-known journalist A. Plyushchev, from Ekho Moskvy:

> Well, you know, I once talked to A. Volozh, the head of Yandex, and that was before the law on aggregators was passed. And he told me that if the law was adopted, he would close the service. (...) Well, the law was softened a bit, and the service, as you can see, did not close. I still doubt if that was the right decision. Because, well, I think, unfortunately, the state did everything possible to manipulate both the media and extraction in search engines.[13]

In May 2018, in an open letter to Yandex CEO Yelena Bunina, A. Plyushchev advised her to shut down the Yandex.News service or to rename it Yandex. Propaganda.[14]

However, closing the aggregator is not the only option. Excluded from Yandex's rankings since 2016, independent media carry out dissemination actions on social networks to bypass the aggregator. They have migrated and relocated to other spaces and new types of distribution, disseminating their content on social media such as Facebook, Twitter, Instagram, or Telegram. The example of *Meduza*, a Riga-based online newspaper created by Galina Timchenko after she was fired from the news website Lenta.ru in 2014, is very enlightening here. According to its own metrics, in 2020, traffic came mostly from direct connections and social networks, which is presented as a badge of honor with its traffic being "certified organic." *Meduza* does not obtain any traffic from Yandex.News (compared with Lenta.ru, *Kommersant*, and RBK, which are more dependent on the aggregator). It has an active presence on social networks, which is consistent with the new information practices of the younger generation. Since 2016, a growing gap between how people experience news on Yandex.News and on social networks is noticeable. A media consumption study carried out by the Levada Sociological Center in Russia in February 2020 showed that people over 40 years old get their information mainly from official websites or from television, while younger people (18–39 years old) secure it mostly from social networks.[15]

Another scenario to bypass Yandex.news concerns the creation of an alternative aggregator. In 2019, from abroad, Telegram founder Pavel Durov announced his intention of developing a news aggregator on his platform: "We have a chance to create the first effective and free news aggregator in the history of the Internet," said Durov. "We can start recommending articles from the Recommended Articles block after reading each article in Telegram, gradually bringing it into service with an hourly selection and a global search on all the news in the world" (Eremenko & Brzygalova, 2019). In the context of the

[13] Interview with Aleksandr Plyushchev, Moscow, March 2019.

[14] See https://t.me/PlushevChannel/2533"\t"_blank.

[15] See the study by the Levada Center (2020). These results are coherent with the research on media consumption in Russia done by the audit company Deloitte (2020).

failed blocking of Telegram in Russia, P. Durov announced his aggregator will be beyond the control of the Russian security services and political censorship, unlike local operators. He invited Yandex.News developers to participate in the creation of his service and announced a competition to develop an algorithm from the Data Clustering Contest. Its first round took place in spring 2020 and was won by "Mindful Squirrel" (contestants appear on the platform under animal aliases to ensure fairness and transparency in testing). However, according to experts, "Mindful Squirrel" is actually Ilya Gusev, who works as a machine learning engineer at Yandex.News. In this way, the Telegram news aggregator is built on the skills of Yandex engineers, who themselves contribute to the circumvention of the aggregator they work for. This singular case highlights the agentivity of web engineers circulating in a plural technical world where cooperation is possible beyond the opposition displayed between the major internet actors. They thus contribute themselves to the bypassing of the infrastructures they built.

8.3.4 Online Repression of Local Environmental Movements as a "Sovereignization" Process

Processes of circumventing online constraints are also enacted by "ordinary" citizens and activists in far-off Russian regions. We analyzed one of these processes in the frame of a specific case study: citizens have been fighting since July 2018 against a waste landfill project designed to dispose of half a million tons of Moscow waste per year in a swampy area in a remote site called Shies, 1,200 km north of Moscow. A protest camp was set up and maintained to physically preserve the site, joined by people from all over Russia.

Activists do not themselves mobilize the notion of "digital sovereignty." The phenomenon of RuNet sovereignization is, however, a phenomenon whose effects on protest practices are felt on a daily basis. In other words, there are indeed practices of protection among mobilized inhabitants vis-à-vis the state's digital repression and surveillance, but no discourse on sovereignty or sovereignization as such, either to contest it or to appropriate the term, as we see in activist or indigenous movements in other countries (Couture & Toupin, 2019).

If we consider sovereignty as a discourse, a performative action of the state, sovereignty is "a speech act to (re-)establish the claimant's position as absolute authority, and to legitimise its exercise of power" (Werner & de Wilde, 2001). In the Shies case, the question of authority, power, and the rule of law was raised by habitants when they discovered that forest areas had been cut down near Shies and a building site was under construction. The project was started illegally from the point of view of Russian law, that is, without any state ecological, health, and technical expertise, public hearings, or legislative decree. In response to the Shies mobilization, the state did not question the illegal development project; instead, it repressed protest activities, including online ones.

If the State had forced the project owner to bring the project into conformity with the law, this would have been another form of sovereignization.

The online repressions take place in a political context where uprisings across the Middle East and North Africa (the so-called Arab Spring), Europe (the Indignados in Spain), and the US (the Occupy Wall Street protest) have received a great deal of attention from the Russian government (Nocetti, 2015). Other revolts in post-Soviet countries, such as Ukraine (2013–2014), Armenia (2018), and Belarus (2020), where social media played a prominent role, confirmed this trend. After 2012, the regime started to more closely monitor online media and social platforms. Oligarch Alisher Usmanov's Mail.ru group, with close ties to the Kremlin, bought VKontakte and since, the government has had no difficulty blocking groups or accessing personal data of site users. In this way, Russia develops a strong "data sovereignty," as it attempts to "subject data flows to national jurisdiction [...] with an emphasis on safeguarding national security" (Polatin-Reuben & Wright, 2014: 1). In 2014, with conflict rising in Ukraine, the crackdown against critical voices and opponents in Russia became even greater. Pavel Durov, the VKontakte (the Russia-developed dominant social network in the country) founder, lost control of his company and left the country because of political pressure. Like other local grassroots movements, the Shies one mainly use VKontakte. Activists use it despite the potential privacy and security risks this platform has posed to users since 2014.

The repressive practices against the Shies mobilization can be seen as attempts from the state to reassert its own sovereignty and that of its allies, the private waste sector. Repression related to VKontakte either took place offline, and meticulously documented online by activists in groups, or enacted entirely online. As for the first type, the blockade of fuel transfers and trucks by activists led to conflicts with site guards, with injuries and arrests in the ranks of activists, which in turn led to trials. Other cases of offline repressions documented online were related to the meetings organized by activists. For the second type, repressions were carried out online, or related to the internet directly. They included internet shutdowns at critical moments, seizing activists' audio, video, and computing equipment, blocking, deleting, or hacking groups and personal accounts, and carrying out legal trials based on material related to online groups.

After an initial moment of surprise derived from the first group blockings, the communities devised reaction strategies. At each blocking, a new group was created on VKontakte and activists intensively shared the link with others. Moreover, activists were making clones of VKontakte groups: the contents were copied simultaneously to Telegram and Instagram. A minority of activists exit platforms that implement stricter surveillance regimes and technologies (as VKontakte), moving, for example, to Telegram. But even so, most kept an account on VKontakte. Local activists, as the substantial majority of ordinary citizens, even those who are physically on the front line of local struggles, do not use free software, servers, and encryption-based technologies, as telecommunications, digital, and internet surveillance is the norm and routine for them; further, they do not trust digital services to protect them from privacy threats. They have the belief, inherited from the Soviet times, that "the State knows everything about everyone anyway."

Protest repression tools are continuously experimenting. Each protest case is an opportunity to test and search for effective technologies to block and filter out critical content and hold trials based on online materials. There is a continuum of the infrastructures and territories that are under the authority of the state and that are subject to a reassertion of power in critical situations: from the classic ones, such as landmass (with the landfill project), to digital content. Faced with repression, activists are learning and using new techniques of circumvention.

8.3.5 Google and US-based Tech Giants as "Recommendable" Tools in RuNet Digital Security Practices

Unlike in other so-called authoritarian regimes (e.g., China and Iran), Google remains legally accessible in Russia and is widely used, including by political leaders and pro-government media. This positions Google as a core actor in negotiations on digital freedoms between authorities and actors of civil society in Russia. Its position is further strengthened by the close dependence of the Russian economy and communication networks on internet giants. Indeed, a strong embeddedness of the Russian internet sector in the global IT ecosystem has been highlighted on several occasions, in particular during the aforementioned blocking of Telegram.

Nevertheless, Google's relations with Russian authorities are tense. Although the company has been present on the Russian market since 2005, the Russian authorities began to take a close interest in it after the mobilizations in 2011–2012: YouTube was widely used to disseminate evidence of electoral fraud. Several other cases have subsequently set Google against the Russian state, especially following the law on blocking prohibited content in Russia and the localization of data of Russian citizens on Russian territory. But the peak of the tensions was reached in May 2021, when Google was the first of the Big Tech companies in Russia to take legal action against RKN following the latter's request to remove the links on the demonstrations in support of Alexei Navalny.

In the polarized context of "information warfare," Western sanctions against Russia and a growing divide between civil liberties activists and the pro-government camp, any regulation of global internet companies, often seen as desirable in liberal regimes, is discredited in the eyes of Russian activists for free internet as synonymous with the internet's subordination to state surveillance and a threat to freedom of expression. In contrast to their Western colleagues, Google is considered mostly reliable by activists for internet liberties in Russia. This trust is based on the monitoring of Google's Transparency Reports. As noted by a digital security trainer for civil society NGOs in Russia, "*while for countries (...) participating in the 'five eyes' intelligence alliance, 80 to 90% of requests for information from the authorities are met, for Russia these figures represent only a few %.*"[16] This trust is, of course, not exempt from paradox, since Google Transparency Reports are, with some naïveté, considered here as an authoritative source providing a complete picture of what foreign companies may do with the personal data of RuNet users, neglecting both possible and acknowledged biases that do exist in this kind of documents.

Our contacts rely also on their own databases and measurement tools. For example, the "Map of repression on the Internet" (a project of the Internet Protection Society) lists only a few cases related to internet giants,[17] whereas 95% of them concern posts in VKontakte.[18] As to digital security trainers, they draw on their own internal "incident database": very few incidents involving Google services have been relayed in post-Soviet countries.[19]

While not always being deeply concerned about Google's involvement in "surveillance capitalism," internet freedom defenders point out the same phenomenon for Russian technology companies: "*In Russia, there are two logics of surveillance capitalism. On the one hand, companies that want to collect the maximum amount of behavioral data. On the other hand, there are some traditions and logics of citizen surveillance that allow the authorities to perceive this data as their property. The number of actors who can use it is really unlimited.*"[20] Despite pointing out that Google has fairly similar commercial strategies in a variety of countries, our respondents nevertheless underline the specificities of the Soviet context, marked by the porosity between public and private spheres and the total distrust in political institutions, which arguably still impact post-Soviet societies (Svenonius & Björklund, 2018). Thus, different experts in digital security for civil security actors understand and convey to their audiences the risks associated with the registration of technology companies in the Russian jurisdiction. Thanks to this positive "publicity" by the expert community, Google is used by multiple civil society organizations and activists in Russia in their everyday work for the usability, security, and efficiency of its various services. Indeed, several of our interlocutors pointed out the danger of "physical infiltration" by malicious people that NGOs are

16 Interview with I.S., digital security trainer, Minsk, April 2019.

17 According to our interviewees, these few cases were mainly related to terrorism, hate speech, or telephone fraud. Google would cooperate with the Russian authorities only after eliminating any possibility of its use for repression.

18 Interview with M.K., coordinator of the "Map of repression on the Internet" (project of the NGO Internet Protection Society), April 8, 2020.

19 Interview with I.S., April 2019.

20 A.S. (civic tech ONG), Panel on the regulation of algorithms, conference "Setevoy Sentyabr," September 3–4, 2020.

facing. Services such as Google Workspace (formerly GSuite) allow differentiated access to data for different NGO employees. In addition, many NGOs cannot afford to hire an IT manager to maintain digital architecture. In this case, the use of open-source solutions appears too difficult to them.[21] This situation of dependency upon Google demonstrates that Russian NGOs have little choice, given the chronic lack of resources and various threats from the Russian authorities.

However, the NGOs dependency upon Google is also due to the role played by the company in the technological assistance to the nonprofit sector. Indeed, while having a reputation for being practical, Google services, such as Google Workspace, are quite expensive for NGOs. Thus, Google, with other Big Tech actors, has partnered with NGOs via its global TechSoup[22] program to provide its services and devices (cloud storage, Google "AdWords," YouTube Premium, etc.); as with similar, private-sector promoted initiatives such as Facebook's Free Basics,[23] Google's strategy via such programs likely goes beyond philanthropy and assistance, and may be connected to the well-documented history of cooperation between US tech giants and national security agencies. The example of Teplodigital program also shows the efficiency of the worldwide efforts made by the company to consolidate the hold of its "soft power" beyond conventional means of lobbying, such as a long-term work with the nonprofit sector, in particular, with NGOs defending internet freedom and digital rights, "influential in civil society and devoted to myriad missions, including shaping technology and privacy policy" (Jewler, 2015). Presenting itself internationally as a defender of free speech and a sponsor of human rights organizations and of international Human Rights events, Google is thus criticized to fund "those who might otherwise raise alarms about its practices" (Ibid., 2015).

More specifically for the Russian case, nonprofits' partnerships with Big Tech actors appear paradoxically as a fallback solution, given the particularly tense context in which NGOs function in Russia, operating in quasi-"cold war" conditions, drastically reducing the opportunities for funding by international foundations and favorable to the official hunt for foreign influences. "My state is my main enemy" seems to be a formula that sums up well the polarized quasi-war situation in which the civil activists find themselves in their daily activities as well as in their social and professional representations. This trust in Google is indeed defined by this crude arithmetic of threats and power relations: "the enemy of my enemy is my friend." Thus, the American Net giant is valued for what it is otherwise criticized for: its monopolistic position, which allows it to resist the Russian state and to comply only partially with its legislation.

[21] Ibid.

[22] TechSoup website is www.techsoup.org

[23] Its website can be found at www.facebook.com/connectivity/solutions/free-basics.

8.3.6 "Shadow Libraries" as Knowledge Disseminators, between Conformity and Repression

Online user-generated "shadow" libraries may be seen as troublemakers that challenge the Russian sovereignization project in several ways. First, by disseminating texts without regard to their legal status, they defy the state's increasing willingness to enforce copyright on the Russian web. Second, they challenge the cultural dimension of sovereignty: by creating an autonomous, uncensored text-sharing space, they thwart the Russian government's desire to control the cultural consumption of internet users by filtering their access to cultural goods. And finally, by developing and promoting tools to circumvent website blocking, the administrators and users of shadow libraries contribute to public resistance to the sovereignization project.

Long blamed for numerous copyright infringements, especially by the US Creative industries (Kirya, 2011), Russian federation authorities gradually developed copyright legislation that not only meets global standards, but is aligned with its strictest versions (Alekseeva et al., 2013, p. 69). New internet control tools introduced in the 2010s have ensured its compliance on Russian territory. A year after the FZ-139 law adoption, in 2013, an "anti-piracy law" designed to apply the black-listing and blocking mechanism to copyright-infringing sites entered into force. Mobilizations against the "Russian SOPA" were numerous (Zasursky, 2016, pp. 62–63), and different struggles for digital freedoms converged in a common struggle for a "free RuNet." However, the "anti-piracy" legislation has been reinforced ever since, integrating more actors and amplifying penalties.

In this context, Russian "shadow" mass-literature libraries, access to which was progressively blocked on the Russian territory since 2015, developed different survival strategies. A major concern is to ensure the sustainability and growth of the collections, which depends on the vitality of the community that nurtures it. Major sites, such as Librusec and Flibusta, operate in a Wiki-like way: texts and annotations are uploaded and corrected by the users themselves, thus ensuring the exponential growth of collections. Librusec's administrator, Ilya Larin, relies on both code and text sharing – which he calls "cross-pollination" – to guarantee the survival of the ecosystem. Torrent distribution in one of the alternative dissemination channels. Torrents allow users to download the entire archives onto their computers, accompanied by a program that transforms it into a database for convenient use. Once the full database is installed on the computer, the user may download its updates. Thus, the library's collection is replicated many times and kept not only online, but also offline. Its ability to be restored anytime makes its total disappearance impossible. The server on which the main collection is stored is also of great importance for the security of the library. The legislation of the country the hosting is located in must be sufficiently tolerant of copyright infringements.

Another important concern of these libraries is to ensure access to the collections on the Russian soil. The first way consists of multiplying "mirrors" in locations that are considered safe. For example, the .lib domain, ruled by Emercoin, is regarded as such thanks to its decentralized structure. In its current form, the Domain Name System root is under the centralized authority of Internet Corporation for Assigned Names and Numbers (ICANN, a Los Angeles–based nonprofit). In this system, every DNS record is kept by the DNS provider and can be blocked under political or commercial pressure; however, in a decentralized DNS each record is managed solely by its owner, and is readable by all users on the network[24]. Networks that guarantee anonymity, like Tor and "Invisible Internet Project" (i2p), are also suitable to escape national constraints, which leads shadow libraries to have their "representatives" there[25].

The second way focuses on instructing users. Since the beginning of site blockages, libraries and forums have displayed lists of the technical means to escape the communication barriers created by RuNet service providers at RKN's request. This dissemination of circumvention knowledge seems to be omnipresent and circulates through many channels: mailings, posts on social networks, or YouTube tutorials. The proposed solutions include the change of DNS server, browsers with turbo mode (Opera, Chrome, and Yandex),[26] or embedded VPN, special plug-ins for browsers, VPN services, Tor browser, and the use of anonymizers. Expert community members explain to nontechnical users how each method works and present its advantages and disadvantages (which are usually speed of execution versus simplicity of use). This mastering of circumvention tools today becomes a part of the know-how of every person visiting the shadow libraries.

In addition to the torrents mentioned earlier, library users and administrators compete in creativity to organize the distribution of new archive updates. Here again, the proliferation of means and media is the rule. For example, Librusec.ucoz, a forum common to several shadow libraries and which acts as a safe harbor in case the internal forum is inaccessible, has a section called "Our Tortuga"[27] centralizing the links to the updates of Librusek and Flibusta databases *via* free file-sharing sites.

In parallel to these friendly sites, the communities use social networks and messaging. For example, a bot on the Russian social media VKontakte allowed, for a while, to make a quick search in the shadow libraries and thus

24 See https://roskomsvoboda.org/12118/, accessed May 20, 2024.

25 See https://roskomsvoboda.org/28612/, accessed May 20, 2024.

26 Invented by the developers of the Opera browser in 2009, the turbo mode was intended to increase browsing speed: data is first downloaded to the browser's server, and the user downloads it from there in compressed form. But the fact that the data transits through Opera's server allows this tool to be used for bypassing site blockades: the ISP cannot detect and therefore deny access to banned sites.

27 See http://librusec.ucoz.de/forum/7-171-318"\l"105370"\t"_blank, accessed July 16, 2020.

facilitate access in case of breakdown or blocking.[28] In June 2019, VKontakte and the publishing house Eksmo concluded a settlement according to which the social network has to check the legal status of all the books downloaded by users. However, this did not lead to the disappearance of the bot: in September, it was transferred to a safer storage medium.[29] After the tightening of VKontakte's attitude toward illegal content, some shadow libraries began to actively use Telegram bots to distribute books, since this messenger was known to be tolerant to illegal content, thanks to the libertarian worldview of its owner, Pavel Durov. However, by August 2020, these bots would have stopped working, supposedly as a result of an agreement between Telegram and the Russian authorities.

8.4 CONCLUSIONS

This chapter has sought to provide an analytical overview of the ongoing processes related to infrastructure-based digital sovereignization in Russia, drawing from three years of fieldwork conducted in the frame of the ResisTIC project. Our overview of case studies has highlighted four recurring dynamics in the Russian state's attempt to enforce digital sovereignty by infrastructure, as well as in strategies of circumvention and evasion enacted by different groups of actors, from civil society organizations to technical actors and "ordinary citizens."

First, we have observed how the Russian government seeks to raise a series of obstacles against foreign techniques and alternative infrastructures, considered as "subversive." Second, our research sheds light on the "collateral damage" resulting from the technical implementation of these infrastructure-based coercive measures, and the (often infrastructure-based, as well) attempts to remedy or mitigate this collateral damage; in doing so, it shows in parallel the extent to which such measures are frequently ineffective with respect to their intended purpose (on this point, see also Musiani et al., 2016). Third, we have followed the creation and development of new "digital national champions" under an increasingly close government supervision, which leads to pressures and manipulations exerted by the State on particular platforms and their algorithms, as well as to countermoves that can be surprising from the standpoint of a Europe- or United States-based scholar, such as, the trust in American "Net giants" as powerful actors able to stand up to the Russian government. Finally, we have highlighted the emergence of critique and circumvention initiatives among internet users vis-à-vis "governance by infrastructure," and we have observed how these reactions contribute to the emergence of new forms of "resistance by infrastructure." This approach by case studies provides a nonlinear, nuanced, and complex understanding of the specificities of RuNet

[28] See Flibusta's VK page: https://vk.com/wall-98093156_238, accessed September 2, 2020.
[29] See https://github.com/FlyInk13/FlibustaBot, accessed September 5, 2020.

governance, which mirrors the national conception of digital sovereignty, often described as a strictly centralized, top-down, and efficient information control system. Our chapter has proposed to pay attention to microtechniques of circumvention and shows how the discourse on internet sovereignty (and the subsequent demand for all information control technologies to be "made in Russia") is currently giving way to two important paradoxes in the country. On the one hand, it can lead groups of activists and users whose main priority is to escape the Russian government's surveillance, control, and sovereignization to end up spontaneously subjecting themselves to surveillance, control, and "sovereignization" originating in the United States. On the other hand, it opens up technical and legal opportunities for mundane resistances and the existence of "parallel" RuNets, where particular instantiations of informational freedom are still possible.

8.5 OVERTURE: UKRAINE, INTERNET AS A TOOL (AND BATTLEFIELD) OF WAR?

On February 24, 2022, the Russian military offensive against Ukraine is accompanied by an immediate reinforcement of censorship on the media as well as controls and blockages of the internet in Russia. The process of co-opting the internet as a tool in the warmongering policy of the Russian state is suddenly accelerating and making it possible to tighten the grip on the public space in the context of the war. This justifies the brutal tightening of the network of constraints that already weighed on both the actors and the digital infrastructures in Russia. On the one hand, the law is amended in a more restrictive sense, prohibiting any criticism of the army or any evocation of the term "war" (qualified as "special military operation"). This censorship leads many media to give up their publications. Criminal proceedings are initiated against independent journalists and opponents of the war while the repository of "foreign agents," kept by the Ministry of Justice, is considerably longer.

When it comes to internet infrastructures, the topic of this chapter, the government is blocking international social networks (Facebook, Instagram, etc.) and strengthening its control over local digital players (VKontakte, Yandex, etc.). These decisions come as, under the effect of sanctions, a number of foreign digital operators have left the country and disconnected their infrastructure from the Russian network. The invasion of Ukraine by Russia, and the retaliatory international sanctions, makes visible the manifold dependencies of the Russian surveillance and censorship industry on foreign components, infrastructure, and know-how: for example, the lack of filtering software traditionally supplied by Western firms, such as Sandvine and Nokia, is heavily impacting the monitoring and blocking activities of the Russian government. Furthermore, this results in techno-legal loopholes and gray areas that create both uncertainty and opportunity for technical actors, such as internet service providers. It also leads to paradoxical situations for the government, such as the fact that, despite the discourse on sovereignty and despite the sanctions, the Russian central bank continues to use European certificates in order to give a stamp of approval to the activity of the RuNet technical actors.

While all of these dynamics are currently evolving at a steady pace and conclusions cannot yet be drawn from the situation, one thing is clear: internet governance has never been as close to a "global war" (DeNardis, 2014) as today, and the upcoming months and years will keep on providing illustrations of this problematic trend.

ACKNOWLEDGMENTS

In addition to ResisTIC, several authors (F. Daucé, K. Ermoshina, B. Loveluck, F. Musiani) would like to acknowledge the research project that supports them at the time of this book's publication on the topic of this chapter, DIGISOV "Digital Governance and Sovereignty in a Fractured World: Competing States and Circulating Norms" (2024-2027) ANR-23-CE53-0009-02, funded by the French National Agency for Research (ANR).

9

Brazilian Activism in Mastodon

Sovereignty Discourses between Cyberlibertarianism and State-Centrism

Tales Tomaz

9.1 INTRODUCTION

One of the most resilient elements of the digital culture has been the free and open source software (FOSS) movement, which began with the purpose of developing software whose code is open, modifiable, and shareable. This activism has given birth to well-known initiatives such as Linux operating systems, the web browser Mozilla Firefox, the website creator WordPress, and the web server software Apache and Nginx, which together serve more than 60% of the most popular websites (W3techs.com, 2022). For the movement, technological infrastructure is too important to allow proprietary lock-in, an argument that resembles the rhetoric of control and autonomy over devices, software and data of digital sovereignty discourses (Couture & Toupin, 2019; Pohle & Thiel, 2020). More specifically, it belongs to the "commons digital sovereignty," explained in the introduction of this book, which seeks to create digital public goods from the bottom-up, beyond state and corporate control.

The rise of corporate digital platforms led the FOSS movement to articulate specific sovereignty discourses and practices with regard to social media as well, advancing the model of *federation*. In this model, social networks should adopt open and interoperable protocols, allowing users to reach contacts across different federated networks (Gehl, 2015; Mansoux & Abbing, 2020). Since Elon Musk's takeover of Twitter (now X), this alternative model of social networking has attracted more attention, as its spearhead Mastodon became the favorite destination of millions of Twitter users disappointed with the prospects of Musk's leadership (Chambers, 2022). Mastodon is a Twitter-like software released in 2016 by the German developer Eugen Rochko that allows people to connect to the "Fediverse," the ecosystem of federated social media, accounting for nearly 90% of its current active users according to the stats website "The Federation."[1] Even corporate social media are slowly moving in this direction, as Meta anticipates EU regulation and plans to implement federation with the Fediverse and Mastodon in its newly launched Threads (MacManus, 2023).

There is already scholarly literature on federated social media and, more specifically, Mastodon exploring some social and political aspects: interoperability in the Fediverse as a model for competition in digital markets (Brown, 2020); the restructuration of online social interaction promoted by Mastodon's design choices (Zulli et al., 2020); and internal pressures on Mastodon toward centralization (Raman et al., 2019). A dense discussion about federated social media appears in an essay by Mansoux and Abbing (2020), where they assert that the Fediverse represents a turning point in the politicization of FOSS activism toward a less neutral understanding of technological openness. Such a bold claim opens up the possibility that the Fediverse activism also advances a different understanding of digital sovereignty in comparison with FOSS historical claims. However, to the author's knowledge, no literature on the Fediverse has addressed so far this issue. Furthermore, in countries from the Global South, FOSS activism has articulated digital sovereignty discourses that differ from the widespread narratives in rich countries, with the state as an active player supporting and implementing open technologies to achieve geopolitical sovereignty (Schoonmaker, 2018). Nonetheless, research on federated social media still misses the discussion about the participation of peripheral countries and their own appropriation of sovereignty discourses. This chapter aims to contribute to closing this gap in literature by investigating how Brazilian activists on Mastodon articulate concepts and practices related to digital sovereignty discourses and how this narrative relates to traditional claims within the FOSS movement.

In the first part, I discuss the relations of FOSS activism with digital sovereignty discourses. There is a growing body of literature dealing with the assumptions, implications, complexities, and contradictions of discourses on digital sovereignty, and this chapter will concentrate on the approaches by Stéphane Couture and Sophie Toupin (2019) and Julia Pohle and Thorsten Thiel (2020). In the second part, I analyze the digital sovereignty claims in Brazilian activism around Mastodon. For this, I briefly explain the context of the emergence of federated social media, as well as their political assumptions and implications that are relevant for digital sovereignty discourses. Finally, relying on data about country participation on Mastodon, participant observation and interviews with administrators and moderators of communities oriented to Brazilian people, I sketch an understanding of digital sovereignty by Brazilian Fediverse activists – narratives, actors, and the role

[1] https://the-federation.info. This website hosts statistical data on Fediverse software, operating instances, server location, registered and active users, and is the primary source of all statistical information of Fediverse and Mastodon in this text.

of this technology in fulfilling their normative expectations – and discuss their presence and influence in the global movement, considering specifically the geopolitical dimension of their activism.

9.2 FOSS ACTIVISM IN DIGITAL SOVEREIGNTY DISCOURSES

The roots of the FOSS movement lie in the 1980s, when hacker Richard Stallman (2002) started to develop software under the so-called "copyleft" licenses, that is, whose legal status sought to protect the right of users to further examine the code, modify it, and distribute new versions. Because of the influence of its founder, the ethical thinking emerged from this movement is called by Rappaport (2018) "Stallmanism." Indeed, the hacker culture assigns great importance to some key figures, playfully called "Benevolent Dictators for Life" (BDFL), and Stallman is considered to be the first of them. Since then, the movement consolidated and expanded, playing a decisive role in the emergence of the digital commons and the culture of peer production (Benkler, 2006; Lessig, 2006). Gabriela Coleman (2004) argues that the FOSS movement is ultimately a struggle for freedom of speech by rethinking the naturalness of intellectual property, which in the 1980s had been extended into coding by public regulation in the interest of the corporate software industry. FOSS activists consider that this alliance between state and corporate power restrains freedom to work with computing and coding and, by extension, hackers' freedom to express themselves (Coleman, 2004). Free software participants, thus, struggle to conserve, reinforce, and spread the software through which they communicate, collaborate, and coordinate themselves.

The community that follows the free software principles and ethical thinking is defined by Christopher Kelty (2008) as a "recursive public," "a public that is vitally concerned with the material and practical maintenance and modification of the technical, legal, practical and conceptual means of its own existence as a public" (p. 3). Furthermore, by protecting the right of expression in code, FOSS activism intends to safeguard an important dimension of political freedom. They believe in the necessity to "include within the spectrum of political activity the creation, modification, and maintenance of software, networks, and [related] legal documents," as these forms of expression "can both express and 'implement' ideas about the social and moral order of society" (Kelty, 2008, p. 8). In other words, not only the content expressed by technologies, but also their technical materiality matters, as it creates infrastructures that actually allow for expression and circulation of ideas, sometimes in very unexpected ways. Expanding freedom to use, examine, modify, and share source code is a way of assuring political debate regarding one of the most important realms of contemporary societies, namely the information and communication infrastructure.

Therefore, FOSS activism is full of references to actors and practices that restrain or enable freedom, and is directly oriented to create strategies for politicizing control over the digital infrastructure. These are typical features of digital sovereignty discourses, which "describe various forms of independence, control, and autonomy over digital infrastructures, technologies, and data" (Couture & Toupin, 2019, p. 2305). Nevertheless, digital sovereignty is a highly contested concept, with a large variety of connotations, very different actor arrangements, and competing normative practices (Couture & Toupin, 2019; Pohle & Thiel, 2020). For the structure of my argument, I will follow Couture and Toupin's (2019) categorization with five clusters of discourses, namely "cyberspace sovereignty," "state digital sovereignty," "indigenous digital sovereignty," "social movements and digital sovereignty," and "personal digital sovereignty."

FOSS is an important part of two of these discourses. First, free software appears in the category of *social movements and digital sovereignty*, which is equivalent to the "commons digital sovereignty" explained in the introduction of the book. According to this discourse, social movements should be entitled the capacity and, to a certain extent, even the responsibility to develop technological skills, programs, devices, and content outside the framework of commercial and state-sponsored infrastructures. Most initiatives in this kind of discourse promote FOSS, digital commons, encryption technologies, self-managed servers, among others (Couture & Toupin, 2019). Lately, this discourse centers on the critique of the use and ownership of users' data by the corporate digital platforms, sometimes called GAFAM (Google, Apple, Facebook, Amazon, and Microsoft), whose surveillance business model represents a modern form of dispossession (Gosh & Couldry, 2020; Zuboff, 2019a).

Then, Couture and Toupin (2019) situate FOSS activism in the *personal digital sovereignty* discourse as well, which pleads for autonomy of citizens as individuals. Consumers and users should be empowered to make self-determined decisions facing commercial and state powers, including their own protection against surveillance. Measures in this case include "economic incentives for user-friendly and domestic technology development, but also the introduction of technical features allowing for effective encryption, data protection and more transparent business models" (Pohle & Thiel, 2020, p. 12).

However, the whole debate around technological sovereignty began before FOSS, tracing back to the 1960s and 1970s, when the geopolitical implications of the information and communication technologies were high on the agenda. Couture and Toupin (2019) report discussions in France, Canada, and Australia with the term "sovereignty" linked to technology, formulating an informational version of nationalistic concerns. Countries from the Global South also expressed very specific concerns in the debate. In the late 1970s, Latin American and African countries realized deep inequalities in the information technology sector, especially dependency because of their "lack of development of information productive forces such as computer and software industries" (Schoonmaker, 2018, p. 28). Data about their economies and citizens were stored and processed outside of their jurisdictions, spurring concerns on the perpetuation of global power inequalities and dominance. The discussion around strategies to tackle this power imbalance was a crucial part of the debates in the late 1970s and early 1980s around a New World Information and Communication Order (Schoonmaker, 2018). This history shows that a state-centered technological sovereignty discourse existed before the FOSS movement, and peripheral countries had a very specific position in this debate, underscoring the need of state-led action against global power inequalities.

The popularization of networked communication in the 1990s pumped up another kind of sovereignty discourse, focused rather on the promise of overcoming the state as boundary. Couture and Toupin (2019) call it the *cyberspace sovereignty discourse*. In this narrative, Westphalian nation-states should have no say on what the rules on the internet are supposed to be. Sovereignty here refers mostly to freedom for internet users *from* the state. This kind of discourse reproduces what Barbrook and Cameron (1996) called the Californian ideology, a mash-up of technological determinism and libertarian individualism that shaped technological development in the Silicon Valley. Cyberlibertarians distrust political institutions to a major extent and argue that the decentralization provided by digital technologies allows for better forms of organizing modern societies (Pohle & Thiel, 2020).

It is obvious nowadays that cyberlibertarianism is naïve regarding the power struggles in global capitalism. In fact, after some predominance of the cyberspace sovereignty, the 2010s witnessed a revival of *state digital sovereignty discourses* (Couture & Toupin, 2019; Pohle & Thiel, 2020). In its recent form, the most popular measure is data localization, whereby storage and processing of data should occur within national or regional jurisdictions. Some of these discourses focus more decisively on the economic dimension, highlighting the "autonomy of the national economy in relation to foreign technology and service providers" (Pohle & Thiel, 2020, p. 10). Measures here refer to incentives to the domestic economy and local competitors, usually part of a larger economic policy strategy. Couture and Toupin (2019) report a growing concern on the side of European governments throughout the 2010s, pursuing developments such as encrypted chatting functionalities, national emails, localized data storage, and restriction of European data flow within the continent (Pohle & Thiel, 2020). Despite recognition of the lack of political conditions, some scholars even plead for publicly owned or funded digital infrastructures, following the model of public service media, which could promote more democratic control over the internet (Fuchs & Unterberger, 2021; Morozov, 2019).

As with the early state-centered discourses, the Global South also positions itself considering global power imbalances. Brazil has performed a leading role among liberal democracies, especially under the presidency of Dilma Rousseff, with actions such as data localization and state investment in undersea cables (Schoonmaker, 2018). Much earlier and within a much bigger scope, China realized the need to develop its own state approach to the internet to ensure the achievement of its political, economic, and cultural goals (Jia & Winseck, 2018). Somewhat similar approaches have been either discussed or implemented in countries such as Russia and India.

Finally, Couture and Toupin (2019) identify a further category, the so-called *indigenous digital sovereignty discourses*, arguing for the inclusion of voices and rights of indigenous populations in the realm of digital data. They question, for example, the Western-centric prism of sovereignty based on territory jurisdiction.

All of these discourses articulate a particular arrangement of *governments*, *market economy*, and *civil society* as actors with possible agency over digital infrastructure, software, hardware, data, and content. Governments are addressed as either liberal democracies or authoritarian (and semi-authoritarian) regimes. Market economy is also referred to by two sets of actors: transnational companies headquartered in the United States – mostly the GAFAM – or regional/national market players. The civil society realm is divided into social movements or the individual person, usually addressed as user or consumer. According to Couture and Toupin (2019) and Pohle and Thiel (2020), FOSS actively participates in accounts that pose the first two groups – governments and market economy – as entities that control technologies, whereas the last group – civil society – should reclaim its independence and autonomy. In these accounts, the search and the agency for technological sovereignty come from civil society, not from the Westphalian nation-state or private business looking for economic sustainability. However, I argue in the following section that some peculiarities have to be considered, revealing a more complex participation of FOSS in digital sovereignty discourses.

9.2.1 FOSS in Cyberlibertarian and State Sovereignty Discourses

The first important element for a more complex understanding of FOSS claims on digital sovereignty is its relation with the cyberspace sovereignty discourse. As Coleman (2004) documented almost 20 years ago, hackers and developers often reject any deliberate politicization of their work, but FOSS clearly instantiates many liberal values. While the movement mostly relies on technical and economic rationalities as its justification, this conception is informed by a "taken for granted form of cultural liberalism," expressed in Anglo-European ideas of individual autonomy, self-development, and a value-free marketplace for the expression of ideas (Coleman, 2004, p. 509). Since the consolidation of the surveillance business model of digital platforms, FOSS activism also stresses the liberal value of privacy, which hackers seek to embed in most of their discourses and practices (Mansoux & Abbing, 2020).

In fact, enthusiasts of FOSS and networked communication often emphasize the emancipatory potential of openness and decentralization, a typical reasoning in the liberal toolbox (Benkler, 2006; Lessig, 2006). In his philosophical inquiry on Stallman's argument that proprietary software restricts users' freedom and is unjust, Rappaport (2018) concludes that his ethical thinking poses an intrinsic moral value of freedom and autonomy that aligns with libertarian ethics. Ossewaarde and Reijers (2017) argue that the digital commons presuppose the atomized individual of neoliberal discourses and, at the end of the day, reinforces the cyberlibertarian ideology, a relation that is also constructed by Lund and Zuckerfeld (2020).

Coleman (2004) and Kelty (2008) warn against overstating the role of liberal ideas shaping the movement, as FOSS activism fundamentally begins not with ideologies, but practices of programming. That said, it is justifiable to argue that FOSS activism historically echoes libertarian discourses of cyberspace sovereignty in many aspects.

On the other hand, there are appropriations of FOSS activism, which ascribe a crucial role to the state in implementing technological autonomy and independence, problematizing immediate associations between FOSS activism and neoliberal thought. Recently, European activists have argued on the necessity of purposeful state investment on digital commons and FOSS as a digital sovereignty strategy (Bria, 2020, Reda, 2020). State intervention is required to protect the regional and national freedom to code software (and further forms of expressions alongside the spectrum of the digital commons) from dispossession strategies by foreign actors, fostering local digital industry and enhancing security. Following variations of this reasoning, several European municipalities have increased the presence of FOSS in their infrastructure, with Barcelona showcasing the success of this initiative (Calzada, 2017).

But even before this awakening in Europe, state power has been an active part of tech activism around FOSS activism in countries from the Global South. As early as in the 1980s, such governments articulated resistance to proprietary software and incentives to local and open-source industry. Brazil objected to the US copyright law on software until 1987, conceding after trade barriers to soya exports (Leister & Frazier, 2014). At the level of municipalities, the public sector began to embrace FOSS in the mid-1990s, whereas the federal government adopted it in 2003, under Lula da Silva's administration. His government prioritized FOSS in public schools, and introduced support for hacker events and projects with copyleft licenses (Leister & Frazier, 2014). Much of this effort has been backpedaled since Rousseff's term, but she still pushed forward an agenda of internet neutrality, which converges with FOSS activism in the efforts to expand the digital commons (Schoonmaker, 2018). Besides Brazil, other Latin American countries, such as Uruguay, Ecuador, Bolivia, Venezuela, and Cuba, have passed laws between 2004 and 2013 to migrate governmental data to systems operating with free software (Avila Pinto, 2018). Reportedly, India and Russia also have laws mandating open source software in several layers of state administration (Avila Pinto, 2018).

Thus, FOSS activism cannot be exclusively associated to social movements. FOSS embodies many aspects of cyberlibertarian discourses that should not be ignored, a perspective that could even undermine the organization of collectives such as social movements. At the same time, FOSS also appears on the other side of the sovereignty spectrum in variations of state-led discourses, with an early development in the Global South. State participation in the recursive publics of FOSS might sound contradictory for libertarians, but the referred actors from the Global South have rearticulated freedom discourse "beyond its original focus on individual rights and societal value" toward a geopolitical conception of "freedom within a context of relationships between states in the global economy" (Schoonmaker, 2018, p. 38).

This makes the position of FOSS activism in digital sovereignty discourses more complex, sometimes ambiguous and contradictory, beyond a straightforward identification with the social movements of the "commons digital sovereignty" narrative. Political, economic, and social developments have shaped FOSS, creating different opportunities and threats in this form of tech activism. Furthermore, the role of the Global South and its appropriation of FOSS for technological sovereignty have to be differentiated from general statements, as it not simply reproduces the efforts of US and European activists but also ascribes way more importance to state participation in a geopolitical context.

9.3 FOSS ALTERNATIVE FOR SOCIAL MEDIA PLATFORMS

More recently, FOSS activism has also been concerned with the rise of corporate social media platforms. The business model of these platforms contradicts core values of the movement (Gehl, 2015; Maxigas & Latzko-Toth, 2020). These companies use people's interactions to collect personal data, profile users' behavior, and sell this targeting capacity to advertisers (Gosh & Couldry, 2020; Hildebrandt, 2018; Poell et al., 2019). Because of their need of data, they promote engagement at the expense of other considerations, strive for never-ending expansion of their user base, and adopt proprietary standards in order to gain more control over data collection and processing of information. Platforms are able to use these data to leverage power across several sectors and markets, benefiting from network effects and becoming infrastructure for much of modern life, including services historically associated in Western democracies with public values (Plantin et al., 2018; Taylor, 2021; van Dijck, 2020).

This societal phenomenon can be seen as a loss of control over personal data and a fundamental infringement of the right to privacy. In the liberal tradition, privacy is a human right, not by chance enshrined in the Article 12 of the Universal Declaration of the Human Rights. Understood as a protection against invasive inquiry, privacy is crucial to self-determination, and data-driven platforms seek to undermine it (Hildebrandt, 2018). Research has shown that people desire to control the information digital entities have about them, even if they feel unable to do so (Draper & Turow, 2019).

Digital platforms can also represent a loss of control over data at a societal level. Laura DeNardis (2012) argues that these digital information intermediaries "have diminished the capacity of sovereign nation states and media content producers to directly control information flows," representing "a loss of control over content" (p. 721). Corporate digital platforms shifted to a central position in the public information ecosystem, as they became an important source of information and news consumption for an increasing amount of people over the world, especially in the Global South (Newman et al., 2023). While established media organizations still produce the bulk of the internet content actually consumed, social media platforms organize access to and consumption of this content, involved therefore in real-time decisions about which content is allowed, promoted, or removed (Gillespie, 2018; Jakubowicz, 2015; Napoli & Caplan, 2017). By voluntarily or obligatorily assuming the task to govern content and expression, private social media platforms accrue significant opinion and political power (Belli, 2017; Helberger, 2020). Examples are the constitution of the Facebook Oversight Board and platforms' ban of former US president Donald Trump's accounts in early 2021, as well as the siege by app stores and hosting services of the far-right social network Parler. Given the circumstances, many of these initiatives are welcome and can be justified according to Western standards. But they also point to a deeper question on whether few (US) private corporations should have the power to both amplify and curb speech, even beyond national jurisdictions. Scholarly literature has summarized this aspect as a concern regarding the privatization of the governance (Belli, 2017; DeNardis & Hackl, 2015).

Therefore, loss of control is perceived at both individual and collective levels. Reaction from FOSS activism comes with the argument that social networking does not need to operate this way (Gehl, 2015; Maxigas & Latzko-Toth, 2020). Accordingly, activists have come up with alternatives based on the concept of federation. This concept refers to a communication system where social networks use open and interoperable protocols and software, having the capacity to run independently but still allowing their communities to reach people with accounts in other networks (Brown, 2020). In contrast, in the model of corporate social media platforms, the company enforces its own messaging protocols, operated exclusively in software run on its servers, and this way restricts access to its user base, increasing the company's power over users and their activities. The architecture of federated social media expects to make difficult, if not impossible, such a control and oversight of digital communication by a single entity.

In the last decade, the ActivityPub standard, developed by the World Wide Web Consortium (W3C), has evolved into an established protocol for the social media willing to federate, and this group of federated social media became known as the "Fediverse." On top of this protocol layer, a number of software applications have provided the practical features for users' communication. Created in 2016, Mastodon became the most important Fediverse software, employed by over 90% of active Fediverse users, according to the statistics of the website "The Federation." In December 2022, two months after the conclusion of the Musk deal over Twitter, the Mastodon community had grown from around 500,000 to 2.5 million monthly active users, most of them disillusioned Twitter migrants (Chambers, 2022).

Mastodon reproduces the microblogging functionality of Twitter with the principles of the Fediverse, meaning that any person can host it on their own servers – each server installation is technically called *instance* – and connect to other instances. Each of them, in turn, keep independent administration and moderation, although administrators often coordinate actions. People who do not want to host an instance – the vast majority of current internet users – can register accounts in the hundreds of open ones, being subject to their rules. If the user wants to have another administration or moderation, they can move to other open instances, import their older list of contacts, and remain in touch with them. Differently from corporate social media, Mastodon software does not provide algorithmic curation of content, so that timelines strictly follow chronological order, and content curation depends exclusively on human decision-making, by both moderators and users. Design choices create several possibilities of account and post visibility, allowing users to decide to what extent they want their communication to be public.

The Fediverse explicitly seeks to offer an alternative to corporate control over social media communication, resonating with discussions on digital sovereignty. At a first glance, its decentralized governance might recall libertarian accounts of unfettered individual control over digital data and content. Indeed, a foundational manifesto of federated social media, the text *A people's history of the Fediverse* (Freedombone.net, n.d.) argues that, from the point of view of privacy and security, the ideal approach for everything in the internet would be an individual governance of data, following the peer-to-peer model, with no servers as intermediaries. This way, each peer would be able to make their own decisions about who to connect to and what data to share. However, the text acknowledges that this approach has important drawbacks. It is ultimately inefficient, as it would cause "a lot of duplicated curation effort." Furthermore, it overwhelms individual users who do not possess the interest and the technological knowledge to make these decisions. Federation is then considered a middle ground approach. Data can be collectively governed if there is closer connection between provider and user. This allows for better trust. Offloading preferences to affinity groups improves user experience and reduces cognitive workload.

Federation can be regarded as a further development of the original idea of decentralization in the imaginary of the internet, which would challenge the hierarchical capitalist mode of production and spur emancipatory effects in societies (Benkler, 2006). As already referred in the discourse of cyberlibertarians, decentralized organization should offer "a better tailored response to the complex demands of governing modern societies than is offered by traditional forms of political organization" (Pohle & Thiel, 2020, p. 4). In other words, this imaginary assumes that technical decentralization induces political emancipation. But this understanding has always faced several tensions. In some cases, the decentralized architecture of the internet is simply regarded as a myth, since its approach to information seems to reflect rather design for control, and not decentralization (Galloway, 2004). In addition, some argue that addressing power and conflict requires coordination, so that technical decentralization often leads to centralizing effects (Bodó et al., 2021). Moreover, the internet itself did not evolve as expected into a wholesome decentralized system, displaying some features of decentralization at the infrastructural level (Winseck, 2017), but strong concentration at other levels, such as content distribution (Helberger, 2020; DeNardis & Hackl, 2015). From a critical perspective, it is possible to argue that internet decentralization did not change any structural aspect of information capitalism. Nonetheless, the tension remains, and decentralized network architectures are still seen as a possible response to the dynamics of concentration, centralization, and capture in platform capitalism (Rosnay & Musiani, 2020).

In any case, the Fediverse also diverges from the historical approach of FOSS communities in some aspects. While FOSS communities have historically focused on addressing privacy through security technologies (end-to-end encryption, peer-to-peer topologies, etc.), in the Fediverse, development has focused rather on "building moderation tools, granular visibility settings for posts, and the possibility to block other instances" (Mansoux & Abbing, 2020, p. 133). Fediverse activists usually pose their refusal to automate moderation by means of algorithmic curation as an advantage. For this reason, Mansoux and Abbing (2020) assert that the Fediverse promotes a shift from technical to social understanding of privacy.

Furthermore, Mansoux and Abbing (2020) argue that the Fediverse represents a decisive politicization of FOSS. It departs from naïve notions of neutrality and openness in original FOSS activism, embracing a kind of agonistic pluralism, in Mouffe's (2013) sense, that acknowledges the limits of connection and openness. This is materialized by allowing not only federation, but defederation and instance blocking. This design feature has been systematically used to isolate white supremacists and other far-right extremists that resort to the Fediverse to escape moderation policies from platforms (e.g., when the far-right social network Gab adopted Mastodon software in 2019, most relevant Fediverse instances took a coordinated action to defederate it and avoid user exposure to Gab's content). This way, "non-Western views on democracy, secularism, communities, and the individual" can still express and coordinate themselves, but no group or ideology can claim full acceptance and reach in the public discourse, as there is no centralized public sphere anymore (Mansoux & Abbing, 2020, p. 131). Many of these design choices reflected demands from the LGBTQIA+ community, which saw the universalizing and amplifying features in corporate social media platforms as prone to abuse and harassment (Valens, 2019).

Therefore, the federation expressed by the Fediverse and Mastodon understands itself as a means of transferring power control over online communication from big corporations to communities and social movements, a historical claim of FOSS activism regarding digital sovereignty. At the same time, federated social media evolved in a way that challenges neutral openness in classical FOSS discourses. Because of these characteristics, Mansoux and Abbing (2020) conclude that the Fediverse represents a turning point in the history of the FOSS movement. However, although research identifies a more sophisticated political understanding in Fediverse activism, there is little attention to the dimension of geopolitical power. This is even more striking if one considers the tension North–South in the history of digital sovereignty discourses, including the appropriation of elements of FOSS activism in peripheral countries.

In the following, I analyze Brazilian activism in Mastodon in order to shed some light on this issue. Brazil belongs to the group of Global South and BRICS countries with a relevant history in digital sovereignty debates and, as shown in the following section, has activists engaged with Mastodon as well. Nonetheless, it is not clear the dimension of their activism with regard to the broader Fediverse movement, nor the specific imaginaries of digital sovereignty that fuel these activists in the margins of global capitalism. Learning the role of geopolitical imbalances in the discourses articulated by Brazilian Mastodon activists will help to understand which digital sovereignty can be expected from this FOSS iteration in countries from the Global South.

9.3.1 Brazil in Mastodon

Following a mixed-methods approach, I collected both quantitative and qualitative data between January and June 2021. Quantitative data refer to country location of servers, users, and content production provided by the website "The Federation." These data were cross-checked with the website "Mastodon Instances"[2] and my own observation, having visited all 300 communities with more than 100 users. These data have some shortcomings, but can provide a better understanding of the magnitude of the geopolitical forces shaping Mastodon.[3]

Then, qualitative data help to understand the ideas and practices behind the numbers of Brazilian activism. For the purpose of this research, activists are defined as administrators and moderators of instances. I conducted

[2] https://instances.social.

[3] There are two important limitations regarding this approach of data collection. The website "The Federation" works in an opt-in basis, meaning that instance administrators have to flag their intent to participate in the statistics. This way, it can never reflect the whole network. At the same time, most activists rely on these data when talking about the size and growth of the Fediverse, especially because most instance operators are engaged with activism and want their activity to be counted into the statistics, turning instance opt-in very likely. A second limitation of this approach is related to the global nature of the FOSS movement, whereby activists articulate themselves relatively independent from national jurisdictions. Most communities have highly mixed membership with no attachment at all to countries, although English remains overwhelmingly important. Not rarely, instance operators even hide their actual location, as it is the case of almost all Chinese instances.

five semi-structured interviews with activists from four (out of six then active) instances oriented to Brazilian people or Brazilian-Portuguese speakers, including the two largest ones. Administrators were asked about the reasons for creating a Mastodon instance, their views on the actors actually controlling digital social networking, the necessary practices to achieve the desired condition, and in which sense Mastodon contributes to this. As requested by most interviewees, I have done my best effort to safeguard their anonymity by not referring to any name, gender, role, and instance affiliation (see Appendix 1 for the interview protocol).

9.3.2 Brazilian Instances

Despite the global nature of the FOSS movement and Mastodon, many activists engage in nation-related practices. At the time of data collection, the active Mastodon communities oriented to Brazilian people or Brazilian-Portuguese speakers were "Masto.donte.com.br," "Mastodon.com.br," "Ursal.zona," "Colorid.es," "Bantu.social," and "Brasileiros.social" (see Table 9.1 and Figures 9.1 to 9.5).

The community "Brasileiros.social" was oriented to far-right supporters of former Brazilian president Jair Bolsonaro, had very low (apparently coordinated and unauthentic) activity, and was either silenced or blocked by the other networks. In late 2021, it was discontinued following up a scandal with the publication of classified documents in the instance (Poder360, 2021). All other communities were organically active and federated with one another. As evident in the descriptions, three of them ("Ursal.zona," "Colorid.es," and "Bantu.social") were oriented toward specific social movements and highly moderated. The other two instances ("Masto.donte.com.br" and "Mastodon.com.br") were more generic, but had moderation explicitly oriented to curb hate speech, harassment, and abuse, especially toward minorities and marginalized groups. For this reason, despite their different goals, these five communities were federated with one another.

TABLE 9.1 *Brazilian Mastodon instances: users and posts*

Instance	Total Users	%	Monthly Active Users	%	Posts	%
masto.donte.com.br	454	14.6%	402	33.1%	380957	60.9%
mastodon.com.br	1482	47.7%	307	25.2%	64245	10.3%
ursal.zona	477	15.3%	294	24.2%	107033	17.1%
colorid.es	618	19.9%	161	13.2%	53577	8.6%
bantu.social	30	1.0%	30	2.5%	19297	3.1%
brasileiros.social	41	1.3%	22	1.8%	335	0.1%
TOTAL	3,102		1,216		625,444	

Source: Compilation by the author, based on data available at https://the-federation.info. Latest update in June 2021.

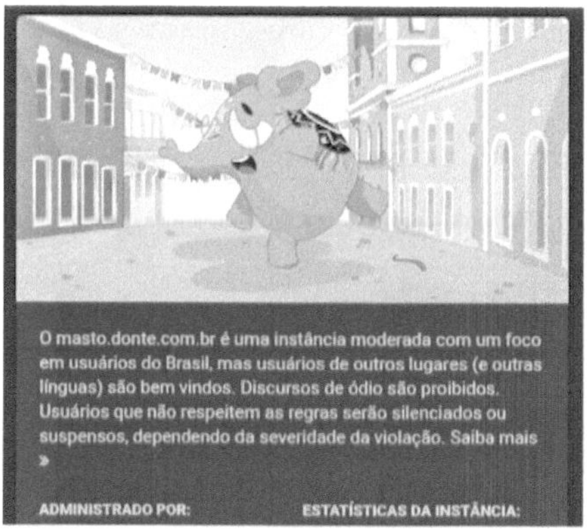

FIGURE 9.1 About page of masto.donte.com.br Translation: "Masto.donte.com.br is an instance focused on Brazilian users, but users from other places (and languages) are welcome. Hate speech is prohibited. Users who do not respect the rules will be silenced or suspended, depending on the severity of the violation."

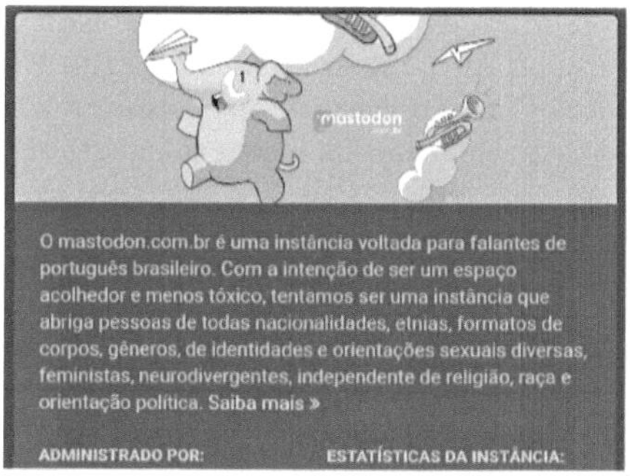

FIGURE 9.2 About page of mastodon.com.br Translation: "Mastodon.com.br is an instance oriented to Brazilian-Portuguese speakers. Aiming to be an inviting and less toxic space, we intend to be an instance that welcomes people from all nationalities, ethnic groups, body formats, genders, diverse sexual identities and orientations, feminists, neurodivergents, independently from religion, race and political orientation."

FIGURE 9.3 About page of ursal.zona Translation: "URSAL.zone is a moderate instance focusing on progressive, feminist and anti-fascist activists in Latin America opposed to all forms of oppression, exploitation and humiliation among human beings. Hate speech, propagation of lies and commercial pornography are prohibited. Read our Code of Conduct for more information."

FIGURE 9.4 About page of colorid.es Text retrieved from their official English version: "Colorid.es (from colorides, 'colorful people') is an instance focused on the queer/LGBTQIAPN+ community. Anyone can make an account, but don't be surprised if you encounter few het, cis and perisex people here. We take our rules seriously, so please read that section before making an account. Also, this is an instance primarily for Portuguese speakers. People who don't speak Portuguese or who will also speak in other languages are welcome, though, as long as our moderation team can handle it!"

FIGURE 9.5 About page of bantu.social Translation: "Mastodon instance focused on non-white Brazilian people."

9.3.3 Restoring Social Movements' Autonomy Over Online Communication

In the Brazilian Mastodon activism, there is a clear arrangement of actors and a corresponding narrative on who has and should have control and autonomy over digital infrastructure, content, and data. Interviewees strongly endorse the critique that corporate digital platforms, the GAFAM, have excessive control over current online communication, reproducing the surveillance capitalism thesis (Zuboff, 2019b). They affirm that big companies are "monopolizing" (interviewee I2) the internet and harming the autonomy of citizens, who have to surrender their personal data to few stakeholders mostly located in foreign countries (interviewees I1, I2, I3, I4, and I5). But they also reveal concerns regarding the way state power can make use of the centralized data provided by few market companies, not only in authoritarian regimes, but also in liberal democracies, especially by the United States (interviewee I4).

While discussing this dominance, they advance a classical argument of FOSS communities: the nostalgia regarding the early days of the decentralized internet, which frames their normative expectations. All interviewees, at some point of conversation, refer to the need of returning to a stage of networked communication when the forces of commercialization did not colonize most online activities. Illustrating this argument, one interviewee said: "We have lost this spirit of the beginning of the internet, when you used IRC [messaging application], those obscure fora... And the data you put there were not monetized. These were discussions for the sake of discussions" (interviewee I4).

Accordingly, activists believe that the ideal situation would be the individual having full control of their social media data. An interviewee said: "Ideally control would be in the hands of users as individuals, at least controlling their own data" (interviewee I1). But collectives of the civil society are mentioned more often as appropriate agents of autonomy struggle in the digital realm. When asked about "sovereignty for whom," interviewees focused on the collective organization and digital emancipation of the LGBTQIA+ community, people of color, people with disabilities, and indigenous people (interviewees I1, I2, I4, and I5). Some activists argue that these social movements should incorporate struggles for control over the digital infrastructure as part of their own struggles. One interviewee even asked: "Isn't it absurd how progressive groups organise themselves on Facebook? It's like Jews saying 'let's go to Auschwitz, we organise ourselves there and fight against the Nazis'" (interviewee I2).

This weighed approach regarding the roles and responsibilities of individuals and collectives shows that current Mastodon activism in Brazil is aware of the limitations of an unfettered individualist approach. In this sense, it distances itself from cyberlibertarian accounts that, as seen before, have historically marked much of FOSS activism. Activists fear excessively burdening citizens and users. Despite their appreciation of individual autonomy, they believe that responsibility – and the most promising results – lies on collective structures of governance (interviewees I1, I2, I4, and I5).

Furthermore, although activists concentrate on the agency of collectives from the civil society, they do not discard participation of the state in online affairs. Nothing close, however, to strong claims of state sovereignty discourses. For example, Brazilian administrators and moderators see no point in the main measure of the state digital sovereignty discourse, namely data localization (interviewees I2, I4, and I5). Server location of the Brazilian instances already indicates their flexible approach in this regard, as only one of the six communities is hosted in Brazilian territory. All others are in either the United States or Canada.

Interviewed activists are also skeptical of other ideas from the toolbox of state sovereignty discourses, such as publicly owned and managed social networking. None of them showed support to this measure, some were actually surprised about the possibility of such a debate. This does not mean that Brazilian administrators and moderators see no role for the state. "I don't think that having a publicly-funded instance would be an advantage. Instead, it would be a good advantage if we had grants to support developers working on free software in order to bring this knowledge [to the country]. [Other possibility would be] funding for a research centre on the Fediverse at a Brazilian university" (interviewee I1). In addition, activists claim for public regulation to enforce transparency, an approach that later became central in the parliamentary proposal to regulate digital platforms (Tomaz, 2023). "Governments should not control what kinds of data are consumed, where they are transferred to or where they should be stored, but demand more transparency from these companies [digital platforms]," complemented another interviewee (interviewee I2). Thus, activism shows concern regarding the privatization of the governance of the public sphere, but from a perspective that is more akin to liberal discourses, whereby the role of the state is to offer good conditions for allowing the civil society to create its own solutions. In the case of social networking, this means regulating big business, investing in local technical knowledge, and providing population with appropriate media and data literacy (interviewees I1, I2, and I5).

Most interviewees appreciate what Mastodon offers to fulfill their normative expectations, namely to restore civil society control over social networking. Following the reasoning of the text *A people's history of the Fediverse* (Freedombone.net, n.d.), interviewees adopt the argument that the Fediverse provides the conditions for a middle ground approach. It rejects platform centralization, but does not burden too much the individual. "Mastodon is a halfway, so to say, a transitional stage where power moves from the private hand to the collective, so you would be able to make collectives that can pull that power back to the user and eventually return it fully to the user," said an interviewee (interviewee I1).

Furthermore, they value Mastodon's rejection of algorithmic curation, which promotes more transparency regarding data. "Mastodon, despite all its problems and they are many, makes it easier to have some order because it is real people moderating, not algorithms, not big companies, not people who want your engagement for the good or the evil as long as it generates profit," says an interviewee (interviewee I2). This confirms Mansoux and Abbing's (2020) point on the shift to a social understanding of privacy and control.

However, the emphasis on technical affordances can still be felt in much of the conception of Brazilian administrators and moderators. This is the case when they relegate state-related investment to the technical development of free software, undermining the conditions for a political debate about publicly owned and managed instances. Another evidence comes from the fact that only one of the interviewees has no background as software developer (interviewee I3). By highlighting the technical aspect of federated social media, Mastodon activism risks reproducing some aspects of the belief in technological determinism that fueled the cyberspace sovereignty discourse.

9.3.4 Pitfalls of Resistance from the Margins

Finally, I address here the extent to which peripheral countries participate in Fediverse activism, shaping and adapting it to their specific demands. A simple comparison between the Brazilian internet population (around 160 million users in an overall population of over 210 million people) and the number of participants in Brazilian instances of Mastodon (merely 1,200 active users) exemplifies how fringe federated social media still are. The movement struggles to achieve any critical mass that would be able to meaningfully influence digital sovereignty in FOSS terms. Network effects favoring established commercial players and digital resignation, among other factors, play against such a community-led initiative. The long-term effects of the Twitter takeover by Elon Musk are yet to be seen, as this fact can be a game changer.

Even within the Fediverse itself, Brazil seems to be far away from the prominent role it has played in the broader FOSS movement in the past. Indeed, the whole Global South falls short of the contribution to the recursive public of the Fediverse. Despite constant growth since 2016, Mastodon remains largely concentrated in Europe and North America. In 2021, the United States, France, and Germany hosted 65% of all servers. Adding up Japan, this comes nearly to 80% of Mastodon instances concentrated in four rich countries. The Global South, on the other hand, is underrepresented. At that time, Brazil run 0.4% of the instances, and only China, another BRICS country, performed better (see Table 9.2). There is no evidence that this power imbalance has changed since the beginning of the Musk-motivated Twitter migration. The fivefold growth of active users since then remains astoundingly concentrated on the US and Europe. This clearly contradicts the history of geopolitical engagement of peripheral countries with FOSS, even more striking as the internet infrastructure itself has been tipping in the last two decades toward the BRICS and the Global South (Winseck, 2017).

My research does not allow to draw definitive conclusions on the reasons for this, but certainly economic constraints play a role. Costs of operating small instances, between 30 and 200 active users, vary between 50 and 400 dollars a year, and poor economies will certainly lack financial resources to sustain such a voluntary, non commercial effort. However, the governance structure of Mastodon also contributes to this situation. Despite the ideological stance for decentralization, governance is still centralized in key figures, undermining possibilities and interest of activism from the margins. Some

TABLE 9.2 *Participation of countries in Mastodon in 2021: instances, users, and posts*

Country	Instances	%	Active Users	%	Posts	%
Top countries in terms of instances						
US	581	24.37%	68,725	15.72%	52,177,794	14.53%
France	577	24.20%	51,340	11.74%	22,521,403	6.27%
Germany	394	16.53%	108,065	24.71%	52,035,253	14.49%
Japan	345	14.47%	118,101	27.01%	207,467,657	57.78%
China	101	4.24%	26,986	6.17%	7,601,084	2.12%
Canada	68	2.85%	3,691	0.32%	1,941	0.44%
UK	48	2.01%	7,036	0.62%	3,951	0.90%
Comparison with Brazil						
Brazil	8	0.34%	1,224	0.28%	628,424	0.18%
TOTAL	2,380		437,822		358,749,149	

Source: Compilation by the author, based on data available at https://the-federation.info. Latest update in June 2021. In this table, I consider only instances with more than one monthly active user.

activists criticize Rochko's management and development of Mastodon as a reproduction of the "Benevolent Dictator For Life" model (Valens, 2019), an opinion shared by a moderator of a Brazilian instance who has engaged over years with Mastodon governance: "He [Eugen Rochko] is a very privileged person, who has a corresponding worldview that sometimes make it difficult for him to accept other perspectives" (interviewee I4). Reflecting on the development structure of Mastodon around a "benevolent dictator" and the overwhelming majority of Anglo-American white people, this interviewee reports that marginalized groups coming from the global periphery resist to join it: "This [the difficulties to participate in Mastodon] is especially true if we look at black people, indigenous peoples and many other marginalized groups who have several problems to express themselves and be heard by those who develop the software and moderate the communities" (interviewee I4). This interviewee complements: "The very few Black people who are on Mastodon now are there for the sake of resistance" (interviewee I4). According to this interviewee, it is common that persons from these countries and social groups come from Twitter and join a Mastodon instance for a while but, after perceiving its whiteness, return to Twitter, where there are already established communities such as the Black Twitter.

Thus, even if the Fediverse might be celebrated by its possibilities of decentralization, the lack of participation of the Global South in Mastodon brings again to the fore the shortcomings of merely technical approaches. More than openness and federation, politicization of social media infrastructure requires collaboration, negotiation, and explicit choices at all possible layers. "The code might be open, but there is no real collaboration if Eugen [and the small group of developers around him] is not open to discussion," complemented the same interviewee (interviewee I4).

Despite the hurdles to actively participate in and shape the ecosystem of federated social media, Brazilian administrators and moderators see positive repercussions in their country, especially for the marginalized groups of populations. One interviewee reinforces this idea: "White, European, North American people still dominate the internet. Federated social media allow us to reach these marginalized people which Facebook and Elon Musk don't know. Marginalized people fighting together with marginalized people" (interviewee I2). This must be read, of course, as optimism regarding the potential of alternative social media, and not as a factual observation, as Fediverse figures still do not allow to affirm any significant reach. At best, they suggest more autonomy and independence for some individuals within these collectives.

If, on the one hand, Brazilian collectives of civil society are meant to be empowered, the nation-state in its territorial sense, on the other hand, is not thought of as an actor that could enjoy more sovereignty with the Fediverse, weakening once more state digital sovereignty claims. The dismay in face of Bolsonaro's ultraconservative government at the time of the interviews and the perception that the independence of Brazilian institutions was under threat, as some interviewees explicitly expressed (interviewees I1, I2, and I4), might have increased skepticism regarding strong sovereignty measures by the state, such as data localization and publicly funded internet services. Only one instance, "Ursal.zona," considers the necessity of a more active role of the nation-state in the development of an independent Brazilian and Latin American digital communication.

This emphasis on collectives of the civil society when thinking about the Global South, instead of the territorial framing of nation-states, represents a reformulation of collective struggles that often favors cross-country allegiances around shared experiences and subjectivities over national solidarity. This is in line with late resignifications of the Global South beyond its geographical categories (Mahler, 2018). Nonetheless, there is also a risk in this approach, namely to excessively minimize the geopolitical dimensions of technological power. The business model of tech companies benefits from and reproduces, at least to a certain extent, the old patterns of colonialism and exploitation from the Northern nation-states, as scholars have increasingly argued (Avila Pinto, 2018; Couldry & Mejias, 2019). In fact, geopolitical power imbalance has been a matter of concern in digital sovereignty discourses from the Global South, including those which have focused on FOSS as part of the strategy (Schoonmaker, 2018), but it is almost non-existent in the discourse and practices of Mastodon activism in Brazil. Federated social media activists would provide an even richer contribution to the politicization of social media infrastructure if they could integrate into their framework a geopolitical dimension that acknowledges nation-state as a site of struggle, which also bears the capacity to tackle power imbalances and protect its citizens from exploitation.

9.4 CONCLUSION

In this chapter, I proposed to understand the digital sovereignty claims in Brazilian activism on Mastodon. Clearly this activism has a well-organized narrative and advances a politicized notion of digital social networking that differs from the alleged neutrality of the FOSS movement. It distances itself from individual claims of sovereignty by reinforcing the role of collectives of civil society in the management of the digital resources. The state is not rejected *tout court*. Activists expect it to regulate big business, making it more transparent, and support free software initiatives, which could expand the spectrum of alternative social media. But they clearly do not see an active role by the state such as operating publicly funded networks. Considering Couture and Toupin's (2019) categorization, Brazilian activism positions the Fediverse in *social movements and digital sovereignty discourses*, roughly equivalent to the "commons digital sovereignty" explained in the introduction of the book.

However, Brazil and other peripheral countries still lag behind in their capacity of shaping the development of federated social media in the benefit of their populations. Shortcomings in the project, such as economic constraints in hosting networks and the predominance of male, white, Anglo-European people in both governance and usage, undermine participation from marginalized groups. In addition, Brazilian activism still attaches little value to the geopolitical dimension of struggles regarding social media, missing a historical contribution of technological sovereignty claims from the Global South and possibly a broader understanding of the conditions that sustain current power imbalances. Even if state sovereignty does not belong to the core concerns of Fediverse activists, it is unlikely that the sovereignty they aim at, namely of social movements, will succeed without resisting the nearly universal reach of corporate social media. This will require at least some alliance with local political and economic powers, without which federated online communication will continue to be a paper tiger fighting the enormous economic and intellectual resources available in the core of capitalism. At the time of writing, even after Musk has taken several controversial decisions, Twitter still has a hundred times more active users than Mastodon. Facebook, thousandfold.

Brazilian activism on Mastodon represents, therefore, a further step in the politicization of the FOSS movement and the commons digital sovereignty, away from any value-neutral thinking. On the other hand, it is departing from the historical politicization of global inequalities in technological power promoted by earlier FOSS appropriations in the Global South, which stressed the inexorable reality of state power in the reproduction of digital inequalities and upheld *counterpower at the same level.*

Appendix I

Interview Protocol

This is the interview protocol for the chapter "Brazilian Activism in Mastodon: Sovereignty Discourses between Cyberlibertarianism and State-Centrism." It is mostly based on the interview protocol refinement framework (IPR) for semi-structured interviews (Castillo-Montoya, 2016). All interviews were conducted in Brazilian Portuguese between native speakers. Therefore, the scripts and the questions below are a translation of the original ones, whose correctness and accuracy are entirely under the author's responsibility.

The interviews aimed at providing data to answer the following research question (RQ):

RQ 1: How do Brazilian activists on Mastodon articulate concepts and practices related to digital sovereignty discourses?

This RQ was broken down into the following units:

RQ 1.1: What are and should be the digital stakeholders with sovereignty?
RQ 1.2: What are and should be the relevant digital practices for achieving sovereignty?
RQ 1.3: What is the contribution of Mastodon activism to empower the desired digital stakeholders and promote sovereign digital practices?

The interview questions (IQ) are related both to these sub-research questions and to background information (BI).

PART I – Script prior to the interview					
Thank you for your time to participate in this interview. We have already talked about the basics of this interview in our [Mastodon] message exchanges, but I'd like to make an official introduction. My name is Tales Tomaz, I am a researcher at the University of Salzburg and I'm working now on an article about digital sovereignty and federated social media, within the scope of a project of a research group at FGV. It will be presented in a conference in July. Depending on the results, this article might become a book chapter published in English. I will let you know in case this happens. For the sake of accuracy, I would like to record our talk, if you have nothing against it. Data will be deleted immediately after the conclusion of this project. If you don't understand any question, no problems, I can repeat or ask it in other words.					
PART II – Interview questions on personal involvement/practices					
		BI	RQ 1.1	RQ 1.2	RQ 1.3
IQ 1	What is your area of professional activity?	x			

<table>
<tr><td>IQ 2</td><td>For administrators:
For how long does the instance XXX exist?</td><td>x</td><td></td><td></td><td></td></tr>
<tr><td>IQ 3</td><td>For administrators:
How did you become an instance administrator?
For moderators:
How did you become a Mastodon moderator?</td><td>x</td><td></td><td></td><td></td></tr>
<tr><td>IQ 4</td><td>What are your main activities in the management of the instance?
How many weekly hours do you dedicate? Do you have help?</td><td>x</td><td></td><td></td><td></td></tr>
<tr><td>IQ 5</td><td>Did you have previous experience with FOSS?</td><td>x</td><td></td><td></td><td></td></tr>
<tr><td colspan="6">PART III – Short introduction to theoretical concepts</td></tr>
<tr><td colspan="6">When talking about digital sovereignty, we are talking about independence and autonomy over digital infrastructure and content. We usually talk about the following stakeholders:
• States
  o Public authorities in liberal democracies (e.g., the United States, European Union, and Brazil)
  o Governments of authoritarian or semi-authoritarian regimes (e.g., China and Russia)
• Private companies
  o Transnational big techs (e.g., Facebook and Alphabet/Google)
  o Private national companies
• Civil society
  o Collectives (e.g., NGOs, unions, churches, and social movements)
  o Individual users

There are different narratives about who (among these stakeholders) currently holds control and autonomy, who should have this control and autonomy, and how this should be achieved. I want to know how Mastodon situates itself in these narratives.</td></tr>
<tr><td colspan="6">PART IV – Interview questions on concepts and understanding of digital sovereignty</td></tr>
<tr><td></td><td></td><td>BI</td><td>RQ 1.1</td><td>RQ 1.2</td><td>RQ 1.3</td></tr>
<tr><td>IQ 6</td><td>In your opinion, who holds currently more control and autonomy over communication in social media?</td><td></td><td>x</td><td></td><td></td></tr>
<tr><td>IQ 7</td><td>In your opinion, who should have more control and autonomy over communication in social media?</td><td></td><td>x</td><td></td><td></td></tr>
</table>

IQ 8	Does Mastodon help to give more control and autonomy to these stakeholders? How?				x
IQ 9	In your opinion, is the location of communication data, in other words, where our data is located, important? *If yes*: Then, with whom (among these stakeholders)? Does Mastodon help in this? *If no*: next question		x	x	x
IQ 10	In your opinion, is the offer of this kind of service [microblogging and social media] by domestic stakeholders important? *If yes*: Then, by whom (among these stakeholders)? Does Mastodon help in this? *If no*: next question		x	x	x
IQ 11	In your opinion, is the adoption by the user of practices that promote more data protection important? *If yes*: Does Mastodon help in this? *If no*: next question		x	x	x
IQ 12	Do you see Mastodon's potential of contribution to Brazil in the current scenario of digital platforms? For whom (among these stakeholders)?				x
IQ 13	Is there a role for the public power (especially in Brazil) in expanding the model of relation to digital infrastructure and content presented by Fediverse and Mastodon? *If yes*: Which? *If no*: closing remarks		x		x

PART V – Closing remarks

Thank you for your time and patience. Now I'm stopping the recording. As said, raw data will be deleted immediately after the conclusion of this project and will not be used in further works. If needed, I will contact you once again for another interview. When my paper is revised and ready for publication, I will send it to you. If it will become a book chapter, I will let you know. Thanks again!

10

Conclusion

Digital Sovereignty in the BRICS: Structuring Self-Determination, Cybersecurity, and Control

Luca Belli and Min Jiang

10.1 INTRODUCTION: DIGITAL SOVEREIGNS OR DIGITAL SUBJECTS?

This chapter acknowledges both the fluidity and complexity of the notion of digital sovereignty, while also highlighting the necessity of digital sovereignty strategies, policies, and governance mechanisms, envisaged especially by leading emerging economies. As we discuss in the introductory chapter, digital sovereignty suffers from a lack of a consensus regarding both the substance and contours of the concept. In this regard, the analysis of various conceptualizations of this notion as well as its concrete implementations in BRICS countries allows us to move beyond the conventional, normative, state-centric approach toward "sovereignty" that dominates in Western scholarly, policy, and popular debates. Doing so also allows us to engage with how "digital sovereignty" is perceived and practiced in reality by not only nation-states but also empowered individuals, companies, indigenous populations, activist groups, and even supranational entities including the BRICS.

In this spirit, the chapter notes that digital sovereignty narratives and initiatives play a pivotal role in fostering self-determination,[1] while increasing cybersecurity capabilities and strengthening the capacity to exercise control over digital infrastructures and data of the various types of "digital sovereigns." Importantly, depending on the conception of digital sovereignty

[1] As pointed out in the introductory chapter of this volume, this work stresses the instrumental role of digital sovereignty in the achievement of the internal dimension of self-determination, that is, the right to freely determine and pursue one's economic, social, and cultural developments, including by independently choosing, developing, and adopting digital technologies. Such conception also includes the fundamental right to "informational self-determination" enshrining the individuals' faculty to exert control over their personal data, as an expression of the human right to have and develop a personality. See Chapter 1, note 1.

that we decide to utilize and the initiatives at stake, a "digital sovereign" can be an individual, a community, a corporation, a state, or even a supranational organization.[2]

Indeed, the examples analyzed in this volume illustrate how individuals, communities, corporations, states, and supranational organizations can become digital sovereigns by understanding, developing, and regulating the use of digital technologies, according to their needs, aspirations, and values. Conversely, aspiring digital sovereigns can be turned into digital subjects when there is insufficient understanding, development, or command of such technologies even when "digital sovereignty" policies and plans are formally adopted.

As we contend along the chapters of this book, digital sovereignty is a multifaceted and contested concept. It may be considered something positive or negative, depending on who the sovereign entity is, and how the entity decides to structure its sovereignty capability. It is important to emphasize that remarkably similar policies may be aimed at defending a nation from cyberattacks or surveilling it, may strive to promote local talent, fostering the development of indigenous technologies, or blatantly enact protectionist agendas, preserving the position of cronies. Chiefly, the positive or negative assessment of this concept will strongly rely on how the construction and deployment of digital sovereignty affects the rights and agency of others. As such, the digital sovereignty label indicates the idea that digital sovereigns assert their agency, authority, and capacity to "pursue their economic, social and cultural development"[3] through the digital technologies they use. Such a vision introduces a new element of complexity, dependent on the *capability* of a sovereign entity to understand and exercise power through technology without being necessarily bound to a specific territory. These elements challenge the traditional state-centric conceptions of sovereignty, which rely on a nation-state's domestic authority and control over a given population in a specific territory and its monopoly in the definition of international legal instruments, alliances, and exercise of military power.

The concept of digital sovereignty does not obliterate the importance of the above-mentioned elements but brings to the fore the essential role of technology systems in expanding authority, self-determination, and control. In this perspective, a digital sovereign is the entity that owns, operates, and, ultimately,

[2] For instance, digital sovereignty was recognized as a priority for the European Union, which is a supranational organization. In a statement just prior to her appointment as president of the European Commission, Ursula von der Leyen, called for Europe to achieve "technological sovereignty in some critical technology areas" stating that "Europe must have (the technological capacity) to make its own choices, according to its own values, respecting its own rules" while not hiding the explicit ambition that Europe "define standards for this new generation of technologies that will become the global norm." (von der Leyen, 2020).

[3] See the definition of the fundamental right to self-determination in Article 1 of the *Charter of the United Nations* as well as in Article 1 of both the *International Covenant on Economic, Social and Cultural Rights* and the *International Covenant on Civil and Political Rights*.

has the capacity to understand, regulate, and control the technology can and will be used. To appreciate the breath and relevance of digital sovereignty, it is therefore useful to emphasize the "structural power" of (digital) technology. The structural power concept was first elaborated by political scientist Susan Strange in *States and Markets* (1988). In her vision, power can be exercised not only through command and control and the ability to compel someone to do something by establishing regimes that regulate societies but also through the power to shape the structures defining the frameworks within which people, corporations, and states relate to each other.

Strange's conception of structural power can be seen as a sovereign entity's capability to shape the bureaucratic, commercial, or even technological "labyrinths" enabling interactions among people, organizations, businesses, and states. The sovereign defines where walls or doors will be in the labyrinth, shaping its "architecture" (Lessig, 1999a, 2006), thus ultimately exercising power by controlling and regulating the capacity of those who use the labyrinth to move and interact. In this sense, Strange's work provides a useful perspective from which we can read Lessig's concept of software and hardware architectures as regulation. Here, architectures act as constraints that can structure (cyber)spaces in both the physical[4] and digital realms, determining whether specific behaviors are allowed by design, and thus playing a regulatory function (Belli, 2022).

Awareness of the use of digital technology for surveillance or "data colonialism" (Benyera, 2021; Couldry & Mejias, 2018) has been matched by the increasing understanding of the central role played by digital technology to structure national economy, society, and governance. Hence, understanding the relevance of the structural power of technology is essential to realizing the relevance of digital sovereignty and, more broadly, the regulatory function of technology (Benyera, 2021; Couldry & Mejias, 2018). It would be either incorrect or hubristic – or both – to argue that the nation-state is the only possible digital sovereign. Indeed, individuals, communities, organizations, and businesses that understand, develop, and deploy digital technologies can all be considered digital sovereigns as they are not only regulated by technologies but also enjoy self-determination thanks to technology and may even be able to elude the implementation of traditional state sovereignty through the exercise of their digital sovereignty.

As this volume demonstrates, especially from a Global South perspective, a very large spectrum of different entities may engage in understanding, developing, and mustering digital technologies. Importantly, as we have stressed previously, the entities that manage to become digital sovereigns are not only states. Community networks built and operated by local communities are interesting examples in this regard, which can be found in several BRICS

[4] An example offered by Lessig is the architecture of the city of Paris, which was reorganized with large avenues by Baron Haussmann to prevent rebellious people from taking control of the city center, as previously happened during the third French revolution of 1848 (Lessig, 2006).

countries. These crowd-sourced, bottom-up networks are excellent examples of entities pursuing a form of Commons Digital Sovereignty, which frequently emerges not only as a community-driven alternative to corporate and state approaches, but as a concrete strategy to cope with the limitations and failures of the traditional public and private approaches.

Internet access infrastructures created by local communities to overcome digital divides and achieve "network self-determination"[5] illustrate that digital sovereignty can stem from the actions of empowered communities, where individuals cooperate to build technology, understand its functioning, and exert control over the local digital infrastructure, thus appropriate the benefits of tech-enabled social, economic, and cultural developments (Belli, 2017). The commons approach to digital sovereignty, with mounting evidence from several BRICS countries including Brazil, India, and South Africa, can be seen as a by-product of communities yearning for network self-determination (Belli & Hadzic, 2022; Belli & Hadzic, 2023; GISWatch, 2018). Indeed, such examples demonstrate that even vulnerable and marginalized communities such as Brazilian *quilomobola*[6] women or rural communities and slum-dwellers in South Africa and India can become the protagonists and participants of their digital futures, learning how to build and use new digital infrastructures and new services for the local communities, based on the needs and characteristics of the local communities.

Indeed, as we have demonstrated in the chapter of this volume, digital sovereignty is not only fostered by states but can also be crafted by local communities. Despite not having explicit digital sovereignty agendas, community networks offer intriguing examples of "good digital sovereignty" (Belli, 2023), illustrating how new digital architectures can be constructed, managed, and self-regulated using a bottom-up approach (Belli, 2017). They tellingly demonstrate that internet connectivity and entire digital ecosystems can be built by the local communities for the local communities, demonstrating that groups of individuals that previously were scarcely connected or totally unconnected can become digitally sovereign. Such commons-based conception of digital sovereignty can not only lead the local community to start understanding the

[5] Network self-determination is defined as the "right to freely associate in order to define, in a democratic fashion, the design, development and management of network infrastructure as a common good, so that all individuals can freely seek, impart and receive information and innovation." The concept is based on the consideration that by freely developing connectivity infrastructure, individuals and communities quintessentially enjoy their fundamental right to self-determine, that is, to "pursue their economic, social and cultural development" through the opportunities that connectivity can offer (Belli, 2017).

[6] Quilombos are communities that emerged as refuges for African enslaved individuals who escaped exploitation during the entire period of slavery in Brazil, established by Portuguese colonizers in the sixteenth century and maintained until 1888. The inhabitants of these communities are called quilombolas. With the adoption of the 1988 Constitution, Brazil enshrined the quilombolas right to own and use the land they were on. Today Brazil has more than fifteen thousand quilombola communities (Zanolli, 2021, pp. 121–128).

functioning and developing digital technology but also strive to shape their economic, social, and cultural developments (Belli, 2017; Belli & Hadzic, 2022; Belli & Hadzic, 2023; Bidwell & Jensen; 2019; GISWatch 2018).

Besides providing access to previously disconnected populations, these community networks also give rise to an ample range of positive externalities, including the construction of new infrastructure with limited investment, the engagement of locals in the development of new self-governance models, the revitalization of social interactions among local community members, and the emergence of new opportunities for accessing information, learning, doing business, and creating employment (Belli, 2017; Bidwell & Jensen, 2019).

In this perspective, these initiatives are real laboratories of digital sovereignty for local communities that experiment with digital technologies to understand their functioning, thus developing a better understanding not only of the technology itself but of the type of governance and regulation compatible with their community. It leads the local communities to develop "good digital sovereignty," thanks to their capacity to understand, develop, and regulate their local digital ecosystems, while connecting them to the global internet (Belli, 2017; Belli & Hadzic, 2023).

It becomes increasingly evident that a comprehensive plan guided by a long-term perspective is essential to the successful implementation of digital sovereignty initiatives. Those who manage to do so may have a better chance of becoming digital sovereigns, where they can avoid or minimize the risks brought by technical and economic dependence on foreign technology. Those who do not may turn into digital subjects (or digitally colonized) by other more powerful digital sovereigns. Unfortunately, the "vision" of digital sovereignty of most states often lacks farsightedness and a holistic approach to this issue.

Importantly, a variety of different goals may be explicitly or implicitly included within digital sovereignty narratives, as digital technologies and their structural power can facilitate enormous social and economic advancements but can also be weaponized against individuals, corporations, and nation-states. In such contexts, this chapter takes a more agnostic approach toward digital sovereignty, exploring a selection of practices and providing insight into what this concept means in practical terms. In this respect, BRICS countries' approaches offer some telling examples of how and why the need for digital sovereignty can emerge as well as how confused, contradictory, and even dysfunctional the implementation of policies aiming at digital sovereignty can be.

10.2 THE EMERGENCE OF THE DIGITAL SOVEREIGNTY DISCOURSE IN THE BRICS

The heterogeneity, cultural richness, and historical backgrounds of the BRICS are also reflected in their diverse approaches to digital sovereignty. The differences in their state digital sovereignty strategies can be partly explained by their divergent political stances.

As noted by Johannes Thumfart's contribution in this volume, Russia and China, and to a lesser extent India, have traditionally played an antagonistic role to the digital superpower, the US, and have structured their approaches to digital sovereignty based on such antagonism. Their clear intention to avoid reliance on US technology is a decades-long strategic choice. Historically, the RIC[7] countries have not only had a strongly suspicious and frequently confrontational attitude toward the US but also associated dependence on US technology with high risks.

A telling example is the existence of alternatives to the Global Positioning Systems (GPS), which was established by the US in the late 1970s. GPS, an essential component of a wide range of digital products and services, plays a critical role for many for military technologies used for defense purposes. Out of the five alternatives to the dominant US system, the first three were developed by Russia, China, and India.[8] The EU and Japan have also decided to create alternative systems in recent years as they become increasingly mindful of how critical it is to be strategically autonomous.[9]

India, Brazil, and South Africa have also strong historical reasons for being particularly attached to their (digital) sovereignty. These span from postcolonial resentments against imperialist attitudes of old colonizers, feeding several decades-long engagements in "South-South cooperation" (The South Commission, 1990)[10] through numerous initiatives, such as the Group of 77, the Non-Aligned Movement and Group of 15, the IBSA Trilateral[11] and,

[7] The RIC Trilateral Alignment was established by Russia, India, and China in 2001 (O'Donnell & Papa, 2021).

The RIC Trilateral Alignment is not the only official club created by BRICS countries before the BRICS: in 2003, India also cofounded the IBSA Trilateral, together with Brazil and South Africa (see note 212, below), and in 2017, India also joined the Shanghai Cooperation Organization (SCO), a larger alignment that also includes China and Russia.

[8] The Global Navigation Satellite System (GLONASS) was developed by Russia in the 1980s; China started the development of the BeiDou Navigation Satellite System (BDS) in the 2000s; India launched the development of the Navigation with Indian Constellation (NavIC) in the 2010s.

[9] The EU Galileo system and the Quasi-Zenith Satellite System (QZSS) led by Japan were developed since 2015.

[10] Already in 1990, the seminal Report of the South Commission called for South-South cooperation, emphasizing that "the emerging development patterns of the North clearly suggest that the Northern locomotive economies will not pull the train of Southern economies at a pace that will satisfy its passengers – the people of the South. The locomotive power has to be generated to the maximum extent possible within the economies of the South themselves." (The South Commission, 1990, p. 286). The South Commission, formally established in 1987, fostered discussions among intellectual and political leaders from the South and evolved into the South Centre, an intergovernmental organization established in 1995. www.southcentre.int/.

[11] Little known to the public, IBSA is a trilateral forum that brings together India, Brazil, and South Africa to foster consultation and coordination on global and regional political issues; collaboration on concrete projects; and assisting other developing countries through the IBSA Fund. See www.ibsa-trilateral.org/. This organization become well known to internet

finally, the BRICS grouping.[12] These countries also harbor strong sensitivities stemming from the US abuses of its dominant position in the digital realm.

Such egregious abuses have pushed the BRICS to seek alternative paths of digital development and policymaking. Notably, former NSA contractor Edward Snowden revealed the Brazilian head of state Dilma Rousseff herself was personally a victim of illegal wiretapping (MacAskill & Dance, 2013). Such an episode represented a true wake-up call for the BRICS grouping. Indeed, post-Snowden, BRICS nations have been reorganizing their postures to enhance their cooperation on digital matters – especially in cybersecurity (Belli, 2021a, 2021b, 2021c) – as a reaction to the unlimited digital sovereignty exercised by the US globally.

Snowden revelations exposed the strategic risks associated with the massive use and dependence on foreign technologies. The real costs of "free services" are paid de facto by granting a license to large-scale collection of personal data as well as the consequent loss of privacy, competition, sovereignty, and informational self-determination.[13] However, it may be argued that the actor mainly responsible for the global awakening of the risks associated with the "weaponization" of digital policies was the Trump Administration that frequently targeted adversaries with several executive orders (Jiang, 2019) accompanied by bombastic announcements via social media.

Indeed, the periodic use of executive orders in prohibiting US tech firms from supplying software or hardware components to Chinese manufacturers such as ZTE and Huawei has led many governments and businesses around the world to reconsider their supply chains and grasp the importance of digital sovereignty in terms of strategic autonomy, self-sufficiency, and

governance scholars in 2011, when it put forward a proposal for a UN Committee for Internet-Related Policies, which was strongly contested at that year's UN Internet Governance Forum and, despite the contestations, endorsed by the Indian Government at the 66th Session of the UN General Assembly in October 2011 (Belli, 2011).

[12] The G77 was established in 1964 as a developing countries' interest group. G15 emerged within the Non-Aligned Movement in 1989. The IBSA Trilateral was created in 2003. BRICS was formed in 2009. They have all been considered "locomotives of the South" defined by the Report of the South Commission, raising hopes of an alternative to the world order imposed by the Global North. A compelling review of how and why such groupings were created as well as the subsequent South-South cooperation attempts is provided by V. Prashad in "Poorer Nations: A Possible History of the Global South" (2012).

[13] Since the early 1980s, the fundamental right to "informational self-determination" has become a cornerstone of personal-data protection, starting to be consecrated as an expression of the right to free development of the personality. Particularly, in 1983, the landmark "Census" decision of the Federal Supreme Court of Germany (1983) stressed that the right to informational self-determination underpins "the capacity of the individual to determine the disclosure and use of his/her personal data," thus ascribing to individuals the right to choose what personal data about themselves can be disclosed, to whom, and for what purposes such data can be used. The principle is considered to be a cornerstone of modern data protection and is explicitly enshrined by art. 2 of the Brazilian General Data Protection Law as one of the founding elements of the Brazilian data protection framework (CyberBRICS, 2020).

self-determination.[14] While such concerns have been particularly acutely felt among BRICS countries, many Western countries shared them as well, especially at the EU level (von der Leyen, 2020).

Recent years have witnessed the considerable transformation of the perception of digital sovereignty from an initial negative connotation associated with authoritarian ambition to a more positive conceptualization for recognizing its relevance in community, national, and international agendas. A growing chain of events has shown there are concrete risks associated with the inability to exercise digital sovereignty, thus being subject to the unilateral decisions of those able to assert agency, power, and control over digital infrastructure, data, services, and protocols. Indeed, the notion of digital sovereignty gradually progressed from a niche concept, primarily supported by China and few other developing countries, and frequently purported as an autocratic cliché, to a mainstream issue now advocated by EU leaders as an essential tussle to reassert strategic autonomy.

10.3 RESISTING FOREIGN ESPIONAGE, MEDDLING, AND SANCTIONS

We must note that the various initiatives that emerged over the past decade in the BRICS countries and beyond to pursue digital sovereignty have not been merely motivated by a mere desire to avoid US espionage. On the contrary, the increasing awareness of the US's invasive behaviors through its technological apparatus has led BRICS countries to realize that without alternatives, their technological disadvantage would have led to irreversible economic dependence and ultimately (digital) colonization.

First, on top of fearing being victim of weaponized digital policies, countries around the world understand that the main concerns raised by Edward Snowden in 2013 remain substantially unchanged. In July 2020, the European Court of Justice (ECJ) in its Schrems II case invalidated the Trans-Atlantic transfer of personal data from the EU to the US due to the nature of US government access to data held by American corporations under existing intelligence activities. Particularly the Court held that such activities undermine "the minimum safeguards resulting, under EU law, from the principle of proportionality, with the consequence that the surveillance programmes based on those provisions cannot be regarded as limited to what is strictly necessary" (*Data Protection Commissioner* v *Facebook Ireland Ltd*, 2020, para 184).

To understand why the digital sovereignty sentiments have been growing globally, motivated by mistrust toward dominant US technologies, it is instructive to consider the normative analysis of the ECJ. Section 702 of the Foreign Intelligence Surveillance Act (FISA) authorizes the collection, use, and

[14] See the first chapter of this book but also the detailed analysis offered by A. Chander and H. Sun (2022).

dissemination of electronic communications content stored by US platforms (such as Facebook, Google, and Microsoft) or transported across the internet's "backbone" infrastructure, thus compelling US connectivity providers (such as AT&T and Verizon) to cooperate with national intelligence agencies (*Data Protection Commissioner* v *Facebook Ireland Ltd*, 2020, para 184).[15]

The reactions that this situation triggered in the BRICS countries are tellingly illustrated by former Brazilian President Dilma Rousseff's opening remarks at 68th UN General Assembly, describing the NSA scandal in the following terms:

> As many other Latin Americans, I fought against authoritarianism and censorship, and I cannot but defend, in an uncompromising fashion, the right to privacy of individuals and the **sovereignty of my country**.
>
> In the absence of the right to privacy, there can be no true freedom of expression and opinion, and therefore no effective democracy. In the absence of the **respect for sovereignty**, there is no basis for the relationship among Nations.
>
> We face, Mr. President, a situation of grave violation of human rights and of civil liberties; of invasion and capture of confidential information concerning corporate activities, and especially of **disrespect to national sovereignty**. (Rousseff, 2013) [emphasis added]

It is in this context that BRICS countries have started some of their most ambitious initiatives aimed at reasserting digital sovereignty, both independently and as a grouping. Since the BRICS Summit issued the *2013 eThekwini Declaration and Action Plan* in Durban, South Africa, BRICS nations have made explicit their desire to enhance their cooperation on cybersecurity, expressing for the first time their desire "to contribute to and participate in a peaceful, secure, and open cyberspace" while calling for the elaboration of "universally accepted norms, standards and practices" (BRICS, 2013). Consequently, BRICS leaders established the "Working Group of Experts of the BRICS States on security in the use of ICTs" with a mandate to, inter alia, "develop practical cooperation with each other in order to address common security challenges in the use of ICTs" (BRICS, 2015).

Individual initiatives also followed suit as the governance, regulation, and development of digital technologies have swiftly gained prominence in each BRICS country's agenda. In 2014, Brazil approved its Internet Rights Framework (Marco Civil da Internet) to regulate *inter alia* data protection in the online environment and agreed to start the construction together with the EU of EllaLink,[16] a new submarine fiber-optic cable. This cable connects Seixas, Portugal directly with Fortaleza, Brazil without having to pass through Miami, US, where all previous submarine cable landed as part of US telecom backbone. The inauguration of EllaLink in June 2021, after several years of

[15] See notably the ECJ considerations on the PRISM and UPSTREAM surveillance programs, regulated by Section 702 of the FISA and Executive Order 12333.

[16] For more information about EllaLink, see https://ella.link.

development, is an example of an infrastructure initiative aimed at strengthening digital sovereignty to enhance strategic autonomy from US technology while reducing dependency on US suppliers.

The considerable time and financial cost of the initiative, however, are also a stark reminder of how complex it is to build such strategic autonomy, how necessary it is to adopt a systemic long-term plan, and how difficult it is to maintain a particular digital sovereignty stance in an unstable geopolitical environment. Understanding how digital technologies works, crafting a sound and comprehensive strategy to frame their governance, securing adequate resources to implement such a strategy, and having a stable environment to avoid disruption are key elements in implementing digital sovereignty, be it exercised by individuals, communities, corporations, states, or supranational entities. Such elements are much easier to crystallize in countries that enjoy strong political stability and a systemic approach to technology, while they are much rarer in countries where administrations lack technological understanding and subsequently hold radically different – or frequently contradictory – postures toward digital sovereignty.

Within BRICS, China is clearly a country enjoying relative political stability, systematic governance, and deployment of digital technologies. However, even the presence of these elements does not guarantee the achievement of digital sovereignty without a long-term plan. For example, in Russia, the regulation of internet infrastructure and calls for cyber sovereignty started to appear as early as the 2010s. Since then, a number of initiatives have been gradually implemented over the subsequent decade with the goal of achieving digital self-sufficiency and enhancing the country's digital cyber-control, cyber-defense, and offense capabilities. Importantly, Russia, China, and other members of the Shanghai Cooperation Organization (SCO) released the first version of their International Code of Conduct for Information Security, updated in 2015, stressing that "policy authority for Internet-related public policy issues is the sovereign right of States." (Ministry of Digital Development, Communications and Mass Media of the Russian Federation, 2015).[17]

In 2012, Russia established a legal framework for website blocking and in 2015 introduced data localization provisions, which mandate the storage of personal data in servers located in the national territory (Shcherbovich, 2021). These policies laid the ground for the institutionalization of the "internet sovereignty" discourse, articulated by Deputy Chairman of the State Duma Irina Yarovaya and consecrated into legislation in 2019, frequently dubbed

[17] Already in 2015, Russia announced its willingness to develop a "independent" mobile operating system reduce and ideally break the iOS and Android duopoly by Apple and Google. Notably, the Russia Ministry of Telecommunications adamantly supported the use of Free and Open Software as the base "for creation of international industrial consortium for development of alternative software products [...] relying on collaboration with BRICS-countries" (Ministry of Digital Development, Communications and Mass Media of the Russian Federation, 2015).

as "Yarovaya Law" (Shcherbovich, 2021). Russia has dedicated considerable efforts to territorialize its digital infrastructure[18] and exert control over information flows in a bid to not only assert control over the national digital environment but also resist foreign cyberattacks and skirt the disruptive effects of foreign sanctions. The establishment of a national segment of the internet, known as the "RuNet," heavily reliant on the adoption of Russian hardware and software facilitates the pervasive control of information flows by Russian Internet Service Providers, while also providing strategic autonomy to a country that has massively bet on digitalization.

It is important to note that the Russian case illustrates the juxtaposition of cybersecurity, digital sovereignty, and (social) control narratives. Undeniably, the Russian government has frequently utilized the same measures that are branded as enhancing digital sovereignty to monitor Russian citizens and unduly block undesired content online.[19] As argued in this book by Olga Bronnikova and colleagues, the implementation of the various iterations of SORM (System for Operative Investigative Activities) illustrates how digital sovereignty and cybersecurity discourse may also represent a convenient way to expand national surveillance operations.

However, the Russian push for the "sovereignization of the internet" (Grover & Thomas, 2021) has been justified not only by the fear of foreign meddling exposed by Snowden revelations or the willingness to control online speech but also by the increasing need to develop a self-sufficient national network able to resist the disruption of foreign sanctions and mitigate foreign cyberattacks on national digital infrastructure as seen in Russia's ongoing war in Ukraine. For instance, in June 2019, the *New York Times* reported that the US Cyber Command was stepping up its "digital incursions" into Russia's electric power grid in accordance with the Command's attributions to "conduct clandestine military activity to deter, safeguard or defend against attacks" (Sanger & Perlroth, 2019).

Concrete initiatives aimed at constructing digital sovereignty in Russia have emerged partly out of the need for survival. This is the case of Mir,[20] a Russian

[18] Here the term "digital infrastructure" should be considered as any physical and logical asset, that is, not only the physical infrastructure aimed at providing connectivity, but also the protocols and applications that facilitate communications, as it is generally understood in science and technology studies.

[19] This has been stated unequivocally by the European Court of Human Rights – to which Russia is subject, as a member of the Council of Europe – that, in four different judgments delivered in June 2020, criticized the Russian law for allowing the government to take down or block online content without requiring a court order. An interesting analysis of the four judgments (*Flavus and Others* v. *Russia*, *Bulgakov* v. *Russia*, *Engels* v. *Russia*, and *Vladimir Kharitonov* v. *Russia*) is offered by G. Grover and A. Thomas (2021).

[20] See the dedicated section on the website of the Bank of Russia www.cbr.ru/eng/psystem/. Mir literally means "peace" or "world" in Russian. Interestingly, the Mir payment system has the same name of the space station, operated from 1986 to 2001 by the Soviet Union and later by Russia.

payment system established in 2014 to overcome total denial of e-payment service imposed on Russian banks by US-based Visa and MasterCard. After the annexation of Crimea, US sanctions against Russia left millions of Russian customers with no access to credit card services. As a response, the Central Bank of Russia established Mir that is fully operated by the Russian National Card Payment System, a subsidiary of the Central Bank of Russia. This episode demonstrated that digital sovereignty initiatives often emerge out of the perceived risks of disruption and the possible weaponization of foreign technologies on which a country, an individual, a community, or a corporation relies.

Similar considerations can be seen in the ambitious plan of BRICS countries, chiefly China and Russia, to develop their own national digital currencies[21] in a bid to compete with and reduce dependence on the US dollar at the international level, enabling a process of "dedollarization" (Huang, 2020). Furthermore, as stressed by Hariharan and Natarajan in this volume, the consequences of the Visa-MasterCard episode are far from trivial and represented a further wake-up call for the BRICS nations, only one year after the NSA scandal. Increasingly aware of the risks linked to overreliance on foreign technology, India launched the development of its indigenous payments system, the Unified Payments Interface (UPI) and the National Payments Corporation of India (NPCI), as well as the Digital India[22] program. As we will argue in the following section, the ultimate goal of the latter plan is the development of a digital public infrastructure (DPI) that enables India's digital transformation by fostering the emergence of a sound national digital ecosystem and reducing the country's reliance on foreign hardware and software, thus reasserting digital sovereignty.

Lastly, it is also interesting to note that similar concerns and increasing alignment of Russia and India regarding the relevance of their digital sovereignty on electronic payment systems also emerged from the countries' explicit political statements. Indeed, in late 2021, India and Russia expressed interest in enhancing their cooperation toward the mutual acceptance of national payment systems within their respective national payment infrastructures, promoting "interaction of Unified Payments Interface (UPI) and the Faster Payments System of the Bank of Russia (FPS). [In this occasion, t]he Russian Side invited Indian credit institutions to connect to the financial messaging system of the Bank of Russia to facilitate faultless interbank transactions" (Ministry of External Affairs of India, 2021).

Importantly, the relevance of digital payments systems is fundamental from a state digital sovereignty perspective, especially for giant countries with large populations such as the BRICS. On the one hand, e-payments have been traditionally controlled by dominant US providers such as Visa and MasterCard,

[21] A detailed analysis of the ongoing BRICS initiatives in this context can be found consulting the recording of the "BRICS Conference – Central Bank Digital Currencies" (CyberBRICS, 2022).

[22] Digital India was launched in 2015. See www.digitalindia.gov.in.

thus creating an enormous vulnerability for all countries relying on such systems, as the abovementioned Russian example illustrates tellingly. On the other hand, electronic payments have garnered major relevance due to the enormous amount of data and revenue they generate. Aware of the strategic importance of e-payments, BRICS nations have heavily invested in this data-intensive sector.

In less than a decade, China, India, and Brazil have become global leaders in instant online payments, leapfrogging virtually all developed countries (ACI Worldwide & Global Data, 2022).[23] India and China have achieved the first and second positions of the global ranking of countries with highest number of real-time online payments. Even more impressively, Brazil has reached the top ten of the ranking, starting from the bottom, in only two years since the introduction in 2020 of Pix, its national digital payment system established by the Brazilian Central Bank.[24] Although not always mentioned explicitly, digital sovereignty is becoming the key concern underpinning new digital payment initiatives in the BRICS. Pix is now used by 70% of Brazilians to transfer money at no cost, while before its introduction the only available option to process instantaneous electronic payments was to use the networks of foreign e-payment giants such as Visa and MasterCard, which charge a 3% fee on each transaction besides centralizing data collection of all their users (Belli, 2023). These latter points are the main reasons why the development of public digital infrastructures such as Pix are enormously relevant from a "good digital sovereignty" perspective: it democratizes digital payments, reduces market and data concentration, and provides unique insight onto the national economy to the Central Bank of Brazil (rather than to two foreign actors), thus reverting a trend many scholars have defined as data colonialism (Belli, 2023).

This concern was evident in the Brazilian Central Bank's order to suspend the plan of WhatsApp – the dominant instant messaging app in Brazil, owned by the US conglomerate Meta – to introduce the app's own payment system several months before the release of the Pix payment system (Mandl & Versiani, 2020). The rationale of the Brazilian Central Bank's order is that the first mover advantage of WhatsApp – the use of which is subsidized to consumers by all Brazilian operators in the context of the so-called "zero-rating" schemes[25] – would have created "irreparable damages" to competition,

[23] Particularly interesting and up-to-date data are available in the ACI Worldwide and Global Data reports on "Prime-Time for Real Time," which track and analyze real-time payments volumes, growth, and dynamics of 48 global markets.

[24] According to the ACI Worldwide and Global Data report mentioned at n.42, "Brazil's Pix system has gotten off to a flying start, passing a billion transactions within months of launching and continuing to go from strength to strength. There are now more than 100 million Pix users" (ACI Worldwide & Global Data, 2022, p. 8).

[25] For a detailed analyses of zero-rating practices, see www.zerorating.info. For an updated overview of the practices in Brazil, see Instituto Brasileiro de Defesa do Consumidor [IDEC] and Instituto Locomotiva (2021).

privacy, and data protection in Brazil. Hence, the suspension of WhatsApp's plan was necessary to "preserve an adequate competitive environment that can ensure the functioning of a payment system that is interoperable, fast, secure, transparent, open, and cheap" (Banco Central do Brasil, 2020).

We are witnessing a new generation of techno-regulatory initiatives that aim at embedding digital sovereignty into technology. This new approach to policy and regulation by technology, seen from the BRICS experiences, deserves academic, policy, and public attention. While not necessarily a trend toward techno-authoritarianism where technology becomes an instrument of control, embedding digital sovereignty into technology can also be a positive exercise of self-determination. The India Stack, for instance, fosters the digitalization of the entire country through the development of digital public goods based on open source technology. It is a fascinating example of digital sovereignty fostered by the state but implemented in a decentralized way by technologists through technology, no less effective than state policy. This and other initiatives from BRICS and the Global South need to be carefully studied and understood by researchers, policymakers, and civil society advocates alike, as it holds promise to a future shape of governance, policy, and regulation.

10.4 RESISTANCE TO DATA COLONIALISM OR CONSTRUCTION OF DIGITAL PROTECTIONISM?

Digitalization can enable important benefits but depending on how such a process is structured, it may also entail considerable risks for state digital sovereignty. Such considerations particularly relate to extensive adoption of foreign software, introducing risks spanning from unsustainable dependence of both private and public sectors on foreign technology to various threats to national security, uncontrolled extraction of strategic national resources – notably (personal) data of entire populations and economic sectors – and unfair competition. In this perspective, as we have noted in the introduction, Brazil was a pioneer of software autonomy through a Commons Digital Sovereignty stance more than two decades ago.

Indeed, the Lula administrations of the 2000s realized that by being a mere software consumer, Brazil was facing an unsustainable future, destined to be a digital vassal like most other countries. In retrospect, the Free Software policies adopted by Brazil 20 years ago – and unwisely reversed, under the Temer administration – were remarkably forward-looking in reducing software dependency and public expenditure, while enhancing security and control over Brazilian digital infrastructures. Even if these policies have never been explicitly labeled as "digital sovereignty," they are some of the earliest and strongest examples of State Digital Sovereignty.

It is also necessary to stress that digital sovereignty policies may also be primarily driven by economic protectionism. Indeed, a further element of complexity in digital sovereignty discussions is the potential protectionist dimension. Digital sovereignty narratives lend themselves well to the inclusion – and to some extent confusion – of a variety of goals, including resistance to data colonialism (Ávila, 2018), the implementation of digital development agendas, the establishment of protectionist measures, the tightening of social control, and political exploitation of post-colonial resentments.

Digitalization can enable important benefits but, depending on how such a process is structured, it may also entail large risks. China and India provide interesting insight in this regard. While the Snowden revelations have triggered vitriolic reactions in the Brazilian government and boosted Russian plans for "internet sovereignty," the Chinese authorities perceived them as exposing China's vulnerable position as long as it relied on foreign technology. The Chinese approach to digital technology has been extremely cautious, understanding not only the potential of digital technologies to foster development but also the importance to assert control at the national level.

From the perspective of the Chinese authorities, the 2013 Snowden revelations and the 2014 US sanctions on Russia have exposed both external and internal threats. The reliance on and limited control of foreign technologies undoubtedly created vulnerabilities for both external and internal actors. Furthermore, China perceived its strategic disadvantage in a global digital economy dominated by US technologies, as well as a situation of weakness in a global digital governance landscape dominated by Western actors' narratives. Clearly, in the Chinese authorities' view (Arsène, 2016), this situation called for an immediate and organized reaction, carefully blending policies, politics, and developmental approach to redefine Chinese digital sovereignty.

In 2014, the Xi Jinping administration established the Cyberspace Administration of China (CAC) and the Central Commission for Cybersecurity and Informatization, creating a new cybersecurity and informatization *xitong*, a cluster of institutions with various digital-related competences, which has been personally chaired by Xi Jinping to date (Creemers, 2020). In the same year, the first World Internet Conference (WIC) was organized, creating a China-led global multi-stakeholder forum on digital governance. The first *Wuzhen Declaration*, proposed as a WIC outcome, featured "cyber sovereignty" in a prominent position among the advocated principles. In the following year, at the opening ceremony of the WIC 2015, President Xi Jinping himself stressed the importance of every country's right "to choose its online development path, its network management model and its public Internet policies, and to equal participation in international cyberspace governance" (Xi, 2015).

Simultaneously, China started paying more close attention to digital innovations. It is hoped through innovations Chinese researchers, developers, and ultimately the Chinese state could achieve a sovereign position rather than relying on existing Western, mainly US, technologies. Due to reduced production costs and increasing advancement in Chinese technology competitiveness, the production and large-scale exportation of Chinese hardware seemed to have solidified and expanded the Chinese state's digital sovereignty. Not surprisingly, the Internet of Things (IoT), featured as a prominent area of the "Made in China 2025" strategic plan in 2015, aimed to expand China's development of connected devices to reach 95% of the market by 2025. Such ambitious goals were part of the comprehensive "Digital Silk Road" initiative and the larger Belt and Road Initiative (Jiang, 2021).

Artificial Intelligence (AI) appears to be another area of essential importance for the preservation and expansion of Chinese digital sovereignty. The Chinese State Council issued an *AI Development Plan* in July 2017, prompting various initiatives from local governments and businesses to establish AI funds and local plans with the goal of becoming the world's "primary" AI innovation center by 2030 (Ding, 2018). The goal of such a plan aims to reproduce the success of the State Council 2015 Plan for "mass entrepreneurship and mass innovation" that created thousands of technology incubators, entrepreneurship zones, and government-backed funds in attracting an enormous level of private venture capital.[26] At the same time, since 2018 China has started piloting the inclusion of computer coding in the curricula for primary and middle school students. Since 2020, such curricula were incorporated into national planning, denoting a clear understanding of the key role of digital capacity building to achieve full digital sovereignty (Zou, 2020): only a country whose population knows how to develop and use digital technologies can truly be digitally sovereign.

Hence, apart from the yearning to resist US intelligence programs, BRICS countries initiatives demonstrate that an equally, if not more, relevant preoccupation is the preservation and expansion of the local digital economy while avoiding digital colonization. However, understanding, planning, coherence, and implementation capabilities of each BRICS country vary enormously, spanning from a holistic Chinese approach to more fragmented or even unorganized postures.

BRICS policies and initiatives also vary in their understanding of the structural power of technology. As mentioned in the introduction of this chapter, awareness of the structural power technology plays is essential to understand the relevance of digital sovereignty and, chiefly, how to organize the concrete implementation of this multifaceted notion. However, not all BRICS countries and the individuals, the entities, and communities that compose them may have achieved the same understanding of this issue. Due to their reduced size and power (whether a BRICS member or not), they may not even be able to elaborate any measure to resist digital colonization, even if they wished to do so.

[26] The State Council directives were issued as a response to Prime Minister Li Keqiang call for "mass entrepreneurship and mass innovation" on September 10, 2014, during the 2014 edition of the World Economic Forum's "Summer Davos" in the coastal Chinese city of Tianjin (Lee, 2018, p. 70).

In this context, Vashishta Doshi and Henrique Delgado's contribution to this volume reminds us that US technology providers are at the core of the digital economy. It is through the likes of tech giants such as the notorious GAFAM (Google, Amazon, Facebook, Apple, and Microsoft) and more recently OpenAI and Nvidia that the US maintains an upper hand in the technology field, exercises its digital sovereignty, and expands this power globally. Reliant on US digital infrastructures, middle powers such as Brazil and India as well as most other countries find themselves in a situation of at least partial digital colonization, where the only available option to undertake a "digital transformation" is the use of foreign digital products and services.

In this perspective, the Digital India initiative focuses on the three digital architecture layers that are considered essential enablers of digital sovereignty: expansion of connectivity, digitization of public services, and establishment of DPI. The Indian government is aware of not only the key role of digital connectivity but also the fact that not all types of internet access offerings are equal and existing differences may have enormous impact on national and community digital sovereignty. It is interesting to note that one of the most assertive and impactful digital sovereignty measures established by India over the past decade has been the adoption of strict Net Neutrality regulation in 2016, prohibiting the so-called "zero-rating"[27] practices where a few dominant US platforms such as Facebook offered "free" access to the unconnected population as a purported inclusive access initiative (Belli, 2017a).

While these plans were heralded as a way to "connect the unconnected" by their proponents, the opponents to such practices have stressed that sponsoring access to a few dominant apps would have exacerbated the dominance by a few foreign commercial actors. Simultaneously these practices can considerably increase data concentration in the hands of the few sponsored platforms, creating strong dependence on such services in the entire (developing) world (Belli, 2017a). To understand the zero-rating services especially in low- and middle-income countries where average individuals cannot afford internet access fees, it must be considered that for the largest application providers, it is worth sponsoring internet access limited to their applications to enlarge and retain user base to perpetuate user dependency on such applications.[28]

We may fairly assume that when the Indian government decided to prohibit the zero-rating practices, one of the main goals was not only to preserve internet openness, competition, and free expression, but a key consideration behind India's decision to prohibit zero-rating services was mainly to avoid the concentration of Indian internet users and the consequent collection of Indian user data in a few foreign apps, capable to exert enormous control, extract

[27] For an analysis of zero-rating practices, see www.zerorating.info.

[28] The importance for businesses to "hook" users into their applications, through an ample range of techniques including also addictive interface configurations, is eloquently presented by N. Eyal (2014).

enormously valuable insights and profits under foreign tax law, store user data in foreign servers, enhance foreign software and AI development thanks to such data, and sharing them with foreign intelligence agencies through numerous programs revealed by the Snowden episode.

Hence, the 2016 order of the Telecommunications Regulation Authority of India (TRAI) prohibiting zero-rating practices denotes the same "digital sovereignty" rationale applied by the Brazilian Central Bank to the suspension of WhatsApp Payments to preserve openness, competition, and data privacy in the Brazilian digital payment system. Indeed, BRICS institutions seem to have an increasingly sophisticated understanding of the digital colonization dynamics underpinning the provision of "free services" by dominant foreign tech giants, notably regarding the fact that such services, presented as free, are de facto paid with a waiver on the individuals' and country's possibility or ability to exercise sovereignty over data (Belli, 2021b).

Clearly, the use of foreign technology is not something negative per se as long as such technology does not become a Trojan horse aimed at undermining capability of the user – be this an individual, a corporation, a specific community, or a country – to exercise (digital) self-determination. In this spirit, the considerable increase in digital policies and notably data-related regulations in the BRICS in recent years may be seen as a clear reassertion of digital sovereignty to protect critical national resources. It is useful to recall that together Brazil, Russia, India, China, and South Africa are home to 3.2 billion people, representing roughly 42% of the world's population. In effect, BRICS countries sit on 42% of "the most valuable resource" (The Economist, 2017) on the planet: personal data (Belli, 2021a, 2021b).

Members of the BRICS grouping are aware not only that they are the main producers of personal data but also that higher levels of connectivity concretely would produce more wealth and productivity.[29] They have also developed an increasing understanding that digital services provided by foreign corporations and portrayed as "free" are not exactly so, but rather paid with an open-ended license to extract personal data and, ultimately, undermine state and individual digital sovereignty. This situation has become even more palpable in the context of the ongoing "scramble for data," launched by dominant tech businesses. This rush to offer "free" digital services to developing countries may indeed be seen as a strategy to be the first in capturing the attention of poor users and drilling as much data as possible out of

[29] According to the World Bank, 10% increase in broadband penetration can result in a gross domestic product growth of up to 3.2%, with benefits ranging from the generation of services and jobs to an increase in family income (World Bank, 2016). The Organization for Economic Cooperation and Development and the Inter-American Development Bank have underscored that the expansion of connectivity generates greater availability and efficient use of services, enhancing social inclusion, increasing productivity, and improving governance (Organization for Economic Cooperation Development and Inter-American Development Bank, 2017).

entire populations who frequently lack data protection frameworks to prevent undue exploitations. The indigenous populations are increasingly seen by the new digital colonizers as convenient data wells.

As argued in this book, digital infrastructures play a particularly relevant role to structure digital sovereignty. Hence, it is obvious that India's Net Neutrality regulation, its ban of zero-rating services, together with the Digital India program have been essential to reducing India's exposure to foreign digital sovereignty and building its own. The simultaneous promotion of connectivity and ban of zero-rating practices paved the way to the entrance of Reliance Jio, a new domestic player, in India's mobile internet market, which with its low-rate offering managed to reduce gigabit prices by almost 95%, double the number of connected Indians and increase more than twentyfold data consumption in less than 5 years.[30] To capitalize on such a staggering expansion of connectivity infrastructure, Digital India fostered the creation of a set of Application Programming Interface (APIs)[31] commonly referred to as the "India Stack"[32] that play a key role in India's DPI, on top of which new home-grown digital services can be built.

10.5 DISORDERED APPROACHES TO DIGITAL SOVEREIGNTY

BRICS countries have developed an understanding of the strategic importance of data, software, and infrastructures to constructing digital sovereignty. Data is an essential resource used as raw material to develop AI applications by powering highly complex algorithms. Software, on the other hand, plays an essential role in creating "high-growth, high-margin, highly defensible businesses" (Andreessen, 2011) as an increasingly large number of industries are redefined by software. From the automation of agriculture and manufacturing to the digitization of public services and personal apps in our smartphones. "Software is eating the world" famously stated by Marc Andreesen. The stellar market evaluation of some technology giants means that in practical terms if a digital sovereign – be it a corporation or a nation-state – can exercise control over popular software, it may earn very large returns on investments. Conversely, one is likely to perpetually pay a usage fee along with the contractual conditions unilaterally defined by the digital sovereign over digital infrastructure, data, services, and protocols.

This latter point is of utmost importance, especially when industry segments are increasingly automated by large-scale usage of software (or AI). When the software in question is not owned by the user, it is highly likely that in the long

[30] Compare the Indian Telecom Services Performance Indicator Report developed by the Telecom Regulatory Authority of India www.trai.gov.in/release-publication/reports/performance-indicators-reports.

[31] An API is a piece of software that allows different software applications to interact and exchange data, according to the specifications established by the API.

[32] See www.indiastack.org/.

term, the main beneficiary of such automations will be the software producer, that is, the digital sovereign. Admittedly software automation will generate efficiency gains for users and price will likely decrease, and some services may even be provided "for free." However, when such services are not paid with money by users, they are paid with user data. This shift in payment either through a fee to the software provider or through personal data or both is the de facto payment with the user's individual sovereignty, which entails a choice between self-determination and dependency.

It is understandable that different digital sovereigns, as with their different capacity to muster, develop and deploy digital infrastructure, data, service, and protocols, follow their own agendas and interests, which frequently conflict with those of others. Several BRICS countries, notably Russia, India, and China (RIC), have developed an increasingly systemic thinking about digital sovereignty that can lead to positive or negative outcomes. Brazil and South Africa, on the other hand, may have had intended to do so but have struggled to develop or implement a coherent vision, due to unstable political environments, inconsistent policies, or timid implementation of such policies.

Brazil offers, again, a telling tale. While it reacted vehemently when attempts in undermining its digital sovereignty were revealed, its posture denotes a certain disorder, typical of most politically unstable countries aspiring to achieve digital self-determination and independence from foreign technology. The fact is that shortly after condemning NSA surveillance, former President Dilma Rousseff actively promoted the zero-rating service offered by Facebook in Brazil (Belli, 2015), thus opening the path for the digital colonization of the country[33] by a foreign corporation. That Facebook to date has been cooperating with US intelligence agencies such as the NSA suggests President Rousseff's promotion of free-rating services can be now seen as a willful waiver of Brazil's state digital sovereignty.

It is interesting to note that, according to recent research by the Brazilian Institute for Consumer Protection (IDEC), 85% of Brazilian mobile users have prepaid plans including limited data volumes and zero-rated social networks (typically WhatsApp and Facebook) (IDEC & Instituto Locomotiva, 2021). Due to the subsidized nature of such apps, this enormous part of the Brazilian population utilizes the internet primarily to access US-based social media, especially in the last part of a month when the data allowance is entirely consumed and the only accessible applications are the zero-rated ones, which become also the only ones with concentrated data collection. It is difficult to think that the Brazilian government does not realize that this

[33] It is important to stress that, despite multiple years of permissive attitude of Brazilian regulators toward zero-rating, this practice amounts to preferential treatment of applications, which is prohibited under Brazilian net neutrality norms, such as art 9 of the Internet Civil Framework and art 9 of Decree 8771/2016.

situation implies the cession to foreign actors the right to extract personal data from the entire connected population and generate enormous and nearly untaxed profit with value generation on foreign servers.

Another remarkable example illustrates the confused and even conflicting Brazilian approach to digital sovereignty. In the context of its privatization program, the Bolsonaro administration announced in 2019 the intention to sell two public enterprises deemed the crown jewels of Brazilian IT: the Federal Data Processing Service or *Serviço Federal de Processamento de Dados* (Serpro) and the Information Technology for Pensions Corporation or *Empresa de Tecnologia e Informações da Previdência* (Dataprev). Serpro is the largest government-owned corporation of IT services in Brazil, created in 1964 to modernize strategic public sector. Dataprev is a Brazilian public company, responsible for managing the Brazilian Social Database with five software development units and three data centers throughout the country. Both are under the control of the Ministry of the Economy.

These corporations including the software they produce and the enormous databases they control are highly valuable strategic assets in terms of digital sovereignty. While selling these corporations to foreign investors could generate considerable financial gains, it would also incur many unintended consequences for Brazil's state digital sovereignty. After several years of feasibility studies, the Brazilian Congress has kept postponing selling these state assets until it reached the electoral period when the sale of state-owned enterprises becomes de facto impossible (Lobo, 2022). The strategy of the Brazilian Congressmen has been effective, even unorthodox, to achieve the preservation of the two public companies and their digital assets. However, the episode goes far beyond highlighting the lack of understanding of the implications of digital sovereignty of the Bolsonaro administration. It explains tellingly the dependency of digital sovereignty on politics and public policies.

Such dependency became clear with the recent change at the helm of the Brazilian federal government. One of the first executive orders adopted by the new Lula administration has suspended the privatization of public companies deemed as nationally strategic assets, including Serpro and Dataprev (Presidência da República, 2023). While such reversal indicates a welcomed renewed sensitivity to digital sovereignty issues, it also proves that in most countries as in Brazil digital sovereignty policies are ultimately a function of politics.

Corporate digital sovereigns – typically large business actors – build and manage expansive digital infrastructures with their own agendas to fostering self-interest that may conflict with the interest of other sovereign entities using the technology they supply, which could include their users, advertisers, and the public they purportedly serve. Further, private developers of digital infrastructures may become proxies for the expansion of State Digital Sovereignty where they are headquartered. As demonstrated by the Snowden revelations and as contended by Stefano Calzati in his contribution for this book, the expansion of digital infrastructures and services overseas makes it possible for a given state to project its digital sovereignty well beyond its borders, whether American or Chinese.

It is also essential to note that initiatives branded as digital sovereignty may be frequently used to disguise ambitions to intensify control through digital means. The reader might think of China and Russia as frequently suggested examples in this sense, but such ambitions are rather widespread well beyond these two countries. As stressed by Enrico Calandro's contribution to this volume, South African digital sovereignty discourse finds itself at the crossroad of securitization and ICT development, as happens in many other African countries.

South African authorities as well as other developing countries have a considerable opportunity to construct solid basis for digital sovereignty through more modernized digital policies to properly regulate the functions and consequences of ICTs. For South Africa, the state construction of digital sovereignty aims to enhance self-determination, cybersecurity, and the rule of law in the digital environment. At the national level, South Africa has also stressed "data ownership, data sovereignty, and data protection are critical elements for the digital economy" (Department of Communications & Digital Technologies, 2021, p. 20). In April 2021, the South African government presented its Draft National Data and Cloud Policy Data, which explicitly recognizes that and "seeks to strengthen the capacity of the State to deliver services to its citizens, ensure informed policy development based on data analytics, as well as promote South Africa's data sovereignty and the security thereof" (Department of Communications & Digital Technologies, 2021, p. 8).

As for any government, however, it is also very tempting to utilize the digital sovereignty narrative to expand state control over computer systems and digital communications, facilitating surveillance and online censorship. For instance, in October 2019, South Africa adopted the Films and Publications Amendment Act (2019), dubbed "Internet Censorship Law" (Vermeulen, 2022), which allows the South African content regulation authority, the Film and Publication Board, to request the removal of any content deemed harmful. It went into effect in 2022. According to the law, any internet service provider (ISP) with knowledge that its service is being used to distribute or host content that incites imminent violence, serves as propaganda for war, advocates hatred against a person or an identifiable group, or sexually exploits children must immediately remove the content and communicate the identity of the person who published the prohibited content to the Film and Publications Board or the South African Police Services.

South Africa offers an interesting example. On the one hand, the country has recently enacted and adopted progressive data protection and cybersecurity legislations. On the other hand, it has simultaneously established a securitization agenda and increasing censorship measures in reaction of cyber threats (Belli, 2021c). Similarly, while South Africa is home to several outstanding examples of Commons Digital Sovereignty, spanning from community networks to smart villages, led by empowered local communities, it also simultaneously advocates a number of "Fourth Industrial Revolution" policies opening the path to a large number of data colonialism practices (Benyera, 2021).

10.6 CONCLUSION: DIGITAL SOVEREIGNTY OPTIONS

An agnostic approach to digital sovereignty in the BRICS acknowledges that different digital sovereigns may pursue self-determination, cybersecurity, and control with different goals and outcomes. These leave us fundamentally with three options to structure digital sovereignty. The first one is a form of hard digital sovereignty amounting to near digital isolation of the digital sovereign in order to exercise the highest possible level of control and the establishment of tightly controlled gateways to regulate information exchanges. This option might be the most effective choice for isolated communities willing to create their own intranets to communicate among themselves without necessarily communicate with the rest of the world – as even some community networks do (Belli, 2017; GISWatch, 2018) – or countries eager to build strong control on their national segment of the internet and tightly regulate communications, such as China and Russia, but it can only be afforded in the long-term by those that can manage to be digitally self-sufficient and thrive, even while being relatively isolated.

The second option, which is ideal in the opinion of these authors, would be shared global rules to frame and regulate digital technologies and their uses, providing a leveled regulatory playing field, so that any entity would have an incentive to cooperate rather than engaging into antagonist behaviors. Unfortunately, while this option would be ideal, it seems highly unlikely it could be easily reached, given the considerable conflicting interests at stake, the lethargic times of international policymaking, the considerable intellectual and financial resources needed to implement this option in practice, and the democratic deficit of which many intergovernmental organizations – on which such option would have to rely – are frequently accused.

The third and final option seems also possible and palatable. It consists of the establishment of regional blocks or aligned groupings that share common – or at least (legally) interoperable (Belli & Doneda, 2022; Belli & Zingales, 2023) – regulatory frameworks and technological tools. Such groups may limit information flows and technology exchanges with other blocs to the few sectors where shared agreements exist. This option would be less ideal than the establishment of shared global norms and technologies, but would have the benefit of facilitating international exchange, attracting entities with less restrictive digital sovereignty thinking toward other areas, thus increasingly enlarging overlapping areas of interest. As such, different areas would also compete, attracting an ever-larger number of entities and expanding their system globally.

This latter option seems particularly interesting for BRICS countries in light of the grouping's recent expansion (BRICS, 2023) as well as their commitment to enhance cooperation on digital policy frameworks with particular regard to cybersecurity issues. At the 15th BRICS Summit, chaired by South Africa in August 2023, the grouping's heads of states "have decided to invite the Argentine Republic, the Arab Republic of Egypt, the Federal Democratic Republic of Ethiopia, the Islamic Republic of Iran, the Kingdom of Saudi Arabia and the United Arab Emirates to become full members of BRICS from January 1, 2024" (BRICS, 2023). It is clear that the inclusion of these new partners in the grouping hopes to expand the BRICS role as a gathering hub of Global South regional leaders, especially by strengthening the presence in Africa (e.g., Ethiopia hosts the headquarter of the African Union) and including some the most influential countries from the Middle East region, which have already acquired significant global relevance. Such a move becomes particularly relevant in the context of the Ukraine and Gaza wars, which have created enormous instability and prompted many countries to reassess and redefine their strategic alliances and their value chains, desperately looking for strategic autonomy and stability.

Such a scenario has obvious ramifications in digital affairs. In this context of the recent cybersecurity, commitments of the BRICS leaders sound prescient. Indeed, since the New Delhi Declaration, issued as an outcome of the 2021 BRICS Summit, the bloc's leaders expressed the intention to:

> [...] advance practical intra-BRICS cooperation in this domain, including through the implementation of the BRICS Roadmap of Practical Cooperation on ensuring Security in the Use of ICTs and the activities of the BRICS Working Group on Security in the use of ICTs, and underscore[d] also the importance of establishing legal frameworks of cooperation among BRICS States on this matter and acknowledge[d] the work towards consideration and elaboration of proposals, including on a BRICS intergovernmental agreement on cooperation on ensuring security in the use of ICTs and on bilateral agreements among BRICS countries (BRICS, 2021).

The elaboration of such legal frameworks and intergovernmental agreement would be a useful test bed to gauge the extent to which such cooperation can exist in practice. Cybersecurity issues, and notably cybercrime, as well as most digital policies that would fit into the large state digital sovereignty umbrella, are intimately intertwined with strong economic and political interests of each digital sovereign and grounded on quintessentially domestic cultural and legal particularities. The attractiveness of the BRICS bloc remains unchanged, even if some of the countries might have underperformed the original predictions that led to the creation of this bloc. Such attractiveness would notably increase, should BRICS countries create a BRICS digital sovereignty area with shared and compatible digital policies.

A scenario where the BRICS promote legal interoperability would allow the grouping to act as a platform to conjugate digital sovereignty with openness and inclusion (Belli & Doneda, 2022; Belli & Zingales, 2023). This could be an even more powerful strategy considering the current context of expansion of the BRICS through the BRICS+ initiative (Razumovsky, 2022). On the one hand, this scenario would allow the BRICS to fulfill its fundamental mission of fostering international cooperation and building a multipolar order and inclusive global governance, led by the Global South for the benefit of developing countries. On the other hand, this would also allow the BRICS to act both as an "integrator of integrators," fostering the interoperability of regional projects where the participating countries are leaders (Eurasian Economic Union, Mercosur, and South African Customs Union) and as a "union of regionalisms," where regional associations (African Union, Community of Latin American and Caribbean States, and SCO) can interoperate thanks to compatible normative frameworks (Razumovsky, 2022). Sovereignty and openness can and should be seen as mutually reinforcing rather than as antithetic goals that can and should be pursued simultaneously. BRICS have the potential to demonstrate that the Global South can lead in digital governance, promoting openness while preserving sovereignty: as former Brazilian President Luiz Inacio Lula da Silva – generally known as Lula – noted, "the logic behind BRICS [is] to do something different and not copy anybody [...] trying not to be dependent" (Escobar, 2019; Prashad 2012).[34]

[34] It is useful to remember that many Global South countries have been denied the full enjoyment of human rights, democracy, and rule of law by Western colonizers and suffered remarkably abusive treatments for many decades or even centuries. Often, these countries gained independence only after incredibly violent wars that in some cases lasted many years and ended less than fifty years ago. For a brief but detailed description of the geopolitical changes from 1900 to 2000, see The National Archives (n. d.).

References

Accenture. (2020). *Insight into the cyber threat landscape in South Africa*. https://is.gd/f9xSSU

Acharya, A. (2014). *The end of American world order*. Cambridge, UK: Polity Press.

ACI Worldwide and Global Data. (2022, April). *Prime time for real-time global payments report*. https://is.gd/7cebv6

Agbebi, M. (2018). China in Africa's telecom sector: Opportunities for human capital development? A case of Huawei in Nigeria. *Human Resource Development International*, 21(5), 532–551.

Aggad, F. (2021, February 8). Africa's digital transformation risks becoming trapped in geopolitical competition. *Mail & Guardian*. https://is.gd/OKnSH3

Al Jazeera. (2021, January 26). India to impose permanent ban on dozens of Chinese apps: Reports. *Al Jazeera*. https://is.gd/KLFne3

Alekseeva, A., Zasurskij, I. et al., (Eds.) (2013). *Transformacija avtorskogo prava v internete. zarubezhnye tendencii, biznes-modeli, rekomendacii dlja Rossii (Copyright transformation on the internet. Foreign trends, business models, recommendations for Russia)*. Moscow: Associacija Internet-izdatelej.

Allen, K. (2019). *Does Africa risk being left behind in the digital security debate?* Dakar International Forum on Peace and Security in Africa. https://is.gd/CjvJpO

Allison, G. (2017). *Destined for war: Can America and China escape Thucydides's Trap?* New York: Houghton Mifflin Harcourt.

Amnesty International. (2019, December 11). Russian feminist activist fined for "gay propaganda" and facing criminal "pornography" charges. *Amnesty International*.

Amsden, A. (2001). *The rise of "the rest": Challenges to the west from late-industrializing economies*. Oxford, UK: Oxford University Press.

An, N. (2020). China's responses to the US war on terror: A perspective and agenda of Internet geopolitics. *Tijdschrift Voor Economische En Sociale Geografie*, 111(5), 758–770.

Anđelković, L. (2017). The elements of proportionality as a principle of human rights limitations. *Facta Universitatis, Series: Law and Politics*, 15(3), 235–244.

Andreessen, M. (2011, August 20). Why software is eating the World. *The Wall Street Journal*. https://is.gd/UjaIld

Angelidou, M. (2017). The role of smart city characteristics in the plans of fifteen cities. *Journal of Urban Technology*, 24(4), 3–28.

Anghie, A. (2007). *Imperialism, sovereignty and the making of international law*. Cambridge: Cambridge University Press.

Anshan, L. (2007). China and Africa: Policy and challenges. *China Security*, 3(3), 69–93.

Aris, S. (2008). Russian–Chinese relations through the lens of the SCO. *Russia/NIS center*. https://is.gd/Kytr2y

Armijo, L. E., & Katada, S. N. (2014a). New kids on the block: Rising multipolarity, more financial statecraft. In L. Armijo & S. Katada (Eds.), *The financial statecraft of emerging powers: Shield and sword in Asia and Latin America (International political economy series)* (pp. 1–20). New York: Palgrave Macmillan.

Armijo, L. E., & Katada, S. N. (2014b). Theorizing the financial statecraft of emerging powers. *New Political Economy*, 20(1), 42–62.

Armijo, L. E., & Roberts, C. (2014). The emerging powers and global governance Why the BRICS matter. In R. Looney (Ed.), *Handbook of emerging economies* (pp. 503–524). New York: Routledge.

Arsène, S. (2015). Internet domain names in China: Articulating local control with global connectivity. *China Perspectives*, *2015*(4), 25–34.

Arsène, S. (2016). Global internet governance in Chinese academic literature: Rebalancing a hegemonic world order? *China Perspectives*, 2, 25–35.

Arsène, S. (2018). The Chinese ICT development strategy in Africa: Transparency, sovereignty and soft power. In S. Kalathil (Ed.), *Diplomacy, development and security in the information age* (pp. 51–61). https://is.gd/isgr4d

Arya, V. (2020, July 27). Securing India's digital sovereignty. *BW Businessworld*. https://is.gd/Xq1wzx

ASEAN. (2012). *ASEAN Telecommunications and Information Technology Ministers Meeting (TELMIN): Framework on personal data protection*. ASEAN. https://is.gd/iGIo52

ASEAN. (2022). *ASEAN data management framework: Data governance and protection throughout the data lifecycle*. ASEAN. https://is.gd/DWPKAc

Asmolov, G. (2020). Runet in crisis situations. In S. Davydov (Ed.), *Internet in Russia: A study of the Runet and its impact on social life* (pp. 231–250). Cham: Springer.

Associated Press. (2005, November 18). Tech summit ends with Internet control in question despite agreement. *VailDaily*. https://is.gd/8d5CGj

Avila Pinto, R. (2018). Digital sovereignty or digital colonialism? New tensions of privacy, security and national policies. *Sur: International Journal on Human Rights*, *15*(27), 15–28.

Ayers, E. (2016). *Rethinking sovereignty in the context of cyberspace: The cyber sovereignty workshop series*. Carlisle Barracks, PA: U.S. Army War College.

Baasanjav, U. B. (2014). Linguistic diversity on the internet: Arabic, Chinese and Cyrillic script top-level domain names. *Telecommunications Policy*, *38*(11), 961–969.

Babic, M., Fichtner, J., & Heemskerk, E. M. (2017). States versus corporations: Rethinking the power of business in international politics. *The International Spectator*, *52*(4), 20–43.

Bai, C., & Lei, X. (2020). New trends in population aging and challenges for China's sustainable development. *China Economic Journal*, *13*(1), 3–23.

Bailey, R., & Parsheera, S. (2018, September). *Data localisation in India: Questioning the means and ends* (Working Paper No. 242). National Institute of Public Finance and Policy.

Bailey, R., & Parsheera, S. (2021). Data localization in India: Paradigms and processes. *CSIT*, 9(3), 137–150.
Banco Central do Brasil. (2020, June 23). *Nova solução de pagamentos depende de prévia autorização do BC.* https://is.gd/lYs73N
Barbrook, R., & Cameron, A. (1996). The Californian ideology. *Science as Culture*, 6(1), 44–72.
Bardhan, P. (2023). Unmasking India's crony capitalist oligarchy. *Project Syndicate.* https://is.gd/e9ov5s
Barlow, J. P. (1996). *Declaration of the independence of cyberspace. Electronic frontier foundation.* www.eff.org/cyberspaceindependence
Barma, N., Ratner, E., & Weber, S. (2014). Welcome to the world without the West. *The National Interest.* https://is.gd/WcyCdR
Baruah, P. (2016, November 16). How AP Hota created Amul of Indian finance. *The Economic Times.*
Basu, A. (2019, November 7). India's role in global cyber policy formulation. *Lawfare.* https://is.gd/doLRXo
BBC. (2014, March 21). Visa and MasterCard block Russian bank customers. www.bbc.com/news/business-26678145
BBC. (2019, November 22). Chaayos cafe: Indian cafe's facial recognition use sparks anger. *BBC.* www.bbc.com/news/world-asia-india-50499380
BBC. (2020, December 26). Chinese economy to overtake US "by 2028" due to Covid. *BBC.* www.bbc.com/news/world-asia-china-55454146
BBC. (2021a, February 28). Has China lifted 100 million people out of poverty? *BBC.* www.bbc.com/news/56213271
BBC. (2021b, January 30). India protests: Internet cut to hunger-striking farmers in Delhi. *BBC.* www.bbc.com/news/world-asia-india-55872480
Belli, L. (2011, November 7). Internet governance v. Internet government. *MediaLAWS.* www.medialaws.eu/internet-governance-v-internet-government/
Belli, L. (2015, April 20). From net neutrality to net feudality. *MediaLAWS.* www.medialaws.eu/from-net-neutrality-to-net-feudality/
Belli, L. (2017). Network self-determination and the positive externalities of community networks. In L. Belli (Ed.), *Community networks: The internet by the people for the people: Official outcome of the UN IGF dynamic coalition on community connectivity.* FGV. https://is.gd/SuKDFg
Belli, L. (2019). Network neutrality, zero-rating and the Marco Civil da Internet. In L. Belli & O. Cavalli (Eds.), *Internet governance and regulations in Latin America* (pp. 163–190). Rio de Janeiro: FGV Direito Rio.
Belli, L. (2021a). BRICS countries to build digital sovereignty. In L. Belli (Ed.), *CyberBRICS: Cybersecurity regulations in the BRICS countries* (pp. 282–292). London: Springer-Nature.
Belli, L. (Ed.) (2021b). *CyberBRICS: Cybersecurity regulations in BRICS countries.* Berlin, Germany: Springer.
Belli, L. (2021c). Cybersecurity policymaking in the BRICS Countries: From addressing national priorities to seeking international cooperation. *The African Journal of Information and Communication*, 28, 1–14. https://is.gd/4lYPST
Belli, L. (2022). Structural power as a critical element of digital platforms' private sovereignty. In E. Celeste, A. Heldt, & C. Iglesias Keller (Eds.), *Constitutionalising social media.* Hart. https://is.gd/yb6tfh

Belli, L. (2023). *Building good digital sovereignty through digital public infrastructures and digital commons in India and Brazil.* G20's Think20 (T20). https://is.gd/BDCXss

Belli, L., & Doneda, D. (2022). Data protection in the BRICS Countries: Legal interoperability through innovative practices and convergence. *International Data Privacy Law*, *13*(1), 1–24.

Belli, L., & Hadzic, S. (Eds.) (2022). *Community networks as enablers of human rights. Official outcome of the UN IGF dynamic coalition on community connectivity.* www.intgovforum.org/en/filedepot_download/45/24008

Belli, L., & Hadzic, S. (2023). *Community networks: Building digital sovereignty and environmental sustainability.* Official Outcome of the UN IGF Dynamic Coalition on Community Connectivity. https://is.gd/cB2VLm

Belli, L., & Zingales, N. (2023). Interoperability to foster open digital ecosystems in the BRICS countries. In Chinese Academy of Cyberspace Studies, Xinhua Institute, China Institute of International Studies (Eds.), *Shared vision for the digital world: Insights from global think tanks on jointly building a community with a shared future in cyberspace.* Beijing, China: The Commercial Press. [In Chinese].

Benhamou, B., & Sorbier, L. (2006). Souveraineté et réseaux numériques. *Politique étrangère, Automne*, *3*. https://is.gd/QJRrGb

Benkler, Y. (2006). *The wealth of networks: How social production transforms markets and freedom.* New Haven, CT: Yale University Press.

Bennett, L. W., & Sederberg, A. (2013). *The logic of connective action: Digital media and the personalization of contentious politics.* Cambridge: Cambridge University Press.

Benyera, E. (2021). *The fourth industrial revolution and the recolonisation of Africa: The coloniality of data.* New York: Routledge.

Bhandari, V., Kak, A., Parsheera, S., & Rahman, F. (2017). An analysis of Puttaswamy: The supreme court's privacy verdict. *IndraStra Global*, *11*, 1–5.

Bhuiyan, A. (2014). *Internet governance and the global south: Demand for a new framework.* New York: Palgrave Macmillan.

Bidwell, N., & Jensen, M. (2019). *Bottom-up connectivity strategies: Community-led small-scale telecommunication infrastructure networks in the global South.* Association for Progressive Communications.

Biju, P. R. (2019). *Political internet: State and politics in the age of social media.* Place of publication not identified: Routledge India.

Birch, K., Cochrane, D., & Ward, C. (2021). Data as asset? The measurement, governance, and valuation of digital personal data by Big Tech. *Big Data & Society*, *8*(1), 1–15.

Biswas, S. (2021, February 12). The Indian government's war with Twitter – BBC News. *BBC News*. https://is.gd/9tRklL

Black, J. L. (2021). *Russia after 2020: Looking ahead after two decades of Putin* (1st ed.). Routledge.

Boas, T. C. (2000). The dictator's dilemma? The internet and U.S. policy toward Cuba. *The Washington Quarterly*, *23*(3), 57–67.

Bodó, B., Brekke, J. K., & Hoepman, J.-H. (2021). Decentralisation: A multidisciplinary perspective. *Internet Policy Review*, *10*(2). https://policyreview.info/concepts/decentralisation

Bodomo, A. (2009). Africa-China relations: Symmetry, soft power and South Africa. *The China Review: An Interdisciplinary Journal on Greater China*, *9*(2), 169–178.

Bodoni, S., Colten, J., & Bloomberg. (2021, December 9). Amazon hit with a massive new antitrust fine – this time $1.2 billion for steering vendors to use its shipping service. *Fortune*. https://is.gd/qkzM6E

Bond, S. (2022, February 28). Facebook and Tiktok block Russian state media in Europe. *NPR*. https://is.gd/824rTz

Borger, J., Lewis, P., & Mason, R. (2014, July). EU and US impose sweeping economic sanctions on Russia. *The Guardian*. https://is.gd/Dhotum

Borgonovi, F., Centurelli, R., Dernis, H., Grundke, R., Horvát, P., Jamet, S., … Squicciarini, M. (2018). *Bridging the digital gender divide*. https://is.gd/QbLkPp

Bradford, A. (2020). The Brussels effect: How the European Union rules the world. In *The Brussels effect* (pp. 235–264). New York: Oxford University Press.

Braithwaite, J., & Drahos, P. (2000). *Global business regulation*. Cambridge University Press.

Brake, D. R. (2017). The invisible hand of the unaccountable algorithm: How Google, Facebook and other tech companies are changing journalism. In J. Tong & S.-H. Lo (Eds.), *Digital technology and journalism: An international comparative perspective* (pp. 25–46). Berlin: Palgrave Macmillan.

Bratton, B. (2016). *The stack*. Cambridge, MA: MIT Press.

Bria, F. (2020, March 9). *Putting tech and innovation at the service of people and the green transition*. Medium. https://is.gd/qlDqpE

BRICS. (2013). *eThekwini Declaration and Action Plan*. https://is.gd/H3LS8z

BRICS. (2015). *VII BRICS Summit – Ufa Declaration*. https://is.gd/QEUJaw

BRICS. (2021). *XIII BRICS Summit-New Delhi Declaration*. BRICS. https://is.gd/1LDrep

BRICS. (2023). *XV BRICS Summit Johannesburg II Declaration*. In Sandton, Gauteng, South Africa. https://is.gd/wbWiXA

Broeders, D., & van den Berg, B. (2020). *Governing cyberspace: Behavior, power, and diplomacy*. London: Rowman & Littlefield.

Brousseau, E., Marzouki, M., & Méadel, C. (2012). Governance, networks and information technologies: Societal, political, and organizational innovations. In Eric Brousseau, Meryem Marzouki & Cécile Méadel (Eds.), *Governance, regulations and powers on the Internet* (pp. 3–36). Cambridge: Cambridge University Press.

Brown, I. (2020). *Interoperability as a tool for competition regulation*. OpenForum Academy. https://doi.org/10.31228/osf.io/fbvxd

Bruner, C. M. (2008). States, markets, and gatekeepers: Public-private regulatory regimes in an area of economic globalization. *Michigan Journal of International Law*, 30(1), 125–176.

Burke, J. (2023, October 16). China and Russia harden positions on Gaza as war stirs geopolitical tensions. *The Guardian*. https://is.gd/Cyn3kq

Burman, A., & Sharma, U. (2021, April). *How would data localization benefit India?* Carnegie Endowment for International Peace. https://is.gd/oUpf4v

Business Insider India. (2021, February 13). Twitter suspends 90–95% of accounts listed by Indian government. *Business Insider India*. https://is.gd/7gtdgz

Buzan, B., Wæver, O., & De Wilde, J. (1998). *Security: A new framework for analysis*. Boulder: Lynne Rienner Publishers.

Calandro, E. (2015). *Governing regional telecommunication networks in a developing region: The SADC case*. Cape Town: University of Cape Town.

Calandro, E., & Berglund, N. (2021). *Towards converging African positions on international cybersecurity?* African participation in multilateral and multistakeholder processes. [Unpublished paper]
Calzada, I. (2017). The techno-politics of data and smart devolution in city-regions: Comparing Glasgow, Bristol, Barcelona, and Bilbao. *Systems*, 5(1), 1–18.
Calzati, S. (2020a). Decolonising "data colonialism": Propositions for investigating the realpolitik of today's networked ecology. *Television & New Media*, 22(8). https://doi.org/10.1177/1527476420957
Calzati, S. (2020b). China, Africa, and the West: A geopolitical assessment of Huawei's crisis communication on social network. *International Journal of Communication*, 14, 1–21.
Cao, B. (2018). 跨境数据传输的立法模式与完善路径 – 从《网络安全法》第37条切入 [Legislative models and perfection approaches of cross-border data transfer: From Article 37 of the cybersecurity law]. 西南民族大学学报（人文社科版）*[Journal of Southwest Minzu University (Humanities and Social Sciences)]*, 39(9), 94–100.
Cardullo, P., & Kitchin, R. (2019). Smart urbanism and smart citizenship: The neoliberal logic of "citizen-focused" smart cities in Europe. *Environment and Planning C: Politics and Space*, 37(5), 813–830.
Carlsson, U. (2003). The rise and fall of NWICO: From a vision of international regulation to a reality of multilevel governance. *Nordicom Review*, 24(2), 31–67.
Carrai, M. A. (2021). The RCEP and a geopolitical pivot to the Asia-Pacific. *AfronomicsLAW*. https://is.gd/QISMqI
Cartwright, M. (2020). Internationalising state power through the internet: Google, Huawei and geopolitical struggle. *Internet Policy Review*, 9(3), DOI: 10.14763/2020.3.1494
Cascais, A. (2019). How China benefits from Africa's smartphone boom. *Deutsche Welle*. https://is.gd/bfxzhp
Castillo-Montoya, M. (2016). Preparing for interview research: The interview protocol refinement framework. *The Qualitative Report*, 21(5), 811–831.
Cerulus, L. (2019, February 4). Europe eyes privacy clampdown on China. *Politico*. https://is.gd/xYNFxd
CGI. (2023). *92 milhões de brasileiros acessam a Internet apenas pelo telefone celular, aponta TIC Domicílios 2022*. https://is.gd/HwartR
CGTN. (2022a, May 20). Rediscover the value of BRICS under "three pillars." *CGTN America*. https://is.gd/c4pqLy
CGTN. (2022b, May 21). The heat: BRICS meeting. *CGTN America*. https://is.gd/pJEszZ
Chadwick, A. (2006). *Internet politics: States, citizens, and new communication technologies*. Oxford, UK: Oxford University Press.
Chakravarti, A. (2021, March 4). India saw highest number of internet shutdowns in the world in 2020. *India Today*. https://is.gd/S9pUu7
Chamber of Deputies. (2016). *The Brazilian civil framework of the internet*. Edições Câmara.
Chambers, T. (2022). *A snapshot of the #TwitterMigration*. Dewey Square Group.
Chander, A. (2020). Is data localization a solution for Schrems II? *Journal of International Economic Law*, 23(3), 771–784.
Chander, A., & Sun, H. (2022). Sovereignty 2.0. *Vanderbilt Journal of Transnational Law*, 53(4), 283–324.

Chander, A., & Sun, H. (Eds.) (2023). *Data sovereignty: From the Digital Silk Road to the return of the state*. Oxford, UK: Oxford University Press.

Chen, Y. C. (2017). *Managing digital governance: Issues, challenges, solutions*. New York: Routledge.

Cheru, F., & Obi, C. (2010). *The rise of China and India in Africa: Challenges, opportunities and critical interventions*. https://is.gd/WOQK8K

Cheung, A. (2023). From data subjects to data sovereigns: Addressing the limits of data privacy in the digital era. In A. Chander & H. Sun (Eds.), *Data sovereignty: From the Digital Silk Road to the return of the state* (pp. 89–114). Oxford, UK: Oxford University Press.

Chimni, B. S. (2017). *International law and world order*. Cambridge University Press.

China. (2003, December 10). *Strengthening cooperation, promoting development and moving towards the information society together (statement at the World Summit on the Information Society)*. https://is.gd/CDdYuq

China SCIO. (2023, February 3). China's trade with RCEP members up 7.5% year on year. *The State Council Information Office of the People's Republic of China*. https://is.gd/raEru3

Chinese Academy of Social Science, Qinghua University, Fudan University, Nanjing University, University of International Business and Economics, & Chinese Association of Cybersecurity. (2020). *Sovereignty in cyberspace: Theory and practice (Version 2.0)*. World Internet Conference. https://is.gd/GtEXyH

Chung, J. H. (2002). Challenging the state: Falun Gong and regulatory dilemmas in China. In *Sovereignty under challenge: How governments respond* (pp. 83–108). New Brunswick, NJ: Routledge.

Clinton, H. (2010a). *Remarks on internet freedom*. https://is.gd/GfGLMo

Clinton, H. (2010b). Internet freedom. *Foreign Policy*, 21. https://is.gd/XD3xGj

CNN. (2022). Putin is back on the world stage in BRICS, China-hosted summit. *CNN*. https://is.gd/NNroNE

Cohen, B. J. (2000). *The geography of money* (1st ed.). Cornell University Press.

Cohen, B. J. (2019a). *Between truth and power: The legal constructions of informational capitalism*. Oxford, UK: Oxford University Press.

Cohen, B. J. (2019b). *Currency statecraft: Monetary rivalry and geopolitical ambition* (1st ed.). University of Chicago Press.

Cohen, T. (2021, May 3). Critics of SA government's proposed digital grab idea express deep concerns. *Daily Maverick*. https://is.gd/4RoFag

Coleman, A., & Maogoto, J. N. (2013). "Westphalian" meets "Eastphalian" sovereignty: China in a Globalized World. *Asian Journal of International Law*, 3(2), 237–269.

Coleman, G. (2004). The political agnosticism of Free and Open Source Software and the inadvertent politics of contrast. *Anthropological Quarterly*, 77(3), 507–519.

Comninos, A. (2012). *Intermediary liability in South Africa*. Association for Progressive Communications. https://is.gd/Z7y3bw

Cong, W., & Thumfart, J. (2022). A Chinese precursor to the digital sovereignty debate: Digital anti-colonialism and authoritarianism from the post–Cold War era to the Tunis Agenda. *Global Studies Quarterly*, 2(4), 1–13.

Cook, W. (2018). *East African interoperability: Dispatches from the home of M-Pesa*. Nairobi: CGAP.

Cook, W., & Raman, A. (2019). National payments corporation of India and the remaking of payments in India. In *CGAP Working Paper*. https://is.gd/d6McEy

Cooper, A., Nossal, K., & Higgott, R. (1993). *Relocating middle powers: Australia and Canada in a changing world order*. Vancouver: UBC Press.

Cory, N. (2021). *Before the United States-China economic and Security Review Commission's panel on China's cloud market as part of its hearing "A net assessment of the Chinese Communist Party's economic ambitions, plans, and metrics of future success."* Information Technology and Innovation Foundation.

Cory, N., & Dascoli, L. (2021). (rep.). *How barriers to cross-border data flows are spreading globally, what they cost, and how to address them*. https://is.gd/TqI4Wa

Couldry, N., & Mejias, U. (2018). Data colonialism: Rethinking big data's relation to the contemporary subject. *Television and New Media*, 20(4), 336–349.

Couldry, N., & Mejias, U. (2019). *The costs of connection: How data is colonizing human life and appropriating it for capitalism*. Stanford, CA: Stanford University Press.

Coulthard, S. G. (2014). *Red skin, white masks: Rejecting the colonial politics of recognition*. Minneapolis: University of Minnesota Press.

Couture, S., & Toupin, S. (2019). What does the concept of "sovereignty" mean in digital, network and technological sovereignty? *New Media & Society*, *21*(10), 2305–2322.

Crawford, K. (2020). *Atlas of AI: Power, politics, and the planetary costs of artificial intelligence*. New Haven, CT: Yale University Press.

Creemers, R. J. E. H. (2020). China's conception of cyber sovereignty: Rhetoric and realization. In D. Broeders & B. van den Berg (Eds.), *Digital technologies and global politics* (pp. 107–142). Lanham, MD: Rowman & Littlefield.

CyberBRICS. (2020). *The Brazilian General Data Protection Law – Unofficial English version*. CyberBRICS Project. https://is.gd/IDs5UP

CyberBRICS. (2022, April 11). Conference – Central Bank Digital Currencies. [Video]. https://is.gd/D5X9BA

Cyberspace Administration of China. (2017). 《网络安全法》施行前夕国家互联网信息办公室网络安全协调局负责人答记者问 [Press conference of the cyberspace administration of China before the implementation of the cybersecurity law]. Cyberspace Administration of China. https://is.gd/pbIsG1

Dados, N., & Connell, R. (2012). The global south. *Contexts*, *11*(1), 12–13.

Dattani, K. (2019). "Governtrepreneurism" for good governance: The case of Aadhaar and the India Stack. *Area*, *52*(2), 411–419.

Daucé, F., & Loveluck, B. (2021). Codes of conduct for algorithmic news recommendation: The Yandex. News controversy in Russia. *First Monday*, *26*(5).

Daucé, F., & Musiani, F. (2021). Infrastructure-embedded control, circumvention and sovereignty in the Russian Internet: An introduction. *First Monday*, 26(5). https://firstmonday.org/ojs/index.php/fm/article/view/11685/10122

de Goede, M. (2021). Finance/security infrastructures. *Review of International Political Economy*, 28(2), 351–368.

De Gregorio, G., & Stremlau, N. (2020). Internet shutdowns and the limits of law. *International Journal of Communication*, *14*, 1–19.

Deibert, R., & Rohozinski, R. (2010). Control and subversion in Russian cyberspace. In R. Deibert & J. Palfrey (Eds.), *Access controlled: The shaping of power, rights, and rule in cyberspace* (pp. 15–34). Cambridge, MA: MIT Press.

Deibert, R., Palfrey, J., Rohozinski, R., & Zittrain, J. (2010). *Access controlled: The shaping of power, rights, and rule in cyberspace*. Cambridge, MA: MIT Press.

Deleuze, G. (1992). *Postscript on the societies of control.* October, (Winter), 3–7.

Deloitte. (2020). *Mediapotreblenie v Rossii – 2020 [Media consumption in Russia – 2020].* https://is.gd/uctobp

Demtschenko, M. B. (2020). Women and Tech: How 2020 spotlights the digital divide. *ORF Expert Speak.* https://is.gd/oqJ7n6

DeNardis, L. (2009). *Protocol politics: The globalization of internet governance.* Cambridge, MA: MIT Press.

DeNardis, L. (2012). Hidden levers of Internet control. *Information, Communication & Society*, 15(5), 720–738.

DeNardis, L. (2014). *The global war for internet governance.* New Haven, CT: Yale University Press.

DeNardis, L. (2020). *The Internet in everything: Freedom and security in a world with no off switch.* New Haven, CT: Yale University Press.

DeNardis, L., & Hackl, A. M. (2015). Internet governance by social media platforms. *Telecommunications Policy*, 39(9), 761–770.

Department of Communications & Digital Technologies. (2021). *Draft national policy on Data and Cloud.* https://is.gd/U1BM1f

Department Telecommunications and Postal Services (DTPS) (2016, September 28). National Integrated ICT Policy White Paper. Republic of South Africa. www.gov.za/sites/default/files/gcis_document/201610/40325gon1212.pdf

Desai, A., Manoharan, A., Jayanth, S., & Zack, S. (2023). Public value creation through combined consumption of multiple public services – case of India Stack. *International Journal of Public Administration.* https://doi.org/10.1080/01900692.2023.2243401

Dettmer, J. (2019, November 28). Russia's alternative to western credit cards debuts in London. *VOA News.* https://is.gd/87pSCc

Deutsche Welle. (2013, October 21). Deutsche Telekom plans for a "national internet." *Deutsche Welle.* http://is.gd/yLGeyF

Deutsche Welle. (2018, June 14). *Social media fuels vigilantism and mob attacks in India.* https://is.gd/ZWCYv5

Development Bank of Southern Africa (DBSA). (2023). *Notification of security compromise.* www.dbsa.org/press-releases/notification-security-compromise

Digital Europe. (2017). *DIGITALEUROPE position paper on vulnerability stockpiling.* https://is.gd/QLvQ7k

Digital Public Goods Alliance. (2021). *Financing the digital public goods ecosystem.* https://is.gd/H8uHtD

DigWatch. (2019). 3rd Meeting of the first substantive session of the Open-Ended Working Group (OEWG). Event Report, 10 September 2019. *DigWatch.* https://is.gd/vDIxTQ

DigWatch. (2021). 9th Meeting of the third session of the Open-Ended Working Group (OEWG). Event Report, 12 Mar 2021. *DigWatch.* https://is.gd/y8gKu8

Ding, J. (2018). *Deciphering China's AI dream.* Future of Humanity Institute. www.fhi.ox.ac.uk/deciphering-chinas-ai-dream/

Dixit, P. (2019). Netflix agreed to self-regulate its content in India. Critics say it's censorship. *BuzzFeed News.* https://is.gd/qSZqPp

Dlamini, S., & Mbambo, C. (2019). Understanding policing of cyber-crime in South Africa: The phenomena, challenges and effective responses. *Cogent Social Sciences*, 5(1), 1–13.

Donnan, S., & Mitchell, T. (2016, August 11). Chinese laws prompt global business backlash. *Financial Times*. https://is.gd/1yMyCL

Douglas, B. (2013). *Brazil debates internet law in wake of NSA scandal*. www.bbc.com/news/technology-24899396

Draper, N. A., & Turow, J. (2019). The corporate cultivation of digital resignation. *New Media & Society*, 21(8), 1824–1839.

Duarte, M. (2017). *Network sovereignty: Building the Internet across Indian country*. Seattle: University of Washington Press.

Duncan, J. (2018). *Stopping the spies: Constructing and resisting the surveillance state in South Africa*. Wits University Press.

Duncan, J. (2021). The global significance of South Africa's mass surveillance ruling. About Intel. https://aboutintel.eu/south-africa-surveillance-ruling/

Dunn Cavelty, M., & Egloff, F. (2019). The politics of cybersecurity: Balancing different roles of the state. *St Antony's International Review*, 5(1), 37–57.

Dunn Cavelty, M., & Egloff, F. (2021). Hyper-securitization, everyday security practice and technification: Cyber-security Logics in Switzerland. *Swiss Political Science Review*, 27(1), 139–149.

Ebert, H., & Maurer, T. (2013). Contested cyberspace and rising powers. *Third World Quarterly*, 34(6), 1054–1074.

Economic Times, The. (2015, July 9). Not here to compete with IMF, World Bank: NDB chief KV Kamath. https://tinyurl.com/4hkfx6m7

Economic Times, The. (2023, May 25). Flipkart, Amazon, Reliance to corner Indian ecommerce: Bernstein.

Economist, The. (2017, May 6). *The world's most valuable resource is no longer oil, but data*. https://is.gd/WFMTk5

Economist, The. (2023, October 22). *Why Saudi Arabia and the UAE want to keep links with Israel*. https://is.gd/qgdaBa

Elder, M. (2013, June 19). Russia needs to reclaim its "digital sovereignty" from US, says MP. *The Guardian*. https://is.gd/Bq3YbI

eNCA. (2020). *SA information regulator battling to cope*. https://is.gd/BcCLEY3

Enriques, L., & Gatti, M. (2006). The uneasy case for top-down corporate law harmonization in the European Union. *University of Pennsylvania Journal of International Economic Law*, 27(4), 939–998.

Epstein, C. (2016). Surveillance, privacy and the making of the modern subject: Habeas what kind of corpus? *Surveillance and Embodiment*, 22(2), 28–57.

Eremenko, E., and Bryzgalova, E. (2019). "Durov sozdast agregator novostej" *Vedomosti* (June 7, 2019). https://is.gd/ffDieG

Erie, M. S., & Steinze, T. (2022). The Beijing effect: China's "Digital Silk Road" as transnational data governance. *New York University Journal of International Law and Politics*, 54(1), 1–92.

Ermoshina, K., Loveluck, B., & Musiani, F. (2022). A market of black boxes: The political economy of Internet surveillance and censorship in Russia. *Journal of Information Technology & Politics*, 19(1), 18–33.

Escobar, P. (2019, August 19). BRICS was created as a tool of attack: Lula. *Asia Times*. https://is.gd/hkCkth

EU Cyber Direct. (2021). *Cybercrime at the UN: A primer*.

European Commission. (2021). *The digital services act package*. https://is.gd/StQqlf

European Commission. (n. d.). *Shaping Europe's digital future: Americas.* https://is.gd/z5TopG

European Court of Justice. (2020, July 16). Case C-311/18, *Data Protection Commissioner v Facebook Ireland Ltd, Maximilian Schrems and intervening parties.* https://is.gd/rD8OSg

European Parliament. (2020). Digital sovereignty for Europe. European Parliamentary Research Service. European Parliament. www.europarl.europa.eu/thinktank/en/document/EPRS_BRI(2020)651992

European Union. (2019). Policy and investment recommendations for trustworthy AI. https://is.gd/mFsgj7

Evans, P. (1979). *Dependent development: The alliance of multinational, state, and local capital in Brazil.* Princeton, NJ: Princeton University Press.

Evans, P. (1995). *Embedded autonomy.* Princeton, NJ: Princeton University Press.

Eyal, N. (2014). *Hooked: How to build habit-forming products.* Penguin.

Fair Tax. (2019, December 2). *Tax gap of Silicon Six over $100 billion so far this decade.* https://is.gd/MgsODL

Fang, B. X. (2018). *Cyberspace sovereignty: Reflections on building a community of common future in cyberspace.* Singapore: Springer.

Farrell, H., & Newman, A. L. (2019). Weaponized interdependence: How global economic networks shape state coercion. *International Security*, 44(1), 42–79.

Federal Law 19-FZ. (2021, February 24). *On amendments to the code of administrative offences of the Russian federation.* https://is.gd/PxTMQA

Federal Law 139-FZ. (2012, July 28). *On amendments to the federal law on the protection of children from information harmful to their health and development and to certain legislative acts of the Russian federation.* https://is.gd/2afOIe

Federal Law 242-FZ. (2014, July 21). *Concerning the introduction of amendments to certain legislative acts of the Russian federation to clarify the procedure for processing personal data in information and telecommunication networks.* https://is.gd/nrEre9

Federal Law 374-FZ. (2016, July 6). *On amendments to the federal law "On Combating Terrorism" and to certain legislative acts of the Russian federation with regard to establishing additional measures to counter terrorism and ensure public safety.* https://rg.ru/2016/07/08/antiterror-dok.html

Federal Law 398-FZ. (2013, December 28). *On amendments to the federal law on information, information technology and information protection.* https://rg.ru/2013/12/30/extrem-site-dok.html

Federal Law 531-FZ. (2014, December 31). *On amendments to articles 13 and 14 of the federal law on information, information technologies and information protection and to the code of administrative offences of the Russian federation.* https://rg.ru/2015/01/12/informacia-dok.html

Feldmann, M. (2019). Global varieties of capitalism. *World Politics*, 71(1), 162–196.

Fichtner, J. (2016). Perpetual decline or persistent dominance? Uncovering Anglo-America's true structural power in global finance. *Review of International Studies*, 43(1), 3–28.

Fichtner, J., & Heemskerk, E. M. (2020). The new permanent universal owners: Index funds, patient capital, and the distinction between feeble and forceful stewardship. *Economy and Society*, 49(4), 493–515.

Fijałkowski, L. (2011). China's "soft power" in Africa? *Journal of Contemporary African Studies*, 29(2), 223–232.

FISA Amendments Act Reauthorization Act of 2012. (2012). https://is.gd/cHBlCA

Floridi, L. (2019). Marketing as Control of Human Interfaces and Its Political Exploitation. Available at SSRN: https://ssrn.com/abstract=3834989 or http://dx.doi.org/10.2139/ssrn.3834989

Floridi, L. (2020). The fight for digital sovereignty: What it is, and why it matters, especially for the EU. *Philosophy and Technology*, 33(3), 369–378.

Fontaine, R., & Kliman, D. M. (2013). International order and global swing states. *The Washington Quarterly*, 36(1), 93–109. https://doi.org/10.1080/0163660x.2013.751653

Forbes. (2019). Top 100 digital companies. *Forbes*. https://is.gd/fcpFnp

Freedom House. (2020). *Freedom on the net 2020: South Africa*. https://is.gd/84iVKX

Freedombone.net. (n.d.). *A people's history of the Fediverse*. Freedombone.Net. https://is.gd/8OL48h

Freiberg, P. (2014). "Putin's Russia – On a path to cyber sovereignty?" capstone project for the Master of Arts in Media Communications Program for Webster University. https://is.gd/16nOgV

French, H. (2015). *China's second continent: How a million migrants are building a new empire in Africa*. New York: Vintage Books.

French Ministry of European and Foreign Affairs. (2020, July 31). *Barbed wire on the Internet prairie: Against new enclosures, digital commons as drivers of sovereignty*. French Ministry of European and Foreign Affairs. https://is.gd/O1RRxy

Fuchs, C. (2015). The MacBride report in the twenty-first-century capitalism, the age of social media, and the BRICS countries. *Javnost*, 22(3), 226–239.

Fuchs, C., & Unterberger, K. (Eds.) (2021). *The public service media and public service internet manifesto*. University of Westminster Press.

Gabowitsch, M. (2016). *Protest in Putin's Russia*. John Wiley & Sons.

Gagliardone, I. (2019). *China, Africa, and the future of the Internet*. London: Zed Books.

Gallagher, R., & Burkhardt, P. (2021, July 29). "Death kitty" ransomware linked to south African port attack. *Bloomberg*. https://is.gd/AGtphN

Galloway, A. R. (2004). *Protocol: How control exists after decentralization*. MIT Press.

Gao, H. (2022). Across the Great Wall: E-commerce joint statement initiative negotiation and China. In S. Peng, C. Lin, & T. Streinz (Eds.), *Artificial intelligence and international economic law: Disruption, regulation, and reconfiguration* (pp. 295–318). Cambridge: Cambridge University Press.

Gao, H., & Shaffer, G. (2021). The RCEP – Great power competition and cooperation over trade. *AfronomicsLAW*. https://is.gd/NoSJnk

Garcia, E. V. (2022). *The technological leap of AI and the Global South: Deepening asymmetries and the future of international security*. https://is.gd/4LVX9e

Gehl, R. W. (2015). The case for alternative social media. *Social Media + Society*, 1(2). https://doi.org/10.1177/2056305115604338

Geiger, S., Harrison, D., Kjellberg, H., & Mallard, A. (Eds.) (2014). *Concerned markets: Economic ordering for multiple values*. Edward Elgar.

German Federal Constitutional Court. (1983). Judgment of 15 December 1983, 1 BvR 209, 269, 362, 420, 440, 484/83 [CODICES]. https://is.gd/entUqg

Gershenzon, L. (2016, April 20). *Nothing to aggregate*. Republic. https://republic.ru/posts/66965

Gerth, H. H., & Mills, W. (2009). *From Max Weber*. Routledge.

Gillespie, T. (2018). *Custodians of the internet: Platforms, content moderation, and the hidden decisions that shape social media*. Yale University Press.

GISWatch. (2018). *Global information society watch 2018: Community networks 2018*. Association for Progressive Communications and International Development Research Centre. https://is.gd/6ZgTbG

Global Times. (2020, August 6). Most smartphones in China using Beidou system for location and navigation. *Global Times*. https://is.gd/V6neEX

Globerman, S. (1978). Canadian science policy and technological sovereignty. *Canadian Public Policy/Analyse De Politiques*, 4(1), 34–45.

GLONASS to Be Required for Phones Sold in Russia. (2013, November 12). *GPS World*. https://is.gd/NQKTw2

GNU. (2022). *About the GNU Operating System*. GNU. https://is.gd/yQWoEB

Goldsmith, J., & Wu, T. (2006). *Who controls the Internet? Illusions of a borderless world*. New York: Oxford University Press.

Gómez, R. N. (2014). Cyber-geopolitics. Geopolitical rivalries behind the cyber-threat narratives in the United States. *Herodote*, *152–153*(1), 98–122.

Gong, W. (1998). 信息时代的国际传播:国际关系面临的新问题 [International communication in the information age: News problems faced by international relations]. 国际政治研究 *[International Politics Studies]*, 2, 41–46.

González, M. (2017). Subsea cable to connect Brazil and Spain, bypassing US surveillance. https://is.gd/GFvD5W

Gopakumar, G. (2021). BackRBI puts new payment network plan on hold. *Mint*. https://is.gd/Y586Im

Gosh, D., & Couldry, N. (2020). Digital realignment: Rebalancing platform economies from corporation to consumer. M-RCBG *Associate Working Paper Series, 155*. https://is.gd/VYgNpF

Government of New Zealand. (2016). *Text of the Comprehensive and Progressive Agreement for Trans-Pacific Partnership* (CPTPP). https://is.gd/wC6sb6

Grabel, I. (2017). *When things don't fall apart: Global financial governance and developmental finance in an age of productive incoherence*. MIT Press.

Grimm, D. (2015). *Sovereignty: The origin and future of a political and legal concept* (B. Cooper, Trans.). New York: Columbia University Press.

Gritsenko, D., Wijermars, M., & Kopotev, M. (2021). *The Palgrave handbook of digital Russia studies*. Springer Nature.

Gross, A., & Murgia, M. (2020). China and Huawei propose reinvention of the Internet. *Financial Times*.

Grover, G., & Thomas, A. (2021, February 22). Notes from a foreign field: The European court of human rights on Russia's website blocking. *CyberBRICS*. https://is.gd/7v9fr3

Gu, J., Chuanhong, Z., Vaz, A., & Mukwereza, L. (2016). Chinese state capitalism? Rethinking the role of the state and business in Chinese development cooperation in Africa. *World Development*, *81*(May), 24–34.

Guan, S. (1997). 美国“全球信息高速公路”的实施战略 – 剖析美国学者向美国政府提出的战略性建议 [The implementation strategy of the US global information superhighway – Analyzing US scholars' strategic recommendations to the US government]. 国际政治研究 *[International Politics Studies]*, 4, 82–91.

Gueham, F. (2017). *Digital sovereignty*. Paris: The Fondation pour l'innovation politique.

Guo, H., Bandyopadhyay, S., Cheng, H., & Yang, Y. (2010). Net neutrality and vertical integration of content and broadband services. *Journal of Management Information Systems*, 27(2), 243–276.

Haché, A. (2017). *Technological sovereignty Vol. 2*. Barcelona, Spain: Descontrol. https://is.gd/Ntk8bo

Haggard, S. (2018). *Developmental states*. Cambridge University Press.

Han, P. (2000). 网络时代的哲学问题 [Philosophical questions in the internet age]. *现代哲学 [Modern Philosophy]*, 4, 50–55.

Hansen, L., & Nissenbaum, H. (2009). Digital disaster, cyber security, and the Copenhagen school. *International Studies Quarterly*, 53(4), 1155–1175.

Hariharan, V. (2021). *New umbrella entity: Masterstroke or disaster?* https://is.gd/fNdIuM

Harper, J. (2017, July 23). *Russians protest state censorship of the internet*. Deutsche Welle. https://is.gd/gmwmEm

Havercroft, J. (2011). *Captives of sovereignty*. Cambridge, MA: Cambridge University Press.

Hayden, M. V. (2006). *Testimony to the judiciary committee of the US Senate*. https://is.gd/mQF2aW

He, B. (2019). 欧盟阻断法令情况对中国的启示 [Lessons of the EU's blocking statute for China]. *国际贸易 [International Trade]*, 2019(10), 90–96.

Helberger, N. (2020). The political power of platforms: How current attempts to regulate misinformation amplify opinion power. *Digital Journalism*, 8(6), 842–854.

Helleiner, E. (2019). Still an extraordinary power after all these years: The US and the global financial crisis of 2008. In R. Germain (Ed.), *Susan strange and the future of global political economy: Power, control and transformation* (Ripe series in global political economy) (1st ed., pp. 93–108). Routledge.

Herlo, B., Irrgang, D., Joost, G., & Unteidig, A. (Eds.) (2022). *Practicing sovereignty: Digital involvement in times of crisis*. Bielefeld, Germany: Transcript Verlag.

Hicks, J. (2019, September 29). "Digital colonialism": Why countries like India want to take control of data from big tech. *The Print*. https://is.gd/ZQDDjU

Hildebrandt, M. (2013). Extraterritorial jurisdiction to enforce in cyberspace? Bodin, Schmitt, Grotius in cyberspace. *The University of Toronto Law Journal*, 63(2), 196–224.

Hildebrandt, M. (2018). Primitives of legal protection in the era of data-driven platforms. *Georgetown Law Technology Review*, 2(2), 252–273.

Hinck, R., Cooley, S., & Kluver, R. (2019). *Global media and strategic narratives of contested democracy: Chinese, Russian, and Arabic media narratives of the US presidential election*. New York: Routledge.

Hirschman, A. (1980). *National power and the structure of foreign trade: Expanded edition*. Berkeley: University of California Press.

Hlase, E. P. (2018). *The securitisation of cyberspace in South Africa: The tension between national security and civil liberties*. A mini-dissertation submitted in partial fulfilment of the requirements for the degree Master of Security Studies (MSS), Department of Political Sciences, Faculty of Humanities, University of Pretoria.

Hoffman, J. (2016). Multi-stakeholderism in Internet governance: Putting a fiction into practice. *Journal of Cyber Policy*, 1(1), 29–49.

Holbraad, C. (1986). *Middle powers in international politics*. London: Macmillan.

Hong, Y. (2017). 在发展与安全的平衡中构建数据跨境流动安全评估框架 [Building a framework for security review of cross-border data flows while balancing development and security]. 信息安全与通信保密 *[Information Security and Communications Privacy]*, 2017(2), 36–62.

Hong, Y., & Goodnight, T. (2019). How to think about cyber sovereignty: The case of China. *Chinese Journal of Communication*, 13(4), 1–19.

Hoofnagle, C. J., & Garfinkel, S. (2021). *Law and policy for the quantum age*. Cambridge: Cambridge University Press.

Huang, D., Yuan, H., & Hu, W. (2020). 《数据安全法（草案）》的立法背景、立法定位与制度设计 [The legislative background, legislative positioning and institutional design of the data security law (Draft)]. 信息安全与通信保密 *[Information Security and Communications Privacy]*, 2020(8), 9–15.

Huang, R. (2020, May 25). *China will use its digital currency to compete with The USD*.

Huawei. (2017). *Huawei launches OpenLab in South Africa*. https://is.gd/fFpdDY

Huawei. (2018). *Sustainable report*. https://is.gd/V7vCcI

Huawei. (2019). *Huawei smart city white paper*. https://is.gd/6NbsJA

Hummel, P., Braun, M., Tretter, M., & Dabrock, P. (2021). Data sovereignty: A review. *Big Data & Society*, *8*(1), 1–17.

India Stack. (n.d.). *India Stack*. www.indiastack.org/

Indian Ministry of Electronics & IT. (2023, August 9). *Salient features of the digital personal data protection bill*, 2023. https://is.gd/tGNijs

Indian Ministry of External Affairs. (2015, July 9). *7th BRICS summit – Ufa declaration*. https://is.gd/GBKi1M

Indian Ministry of External Affairs. (2021, September 9). *XIII BRICS Summit – New Delhi declaration*. https://is.gd/ib4Ocy

Indian Ministry of External Affairs. (2023, 9–10 September). *G20 New Delhi Leaders' declaration*. https://is.gd/uRO5W1

Instituto Brasileiro de Defesa do Consumidor [IDEC] & Instituto Locomotiva. (2021). *Barreiras e limitações no acesso à internet e hábitos de uso e navegação na rede nas classes C, D e E*. https://is.gd/zhkWVJ

International Association of Privacy Professionals (IAPP). (2020). Brazilian General Data Protection Law (LGPD, English translation). https://is.gd/a6BNg7

International Federation for Human Rights. (2012). *Shanghai cooperation organization: A vehicle for human rights violations*. www.fidh.org/IMG/pdf/sco_report.pdf

International Federation of Human Rights. (2018). *Russia 2012–2018: 50 anti-democracy laws entered into force within last presidential mandate*. https://is.gd/8Qwwfw

International Institute for Sustainable Development (IISD). (2020). *WTO members highlight benefits and drawbacks of c-commerce moratorium*. https://is.gd/a1zmlY

Internet Freedom Foundation. (2019). *Bihar's internet shutdown orders reveal vague but relatively narrow suspension of mass messaging platforms*. https://is.gd/RswTFJ

Internet Shutdowns in India. (n.d.). https://internetshutdowns.in

Israel, E., & Soto, A. (2013). Brazil's anti-spying Internet push could backfire, industry says. *Reuters*. https://is.gd/wvt6no

ITU-T FG-SSC. (2016). Shaping smarter and more sustainable cities: Striving for sustainable development goals. *International Telecommunication Union (ITU-T), Focus Group on Smart Sustainable Cities (FG-SSC)*. New York: United Nations.

ITweb. (2017, November 24). "Internet Censorship Bill" heading to parliament. *ITweb*. https://is.gd/GeKr8Y

Jakubowicz, K. (2015). New media ecology: Reconceptualizing media pluralism. In P. Valcke, M. Sükösd, & R. G. Picard (Eds.), *Media pluralism and diversity* (pp. 23–53). London: Palgrave Macmillan UK.

Jasanoff, S. (2015). Future imperfect: Science, technology, and the imaginations of modernity. In S. H. Kim & S. Jasanoff (Eds.), *Dreamscapes of modernity: Sociotechnical imaginaries and the fabrication of power* (pp. 1–33). Chicago, IL: University of Chicago Press.

Jawaid, D. (2023). 100 biggest technology companies in the world. *Yahoo! Finance*. https://is.gd/vpbpsk

Jewler, S. (2015, August 25). *Mission creep-y: Google is quietly becoming one of the nation's most powerful political forces while expanding its information-collection empire*. Public Citizen. https://is.gd/QewMpm

Jia, L., & Winseck, D. (2018). The political economy of Chinese internet companies: Financialization, concentration, and capitalization. *International Communication Gazette*, *80*(1), 30–59.

Jiang, M. (2010). Aythoritarian informationalism: China's approach to internet sovereignty. *SAIS Review of International Affairs*, *30*(2), 71–89.

Jiang, M. (2014). The business and politics of search engines: A comparative study of Baidu and Google's search results of Internet events from China. *New Media & Society*, *16*(2), 212–233.

Jiang, M. (2019, June 3). U.S. Ban on Huawei: Superpowers' insecurities and nightmares. *CyberBRICS*. https://is.gd/r2inhf

Jiang, M. (2021). Cybersecurity policies in China. In L. Belli (Ed.), *CyberBRICS: Cybersecurity regulations in the BRICS countries* (pp. 183–226). Cham, Switzerland: Springer.

Jiang, M., & Fu, K. W. (2018). Chinese social media and big data: Big data, big brother, big profit? *Policy & Internet*, *10*(4), 372–392.

Johnson, D., & Post, D. (1996). Law and borders: The rise of law in cyberspace. *Stanford Law Review*, *48*(5), 1367–1402.

Jones, C. I., & Tonetti, C. (2020). Nonrivalry and the economics of data. *American Economic Review*, *110*(9), 2819–2858.

Jordaan, E. (2003). The concept of a middle power in international relations: Distinguishing between emerging and traditional middle powers. *Politikon*, *30*(1), 165–181.

Kalra, A., & Bhattacharjee, N. (2020). Google defers Indian in-app fees after angry startups complain. https://is.gd/RUEeol

Kanth, D. R. (2020). South Africa, India call for development-oriented approach to e-com. *SUNS*, *9250*. www.twn.my/title2/wto.info/2020/ti201209.htm

Kaspersky. (2023a). *In Q2 2023 ransomware attacks in South Africa increased by 10% compared to Q1*. July 26, 2023. https://is.gd/f2UPdo

Kaspersky. (2023b). *Scams with HR credentials spread in recent months*. July 25, 2023. https://is.gd/iFAdjh

Kazeem, Y. (2020). *With over 250,000 cases, misinformation is compromising Africa's Covid-19 response*. Quartz Africa. https://is.gd/QurUpw

Kelkar, V., & Shah, A. (2019). *In service of the republic* (1st ed.). New Delhi: Penguin Allen Lane.

Kelty, C. M. (2008). *Two bits: The cultural significance of free software*. Duke University Press.

Kettemann, M. C. (2020). The normative order of the internet: A theory of rule and regulation online. In *The normative order of the internet* (pp. 131–181). Oxford: Oxford University Press.

Khan, L. (2017). Amazon's antitrust paradox. *The Yale Law Journal*, 126(3), 564–907.

Khera, R. (Ed.) (2019). *Dissent on Aadhaar: Big data meets big brother*. Hyderabad, Telangana: Orient BlackSwan.

Kim, E. (2005). F/OSS adoption in Brazil: The growth of a national strategy. In J. Karaganis & R. Latham (Eds.), *The politics of open source adoption* (pp. 53–60). New York: Social Science Research Council.

King, K. (2010). China's cooperation in education and training with Kenya: A different model? *International Journal of Educational Development*, 30(5), 488–496.

King, K. (2013). *China's aid and soft power in Africa: The case of education and training*. Cambridge: Boydell & Brewer.

Kirya, I. (2011). Le piratage audiovisuel en Russie post-soviétique, entre logiques économiques et culturelles. In T. Mattelart (Ed.), *Piratages audiovisuels* (pp. 239–255). Paris and Louvain-la-Neuve: De Boeck Supérieur.

Kleman, K., Miryasova, O., & Demidov, A. (2010). *Ot obyvateley k aktivistam: zarozhdayushchiyesya sotsial'nyye dvizheniya v sovremennoy Rossii [From the philistines to the activists: The emerging social movements in modern Russia]*. Moscow: Tri kvadrata.

Knowledge at Whalton. (2018, January 17). *The mobile payments race: Why China is leading the pack – for now*. https://is.gd/SYTSTX

Knox, R. (2016). Marxist approaches to international law. In A. Orford & F. Hoffmann (Eds.), *The Oxford handbook of the theory of international law* (pp. 306–326). Oxford: Oxford University Press.

Kodačigov, V. (2021, March 15). *V Iphone ustanovât rossijskij soft. Vedomosti*. https://is.gd/CzbU8j

Koh, H. H. (2008). *Transnational litigation in United States courts*. Foundation Press.

Kokas, A. (2022). *Trafficking data: How China is winning the battle for digital sovereignty*. Oxford, UK: Oxford University Press.

Koopman, C. (2019). *How we became our data: A genealogy of the informational person*. Chicago, IL: University of Chicago Press.

Kovacs, A. (2021). Cybersecurity and data protection regulation in India: An uneven patchwork. In L. Belli (Ed.), *CyberBRICS: Cybersecurity regulations in the BRICS countries* (pp. 133–182). Cham, Switzerland: Springer.

Kovacs, A., & Ranganathan, N. (2019). *Data sovereignty, of whom? Limits and suitability of sovereignty frameworks for data in India* (Working Paper No. 3). Data Governance Network. https://datagovernance.org/report/data-sovereignty

Kovalev, M. (2016). Law and (verbal) order: The politics of Russian obscene language from Soviet Russia to the present day. *Zeitschrift Für Slavische Philologie*, 72(2), 323–347.

Krasner, S. (1999). *Sovereignty: Organized hypocrisy*. New Haven, NJ: Princeton University Press.

Krastev, I., & Holmes, S. (2019). *The light that failed: A reckoning*. Penguin Books.

Krishnan, M. (2018, June 27). Fake social media messages fuel latest mob lynchings in India. *National Herald*. https://is.gd/XQKIzx

Kuehn, K. M. (2018). Surveillance and South Africa. [Review of the book Stopping the spies: Constructing and resisting the surveillance state in South Africa, by J. Duncan.] *The Political Economy of Communication*, 6(2), 94–100.

Kukutai, T., & Taylor, J. (2016). *Indigenous data sovereignty: Toward an agenda (CAEPR)*. Canberra, Australia: ANU Press.

Kupchan, C. (2023, November 8). 6 Swing states in the global South will decide geopolitics. Foreign Policy. https://foreignpolicy.com/2023/06/06/geopolitics-global-south-middle-powers-swing-states-india-brazil-turkey-indonesia-saudi-arabia-south-africa/

Kurbalija, J. (2016). *An introduction to Internet governance* (7th edition). Geneva, Switzerland: DiploFoundation. https://is.gd/2zZ1TE

Kushwaha, N., Watson, B, & Roguski, P. (2020). Up in the air: Ensuring government data sovereignty in the cloud. 2020 *12th International Conference on Cyber Conflict*, Tallinn.

Kwet, M. (2019, November 22). Smart CCTV networks are driving an AI-powered apartheid in South Africa. *VICE*. https://is.gd/jpapxF

Lake, D. A. (2007). Escape from the state of nature: Authority and hierarchy in world politics. *International Security*, 32(1), 47–79.

Lake, D. A. (2011). *Hierarchy in international relations*. Cornell University Press.

Lambach, D. (2019). *The Internet is already fragmented*. Digital Society Blog, The Alexander von Humboldt Institute for Internet and Society (HIIG). https://is.gd/X31jN9

Lambach, D. (2020). The territorialization of cyberspace*. *International Studies Review*, 22(3), 482–506.

Laruelle, M. (2015). *The "Russian world." Russia's soft power and geopolitical imagination*. Center for Global Interests Papers.

Laskai, L., & Segal, A. (2021). The encryption debate in China: 2021 update. *Carnegie Endowment for World Peace*. https://is.gd/PoLV3q

Lawder, D. (2022). Yellen: Not legal for U.S. to seize Russian official assets. *Reuters*. https://is.gd/9qHaGX

Lazer, D. (2006). Global and domestic governance: Modes of interdependence in regulatory policymaking. *European Law Journal*, 12(4), 455–468.

Lee, K.-F. (2018). *AI superpowers: China, Silicon Valley, and the new world order*. Houghton Mifflin Harcourt Company.

Leister, V., & Frazier, M. (2014). *Brazil's role in emerging global open-source initiatives*. 12th Congress of the Brazilian Studies Association (BRASA XII).

Leonard, M., & Shapiro, J. (2020). *Sovereign Europe, dangerous world: Five agendas to protect Europe's capacity to act*. European Council on Foreign Relations. https://is.gd/Cwwos8

Lessig, L. (1999a). *Code: And other laws of cyberspace*. New York: Basic Books.

Lessig, L. (1999b). The law of the horse: What cyberlaw might teach. *Harvard Law Review*, *113*, 501–546.

Lessig, L. (2006). *Code: Version 2.0*. New York: Basic Books.

Levada Center. (2020, February 27). *Istochniki novostej i doverie SMI [Sources of information and trust in the media]*. https://is.gd/UlX4Iw

Lewis, J. A. (2020, October 26). Digital sovereignty in the Time of Conflict. *ORF*. https://is.gd/JA7L1W

Li, A. (2008). China's new policy towards Africa. In R. I. Rotberg (Ed.), *China into Africa: Trade, aid and influence*. Washington, DC: Brookings Institution Press.

Li, H. (2016). 数据本地化立法与数字贸易的国际规则 [The legislation of data localization and the international rules of digital trade]. 信息安全研究 *[Journal of Information Security Research]*, 2(9), 781–786.

Litterick, D. (2005, August 31). Chirac Backs Eurocentric Search Engine. *The Telegraph*. http://is.gd/se2dRa

Liu, J., & Cui, B. (2020). 数据本地化和数据防御主义的合理性与趋势 [Data localization and the legitimacy and trend of data defensivism]. 国际展望 *[Global Review]*, 12(6), 89–107.

Lobo, A. P. (2022, January 12). Câmara quer proibir vendas do Serpro e da Dataprev. *Convergência Digital*. https://is.gd/l8kt27

Lopez, A. (2007). Introduction: The (Post)global South. *The Global South*, 1(1), 1–11.

Lowe, V. (1997). US extraterritorial jurisdiction: The Helms-burton and D'Amato Acts. *International and Comparative Law Quarterly*, 46(2), 378–390.

Lukings, M., & Lashkari, A. H. (2022). *Understanding cybersecurity law in data sovereignty and digital governance: An overview from a legal perspective*. Cham, Switzerland: Springer.

Lumumba-Kasongo, T. (2015). Brazil, Russia, India, China, and South Africa (BRICS) and Africa: New projected developmental paradigms. *Africa Development*, 40(3), 77–95.

Lund, A., & Zukerfeld, M. (2020). *Corporate capitalism's use of openness: Profit for free?* Springer International Publishing.

Lyon, D. (2007). *Surveillance studies: An overview*. Cambridge: Polity Press.

MacAskill, E., & Dance, G. (2013, November 1). NSA files: Decoded. *The Guardian*. https://is.gd/gW7sUF

MacBride, S., & Commissioners. (1980). *Communication and society today and tomorrow: Many voices, one world: Towards a new, more just, and more efficient world information and communication order*. Kogan Page, Unipub, UNESCO. (Reprinted by Kogan Page, 1981 and Rowman & Littlefield Publishers, 2004).

MacKinnon, R. (2012). *Consent of the networked: The worldwide struggle for internet freedom*. New York: Basic Books.

MacManus, R. (2023, July 12). Threads adopting ActivityPub makes sense, but won't be easy. *The New Stack*. https://is.gd/hHIfGr

Mahler, A. G. (2018). *From the Tricontinental to the Global South: Race, radicalism, and transnational solidarity*. Duke University Press.

Maizland, L. (2022, June 14). China and Russia: Exploring ties between two authoritarian powers. *Council on Foreign Relations*. https://is.gd/EhHFQ3

Makundi, H., Huyse, H., & Develtere, P. (2016). Cooperation between China and Tanzania on ICT: Fish, fishing tackle or fishing skills? *Journal of Chinese Economic and Business Studies*, 14(2), 129–149.

Malanczuk, P. (1997). *Akehurst's modern introduction to international law* (7th ed.). London and New York: Routledge.

Mandl, C., & Versiani, I. (2020, June 23). Brazil suspends WhatsApp's new payments system. *Reuters*. https://is.gd/KchWc8

Mann, M., Mitchell, P., Foth, M., & Anastasiu Cioaca, I. (2020). #BlockSidewalk to Barcelona: Technological sovereignty and the social license to operate smart cities. *Journal of the Association for Information Science and Technology*, 71(9), 1103–1115.

Mansoux, A., & Abbing, R. R. (2020). Seven theses on Fediverse and the becoming of FLOSS. In K. Gansing & I. Luchs (Eds.), *The eternal network: The ends and becomings of network culture* (pp. 124–140). Institute of Network Cultures. https://is.gd/9s4xdp

Maréchal, N. (2018). *From Russia with crypto: A political history of Telegram. Eighth USENIX Workshop on Free and Open Communications on the Internet.* https://is.gd/mbxBRF

Mason, J. (2019, March 14). U.S. considers sanctions to restrict Visa, Mastercard in Venezuela: Official. *Yahoo! Finance.* https://is.gd/lspf4P

Mattioli, D. (2020). *Amazon scooped up data from its own sellers to launch competing products.* https://is.gd/jZX8bk

Maxigas, P., & Latzko-Toth, G. (2020). Trusted commons: Why "old" social media matter. *Internet Policy Review*, 9(4). https://is.gd/wvosA7

Mazzucato, M. (2013). *The entrepreneurial state.* London: Anthem Press.

Mazzucato, M. (2018). *The entrepreneurial state.* Penguin Books.

Mburu, J. (2018). *The rise of a new dawn in Kenya's payments system.* Nairobi: FSG Kenya.

McCarthy, D. R. (2015). *Power, information technology, and international relations theory: The power and politics of US foreign policy and the internet.* New York: Palgrave Macmillan.

McKenzie, B. (2022, June 1). How the European Union's General Data Protection Regulations influenced data privacy law in Africa. *Baker McKenzie.* https://is.gd/RoTfT7

McKune, S. (2011, 2015). *An analysis of the international code of conduct for information security.* https://openeffect.ca/code-conduct/

McKune, S., & Ahmed, S. (2018). Authoritarian practices in the digital age: The contestation and shaping of cyber norms through China's internet sovereignty agenda. *International Journal of Communication, 12*, 3835–3855.

Meagher, D. (2020). Caught in the economic crosshairs: Secondary sanctions, blocking regulations, and the American sanctions regime. *Fordham Law Review, 89*(3), 999–1030.

Mehta, A. (2020, August 24). Delhi riots: The link between misinformation and radicalisation. *The Wire.* https://is.gd/Lfwgze

Mekouar, D. (2020). *Here's where the internet actually lives.* https://is.gd/OFBejh

Meyer, J. A. (2008). Second thoughts on secondary sanctions symposium article. *University of Pennsylvania Journal of International Law, 30*(3), 905–968.

Miao, S. (2021). 《阻断外国法律与措施不当域外适用办法》的属事适用范围 [On the subject matter of Chinese blocking rules]. 国际法研究 *[Chinese Review of International Law], 2021*(2), 44–62.

Miao, W., Jiang, M., & Pang, Y. (2021). Historicizing Internet regulation in China: A meta-analysis of Chinese Internet policies (1994–2017). *International Journal of Communication, 15*, 2003–2026.

Michel, C. (2021, February 3). *Digital sovereignty is central to European strategic autonomy – Speech by President Charles Michel at "Masters of digital 2021"* online event. European Council. https://is.gd/mm4ysK

Micheli, M., Ponti, M., Craglia, M., & Berti Suman, A. (2020). Emerging models of data governance in the age of datafication. *Big Data & Society*, 7(2), 1–15.

Miéville, C. (2006). *Between equal rights: A Marxist theory of international law.* Haymarket Books.

Milakovich, M. (2012). *Digital governance: New technologies for improving public service and participation.* New York: Routledge.

Ministry of Digital Development, Communications and Mass Media of the Russian Federation. (2015, May 15). *International consortium for development of new mobile operating system is being formed now*. https://digital.gov.ru/en/events/33225/

Ministry of Foreign Affairs of India. (2021, December 6). *India-Russia joint statement following the visit of the President of the Russian Federation*. https://is.gd/oOL5e1

Mohammad-Arif, A., Naudet, J., & Jaoul, N. (2020). The Hindutva turn: Authoritarianism and resistance in India. *South Asia Multidisciplinary Academic Journal*, *24/25*. http://journals.openedition.org/samaj/6632

Mohan, G., & Lampert, B. (2013). Negotiating China: Reinserting African agency into China-Africa relations. *African Affairs*, *112*(446), 92–110.

Morozov, E. V. (2011). *The net delusion: The dark side of internet freedom* (1st ed.). New York: Public Affairs.

Morozov, E. V. (2019). Digital socialism? The calculation debate in the age of big data. *New Left Review*, *116/117*, 33–67.

Mortensen, S. A. (2016). Discursive propagation in Putin's Russia: Prohibiting "propaganda of non-traditional sexual relations." *Zeitschrift Für Slavische Philologie*, *72*(2), 349–381.

Mouffe, C. (2013). *Agonistics: Thinking the world politically*. Verso.

Mueller, M. (2004). *Ruling the root: Internet governance and the taming of cyberspace*. Cambridge, MA: MIT Press.

Mueller, M. (2010). *Networks and states: The global politics of Internet governance*. Cambridge, MA: MIT Press.

Mueller, M. (2017). *Will the internet fragment? Sovereignty, globalization and cyberspace*. Cambridge, UK: Polity Press.

Mueller, M. (2019). Against Sovereignty in Cyberspace. *International Studies Review*, *22*(4), 1–23.

Mueller, M. (2020). *Sovereignty and cyberspace: Institutions and internet governance*. https://is.gd/ePcCOH

Mukerjee, S. (2016). Net neutrality, Facebook, and India's battle to #SaveTheInternet. *Communication & The Public*, *1*(3), 356–361.

Mungadze, S. (2019, October 3). *Controversial Internet censorship Bill now law*. ITWeb. Johannesburg. https://is.gd/VKQqNu

Murau, S., Pape, F., & Pforr, T. (2021, February). The hierarchy of the offshore US-dollar system: On swap lines, the FIMA repo facility and special drawing rights. *Boston University Global Development Policy Center*. https://is.gd/WLgJ8p

Musiani, F. (2013/5). *Nains sans géants. Architecture décentralisée et services Internet*. Presses des Mines.

Musiani, F. (2018). L'invisible qui façonne. Études d'infrastructure et gouvernance d'Internet. *Tracés. Revue de Sciences humaines*, *35*, 161–176.

Musiani, F., Cogburn, D. L., DeNardis, L., & Levinson, N. S. (Eds.) (2016). *The turn to infrastructure in Internet governance*. New York: Palgrave Macmillan.

Musiani, F., Loveluck, B., Daucé, F., & Ermoshina, K. (2019). "Digital sovereignty": Can Russia cut off its Internet from the rest of the world? *The Conversation France*.

Musyimi, C., Malechwanzi, J., & Luo, H. (2018). The Belt and Road Initiative and technical and vocational education and training (TVET) in Kenya: The Kenya-China TVET project. *Frontiers of Education in China*, *13*(September), 346–374.

Mutsvairo, B., & Ragnedda, M. (Eds.) (2019). *Mapping the digital divide in Africa: A mediated analysis*. Amsterdam: Amsterdam University Press.

Napoli, P., & Caplan, R. (2017). Why media companies insist they're not media companies, why they're wrong, and why it matters. *First Monday*, 22(5).

Narlikar, A. (2021). Must the weak suffer what they must? In D. Drezner, H. Farrell, & A. Newman (Eds.), *The uses and abuses of weaponized interdependence* (pp. 289–304). Washington, DC: Brookings Institution Press.

National Archives. (n.d.) *Maps in time from 1900 to 2000*. https://is.gd/SC3Aso

National Archives. (2021, January 5). "*Executive order addressing the threat posed by applications and other software developed or controlled by Chinese companies.*" Trump White House, National Archives. https://is.gd/IR2hYu

Ndzendze, B. (2021, January 26). Beyond the digital cold war: Technology and the future of US-African engagement under Biden. *Mail & Guardian*. https://is.gd/2Mr7TM

Nechushtai, E., & Lewis, S. C. (2019). What kind of news gatekeepers do we want machines to be? Filter bubbles, fragmentation, and the normative dimensions of algorithmic recommendations. *Computers in Human Behavior*, 90, 298–307.

Negro, G. (2020). A history of Chinese global Internet governance and its relations with ITU and ICANN. *Chinese Journal of Communication*, 13(1), 104–121.

Nemroff, C. (2018). *Explanation of vote on a third committee resolution on countering the use of information and communication technologies for criminal purposes*. United States Mission to the United Nations. https://is.gd/UmmIdl

New Development Bank (NDB). (2022). *NDB'S member countries*. www.ndb.int/about-us/organization/members/

Newman, N., Fletcher, R., Eddy, K., Robertson, C. T., & Nielsen, R. K. (2023). *Digital News Report 2023*. Reuters Institute for the Study of Journalism. https://is.gd/x7JFiW

Ngqakamba, S. (2021, September 9). Justice department's IT system brought down in ransomware attack. *News24*. https://is.gd/9q5Mrj

Nocetii, J. (2015). Contest and conquest: Russia and global internet governance. *International Affairs*, 91(1), 111–130.

Nocetti, J. (2017, July 17). *Securitising Putin IV: The rationale behind Russia's new "digital laws."* https://is.gd/wcjChh

Nonnecke, B. (2016). The transformative effects of multistakeholderism in Internet governance: A case study of the East Africa *Internet governance forum*. *Telecommunications Policy*, 40(4), 343–352.

Norris, P. (2001). *Digital divide: Civic engagement, information poverty, and the Internet worldwide*. Cambridge, UK: Cambridge University Press.

NPC & Central Committee of the CPC. (2016). *Outline of the 13th five-year plan for national economic and social development of the People's Republic of China (2016–2020)*. https://is.gd/2eZ7aT

NPCI. (2021). Standard operating procedure (SOP) – Market share cap for third party application providers (TPAP). *NPCI*. https://is.gd/QqJsEI

NPCI. (n.d. -a). An introduction to NPCI and its various products. *NPCI*. www.npci.org.in/who-we-are/about-us

NPCI. (n.d. -b). UPI product statistics. *NPCI*. www.npci.org.in/what-we-do/upi/product-statistics

NPCI. (n.d. -c). UPI live members. *NPCI*. www.npci.org.in/what-we-do/upi/live-members

NPCI. (n.d. -d). UPI 3rd party apps. *NPCI*. www.npci.org.in/what-we-do/upi/3rd-party-apps

NPCI. (n.d. -e). UPI Ecosystem Statistics. *NPCI.* www.npci.org.in/what-we-do/upi/upi-ecosystem-statistics

NPCI. (n.d. -f). Committees. *NPCI.* www.npci.org.in/who-we-are/committee

Nye, J. S., & Owens, W. A. (1996). America's information edge. *Foreign Affairs*, 75(2), 20–36.

O'Donnell, F., & Papa, M. (2021). India's multi-alignment management and the Russia–India–China (RIC) triangle. *International Affairs*, 97(3), 801–822.

O'Neill, J. (2001). *Building better global economic BRICs.* Goldman Sachs. https://is.gd/IOgg7x

Oates, S. (2013). *Revolution stalled: The political limits of the Internet in the post-Soviet sphere.* Oxford, UK: Oxford University Press.

Oatley, T., Winecoff, W. K., Pennock, A., & Danzman, S. B. (2013). The political economy of global finance: A network model. *Perspectives on Politics*, 11(1), 133–153.

Obendiek, A. (2021, May 12). *Take back control? Digital sovereignty and a vision for Europe* (Policy Paper). Hertie School Jacques Delors Centre. https://is.gd/un3sl2

Observer Research Foundation (ORF). (2021, August 1). *Digital BRICS: A new framework for cooperation on technology and innovation.* https://is.gd/USfmdV

OECD. (2022). *Personal data protection at the OECD.* https://is.gd/gngiuL

Oreglia, E. (2012). *Africa's many Chinas.* Report on the Chinese presence in Africa for Intel.

Organization for Economic Cooperation [OECD] and Development and Inter-American Development Bank [IDB]. (2017). *Broadband policies for Latin America and the Caribbean: A digital economy toolkit.* https://is.gd/4sTxPb

Ossewaarde, M., & Reijers, W. (2017). The illusion of the digital commons: "False consciousness" in online alternative economies. *Organization*, 24(5), 609–628.

Palladino, N., & Santaniello, M. (2021). *Legitimacy, power, and inequalities in the multi-stakeholder Internet governance: Analyzing IANA transition.* Cham, Switzerland: Palgrave Macmillan.

Parfitt, R. (2019). *The process of international legal reproduction: Inequality, historiography, resistance.* Cambridge University Press.

Parliament of the Republic of South Africa. (2022, July 31). Electronic Communications and Transactions Act, No. 25 of 2002. www.gov.za/documents/electronic-communications-and-transactions-act

Pâtin, A. (2021, January 26). *Učeniâ po rabote suverennogo Interneta otložili do konca pandemii.* https://is.gd/thdisu

Peškova, T. (2020). Radi celej Putina vlasti pritormoziat zakon Yarovoj. *Cnews.* https://is.gd/ASRosA

Petry, J., Fichtner, J., & Heemskerk, E. (2019). Steering capital: The growing private authority of index providers in the age of passive asset management. *Review of International Political Economy*, 28(1), 152–176.

Philpott, D. (2003). Sovereignty. *Stanford Encyclopedia of Philosophy Archive.* https://plato.stanford.edu/archives/sum2016/entries/sovereignty/

Philpott, D. (2020). Sovereignty. In E. N. Zalta (Ed.), *The Stanford encyclopedia of philosophy (Fall).* https://is.gd/ccZzpg

Plantin, J.-C., Lagoze, C., Edwards, P. N., & Sandvig, C. (2018). Infrastructure studies meet platform studies in the age of Google and Facebook. *New Media & Society*, 20(1), 293–310.

PMJDY (Pradhan Mantri Jan Dhan Yojana). (2023). Pradhan Mantri Jan – Dhan Yojana. https://pmjdy.gov.in/account

Poder360. (2021, August 13). *Irmão do ajudante de ordens de Bolsonaro vazou inquérito da PF, diz jornal.* https://is.gd/tBocRe

Poe, M. (2001). Moscow, the third Rome: The origins and transformations of a "pivotal moment." *Jahrbücher Für Geschichte Osteuropas*, 49(3), 412–429.

Poell, T., Nieborg, D., & van Dijck, J. (2019). Platformisation. *Internet Policy Review*, *8*(4), 1–13.

Pohle, J., & Thiel, T. (2020). Digital sovereignty. *Internet Policy Review*, *9*(4), 1–19.

Polanyi, K. (1980/1944). *The great transformation*. New York: Beacon Publisher Group.

Polatin-Reuben, D., & Wright, J. (2014). *An internet with BRICS characteristics: Data sovereignty and the balkanisation of the internet*. 4th USENIX Workshop on Free and Open Communications on the Internet.

Polyakova, A., & Meserole, C. (2019). Exporting digital authoritarianism. *Foreign Policy at Brookings*. https://is.gd/qe2Se9

Prabhu, J. A. (2012). Strands of anti-Westernism in Indian politics. *Swarajyamag*. https://is.gd/tLOdgI

Prashad, V. (2012). *Poorer nations: A possible history of the Global South*. Verso.

PRC Ministry of Commerce. (2020). 商务部令2020年第4号 不可靠实体清单规定 [*Order No.4 (2020) of the Ministry of Commerce: Regulations on the unreliable entities list*]. PRC Ministry of Commerce. https://is.gd/ZkMmvu

PRC Ministry of Commerce, & PRC Ministry of Science and Technology. (2020). 《中国禁止出口限制出口技术目录》调整内容 [Revision of the catalogue of technologies prohibited or restricted from export]. *The State Council, The People's Republic of China*. https://is.gd/Vi8hMz

Presidência da República. (2023, January 2). *Despacho do Presidente da República.* Brazilian Government Official Gazette [Diário Oficial da União], Ed. 1-A, Section 1-Extra A, p. 7. https://is.gd/W9fRpZ

Presidency of the Russian Federation. (2016). Information *Security Doctrine of the Russian Federation*. https://is.gd/uBFMJD

Presidential Commission on the Fourth Industrial Revolution. (2020). *Summary report & recommendations presented by the commission on the fourth industrial revolution.*

Pretorius, L. (2021, February 9). Anatomy of a disinformation campaign: The who, what and why of deliberate falsehoods on Twitter. *Daily Maverick*. https://is.gd/eaTglA

Purnell, N. (2018). Two years ago, India lacked fast, cheap Internet – one billionaire changed all that. *Wall Street Journal*. https://is.gd/VHOLe3

Putnam, T. L. (2016). *Courts without borders: Law, politics, and US extraterritoriality*. Cambridge University Press.

Pytlak, A. (2020a, November 13). Cyber peace and security. *Reaching Critical Will*, *18*(5). https://is.gd/cOtJnF

Pytlak, A. (2020b, May 28). UN security council meeting highlights the cyber peace and security challenges wrought by the COVID-19 pandemic. *Reaching Critical Will*. https://is.gd/SGLtWV

Quinn, B. (2019, May 20). Huawei cut off from Android and US chips amid US ban. *France24*. https://is.gd/qQ7dxd

Radio Liberty Staff. (2010, May 13). *Cyrillic domain names become operational on the internet*. https://is.gd/i93ZUk

Radu, R. (2019). *Negotiating internet governance*. Oxford, UK: Oxford University Press.

Raghavan, V., Jain, S., & Varma, P. (2019). India stack – digital infrastructure as public good. *Communications of the ACM*, *62*(11), 76–81.

Rainsford, S. (2015, January 16). #JeSuisCharlie gets little sympathy in Russia. *BBC News*. www.bbc.com/news/world-europe-30847694

Raman, A., Joglekar, S., Cristofaro, E. D., Sastry, N., & Tyson, G. (2019). Challenges in the decentralised web: The Mastodon case. *Proceedings of the Internet Measurement Conference*, 217–229.

Ramesh, G., Jangid, A., Sivamalai, L., & Rebelly, A. B. (2020). NPCI: Chartering a payment freeway. In *IIM* Bangalore *Research Paper (No. 626)*. Bangalore.

Rappaport, J. (2018). Is proprietary software unjust? Examining the ethical foundations of free software. *Philosophy & Technology*, *31*(3), 437–453.

Ravi, S. (2018, August 27). Is India ready to JAM? *Brookings*. https://is.gd/5kxfp5

Raymond, M., & DeNardis, L. (2015). Multistakeholderism: Anatomy of an inchoate global institution. *International Theory*, *7*(3), 572–616.

Razumovsky, D. (2022, July 14) BRICS: How will the organization get a "Second Wind"? *Valdai Club*. https://is.gd/wdoE54

Razzano, G., Gillwald, A., Aguera, P., Ahmed, S., Calandro, E., Matanga, C., Rens, A., & van Der Spuy, A. (2020). *SADC PF discussion paper. The digital economy and society*. https://is.gd/tnlBvI

Reda, F. (2020, October 12). Edit policy: Wo bleibt Europas Open Technology Fund? [Edit policy: Where is Europe's open technology fund?]. *Heise Online*. https://is.gd/uq4tu4

Regional Comprehensive Economic Partnership Agreement. (2020). *Legal text of the RCEP agreement*, Chapter 12. https://is.gd/BHPoWy

Renz, B., & Smith, H. (2016). *Russia and Hybrid warfare – Going beyond the label*. https://is.gd/RIOqQK

Research ICT Africa. (2015). *Submission on the cybercrime and cybersecurity bill*. https://is.gd/UaBwhQ

Research ICT Africa. (2020). *Digital futures: South Africa's digital readiness for the "fourth industrial revolution."* https://is.gd/6solEG

Research ICT Africa. (2021). Written submission in response to the: PROPOSED NATIONAL DATA AND CLOUD POLICY. https://researchictafrica.net/wp/wp-content/uploads/2021/06/RIA_Submission_DATA_and_Cloud_Policy.pdf

Reserve Bank of India. (2005). Payment systems in India – Vision 2005–08. *Reserve Bank of India*. https://is.gd/tWSuv4

Reserve Bank of India. (2012). Merchant discount rates structure for debit card transactions. *Reserve Bank of India*. https://is.gd/nrJqF9

Reserve Bank of India. (2017). Draft circular – Rationalisation of merchant discount rate (MDR) for debit card transactions. *Reserve Bank of India*. https://is.gd/JQkwSn

Reserve Bank of India. (2019). Policy paper on authorisation of new retail payment systems. *Reserve Bank of India*. https://is.gd/WcVzFY

Resprepo, R. (2013). Democratic freedom of expression. *Open Journal of Philosophy*, *3*(3), 380–390.

Reuters. (2021a, May 13). South African regulator seeking legal advice on WhatsApp's new privacy policy. *Reuters: Africa*. https://is.gd/cqXAtB

Reuters. (2021b, May 26). Facebook, Twitter told to open databases in Russia by July 1. https://is.gd/WnOxk2

Reuters. (2022, February 15). India adds 54 more Chinese apps to ban list; Sea says it complies with laws. *Reuters*. https://is.gd/nlXQCU

Reviglio, U., & Agosti, C. (2020). Thinking outside the black-box: The case for "algorithmic sovereignty" in social media. *Social Media + Society*, *6*(2), 1–12.

Rinehart, W. (2020, September 14). *Is data nonrivalrous? The Benchmark*. https://is.gd/SPbYQz

Rizzi, A. (2023, September 20). China, Russia, India and the Global South: The era of revenge. *El País*. https://is.gd/EVmqGh

Roberts, S. (2020). Policy brief 1: *Note on WTO moratorium on electronic transmissions*. Industrial Development Think Tank. https://is.gd/bzle4N

Roberts, T. (Ed.) (2021). *Digital rights in closing civic space: Lessons from ten African countries*. Institute of Development Studies. https://is.gd/EH9G33

Robertson, G. (2013). Protesting Putinism: The election protests of 2011–2012 in broader perspective. *Problems of Post-Communism*, *60*(2), 11–23.

Robinson, E. et al. (2017). Telling stories about post-war Britain: Popular individualism and the "crisis" of the 1970s. *Twentieth Century British History*, *28*(2), 268–304.

Robson, D. (2017, March 9). Why China's internet use has overtaken the West. *BBC*. https://is.gd/iVpiJh

Roio, D. (2018). *Algorithmic sovereignty*. [Doctoral dissertation, University of Plymouth]. https://pearl.plymouth.ac.uk/handle/10026.1/11101

Rolf, S., & Schindler, S. (2023). The US–China rivalry and the emergence of state platform capitalism. *Environment and Planning A: Economy and Space*, *55*(5), 1255–1280.

Roskomnadzor. (2021, May 17). *On partial removal of measures to slow down Twitter traffic*. https://rkn.gov.ru/news/rsoc/news73632.htm

Rosnay, M. D. de, & Musiani, F. (2020). Alternatives for the Internet: A journey into decentralised network architectures and information commons. *TripleC: Communication, Capitalism & Critique*, *18*(2), 622–629.

Rousseff, D. (2013, September 24). *Statement by H.E. Dilma Rousseff, President of the Federative Republic of Brazil, at the opening of the general debate of the 68th session of the United Nations General Assembly*. Voltaire Network. www.voltairenet.org/article180382.html

Routley, N. (2019). Ranking the top 100 websites in the world. *Visual Capitalist*. https://is.gd/Sz97XH

Ruijgrok, K. (2021). Understanding India's troubling rise in internet shutdowns. A qualitative and quantitative analysis. *Open Tech Fund*. https://is.gd/NoR5jr

Ruohonen, J. (2020). *The treachery of images in the digital sovereignty debate*. 1–21. http://arxiv.org/abs/2012.02724

SA News. (2019, February 24). South Africa to develop Africa's largest tech hub. *Business Tech*. https://is.gd/31q9lF

Salmon, F. (2020, November 4). *When an ant is too big to fail*. Axios. https://is.gd/HUozqJ

Samuels, E. (2020, February 21). How misinformation on WhatsApp led to a mob killing in India. *Washington Post*.

Sanger, D. E., & Perlroth, N. (2019, June 15) U.S. escalates online attacks on Russia's power grid. *The New York Times*.

Sanzgiri, V. (2023, February 28). Exam excuses and preventive measures fuel internet shutdowns in India. *MediaNama*. https://is.gd/bRmUAq

Sarkar, T., Matam, M., & Grover, G. (2020). *Internet Shutdowns: Threats to Digital Access*. The Centre for Internet and Society. https://cis-india.org/internet-governance/blog/india-digital-freedoms-2-internet-shutdowns

Savelyev, A. (2016). Russia's new personal data localization regulations: A step forward or a self-imposed sanction? *Computer Law & Security Review*, 32(1), 128–145.

Savin, L. (2019a, December 30). *Номос Киберпространства и суверенный Интернет*. https://is.gd/oLycKp

Savin, L. (2019b, December 30). Суверенный Интернет – дело принципиальной важности для национальной безопасности. *News Front*. https://news-front.info/2019/12/30/suverennyj-internet-delo-princzipialnoj-vazhnosti-dlya-naczionalnoj-bezopasnosti/

Schiller, H. I. (1975). Genesis of the free flow of information principles. The imposition of communications domination. *Instant Research on Peace and Violence*, *5*(2), 75–86.

Schmitt, C. (1985). *Political theology: Four chapters on the concept of sovereignty*. Cambridge, MA: MIT Press.

Schneider, F. (2018). *China's digital nationalism*. New York: Oxford University Press.

Schoonmaker, S. (2018). *Free software, the internet, and global communities of resistance*. Routledge.

Schwartz, H. M. (2019). Strange power over credit; or the enduring strength of US structural power. In R. Germain (Ed.), *Susan strange and the future of global political economy: Power, control and transformation* (Ripe series in global political economy) (1st ed., pp. 69–72). Routledge.

SCO. (2005, July 5). *Declaration by the heads of the member states of the Shanghai cooperation organization in Astana*. http://eng.sectsco.org/load/197543/

SCO. (2006, June 15). *Statement on international information security*. http://eng.sectsco.org/load/197770/

SCO. (2007, August 16). *Bishkek declaration*. http://eng.sectsco.org/load/197905/

SCO. (2009, June 16). *Agreement of SCO on cooperation in the field of ensuring the international information security*. https://is.gd/u62bkg

SCO. (2010, June 10). *Tashkent declaration*. http://eng.sectsco.org/load/199082/

Scott, M., & Birnbaum, E. (2021, June 30). How Washington and Big Tech won the global tax fight. *Politico*. https://is.gd/9wMsq7

SEACOM. (2023). *SA has highest number of ransomware and email attacks in Africa*. January 20, 2023. https://is.gd/ILQpAp

Segal, A. (2017). *The hacked world order: How nations fight, trade, maneuver, and manipulate in the digital age* (2nd ed.). New York: PublicAffairs.

Sengupta, D. (2011, June 7). ICANN allows India to register website addresses in seven regional languages. *The Economic Times*.

Shah, N. (2021). Digital infrastructure, liminality, and world-making via Asia: (Dis) information blackouts: Politics and practices of internet shutdowns. *International Journal of Communication*, *15*, 2693–2709.

Shahbaz, A. (2018). *Freedom of the net 2018: The rise of digital authoritarianism*. Freedom House. https://is.gd/QGRohq

Shang, S. (2021). 中国域外规制体系的建构挑战与架构重点 – 兼论《阻断外国法律与措施不当域外适用办法》[Challenges and keys to China's extraterritorial regulatory system: Also a commentary on rules on counteracting unjustified extraterritorial application of foreign legislation and other measures]. 国际法研究 *[Chinese Review of International Law]*, 2021(2), 63–80.

Shapshak, T. (2021, May 12). Facebook to be summonsed before South Africa's parliament over "harmful misinformation." *Forbes*. https://is.gd/w4bjbF

Sharma, L., & Natarajan, S. (2020). *Restoring agency: Modified choice approach*. Bangalore.

Sharma, L., Natarajan, S., & Udhayakumar, K. (2020). *Last mile access: Building offline Architectures for better reach to the state*. https://is.gd/o6hXiD

Shcherbovich, A. (2021). Data protection and cybersecurity legislation of the Russian federation in the context of the "sovereignization" of the internet in Russia. In L. Belli (Ed.), *CyberBRICS: Cybersecurity regulations in the BRICS countries* (pp. 67–131). Cham: Springer.

Sheehan, M., & Du, S. (2022, December 9). *What China's algorithm registry reveals about AI governance*. Carnegie Endowment. https://is.gd/kcimIH

Sheik, S. (2021, December 1). *Alert | The Cybercrimes Act has finally commenced*. Michalsons. https://is.gd/DLxAqs

Shen, X. (2013). *Private Chinese investment in Africa: Myths and realities*. World Bank. http://dx.doi.org/10.1596/1813-9450-6311

Sherman, J. (2019, February 4). *India's digital path: Leaning democratic or authoritarian?* https://is.gd/AWWuYN

Sherman, J. (2021). *Reassessing RuNet: Russian Internet isolation and implications for Russian cyber behavior*. Atlantic Council. https://is.gd/rcJobJ

Sherman, J., & Morgus, R. (2018, November 19). *Breaking down the vote on Russia's new cybercrime resolution at the UN*. https://is.gd/Ke77nA

Shi, Y. (2018). 主权的网络边界 – 以规制数据跨境传输的视角 [Network borders of sovereignty: From the perspective of regulating cross-border data transmission]. 情报杂志 *[Journal of Intelligence]*, 37(9), 160–166.

Siebert, Z. (2021). Digital sovereignty – The EU in a contest for influence and leadership. *Heinrich Böll Stiftung Brussels. https://is.gd/2FbcLb*

Sinclair, T. J. (2008). *The new masters of capital: American bond rating agencies and the politics of creditworthiness*. Cornell University Press.

Singh, S. (2013). India and the SCO. Better late than never. In M. Fredholm (Ed.), *The Shanghai cooperation organization and Eurasian geopolitics: New directions, perspectives, and challenges* (pp. 162–175). Copenhagen: NIAS Press.

Sivetc, L. (2021). Controlling free expression "by infrastructure" in the Russian Internet: The consequences of RuNet sovereignization. *First Monday*, 26(5).

Slobodian, Q. (2020). *Globalists: The end of empire and the birth of neoliberalism*. Harvard University Press.

Sly, L. (1997, June 26). *Reliving the opium war*. https://is.gd/Jr5Zf6

Smit, H., Johnson, C., Hunter, R., Dunn, M., & van Vuuren, P. F. J. (2019). *Africa's digital platforms and financial services. An eight-country overview*. Insight2inpact. https://is.gd/La5uDn

Smith, C. (2023). RSAWEB victim of cyberattack as wave of ransomware attempts hits SA in past week. https://is.gd/hwrQmx

Smith, M. L. (2018). Putting critical realism to use in ICT4D research: Reflections on practice. *The Electronic Journal of Information Systems in Developing Countries*. 84(6), e12052. https://doi.org/10.1002/isd2.12052

Smith, M. L., Zidar, O., & Zwick, E. (2023). Top wealth in America: New estimates under heterogeneous returns. *The Quarterly Journal of Economics*, 138(1), 515–573.

Smuha, N. A. (2021). From a "race to AI" to a "race to AI regulation": Regulatory competition for artificial intelligence. *Law, Innovation and Technology*, *13*(1), 57–84.

Snyder, T. (2018a). *The road to unfreedom: Russia, Europe*. New York: Tim Duggan Books.

Snyder, T. (2018b, March 16). Vladimir Putin's politics of eternity. *The Guardian*. https://is.gd/6EzzRT

Soldatov, A., & Borogan, I. (2015). *The red web: The struggle between Russia's digital dictators and the new online revolutionaries*. PublicAffairs.

Soldatov, A., & Borogan, I. (2016, November 29). Putin brings China's Great Firewall to Russia in cybersecurity pact. *The Guardian*. https://is.gd/8TG9qX

Soldatov, A., & Borogan, I. (2018). Russia's approach to cyber: The best defence is a good offence. In N. Popescu & S. Secrieru (Eds.), *Hacks, leaks and disruptions. Russian cyber strategies* (pp. 15–24). EU Institute for Security Studies. https://is.gd/jp8oUo

Souleimanov, E., & Horák, S. (2006). Islam, Islamism, and terrorism in the Northern Caucasus and Central Asia: A critical assessment. In U. Schlichting (Ed.), *OSCE yearbook: Yearbook on the organization for security and co-operation in Europe* (pp. 271–287). Hamburg: Nomos Verlaggesellschaft.

South African Banking Risk Information Centre (SABRIC). (2020). *SABRIC annual crime stats 2019*. https://is.gd/fBEVJO

South African Banking Risk Information Centre (SABRIC). (2021). *SABRIC annual crime states 2020*. https://is.gd/6KBi3Z

South African Government. (n.d.). Fake news – Coronavirus COVID-19. https://is.gd/2nCMQc

South Commission, The. (1990). *The challenge to the South: The report of the South Commission*. Oxford, UK: Oxford University Press.

Sparks, C. (2014). Deconstructing the BRICS. *International Journal of Communication*, *8*, 392–418.

Srivastava, S. (2022). *Hybrid sovereignty in world politics*. Cambridge, UK: Cambridge University Press.

Srnicek, N. (2016). *Platform capitalism*. London: Polity Press.

Stadnik, I. (2021). Control by infrastructure: Political ambitions meet technical implementations in RuNet. *First Monday*, *26*(5).

Stallman, R. M. (2002). *Free software, free society: Selected essays of Richard M. Stallman*. Free Software Foundation. https://is.gd/R67I8Y

Standnik, I. (2019). *Sovereign Runet: What does it mean?* (White paper). Internet Governance Project of Georgia Tech School of Public Policy. https://is.gd/VHA2hN

Stanford PACS. (2020). *Reclaiming digital infrastructure for the public interest*. Stanford, CA: Stanford PACS.

Starrs, S. (2013). American economic power hasn't declined-it globalized! Summoning the data and taking globalization seriously. *International Studies Quarterly*, *57*(4), 817–830.

Statista. (2021). *Market share of mobile device vendors in South Africa from January 2019 to June 2021*. https://is.gd/NwxWry

Statista. (2024, February 13). BRICS and G7 countries' share of the world's total gross domestic product (GDP) in purchasing power parity (PPP) from 2000 to 2023. *Statista*. https://is.gd/a3LGbg

Stoll, C. (1989). *The cuckoo's egg: Tracking a spy through the maze of computer espionage.* New York: Doubleday.
Stored Wire and Electronic Communications and Transactional Records Access, 18 U.S.C. § 2701 (1986). https://is.gd/c4O1Ow
Strange, S. (1988). *States and markets.* Continuum International Publishing Group.
Stuenkel, O. (2014). *Can the BRICS avoid the "Power South vs. Poor South" dynamic?* https://is.gd/HBWldR
Stuenkel, O. (2016). *Post-Western world: How emerging powers are remaking global order.* London, UK: Polity Press.
Stuenkel, O. (2020). *The BRICS and the future of global order* (2nd ed.). London, UK: Lexington Books.
Subramanian, A., & Felman, J. (2022). Why India can't replace China. *Foreign Affairs.* https://is.gd/noJwQP
Sukumar, A. M. (2021, February 5). Designing digital public goods and playgrounds in India: The need for theoretical and contextual analysis. *Isprit.* https://is.gd/uCykys
Svenonius, O., & Björklund, F. (2018). Explaining attitudes to secret surveillance in post- communist societies. *East European Politics*, 34(2), 123–151.
Swart, K. (1962). "Individualism" in the mid-nineteenth century (1826–1860). *Journal of the History of Ideas*, 23(1), 77–90.
Szonyi, M. (2009). Secularization theories and the study of Chinese religions. *Social Compass*, 56(3), 312–327.
Szyszczak, E. (2006). Experimental governance: The open method of coordination. *European Law Journal*, 12(4), 486–502.
Tan, H. (2023). Russia says its economy did better than expected, one year into the Ukraine war. But experts say there's a red flag behind the announcement. *Business Insider.* https://is.gd/JUuJD4
Tang, X. (1998). 当今世界的信息控制权 [The right to control information in contemporary world]. *探索与争鸣 [Exploration and Free Views]*, 9, 16–18.
Taylor, I. (2006). China's oil diplomacy in Africa. *International Affairs*, 82(5), 937–959.
Taylor, L. (2013). *The scramble for Africa's data: Resource grab or development opportunity?* https://is.gd/vfD2jz
Taylor, L. (2021). Public actors without public values: Legitimacy, domination and the regulation of the technology sector. *Philosophy & Technology*, 34, 897–922.
Taylor, L., & Broeders, D. (2015). In the name of development: Power, profit and the datafication of the global south. *Geoforum*, 64(August), 229–237.
Telecommunications and Postal Services. (2016). *National integrated ICT policy white paper.* https://is.gd/94XZaX
Tellis, A. J. (2018, November 1). *Narendra Modi and U.S.–India relations.* Carnegie Endowment for International Peace. https://is.gd/pKh8wh
Thumfart, J. (2022). The norm development of digital sovereignty between China, Russia, the EU and the US: From the late 1990s to the Covid-crisis 2020/21 as catalytic event. In D. Hallinan, R. Leenes, & P. de Hert (Eds.), *Data protection and privacy: Enforcing rights in a changing world* (pp. 1–44). Oxford: Hart Publishing.
Thumfart, J. (2024a). Digital rights and the state of exception. Internet shutdowns from the perspective of just securitization theory. *Journal of Global Security Studies*, 9(1), ogad024. https://doi.org/10.1093/jogss/ogad024

Thumfart, J. (2024b). *The liberal internet in the postliberal era: Digital sovereignty, private government, and practices of neutralization.* Basingstoke: Palgrave Macmillan.
Thussu, D. K. (2015). Digital BRICS: Building a NWICO 2.0? In K. Nordenstreng & D. K. Thussu (Eds.), *Mapping BRICS media* (pp. 242–263). Cham: Routledge, Taylor & Francis Group.
Tiezzi, S. (2020, September 10). China's bid to write the global rules on data security. *The Diplomat.* https://is.gd/mmhYlV
Tillin, L. (2013). National and subnational comparative politics: Why, what and how. *Studies in Indian Politics*, *1*(2), 235–240.
Tilly, C. (1975). *The formation of national states in Western Europe.* Princeton, NJ: Princeton University Press.
Tilly, C. (2002). *Stories, identities, and political change.* Rowman & Littlefield.
Timmers, P. (2020). *When sovereignty leads and cyber law follows.* Directions Cyber Digital Europe. https://is.gd/rZop6P
Timoteo, M., Verri, B., & Nanni, R. (Eds.) (2023). *Quo vadis, sovereignty? New conceptual and regulatory boundaries in the age of digital China.* Berlin, Germany: Springer.
Tocci, N. (2023, September 20). War in Ukraine is revealing a new global order – and the "power south" is the winner. *The Guardian.* https://is.gd/bX3cia
Tomaz, T. (2023). Brazilian fake news bill: Strong content moderation accountability but limited hold on platform market power. *Javnost – The Public*, 30(2), 253–267.
Tsourapas, G. (2020). Global autocracies: Strategies of transnational repression, legitimation, and co-optation in world politics. *International Studies Review*, 23(3), 616–644.
Turner, F. (2006). *From counterculture to cyberculture: Stewart brand, the whole Earth network, and the rise of digital utopianism.* Chicago, IL: University of Chicago Press.
Tzouvala, N. (2020). The ordo-liberal origins of modern international investment law: Constructing competition on a global scale. In J. D. Haskell & A. Rasulov (Eds.), *New voices and new perspectives in international economic law* (pp. 37–54). Cham: Springer International Publishing.
UN Finance Center for South-South Cooperation. (2023). *Global South Countries (Group of 77 and China).* Finance Center for South-South Cooperation. https://is.gd/AuVGMO
UNCTAD. (2019, September). Digital economy report 2019. *United Nations Publications.* https://is.gd/tdMtOp
UNESCO. (1945). *UNESCO Constitution.* https://is.gd/tjXRI7
United Nations Conference on Trade and Development (UNCTAD). (2019). *UNCTAD research paper No. 29.* https://is.gd/38Peal
United Nations Development Programme (UNDP). (1994). Human development report 1994.
United Nations Development Programme (UNDP). (2015). *The 2030 agenda for sustainable development.* New York: United Nations Development Programme.
United Nations General Assembly. (2020). *Developments in the field of information and telecommunications in the context of international security.* Seventy-fifth session. First Committee. A/C.1/75/L.8/Rev.1
United Nations Office on Drugs and Crime (UNODC). (2020). *Report on the meeting of the expert group to conduct a comprehensive study on cybercrime held in Vienna from 27 to 29 July 2020.* UNODC/CCPCJ/EG.4/2020/2

United Nations Office on Drugs and Crime (UNODC). (2021). *Report on the meeting of the expert group to conduct a comprehensive study on cybercrime held in Vienna from 6 to 8 April 2021*. UNODC/CCPCJ/EG.4/2021/2

USCC (U.S.-China Economic and Security Review Commission). (2022). *Key events and statements summarizing China's position on Russia's invasion of Ukraine*. USCC. https://is.gd/lQ8FUL

Valens, A. (2019, January 18). Mastodon is crumbling – And many blame its creator. *The Daily Dot*. https://is.gd/7NumhA

van der Ploeg, I. (2012). The body as data in the age of information. In K. Ball, K. Haggerty, & D. Lyon (Eds.), *Routledge handbook of surveillance studies* (pp. 176–183). New York: Routledge.

van Dijck, J. (2020). Governing digital societies: Private platforms, public values. *Computer Law and Security Review*, 36, 1–4.

Vermeulen, J. (2022, March 1). Ramaphosa puts Internet censorship law into operation. *My Broadband*. https://is.gd/nHvoHb

Viitanen, J., & Kingston, R. (2014). Smart cities and green growth: Outsourcing democratic and environmental resilience to the global technology sector. *Environment and Planning A*, 46, 803–819.

Vipin, V. N. (2011, July 6). India calls for mechanism to promote IT adoption. https://is.gd/zgRecF

Vogel, D. (1995). *Trading up: Consumer and environmental regulation in a global economy*. Harvard University Press.

von der Leyen, U. (2020). *A Union that strives for more my agenda for Europe: Political guidelines for the next European Commission 2019–2024*. https://is.gd/eVZncc

W3techs.com. (2022, March 1). Usage statistics and market share of web servers, March 2022. W3techs.Com. https://is.gd/jGHWv1

Wade, S. (2018). Privacy concerns focus on tech firms, not government. *China Digital Times*. https://is.gd/CeKiLc

Wakefield, J. (2019, December 24). Russia "successfully tests" its unplugged internet. *BBC News*. www.bbc.com/news/technology-50902496

Wall Street Journal, The (WSJ). (2020). *China Launches initiative to set global data-security rules*. https://is.gd/ixy2av

Wallerstein, I. (1976). Semi-peripheral countries and the contemporary world crisis. *Theory and Society*, 3(4), 461–483.

Wang, K. (2023, June 18). China pushes for Asia-pacific trade agreement membership promises to "actively attract" foreign investment. *South Morning China Post*. https://is.gd/PvAu6q

Wang, M. (2021, April 8). China's techno-authoritarianism has gone global. Washington needs to offer an alternative. *Foreign Affairs*. https://is.gd/86PYUS

Wang, S. (2017). 全国人民代表大会常务委员会执法检查组关于检查《中华人民共和国网络安全法》、《全国人民代表大会常务委员会关于加强网络信息保护的决定》实施情况的报告 [*Report by the law enforcement inspection group on the implementation of the PRC cybersecurity law and the decision of the standing committee of the National People's Congress on strengthening information protection on networks*]. National People's Congress Standing Committee. https://is.gd/oyTlXn

Wang, Y. (2016). 试论网络数据本地化立法的正当性 [Analysis on the justification of cyber data localization legislation]. 西安交通大学学报*(社会科学版) [Journal of Xi'an Jiaotong University(Social Sciences)]*, 36(1), 54–61.

Wang, Y. (2020). Upholding multilateralism, fairness and justice and promoting mutually beneficial cooperation. *Keynote Speech by State Councilor and Foreign Minister Wang Yi at the International Seminar on Global Digital Governance.* Beijing, September 8, 2020.

Wasserman, H. (2018). Power, meaning and geopolitics: Ethics as an entry point for global communication studies. *Journal of Communication*, 68, 441–451.

Watson, J. K. (2021). *Cold war reckonings: Authoritarianism and the genres of decolonization* (1st ed.). New York: Fordham University Press.

We Are Social. (2019). *Digital in 2019.* https://is.gd/mGDOoo

Weber, R. H., & Staiger, D. (2017). *Transatlantic data protection in practice.* Cham, Switzerland: Springer.

Weber, M., Gerth, C., & Mills, W. (1948). *From Max Weber: Essays in sociology.* New York: Oxford University Press.

Webster, G. (2023). Latest publications by Graham Webster. *DigiChina.* https://digichina.stanford.edu/people/graham-webster/

Weiss, D. (2016). The new Russian legislation on blasphemy and swearing: The parliamentary debates. *Zeitschrift Für Slavische Philologie*, 72(2), 289–321.

Wen, Y. (2021). *The Huawei model: The rise of China's technology giant.* Urbana: University of Illinois Press.

Werner, W. G., & De Wilde, J. H. (2001). The endurance of sovereignty. *European Journal of International Relations*, 7(3), 283–313.

Weymouth, S. (2023). India's personal data protection act and the politics of digital governance. *Atlantic Council.* https://is.gd/3XborJ

White House. (2022, May 24). Quad Joint Leaders' Statement. *The White House.* https://is.gd/GsKROM

Wild, S. (2020). Citing virus misinformation, South Africa tests speech limits. *Undark.* https://is.gd/UwoBwZR

Wilson, T. (2019). Huawei and African union boost relationship with deal. *Financial Times.* https://is.gd/PoFPy5

Winecoff, W. K. (2015). Structural power and the global financial crisis: A network analytical approach. *Business and Politics*, 17(3), 495–525.

Winseck, D. (2017). The geopolitical economy of the global Internet infrastructure. *Journal of Information Policy*, 7, 228–267.

Winter, B. (2013, September 12). Dilma mira empresas de Internet após espionagem dos EUA. *Reuters.* https://is.gd/1FESs8

World Bank. (2016). World development report 2016: Digital dividends. *World Bank.* Washington DC: World Bank.

World Bank. (2022a). *GDP and GDP per capita.* https://data.worldbank.org/

World Bank. (2022b). Poverty and shared prosperity 2022: Correcting course. *World Bank.* https://is.gd/wSuj47

World Economic Forum. (2019). *Federated data systems: Balancing innovation and trust in the use of sensitive data.* https://is.gd/2KPbtt

World Health Organization. (2021). *Infodemic.* https://is.gd/jPvkhq

WorldoMeter. (2023). World population. www.worldometers.info/population/world/

World Population Review. (2023). Global North countries 2023. *World Population Review.* https://is.gd/wGN4Ap

World Summit on the Information Society (WSIS). (2005, November 18). *Tunis Agenda for the Information Society.* https://is.gd/GpPpGD

World Summit on the Information Society (WSIS). (2018). *Leveraging ICTs to build information and knowledge societies for achieving the sustainable development goals (SDGs)*. World Summit on the Information Society (WSIS) Forum 2018 Outcome Document, Geneva: International Telecommunication Union.

Wu, E. (2021). *Sovereignty and data localization*. Belfer Center. https://is.gd/XezLEm

Wu, L. (2021, April 21). China's first lawsuit on facial recognition made verdict. *CGTN*. https://is.gd/UJ94Mp

Xi, J. (2014, April 15). A holistic view of national security. *Qiushi*. https://is.gd/fB5QJR

Xi, J. (2015, December 16). Speech at the 2nd World Internet Conference Opening Ceremony. https://is.gd/7hvvTx

Xi, J. (2019, October 21). *Xi: Internet a joint global responsibility*. World Internet Conference. https://is.gd/J6Rr1T

Xinhua Net. (2015). 学习有方：5个词读懂习近平的网络安全新主张 [Study strategies: 5 keywords to understand President Xi's new proposal on cyber security]. *Xinhua Net*. https://is.gd/w8wKoj

Xinhua News Agency. (2019, February 25). 习近平主持召开中央全面依法治国委员会第二次会议并发表重要讲话 [*Xin Jinping chaired the 2nd meeting of the committee of comprehensively promoting the rule of law and gave an important address*]. The State Council, The People's Republic of China. https://is.gd/XGnmpA

Xinhua News Agency. (2020, November 17). 习近平在中央全面依法治国工作会议上强调 坚定不移走中国特色社会主义法治道路 为全面建设社会主义现代化国家提供有力法治保障 [*Xi Jinping stresses the adherence to the path of the socialist rule of law with Chinese characteristics to support the comprehensive construction of socialist modernization in the meeting on comprehensively promoting the rule of law*]. Xinhua News. https://is.gd/SuLDkR

Xinhua News Agency. (2021, September 17). China officially applies to join CPTPP. *The State Council, The People's Republic of China*. https://is.gd/Vd4AWt

Xu, K. (2019). 数据安全法：定位、立场与制度构造 [Data security law: Location, position and institution construction]. 经贸法律评论 *[Business and Economic Law Review]*, *2019*(3), 52–66.

Xu, W. (2021). 论次级经济制裁之阻断立法 [On blocking statutes for secondary economic sanctions]. 法商研究 *[Studies in Law and Business]*, *38*(2), 187–200.

Xu, Y. C. (2014). Chinese state-owned enterprises in Africa: Ambassadors or freebooters? *Journal of Contemporary China*, *23*(89), 822–840.

Yahoo! News. (2022, March 9). Now interconnecting Brazil and Southern Europe: EllaLink and DE-CIX announce strategic partnership. *Yahoo! News*. https://is.gd/cPO9lY

Ye, Y. (2020). 欧盟《阻断法案》述评与启示 [Commentary on the EU blocking statutes]. 太平洋学报 *[Pacific Journal]*, *28*(3), 50–66.

Yeung, J., Gupta, S., & Jha, M. (2021, September 28). Internet goes dark for millions in Indian state's bid to stop exam cheats. *CNN*. https://is.gd/hHZoj2

Yu, H. & Goodnight, T. (2020). How to think about cybersovereignty: The case of China, *Chinese Journal of Communication*, *13*(1), 8–26.

Yurchak, A. (2013). *Everything was forever, until it was no more: The last Soviet generation*. Princeton University Press.

Zakharova, L. (2020). *De Moscou aux terres les plus lointaines*. Communications, politique et société en URSS. EHESS.

Zanolli, B. (2021). Reflections on sustainability from a Quilombola women led community networks. In L. Belli & S. Hadzic (Eds.), *Community networks: Towards sustainable funding models*. Official Outcome of the IGF Dynamic Coalition on Community Connectivity. Editora FGV. www.intgovforum.org/en/filedepot_download/92/20438

Zasurskij, I. (2016). Novaja model' regulirovanija avtorskih prav. Obshhestvennoe dostojanie i koncepcija obshhego blaga (A new model of copyright regulation. The public domain and the concept of the commons). Associacija Internet-izdatelej.

Zeng, V. (2015, December 18). Albaba's Jack Ma sings praises of Xi's global vision of "internet management." *Hong Kong Free Press HKFP*. https://is.gd/IINJw5

Zhao, T. (2019). *Redefining a philosophy for world governance*. Singapore: Springer Singapore. https://doi.org/10.1007/978-981-13-5971-2

Zhu, N. (2020, October 20). 我们需要一部什么样的个人信息保护法 [What kind of Personal Information Protection Law do we need?]. 法制网 *[Legal* Daily]. www.legaldaily.com.cn/index/content/2020-10/20/content_8332111.htm

Zhu, X., & Dai, Z. (2020). 总体国家安全观视域下《数据安全法》的价值与体系定位 [Value and the systemic positioning of the data security law from the perspective of holistic national security]. *电子政务 [E-Government]*, *2020*(8), 82–92.

Zittrain, J. (2003). Internet points of control. *Boston College Law Review*, 44, 653–688.

Zittrain, J. (2019). *Three eras of digital governance*. SSRN. https://is.gd/ogO9M2

Zondi, S. (2022). *The political economy of intra-BRICS cooperation: Challenges and prospects*. Palgrave Macmillan.

Zou, S. (2020, December 16). Coding to be included in curricula. *The State Council of the People's Republic of China*. https://is.gd/VTz3LD

Zuboff, S. (2019a). Surveillance capitalism and the challenge of collective action. *New Labor Forum*, *28*(1). https://doi.org/10.1177/1095796018819461

Zuboff, S. (2019b). *The age of surveillance capitalism: The fight for a human future at the new frontier of power*. PublicAffairs.

Zulli, D., Liu, M., & Gehl, R. W. (2020). Rethinking the "social" in "social media": Insights into topology, abstraction, and scale on the Mastodon social network. *New Media & Society*, 22(7), 1188–1205. https://doi.org/10.1177/1461444820912533ka

Index

www.ingramcontent.com/pod-product-compliance
Lightning Source LLC
LaVergne TN
LVHW100255210926
848480LV00003B/927
* 9 7 8 1 0 0 9 5 3 1 1 2 2 *